# Religion and Politics in Comparative Perspective

In 2000, religion became resurgent across the globe. In many countries religion is a powerful source of political mobilization, and in some it is a potent social cleavage. Some religions reinforce the state; others provide the space for resistance.

This book contains a series of detailed studies examining religion and politics in specific countries or regions. The cases include countries with one dominant religious tradition and countries with two or more competing traditions. They include Catholicism, Protestantism, Islam, Hinduism, Shinto, and Buddhism. They include states in which religion and politics are closely linked and states with at least a low wall of separation between church and state.

The cases are organized by the type of religious marketplace, but they allow many other comparisons as well. We develop some generalizations from the cases and hope that they will be a fertile source of theorizing for others.

Ted Gerard Jelen is Professor and Chair of Political Science at the University of Nevada, Las Vegas. He is the author of *To Serve God and Mammon: Church-State Relations in the United States* and is the co-author (with Clyde Wilcox) of *Public Attitudes on Church and State* (1995).

Clyde Wilcox is Professor of Government at Georgetown University. His many publications include *God's Warriors: The Christian Right in 20th Century America* (1992) and *Onward Christian Soldiers: The Christian Right in American Politics* (1996, 2nd edition, 2000).

D1413426

# Religion and Politics in Comparative Perspective

*The One, the Few, and the Many*

Edited by

**TED GERARD JELEN**
*University of Nevada, Las Vegas*

**CLYDE WILCOX**
*Georgetown University*

**CAMBRIDGE**
UNIVERSITY PRESS

CAMBRIDGE UNIVERSITY PRESS
Cambridge, New York, Melbourne, Madrid, Cape Town, Singapore, São Paulo

Cambridge University Press
32 Avenue of the Americas, New York, NY 10013-2473, USA

www.cambridge.org
Information on this title: www.cambridge.org/9780521650311

First published 2002
Reprinted 2004, 2006

Printed in the United States of America

*A catalog record for this publication is available from the British Library.*

*Library of Congress Cataloging in Publication Data*

Religion and politics in comparative perspective: the one, the few,
and the many / edited by Ted G. Jelen, William Clyde Wilcox.
p.   cm.
Includes bibliographical references and index.
ISBN 0-521-65031-3 – ISBN 0-521-65971-X (pbk.)
1. Religion and politics.   I. Jelen, Ted G.   II. Wilcox, Clyde, 1953–
BL65.P7 R45   2002
332'.1–dc22

2001037372

ISBN-13   978-0-521-65031-1 hardback
ISBN-10   0-521-65031-3 hardback

ISBN-13   978-0-521-65971-0 paperback
ISBN-10   0-521-65971-X paperback

# Contents

# Contributors

**Timothy A. Byrnes**
Colgate University

**Michele Dillon**
Yale University

**Joel S. Fetzer**
Pepperdine University

**Anthony Gill**
University of Washington, Seattle

**Anne Motley Hallum**
Stetson University

**Ted Gerard Jelen**
University of Nevada, Las Vegas

**Paul Manuel**
St. Anselm College

**Sunil K. Sahu**
DePauw University

**Sussan Siavoshi**
Trinity University, San Antonio

**J. Christopher Soper**
Pepperdine University

**Mehran Tamandonfar**
University of Nevada, Las Vegas

**Aiji Tanaka**
Waseda University, Tokyo

**Maria Toyoda**
Stanford University

**Kenneth D. Wald**
University of Florida, Gainesville

**Clyde Wilcox**
Georgetown University

# Preface

The idea for this book came when Clyde was invited to give a paper for the Japanese Political Science Association meeting on religion and politics in the United States. The conversations that ensued with many of the Japanese political scientists reminded us of the enormous international differences that exist in the relationship between religion and politics. Clyde's enthusiasm and fascination with this experience was repeatedly conveyed to Ted, and it was not long before we were telling each other that the time was ripe for a systematic consideration of the issues raised by Clyde's trip. It was in considering the Japanese case in relation to the United States that we began to plan a larger collection of essays. The fine work that we had read over the years by our colleagues in the Religion and Politics Organized Section of the APSA helped us refine our questions, and has inspired our thinking.

We have assembled an impressive group of scholars, who have provided us with excellent studies of religious politics in different regional and national settings. We regard the chapters in this book as sophisticated in the sense that each author is quite sensitive to the cultural contexts and nuances in which religious politics is practiced in a particular place. We also believe that these works are accessible to readers interested in the different ways in which the sacred and the secular interact, but who are not area specialists or experts in the content of particular religious traditions. We would suggest that our contributors have made religion and politics in non-Western settings slightly less esoteric or exotic, and have provided new ways of approaching religious politics in more familiar national contexts.

We have learned more in the process of producing this book than in any of our other projects. With several of our contributors we engaged in interesting dialogues as we sought to understand the complexities of the cases they were presenting. Like so many scholars who have gone before us, we have been reminded that "God is in the details" while engaged in the editorial process. We have been consistently surprised by unexpected similarities among different cases, and also by the necessity to revise conventional wisdom in response to the valuable insights provided by the contributors.

We thank our contributors for their patience when this project was delayed for a time after the death of Clyde's mother.

This book would not have been possible without the help of many individuals. We would like to thank our editors at Cambridge for their support. Alex Holzman helped us shape the project and revise the book in response to the reviewer's comments. Lewis Bateman and Michael Moscati helped shepherd the book through editorial production.

John Green and anonymous reviewers provided many helpful comments on the prospectus, and two anonymous reviewers read the manuscript and made many helpful suggestions for revision. Three of our contributors (Anthony Gill, Kenneth Wald, and J. Christopher Soper) helped us develop the introduction and concluding chapter. Rachel Goldberg and Ben Webster, both graduate students in the Georgetown Ph.D. program, helped proofread the manuscript and prepare it for submission.

Most importantly, we would like to thank our wives, Elizabeth Cook and Marthe Chandler, for advice, support, and (above all) patience.

This book is dedicated to Nikki, Ron, and Cori Rhode, and to Lucy and Jobie Haney, and to Bob and Betty Wilcox, who were there when Clyde needed them.

# 1

# Religion: The One, the Few, and the Many

*Ted G. Jelen and Clyde Wilcox*

Fifty years ago, many social scientists assumed that "religion in the modern world was declining and would likely to continue to decline until its eventual disappearance" (Casanova 1994, p. 25). In Western Europe levels of public religiosity had declined to low levels, and many assumed this to be the likely path of most societies. Predictions that secularism would soon sweep the United States and the rest of the world were commonplace; by the end of the millennium religion was expected to be confined primarily to less developed societies. At the very least, governments and politics were expected to be freed of the influence of religious elites and citizens.

In 2000, religion is resurgent. George Weigel (1991) argues "the unsecularization of the world is one of the dominant social facts in the late twentieth century." Samuel Huntington (1996) argues "In the modern world, religion is a central, perhaps the central, force that motivates and mobilizes people" (p. 66). Huntington sees a religious revival underway at the end of the twentieth century based partially on recruitment but even more on the reinvigoration of religious traditions. This reinvigoration means that religion is today a source of political mobilization in many nations, and also the source of policy disputes over the relationship between church and state.

Religion is the source of some of the most remarkable political mobilizations of our times. In Iran, Islamic activists led a powerful popular revolution that brought millions of Iranians into the street in a successful effort to overthrow the Shah. Religious leaders then outmaneuvered their secular allies to establish an Islamic state headed by the Ayatollah Khomeini. Today Iran debates limits on the power of religious authorities, while at the same time activists in other countries seek to copy the Iranian revolution, or to pressure their government to pass laws more in accord with the Koran.

In India in 1990, a Hindu nationalist leader donned a saffron-colored robe, climbed into an epic chariot, and started out to lead perhaps a million Hindu on a ten-thousand-kilometer journey. Many of those who followed wore saffron robes, and some wore costumes to resemble the monkey head of Hanuman. Each of them carried a brick, with which they would rebuild Rama's temple on what they believed was its historic site. This was controversial, because the site was already occupied by a Muslim mosque built in the sixteenth century. Although government officials halted the march, the mosque was destroyed soon after.

In the United States, the 2000 presidential election witnessed considerable religious mobilization in a country known around the world for its separation of church and state. Republican Presidential nominee George W. Bush identified Jesus as the philosopher having the greatest influence on his life, and the Bible as his favorite book. While serving as governor of Texas after locking up the GOP nomination, Bush signed a proclamation declaring June 10, 2000 to be "Jesus Day" in Texas (Goodstein 2000). Democratic Presidential nominee Al Gore stated repeatedly that, before making important decisions, he asks himself, "What would Jesus do?" Gore named Senator Joseph Leiberman, an Orthodox Jew, as his running mate. Leiberman explicitly drew attention to his faith early in the campaign, refused to campaign on the Sabbath, and repeatedly endorsed the role of religious and spiritual values in politics (Pooley 2000), and was criticized by some Jewish leaders for injecting religion into politics.

In many nations across the world, religion is the source of important political conflicts. In Chile, the Catholic Church sought the passage of laws that would outlaw street preaching and the registration of small churches, and would limit noise levels outside of religious buildings (Gill 1998). Such measures are transparently designed to harass and restrain the growth and influence of Pentecostal churches in a nation that had previously been virtually entirely Catholic.

In Israel, a political conflict arose over the Torah-mandated practice of *shmita*, which ostensibly requires that the land of Israel lie fallow every seven years. In contemporary Israeli politics, Orthodox rabbis have condemned a variety of methods by which this biblical mandate has traditionally been circumvented (by selling the land to a non-Jew, or asserting that the cultivation of land during the sabbatical year is necessary for national survival). The controversy, occasioned by the proposal that *shmita* regulations be tightened, has exacerbated an already severe cleavage between religious traditionalists and modernists in the world's only Jewish-majority state (Sontag 2000).

Religion can also be the source of resistance to the state. In the United States, the Supreme Court upheld a ban on the practice of publicly broadcast prayer at high school football games. In response, some school districts have elected to defy the Court's ruling in *Santa Fe Independent School District v. Doe* (2000), while citizens in other school districts in the American South have elected to conduct public prayers without the use of the public address system, or without the sanction of the school district (Duggan 2000).

Religion is also a source of international politics. Huntington foresees a future clash of civilizations that are defined primarily by religion and language, and thus places religion as a central force in international relations in the twenty-first century. Clearly the revitalization of religious traditions crosses international boundaries, and creates currents of world politics. Across the globe, many Islamic adherents are demanding that their government and laws adhere to religious teachings, and many national and local movements draw their inspiration from the successes of Islamic activists in Iran. Regimes in countries as diverse as Morocco, Jordan, Indonesia, Algeria, and Bangladesh have responded in different ways to this pressure.

Christian evangelists from Europe and the United States continue to spread their traditions abroad. Catholic and Presbyterian churches are winning converts from Buddhism in South Korea Pentecostal churches are springing up throughout Central America and South America and in parts of Africa, in competition with established Catholic and other denominations. Although Pentecostals remain a minority in Central and South America, in some countries they constitute a majority of those who worship regularly. In Korea and in Latin America, these religious changes have become intertwined with politics, with the new religious traditions providing support, infrastructure, and resources for certain political forces. Baptists are making inroads in Russia, and have provoked a reaction among the Orthodox leadership. Other religious trends are confined to particular countries but have international effects: The surge in Hindu nationalism is confined to India, but its affect on tensions with Pakistan cannot be ignored.

Clearly religion has not withered away, but remains an increasingly vital force in society and politics across the globe. Yet the role of religion in political life, the conflicts between religious groups, and the issue of church and state all differ among countries.

## RELIGION AND POLITICS IN COMPARATIVE PERSPECTIVE

The nexus between religion and politics provides an important focus for studies of comparative politics. First, certain religious traditions may provide a source of cross-national identity and identification, which may well facilitate the task of comparative political analysis. For example,

Liberation theologians in Latin America and former members of the anti-Communist resistance in Poland profess adherence to the same Catholic tradition, making comparisons between the politics of Brazil and Poland potentially useful. The role of the Church in resisting democratization in Spain and in some parts of South America also permits interesting comparisons, whereas these two pairs of cases make interesting contrasts in the role of the Church in promoting democratization.

Similarly, the wide scope of Islam makes it possible to compare the role of religion in politics in nations in which Muslims constitute a large majority of citizens (Iran, Algeria) with areas in which Muslims are a consequential political minority (India, Western Europe). Moreover, regimes across the globe and across religious traditions today confront similar challenges: how to conceive of the proper place for religious authority in the state, how to deal with the demands of orthodox activists of religious majorities, and how to deal with demands of religious minorities.

Yet the sheer diversity of religious traditions, political regimes, and their intersections poses a daunting challenge to scholars seeking to develop cross-national generalizations about religion and politics. Religions differ in their core beliefs and theology. They even differ in the number and nature of their gods, ranging from polytheistic religions, such as Hinduism, to monotheistic religions, such as Christianity, Judaism, and Islam, to arguably nontheistic religions, such as Confucianism, Taoism, Shinto, and Buddhism. They differ in the attention they devote to converting others to the faith, and to secular matters, such as politics. Even within religious traditions there is considerable variation: evangelical Protestants in the United States and Latin America differ theologically with Protestants who dominate northern Europe.

Political regimes differ in the nature of the state, and the openness of the state to input from various aspects of society. Democratic, authoritarian, totalitarian, post-totalitarian, and sultanistic regimes may establish quite different relationships with dominant and minority religious traditions. They differ in the nature and type of authority and legitimacy, the degree of elite and mass pluralism, in their control of important resources, such as media and military, and in countless other dimensions. All of these can affect the relationship between the regime and religious groups, their openness to demands of religious majorities and minorities, their support for secular or religious goals.

Most comparative studies of religion and politics have attempted to manage this enormous potential diversity by focusing on one aspect of the relationship between religion and politics. Jose Casanova's elegant work, *Public Religions in the Modern World* (1994), locates the political context of religion in a struggle against modernity and secularism.

Casanova's theoretical analyses provide a much needed elaboration and refinement of the concept of "secularization," and his case studies demonstrate the various ways in which religious elites can contest or accommodate the forces of modernity. Casanova limits his analysis to the Christian West, and focused entirely on the clash between religion and secularism. This work is indispensable for anyone seeking to understand the relationship between the political and the sacred; it is less useful in helping us to understand the sources of conflict *between* adherents of different religious traditions.

Matthew Moen and Lowell S. Gustafson's edited volume *The Religious Challenge to the State* (1992) is organized around the theme of religion as a source of regime opposition. The essays in that volume show the importance of the prophetic role of religion as a moral critic of the state, and of religious resources and infrastructure in helping resistance movements. Of course, in many countries religion serves to reinforce the regime and traditional sources of economic and social power in the face of such opposition. Religion clearly can serve a public purpose as a source of social cohesion and political legitimacy, as well as being a source of regime opposition.

In *The Fundamentalism Project*, Martin Marty and R. Scott Appleby attempt to examine religion and politics in a variety of contexts, using the concept "fundamentalism" (Marty and Appleby 1991).[1] This ambitious project includes a variety of nations including the United States, most of the Islamic world, and India (Gold 1991). Yet the project also revealed the limits of imposing a single concept across a range of religions, for several of the contributors devoted substantial space to explaining why "fundamentalism" was not an adequate description of their countries or areas. Marty and Appleby suggest that the diverse movements considered "fundamentalist" in *The Fundamentalism Project* may share a Wittgensteinian "family resemblance," and this collection tests the usefulness and limits of a theoretically tight, but possibly anachronistic, set of comparisons.

Lester Kurtz' *Gods in the Global Village* is a sophisticated attempt to describe and explain the political roles of religion in a "modern" world, in which technology and international economic activity have rendered religious homogeneity impossible. Kurtz uses three factors to account for the existence of religious conflict. First, Kurtz suggests that the *content* of particular religious traditions matter. He argues that the great Western

[1] The *Fundamentalism Project* is an ambitious, multivolume project with a large number of contributors. Volumes in this collection include *Fundamentalisms Observed* (1991), *Fundamentalisms and Society* (1993a), *Fundamentalisms and the State* (1993b), *Accounting for Fundamentalisms* (1994), and *Fundamentalisms Comprehended* (1995).

monotheistic traditions of Judaism, Christianity, and Islam are more fertile sources of political conflict than most Eastern traditions because monotheism renders Western religions less amenable to compromise or syncretism. This tendency is exacerbated by the existence of a written, authoritative text, from which the tradition can be renewed and from which competing interpreters of religious authenticity can draw. Second, the *similarity* of competing protagonists in religious conflicts may matter a great deal. For example, Kurtz suggests that "heresy," defined as theological conflict between different interpreters of the same tradition, is qualitatively different from "culture wars" conflicts, in which the plausibility of the very *idea* of religious dogma (as opposed to competing versions of the same dogmatic tradition) is contested. Third, the *history* shared by adherents of different religious traditions may render some forms of religious conflict more or less legitimate. For example, there appears to exist no Buddhist or Confucian equivalent of the Judaic stories of bondage and Egypt, or religiously legitimate warfare to secure the "Promised Land"; nor do Eastern traditions contain ideas similar to the Muslim concept of Jihad. Thus, Kurtz provides some intriguing categories within which religious conflict or cooperation can usefully be compared. Kurtz generates some generalizations that can be explored with the cases that follow. Kurtz does not, in the final analysis, produce a genuinely propositional theory as much as a list of priority variables, which may serve future theoretical efforts in this area.

The Gustavo Benavides and M. W. Daly volume, *Religion and Political Power*, has a very wide theoretical and geographical scope, and contains some superlative case studies. The editors and contributors are quite sensitive to the nuances involved in conceptualizing and describing such abstract concepts as "power" and "religion." Moreover, the case studies exhibit an impressive cultural diversity, as they range across the Sudan, Sri Lanka, the United States, Peru, Iran, the former Soviet Union, and the People's Republic of China. The focus of these essays is somewhat narrow (for example, women's roles in Iran, the political thought of Caesar Chavez), and the individual studies are left uninterpreted.

Taken together, these works show us that the comparative study of religion and politics is important, and that single theories such as secularization, single foci, such as regime opposition, or single concepts, such as fundamentalism, can provide us with a rich understanding of some facets of this relationship. Yet thus far no single theory, focus, or concept has proven useful in understanding the interaction of the sacred and the secular in all countries.

In this book, we have invited a number of experts to describe religious politics in the countries or regions of their specialization. We have asked the contributors to describe the religious composition of the country or region, the political regime(s), and their interaction. We have not imposed any single theory, focus, or concept on these cases, but have invited instead the authors to concentrate on the most important elements of religion and politics in each country or region. These cases can provide data to help develop theories and refine concepts that might be useful in cross-national research on religion and politics.

One of our goals in this volume is to provide a preliminary set of categories through which religious politics in different settings can be compared and contrasted, while remaining faithful to the particular circumstances, history, and institutions in particular nations and regions. In this introductory chapter, we offer a general description of what might be termed the "dependent variable": the nature of religious politics in particular settings. We seek to understand where, whether, and how religion can serve as a source of political cohesion or conflict, as well as the differing forms religious conflict may take.

We also offer here a preliminary description of the "independent variables" that may affect the nature of religious politics in diverse circumstances. We suggest at the outset that the "style" of interaction (or noninteraction) between the sacred and the secular public sphere is likely to be a function of two general variables: the structure of religious markets, and the content and application of different religious belief systems.

## THE NATURE OF RELIGIOUS CONTROVERSY AND CONSENSUS

Our first task in this comparative enterprise is to suggest a set of dimensions along which religious politics can vary across national settings, and to provide a general description of the types of issues that animate religious politics in different nations and cultures. As a conceptual starting point, we divide political roles of religion into two general categories: *priestly* religious politics, in which church and state may stand in a mutually supportive relationship to one another, and *prophetic* religious politics, in which political and religious authority may assume opposed or independent roles (Leege 1993).[2]

Priestly religions may enhance or legitimate political authority in a variety of ways. National or subnational regimes may support particular religions (or may support religious values more generally) in a variety of ways. At one extreme, governments may establish official national religions, such as Islam in Iran, Catholicism in Spain and Ireland, Lutheranism in Sweden, or Anglicanism in England. These national

---

[2] In U.S. politics, this distinction corresponds approximately to the "establishment" and "free exercise" clauses of the First Amendment to the U.S. Constitution.

churches may serve as the source of national identity or regime legitimacy. The national identities of Ireland, Spain, Poland, and many South American countries are tied up with Catholicism; Islam is the very basis of the Iranian state. Judaism is the basis of Israel as well, although it is not an official state religion. Under certain circumstances (perhaps most frequently in situations of regime change, or as a component of independence movements) it may indeed be difficult to distinguish identification with a particular religious tradition (or, to use a Christian anachronism, "discipleship") from citizenship in a state or nation. In the case of Iran, Islam is not only the source of national identity, but a fundamental basis of politics. Sussan Siavoshi notes in her chapter, religious authorities are granted enormous power in the Iranian constitution, but other provisions of that document have opened up a lively debate over authoritarian and democratic impulses.

Some nations have not endorsed a national religion, but provide financial subsides to religious bodies, such as public funding for religious schools. These subsidies may exist only for the dominant religion in the state, for some but not all religions, or for all religions. In the United States, the current controversy over government-funded "vouchers" for private schools has been embroiled in a controversy over whether such indirect government assistance to private schools (most of which are religious) violates the establishment clause of the U.S. Constitution (Jelen and Wilcox 1995; Jelen 2000). However, Monsma and Soper (1999) have shown that the United States is an outlier in this regard, and that many multiparty democracies in fact provide direct or indirect support for religious education. More generally, many Western-style regimes provide a publicly supported space within which members of particular religions can enjoy a certain level of autonomy. Thus even in Lutheran Sweden, Catholics are free to practice their religion, and may establish Catholic schools and charities.

The studies in this book suggest that there are important consequences when religion becomes an important part of regime and national identity. First, a commitment to a shared set of religious symbols or doctrines may be an extremely valuable political resource in times of political upheaval. It seems unlikely that phenomena as diverse as Indian independence in the late 1940s, the fall of the Shah of Iran in 1979, or the demise of Polish communism in the 1990s could have occurred without the leadership provided by elites who invoked specifically religious values. While there are obviously important differences between Mahatma Ghandi, Ayatollah Khomieni, and Pope John Paul II, all three of these religious leaders stand as strong testaments to the power of religion to transform important parts of the world.

Second, some of the chapters that follow suggest that religious identity is often a more potent source of change than of stability. The cases of Poland, Iran, and India suggest that religiously based regimes are subject to competition from both religious and secular sources of opposition. Moreover, in certain settings, such as Spain, Portugal, Chile, and Argentina, a religious tradition (in these cases, Catholicism) may be associated with a discredited former regime. Such associations may undermine both the Church's authority in matters religious, as well as the ability of religion to serve as a source of political legitimacy.

By contrast, the prophetic role of religion assumes that religion can assert a certain level of autonomy and independence from political authority. The apparent simplicity of the biblical admonition to "render unto Caesar that which is Caesar's, and to God that which is God's" may not take into account the fact that jurisdiction over some matters (such as education, marriage, and charity) is often contested between the two realms. In many countries in which more than one religion is practiced, disputes over the autonomy of religious belief and practice are quite common. In the United States the Supreme Court has ruled on a wide array of issues, including the rights of religious groups to avoid military service, to refuse to salute the flag in public schools, to be exempt from laws governing the use of peyote,[3] and to practice animal sacrifice. In 1994, a number of Muslim schoolgirls were expelled from French public schools for wearing head scarves mandated by their religion (Bader 2000). A number of European countries have restricted the religious liberty of so-called cults (such as the Church of Scientology) on the basis of the theory that such religious bodies engage in "brainwashing" (Richardson and Introvigne 2001).

Issues involving individual religious freedom, or the autonomy of minority religious traditions, pose a number of interesting questions. Religious liberty is never absolute, and although there are some prohibitions common to all nations (human sacrifice, for example) the range of limitations on religious freedom is large. In some cases, actual religious worship is prohibited, and members of particular faiths are persecuted. In China, the religious movement Falun Gong has been banned

---

[3] This refers to the Supreme Court's decision in *Employment Division v. Smith*, in which the Court upheld the application of a controlled substances statute to Native Americans who used peyote for sacramental purposes. Since *Smith*, Congress has permitted the use of peyote for religious purposes in all fifty states. However, such a ruling does not affect the decision in *Smith*, which specifically contemplates legislative discretion in this area. However, the enactment by Congress of an exemption falls well short of the assertion of a constitutional right, which presumably would lie beyond the reach of popularly elected legislatures.

by the state and is actively harassed. The Iranian government persecuted Baha'ais, sending many to prison. In other cases, religious groups face barriers to organization and worship, but no clear bans. In Latin America some regulations make it difficult for Pentecostal churches to organize.

Other limitations are on the ability to practice religion publicly, or to display religious identification in visible symbols. In France, religious attire in schools is forbidden in an effort to build a national identity. In the United States, Orthodox Jews were once prohibited from wearing headgear under their helmets because of alleged threats to military discipline.[4] In some nations public rallies of religious groups are banned, but not the private practice of that faith.

Many religious minorities are denied exemption from secular laws even if those laws clash with particular faiths, or make religious activity more difficult. Recently, the U.S. Supreme Court rejected a plea by a Catholic Church to expand the seating capacity of its sanctuary in a violation of zoning ordinances, and local county officials in a suburban county near Washington, D.C. denied Muslim groups exemptions from certain land use requirements to build a mosque.

In other cases, however, religious groups are permitted to disobey certain secular laws that conflict with their faith. The most striking example in this volume is that of India, where national laws on marriage, divorce, alimony, and custody do not apply to Muslims, who instead are governed by their own family law. In this case, the rights of Indian women differ by religious tradition, a source of great conflict in the country. In the United States, members of some religious faiths are exempt from mandatory military service, as are Ultraorthodox Jews engaged in fulltime religious study in Israel.

Another question posed by the matter of religious liberty is whether the denial of a governmental benefit to a religious body counts as a restriction on religious freedom. In the United States, the persistent question of private school vouchers poses the tension between religious establishment and free exercise rather starkly. Would the granting of such vouchers to the parents of children attending private schools (most of which are religious) constitute an unlawful "establishment" of religion, or does withholding such assistance inhibit the "free exercise" of religion? (See Jelen 2000 for a more detailed analysis of this question). Monsma and Soper (1997) argue for the latter position, and compare

---

[4] In 1988, Congress permitted the wearing of religious symbols in military uniform, thus overruling the Supreme Court's decision in *Goldman v. Weinberger*. As was observed with respect to the issue of sacramental use of hallucinogenic drugs, there remains an important distinction between a an act of legislative discretion and the assertion of a fundamental constitutional right.

religious freedom in the United States unfavorably with that of other Western nations (England, Holland, Germany, and Australia). They suggest that religious liberty in the United States is inappropriately inhibited by an overly broad interpretation of the establishment clause, and that the scope of proscribed government support should be narrowed to enhance the "positive neutrality" on which authentic religious liberty depends.

This point can thus be generalized. Modern governments of all types provide a range of services and protections, and the scope of their activity is unprecedented in world history. All governments are thus confronted with the question of which religious beliefs to support and to encourage, and which to regulate and (perhaps) inhibit, and how to do so.

### EXPLANATORY FACTORS

Thus, there exist several dimensions across which the nature of religious politics in diverse settings can be described. However, another of our major goals in this book is to point to ways in which these differences can be explained. We suggest that fruitful avenues of inquiry can be found by investigating the nature of a nation's religious composition, or, to use a term from the contemporary sociology of religion, religious "markets," as well as the content of specific religious creeds and traditions.

### THE STRUCTURE OF RELIGIOUS MARKETS

An important set of comparisons may involve the existence of or extent of religious competition. This issue poses the question of whether the number and relative strength of religious competitors has political consequences.[5] In some national cultures, a single religious tradition is dominant. Many sociologists and political scientists have emphasized the ability of dominant religions to ensure social consensus, and to provide an uncontested web of social and spiritual meanings to citizens. Berger (1969) argued that, in social settings in which there exists widespread agreement over religious values, religion forms a "sacred canopy" within which social and political life can be conducted. Religion is a source of social and political integration, which provides a set of meanings that are taken for granted by most members of a given society.

In recent years, the theoretical scaffolding for this approach has been elaborated through analyses of politics in the United States. For example, James Reichley (1985) suggests that a widely shared Judeo-Christian

---

[5] The assumptions underlying this section are largely drawn from Huntington (1974).

tradition provides substantive values that render democratic political discourse possible. He argues that such a dominant religious tradition creates "a body of shared values through which problems can be mediated" (Reichley 1985: 52). Similarly, Richard Neuhaus (1984) argues that the cultural context is shaped by intuitions about how the world is and ought to be, and claims that, as an empirical matter, such moral judgments inevitably involve religious belief.[6]

Scholars who write in this tradition argue that religious values are sources of social cohesion and stability to the extent that such values are widely shared. Various traditionalist religious movements such as the Hindu resurgence in India, the Christian right in the United States, and Islamic movements in various countries, explicitly seek to "restore" a society in which basic religious and moral questions are not subject to debate. Activists in these movements believe that orthodoxy will create national and social stability, consensus, and meaning.

Yet it is also possible that, in at least some cases, religious bodies in countries with dominant religious traditions may lack the vigor to provide such shared meanings and beliefs. Finke and Stark (1992) have argued that U.S. history suggests that religious monopolies or oligopolies may become "lazy," and take the support of the state and the population for granted. If monopoly religions fail to meet the needs and desires of potential members, then the faith may encounter competition either from other faiths, or from secularism. If a nation's population comes to include large numbers of persons for whom religion is of marginal importance, secular ideologies, such as humanism, may become serious competitors with churches for social prestige and political power.

Thus, we can generate at least two possibilities for nations dominated by a single religious tradition. Religious beliefs may provide a "sacred canopy" within which the conflict of everyday politics can be managed. Alternatively, the possible inactivity of locally or nationally dominant churches may reduce the general religiosity of certain segments of the population. If this is the case, monopoly religions may indeed create the market for secular competition, and thus undermine their own dominance.

In other settings, there are two or more serious religious competitors for social and political power. Some of these cases include nations in which previously dominant religious traditions face new competition. In Europe, Islamic migration has created sizable (and highly visible) reli-

---

[6] Of course, the United States case is not incontrovertibly an instance of a dominant religious tradition, because the Judeo-Christian tradition contains many competing theological strains (Kellstedt and Leege 1993), and because non-Western religions are becoming increasingly visible in the United States.

gious minorities in several nations, while in several nations of South and Central America, Pentecostal missionaries have had remarkable success in luring some of the most religiously active citizens away from the Catholic Church. In other cases competition is more long-standing, as in the Hindu-Muslim split in India or the coexistence of Shinto and Buddhism in Japan. In the United States, religious immigration has increased the number of non-Christians, but no single non-Christian faith has sufficient numbers to contest for dominance. Yet the Christian majority is divided into literally hundreds of different denominations, with substantial theological and moral disagreements.

Recent developments in the sociology of religion have suggested that religious competition generally leads to vigorous religious membership and activity. Much of this newer literature regards the United States as normative (Warner 1993), and has focused on the relationship between contending traditions within Christianity (Finke and Stark 1992; Gill 1998; Iannaccone 1990). Using an explicitly economic metaphor, scholars within this emerging tradition suggest that religious bodies, such as denominations, can usefully be compared to firms in an economy. In contrast to the "lazy monopoly" hypothesis described above, "firms" in competitive religious "markets" must strive to attract adherents in order to survive and prosper. To the extent that such "suppliers" of religious goods respond to the desires of potential members, such religious "shoppers" are more likely to act as "consumers" of religious goods.

If religious bodies are indeed involved in a competition for potential members, it seems reasonable to assume that the providers of religious goods must engage in what might be termed "product differentiation." That is, if religious producers seek to attract consumers, they must provide reasons why their particular products are different from (and superior to) those offered by their competitors. In the United States, there is some evidence that this has in fact occurred. Some have argued that evangelical Protestants in the United States have been especially focused on differentiating their doctrine from their nearest theological competitors (Wilcox 1992; Jelen 1993). For example, a pastor in the General Association of Regular Baptist Churches explained to one of us, in excruciating detail, how his denomination is more authentic than other large Baptist denominations, and a Bible Baptist Fellowship pastor went so far as to claim that some other Baptist denominations were so far removed from correct doctrine that their members might not be truly "saved" and thereby not headed for heaven. Yet religious competition in the United States is more common among theological traditions than between them. A particularistic Baptist church may lure members away from another Baptist denomination or even another evangelical church, but it is unlikely to win many Catholic converts.

The very fragmentation of the U.S. religious market may influence the nature of religious competition there. In democratic political systems, politics is, to a large extent, about "making 51 percent." The building of a majority in a religiously pluralistic culture is difficult, and often requires that theological differences be submerged or deemphasized. Thus the religious imperative to differentiate theology clashes with the political imperative to build coalitions (Bendyna and Wilcox 1996; Jelen 1998).

The market model may have applicability outside of the United States as well. Elsewhere, we have shown that Catholicism is a more potent source of political socialization in Europe in settings in which Catholics constitute a minority (Jelen and Wilcox 1998); a finding which suggests that at least the basic mechanism underlying the market model has applications outside the United States. Similarly, Gill (1998) has used this approach with some success in analyzing political religion in South America. However, the generalizability of the model of "demobilized pluralism" from the United States to other settings may depend on the effects of other variables.

One such variable might be the relative size and political power of various religious traditions in a particular setting. For example, while Sihks and Muslims constitute substantial minorities in India, a very large majority of Indian citizens are Hindus. In such an unequal setting, religious politics may not involve either the necessity for religious product differentiation, or the plausibility of intertraditional coalitions. Similarly, the experience of some nations of Latin America suggests that a formerly dominant Catholic Church will often seek to retain its dominance by either suppressing or co-opting religious competition from evangelical Protestant denominations. Where religious minorities are relatively weak, they may seek some measure of autonomy (either functional or geographical), rather than to engage in overtly political action. Where religious majorities are extremely strong, they may seek to dominate, rather than accommodate, religious competitors.[7]

The market model may not apply in countries in which the competing religions are not plausibly attractive to religious "consumers." While one can easily imagine evangelical Protestants in the United States moving from one Baptist denomination to another, or Brazilian Catholics joining a local Pentecostal church, it strains credulity to suppose that very many citizens of India actually contemplate switching from Hinduism to Islam, or vice versa. It is difficult to imagine two religions with

[7] For example, Pankaj Mishra (2000) has argued that the Indian government largely replaced an ideology of secular multiculturalism with one of "unitary Hindu nationalism."

different conceptions of God(s) and of human sexuality than Hinduism and Islam, and it is doubtful that the market model has any application to this type of religious competition. In other words, it may be necessary and appropriate for scholars seeking a comparative understanding of religious politics to consider the *content* of religious belief. It is to this issue that we now turn.

## THE POLITICS OF THEOLOGY

Thus, a second explanatory dimension of comparison that the cases in this book allow is content of religious belief and practice. To what extent does it matter *which* religious traditions are involved in political affairs, and which combination of creeds, practices, and memberships are politically salient in a particular cultural setting?

Directing attention to the identity and content of religious variables enables us to make two disparate types of comparisons. First, several of the chapters in this book are devoted to examining the politics of two religious traditions with what might be termed "universalist" aspirations: Roman Catholicism and Islam. The importance of these creeds in a variety of political settings may provide a basis for cross-national comparisons across otherwise disparate cultures.

A point of similarity between the universalist creeds may be that both Catholicism and Islam have, at times, provided a transcendent basis for regime transformation. Islam was central to the Iranian revolution of 1979, and the Catholic Church played an essential role in the demise of communism in Poland (Davies 1986). Indeed, the charismatic leadership of a Polish pope was arguably the lynchpin underlying the breakup of the communist bloc in Central and Eastern Europe. Similarly, the availability of religiously-based charisma clearly provided Khomeni with an alternative basis for Iranian nationalism, as well as a rationale for undermining the Shah's project of modernization and Westernization.

Conversely, the universalist nature of Catholicism and Islam may be contrasted with respect to the role of religion in what might be termed "normal politics." Perhaps ironically, the centralized, hierarchical nature of Catholicism may have enabled the Church to adapt to national political cultures where necessary. In particular, the Vatican councils of the late nineteenth and mid-twentieth centuries have provided theological rationales for a political flexibility on the part of national Catholic churches. Vatican I, while asserting the infallibility of the pope in matters of faith and morals, nevertheless constituted a retreat on the part of a formerly hegemonic Catholicism by conceding the existence of a "secular" realm. The Church strengthened its authority in certain areas (such as dogma and personal morality) while retreating from other areas, including national and international politics (Burns 1992). In its relationship with modernity and political liberalism, the Catholic hierarchy took an active role in the compartmentalization and limitation of its own authority (Casanova 1994). Similarly, Vatican II deemphasized the importance of a centralized hierarchy, in favor of a concept of the Church as "the people of God" (Dillon 1999). This shift in emphasis provided a theological rationale for adapting the application of Church dogma to local political cultures.[8] Thus, by way of illustration, the American Church is free to participate in the pluralistic religious culture of the United States by respecting the constitutional separation of church and state, while the Church in postcommunist Poland can attempt to reassert its former role as a source of national identity. Several chapters in this book provide details of other instances in which the Church has negotiated specific arrangements with different political regimes, which provide both support for the Church and limits on its power.

By contrast, the chapters dealing with the politics of Islam in this book suggest that the Islamic resurgence has not yet resulted in a stable accommodation between Islam and secular governments. The demands of Islamic activists have led to a variety of political responses, ranging from revolution to acquiescence. The successes of Islamic revolutions in Iran and Afghanistan led many governments in Arab countries to either suppress or co-opt Islam, or in the case of Egypt, to try to do both. The varied relationships between religion and politics in which Islam is the dominant religion may reflect the strength of the revival of Islamic orthodoxy, a diversity of views within Islam about the proper relationship between religion and the state, or the more decentralized nature of Islam.

Second, a focus on the similarities and differences between creeds in pluralistic religious settings may provide some insight as to the sources and nature of religious conflict. The studies by Hallum (Central America), Gill (South America), Soper and Fetzer (Western Europe) and the editors (United States) of this book suggest that religious competition which is, in some sense, "intramural" can be managed successfully within the normal course of democratic politics. To be sure, Catholic elites in Latin America and evangelical leaders in the United States have sought to enhance their political power and influence, and Catholic reaction to Pentecostal recruitment in Latin American has been openly hostile. However, it seems fair to assert that such controversies are conducted within the norms and rules of parliamentary or presidential multiparty democracies. That is, factions within a society attempt to pass legislation favorable to themselves, or unfavorable to their allies.

---

[8] Arguably, an important aspect of the agenda of Pope John Paul II has been the reversal of this centrifugal tendency in world Catholicism.

Protagonists within these "intra-Christian" disputes seem willing to abide by the rules of the game, and accept, however temporarily, unfavorable outcomes.

In a variety of settings, it seems to be the case that there exist clear limits as to the bounds of acceptable religious competition. The analysis of Western European politics by Soper and Fetzer suggests that, while intra-Christian conflict seems safely domesticated in the national politics of Great Britain, Germany, and France, religion can be mobilized for political ends when questions of Muslim immigration are concerned. Moreover, political elites in these nations have been less than accommodating when dealing with growing numbers of Muslim immigrants.[9]

Similarly, political-religious conflict in India frequently approaches an intensity in which the use of violence is actively contemplated (and occasionally employed) by both Hindus and Muslims. Finally, religion provides the idiom for conflict in the Middle East.

By contrast, religious pluralism in Japan does not appear to have resulted in any appreciable increase in religious conflict. Uniquely among the cases considered here, the analysis of Toyoda and Tanaka show that Japanese religious pluralism has resulted in the melding of the Buddhist and Shinto traditions, a practice known as "syncretism." Many Japanese apparently move effortlessly between the rituals and practices of these two traditions, with no apparent cognitive dissonance or social anxiety.

The contrast between Japan and the other cases is interesting, and suggests several possibilities for further investigation. Japan may be a truly exceptional case, where political and religious elites made a conscious effort to blend Shinto and Buddhism, and where a belief in a single (or even any) deity is not central to either faith. There has been some competition between Buddhism and other faiths in the past in Southeast Asia, and Buddhism does have a missionary tradition.

Alternatively, it may be the case that religious pluralism only results in competition between members of religious traditions when at least one of the traditions is monotheistic. The creeds of Judaism, Christianity, and Islam all regard the Hebrew Scriptures as a sacred text, and the *exclusive* monotheism mandated by the First Commandment renders syncretism quite difficult. In the absence of a theological mandate for exclusivity, a citizen of Japan may experience no more tension between being an adherent of Shinto and a Buddhist than an American would between being a Republican and a third baseman, and this might be the natural state of competition between nonmonotheistic religions. In

---

[9] This also suggests that the relationship between evangelical Christianity and Islam among African Americans in the United States is a topic deserving of further study.

contrast, it is difficult to imagine being a Muslim and a Catholic, or a Pentecostal Christian and a Jew, and these exclusive identities may breed conflict.

The competition between Islam and competitor religions appears to be unusually intense at century's end. Islam is in the midst of a world-wide revival, and Islamic countries, such as Iran and Iraq, play an important part in world politics. The conflict may be especially important in the next decade in Europe, where tensions over Islamic immigration may be exacerbated by the admission of Turkey to the European Union. If Turkey were admitted to the EU, this would grant de facto citizenship to nearly one hundred million Muslims to Britain, France, Germany, and the other nations of Europe. Tensions between Islam and Christianity, Judaism, and Hinduism may be greater today because of the reinvigoration of Islam that is occurring among educated young adherents, and also because of the distinctive life-style requirements of the faith.

## CULTURE WARS: THE POLITICAL ROLE OF RELIGION CONTESTED

In principle, the "canopy" and "pluralist" accounts of the relationship between religion and politics represent simplified, static, and (at least potentially) stable models of the intersection of the sacred and the secular. If a society exhibits a consensus on matters of religious faith, morals, and practice, religion can serve as a source of social cohesion and meaning for a society. Religion can impart legitimacy to prevailing values and practices, by providing a shared framework within which the day-to-day practice of politics can be conducted.

Conversely, pluralist theory teaches us that religion may serve as an essentially private resource for political and social criticism. In a cultural setting characterized by high levels of religious diversity, it may be difficult for the faithful to attract sufficient support for religious or moral judgments to engage in efficacious political participation. It may be difficult for adherents of minority religions to attain public ends via political means, which further suggests that religion in pluralistic societies may ultimately prove to be a private matter. In turn, privatized religion may operate as a sort of sanctuary, within which the citizen's attachment to the state is softened and qualified. In either case, religion operates essentially as a background element, within which the normal "stuff" of politics – conflict, engagement, and mobilization – can occur. In their static states, religious values are not normally protagonists in political debate.

In our view, religion is most likely to become overtly politicized in cases in which the political role of religious belief becomes contested.

The dynamic element of religious politics is most easily observed when consensus about the appropriate social and political function of religion is challenged. In its purest theoretical formulation, this can occur in one of two ways. First, the hegemony of a dominant religious tradition can be challenged by competitors, seeking legal autonomy or equality. If a particular denomination enjoys a quasi-monopoly, its dominant status may be challenged by other religious competitors, or by adherents of a secular ideology. Because the theoretical expectations of the pluralist model suggest that there will be many religiously inactive citizens in non-competitive environments, the existence of religious or secular rivals to a dominant religious tradition seems likely. Conversely, a religious body in a secular or religiously competitive body may seek to establish dominance in the political realm. Often (as in the case of militant Islam in Iran, Hindu nationalism in India, or the Christian right in the United States) the challenge to moral and religious pluralism is often explicitly restorationist, and the rhetoric evokes a mythological past in which a religious consensus reigned. In either case, what James Davison Hunter (1991) has termed a "culture war" may often be the result of situations in which the definition of the religious composition of society becomes contested. Whereas the protagonists in a particular culture war seem likely to vary according to particular contexts and circumstances, the common feature of religiously motivated political conflict seems to be dissensus over the appropriate social role of the sacred.

### PLAN OF THE BOOK

Thus, even a preliminary glance at the political roles of religion in the world today suggests that religion can and does serve a variety of public functions. One purpose of this collection is to determine whether, and to what extent, this bewildering diversity of forms of religious politics can be made to yield serviceable generalizations.

In conducting this survey of religion and politics, we begin with the assumption of Alisdair MacIntyre (1973) that cross-national similarities between different nations and practices are to be discovered, rather than assumed. We have therefore not imposed a single concept or theory on our contributors, but rather asked them to describe the religious and political contexts in the country or region of their study, and to focus on the most interesting questions that arise in those contexts. Although there are many interesting cases that are not covered in this book, the cases included provide a representative variety of the public roles religion can take.

Further, our contributors provide a variety of perspectives and methodological approaches. Some of the chapters are explicitly comparative, and some are organized around a classical, social-scientific, hypothesis-testing model of inquiry. Others are classic case studies that emphasize the unique nature of religious politics in specific cultural and political settings.

We have divided the cases in this book into two sections. The first section consists of nations in which one religious tradition is dominant. In Chapter 2, Timothy Byrnes examines the changing role of the Catholic Church in Poland. Although the Church served as a symbol of the Polish people and played a major role in the overthrow of communism, today the Church's role is contested and it faces new challenges in an increasingly pluralistic political system. In Chapter 3, Michele Dillon suggests that the Catholic Church in Ireland still plays a major role in public life by influencing the culture and shaping expectations. Yet as the Church has entered into political debates using secular reasoning, it may have allowed citizens to conceive of a separation between church and state, and of distinct realms of influence for each. Paul Manuel, in Chapter 4, describes a Catholic monopoly in Spain and Portugal, where past relations between the Church and antidemocratic regimes have discredited the Church's priestly and prophetic role in politics. Yet Catholicism remains an important force in society and politics.

Kenneth Wald in Chapter 5 describes Israel, the world's only Jewish state. He argues that religion is the source of two important conflicts in Israel: over the relationship of religion and the state, largely raised by the Ultraorthodox, and over sacred status of land, an issue that has profound implications for foreign policy.

In Chapter 6, Sussan Siavoshi describes the revolution that deposed the Shah and installed an Islamic republic in Iran. Siavoshi suggests that today there is a lively debate in Iran over the relationship between religion and the state, and that this debate is not merely between secular and religious Iranians but among religious Muslims over the proper nature of political authority in Islam. Mehran Tamadonfar compares the political role of Islam in Egypt, Algeria, and Lebanon in Chapter 7. He suggests that efforts to create Islamic states in these countries have been met with a variety of responses by states, and that the political stance of Islam has been influenced by history and foreign events.

The second section contains studies of nations or regions which are characterized by some degree of religious pluralism, and in which multiple religious traditions may compete for social influence and political power. In Chapter 8, Christopher Soper and Joel Fetzer examine religious politics in France, Germany, and England. Although each is a highly secular country, religion provides a source of political mobilization. These countries differ in the composition of their Christian majorities, and have responded differently to Islamic immigration.

Anthony Gill describes religious politics in South America with a focus on the Catholic Church in Chapter 9. Here the Catholic majority is challenged by the growing strength of Pentecostal Protestant churches. The role of the Catholic Church in shoring up established power relationships and discredited regimes echoes Manuel's description of Iberia, but Gill argues that in South America Catholic elites did eventually help the transformation to democracy. The Church has resisted Pentecostal competition in a variety of ways, including using the regulatory power of the state. In Chapter 10, Anne Hallum describes this same religious competition Central America with a focus on evangelical churches. Pentecostals have served as presidents in Guatemala, although to date their performance has been undistinguished. Yet Hallum argues that the Pentecostal movement has had a small scale but significant impact on the personal politics in the region and on the development of social capital.

Our next two cases provide a sharp contrast. In Chapter 11, Sunil Sahu describes the rise of a Hindu nationalist party in the officially secular state of India. Religious conflict in India has been occasionally violent, and the Hindu majority is increasingly mobilized in politics. Yet the Bharatiya Janata party (BJP) has been constrained once in power by divisions with Hinduism, by the official secular nature of the state, by the need to create electoral majorities, and by the history of church-state policy in India.

In Chapter 12, Toyoda and Tanaka describe the syncretism between Shinto and Buddhism in Japan. This blending is unique among our cases, with many Japanese occasionally including elements of each religion in their lives. The inclusion of Shinto shrines on the grounds of Buddhist temples, and vice versa, is radically different from the tale of the demolition of a Muslim mosque in India to rebuild the temple of Rama. The authors argue that political elites in Japan have consciously blended and manipulated religion to meet national needs, but that when elites tried to build a state Shinto in the twentieth century their success with the people was more limited.

Finally, Wilcox and Jelen describe the case of the United States, where a dazzling array of Christian denominations coexist with many other religious traditions in a country known for separation of church and state and for freedom of religion. Americans are far more religious than their socioeconomic profile would predict, and this has consequences for politics. Moreover, the uniquely porous political parties and decentralized political system allow for multiple entry points for many competing religious groups in American politics.

These diverse cases contain rich detail of the history and cultural context of religious politics. Clearly any account of these countries without understanding these details would be incomplete. In the conclusion (Chapter 14), we seek to draw a few generalizations across these cases, however, which we hope will serve as an impetus to future research.

### REFERENCES

Bader, Jenny Lynn. 2000. "The Miniskirt as a National Security Threat." *New York Times, September 10; WK 3.*

Benavides, Gustavo, and M. W. Daly (eds.). 1989. *Religion and Political Power.* Albany: State University of New York Press.

Berger, Peter. 1969. *The Sacred Canopy: Elements of a Sociological Theory of Religion.* Garden City, NY: Anchor.

Burns, Gene, 1992. *The Frontiers of Catholicism: The Politics of Ideology in a Liberal World.* Berkeley: University of California Press.

Casanova, Jose. 1994. *Public Religions in the Modern World.* Chicago: University of Chicago Press.

Davies, Norman. 1986. *Heart of Europe: A Short History of Poland.* New York: Oxford University Press.

Dillon, Michele. 1999. *Catholic Identity: Balancing Reason, Faith, and Power.* New York: Cambridge University Press.

Duggan, Paul. 2000. "A Few Texas Faithful Stand for Prayer." *Washington Post,* September 2: A1; A10.

Finke, Roger, and Rodney Stark. 1992. *The Churching of America, 1776–1992.* New Brunswick, NJ: Rutgers University Press.

Gill, Anthony James. 1998. *Rendering Unto Caesar: The Catholic Church and the State in Latin America.* Chicago: University of Chicago Press.

Gold, Daniel. 1991. "Organized Hinduisms: From Vedic Truth to Hindu Nation." In Martin E. Marty and R. Scott Appleby (eds.). *Fundamentalisms Observed.* Chicago: University of Chicago Press: 531–93.

Goodstein, Laurie. 2000. "Bush is Coming Under Criticism for Jesus Day Proclamation." *New York Times,* August 6: 14.

Hunter, James Davison. 1991. *Culture Wars: The Struggle to Define America.* New York: Basic Books.

Huntington, Samuel S. 1974. "Paradigms of American Politics: Beyond the One, the Two, and the Many." *Political Science Quarterly* 89: 1–26.

    1996. *The Clash of Civilizations and the Remaking of World Order.* New York: Simon and Schuster.

Iannaccone, Laurence R. 1990. "Religious Practice: A Human Capital Approach." *Journal for the Scientific Study of Religion* 29: 297–314.

Jelen, Ted G. 1998. "Research in Religion and Political Behavior: Looking Both Ways After Two Decades of Research." *American Politics Quarterly* 26: 110–13.

    2000. *To Serve God and Mammon: Church-State Relations in the United States.* Boulder, CO: Westview.

Jelen, Ted G., and Clyde Wilcox. 1995. *Public Attitudes Toward Church and State.* Armonk, NY: M. E. Sharpe.

1998. "Context and Conscience: The Catholic Church as an Agent of Political Socialization in Western Europe." *Journal for the Scientific Study of Religion* 37: 28–40.

Kurtz, Lester. 1995. *Gods in the Global Village: The World's Religions in Sociological Perspective*. Thousand Oaks, CA: Pine Forge Press.

Leege, David C. 1993. "Religion and Politics in Theoretical Perspective." In David C. Leege and Lyman A. Kellstedt (eds.). *Rediscovering the Religious Factor in American Politics*. Armonk, NY: M. E. Sharpe: 3–25.

Leege, David C. and Lyman A. Kellstedt. 1993. "Religious Worldviews and Political Philosophies: Capturing Theory in the Grand Manner Through Empirical Data." In David C. Leege and Lyman A. Kellstedt (eds.). *Rediscovering the Religious Factor in American Politics*. Armonk, NY: M. E. Sharpe: 216–31.

MacIntyre, Alasdair. 1973. "Is a Science of Comparative Politics Possible?" In Alan Ryan (ed.). *The Philosophy of Social Explanation*. New York: Oxford University Press: 171–88.

Marty, Martin E., and R. Scott Appleby. 1991. "Conclusion: An Interim Report on a Hypothetical Family." In Martin E. Marty and R. Scott Appleby (eds.). *Fundamentalisms Observed*. Chicago: University of Chicago Press: 814–42.

(eds.). 1991. *Fundamentalisms Observed*. Chicago: University of Chicago Press.

(eds.). 1993a. *Fundamentalisms and Society*. Chicago: University of Chicago Press.

(eds.). 1993b. *Fundamentalisms and the State*. Chicago: University of Chicago Press.

(eds.). 1994. *Accounting for Fundamentalisms*. Chicago: University of Chicago Press.

(eds.). 1995. *Fundamentalisms Comprehended*. Chicago: University of Chicago Press.

Mishra, Pankaj. 2000. "Yearning to be Great, India Loses Its Way." *New York Times*, September 16: A27.

Moen, Matthew C., and Lowell Gustafson (eds.). *The Religious Challenge to the State*. Philadelphia: Temple University Press.

Monsma, Stephen V., and J. Christoper Soper. 1997. *The Challenge of Pluralism: Church and State in Five Democracies*. Lanham, MD: Rowman-Littlefield.

Neuhaus, Richard John, 1984. *The Naked Public Square: Religion and Democracy in America*. Grand Rapids, MI: Eerdmanns.

Pooley, Eric. 2000. "Gore's Leap of Faith." *Time*, August 21: 24–9.

Reichley, A. James. 1985. *Religion in American Public Life*. Washington, D.C.: Brookings.

Richardson, James T., and Massimo Introvigne. 2001. "Brainwashing Theories in European Parliamentary and Administrative Reports on 'Cults' and 'Sects.'" *Journal for the Scientific Study of Religion* 40: 143–68.

Sontag, Deborah. 2000. "In Israel, Suddenly Cucumbers Are Not Kosher." *New York Times*, September 10: 3.

Warner, R. Stephen. 1993. "Work in Progress Toward a New Paradigm for the Sociology of Religion in the United States." *American Journal of Sociology* 98: 1044–93.

Weigel, George. 1991. "Religion and Peace: An Argument Complexified." *Washington Quarterly* 14: 27.

Wilcox, Clyde. 1992. *God's Warriors: The Christian Right in Twentieth Century America*. Baltimore: Johns Hopkins University Press.

In this chapter, Timothy Byrnes provides a dramatic illustration of the distinction between the "prophetic" and "priestly" roles of religion. This analysis suggests that Catholicism was a powerful prophetic voice during the communist era in Poland, but that the Church has been largely rebuffed in its attempts to assert a "priestly" function in the postcommunist period. Historically, Poland's sovereignty has been contested and limited by powerful outside neighbors, most recently, the Soviet Union. During such periods, Polish Catholicism has been a symbol of Polish national identity. In the post-communist era, the Polish Church finds its formerly dominant political role challenged by forces which are neither specifically Catholic nor generally religious, but which are nevertheless authentically "Polish." The Church is but one player – formidable, but hardly invincible – in an increasingly democratic, pluralistic, political system.

# 2

## The Challenge of Pluralism

### *The Catholic Church in Democratic Poland*

#### *Timothy A. Byrnes*

The political role of the Catholic Church in Poland has been fundamentally reshaped by the fall of communism and the rise of democracy
in East Central Europe. Communist rule the Catholic Church to identify
itself with the interests of the Polish nation and with opposition to a
regime imposed from the outside. This political role has been questioned,
critiqued, and even discarded after the transition to democracy. The
Church suffered horribly under communism, but democracy and pluralism have posed challenges and raised obstacles that in the long run may
be more threatening to the Church's role in society than anything offered
by communism. This chapter is an examination of both this change in
context, and of these challenges that have been the result.

### TRADITION AND HISTORY

Patrick Michel wrote that "it was Soviet practice itself that assigned
religion its potential role in Eastern Europe, and now that this practice
no longer exists, the role allocated to religion can only undergo a total
redefinition" (Michel 1992: 339–44). In the Polish case, the role of the
Catholic Church was assigned in Poland not only by Soviet practice, but
also by the invasions, partitions, and occupations that have dominated
Polish history for the past two centuries. Poland was partitioned and
wiped from the map from 1795 to 1918. It was invaded and brutally
occupied by Nazi Germany in 1939. And it suffered under Soviet
imposed communism until 1989 (Davies 1982). Throughout that period,
the Catholic Church survived and at times even thrived by presenting
itself as the only authentically indigenous institution in Polish society
(Szajkowski 1983).

In this connection, Ewa Morawska has called the Church the "traditional carrier of Polish civil religion," and the "major public spokesman

for Polish civil society" (Morawska 1987: 228).[1] The Church's persistent identification with, and support for, the interests of an autonomous Polish nation was the backbone of the Church's political role in the years leading up to the fall of communism.

That political role was concrete in that the Church offered the nation everything from free space for the exploration of Polish history and culture to meeting halls and communication equipment necessary for political mobilization. But the Church's political role was also deeply symbolic in that it served as a living exemplar of independence and what many Poles called authenticity. As a Polish student put it: "For us the church signifies patriotism, tradition, continuity, and stability" (Weschler 1982: 20). For many anticommunist dissidents, the Catholic Church was a model of how a healthier civil society might conduct itself. Although he did not generally trust the church, Adam Michnik was impressed by the Church's willingness and ability to act at times as though the regime was not there – saying Mass, celebrating traditional national holidays, asserting in many ways, large and small, the basic freedoms of both individual and national life (Michnik 1993).

In time, the activism that grew out of the assertion of this autonomy came to form the basic frame of political opposition, picked up with much more fervor and purpose by Solidarity in the late 1970s and throughout the 1980s. The Church's Millenial Novena of 1966 was a seminal event in the cycle of protest that led to profound political change in Poland (Osa 1997: 339–65). The Polish Pope's visit in Spring 1979 reinforced and made ever more visible the church's "counterhegemonic subculture," its status as a kind of alternative Polish authority structure (Kubik 1994: 4). The Church was a central locus of both Polish nationalism and autonomous organization, and it was therefore able to set the stage for not only the emergence of Solidarity as a viable political opposition, but also for the earth-shattering events that took place throughout the region in 1989.

## THE RETURN OF DEMOCRACY

This role, both symbolic and concrete, was unlikely to survive the revolution of 1989. The political role of the Catholic Church, after all, was forged in opposition. When opposition was no longer necessary because of the stunning victory of the Church and its allies, the Church had to reorient itself to the new realities of postcommunist Poland. During the first heady days after the fall of communism, the Church enjoyed substantial structural advantages over other actors. The Catholic Church

---

[1] Maryjane Osa, on the other hand, has sounded a cautionary note, reminding us just how complex, and at times even ambivalent, the relationship between Church and nation has actually been across the whole span of Polish history (Osa 1989: 268–99).

was, in the early 1990s, the most organized and most coherent institutional presence in a rather chaotic political environment. As a result, the church was able to reap the benefits of its prominent opposition to a now thoroughly discredited former regime. Religious education was returned to public schools; abortion was criminalized and restricted; and a concordat with the Vatican was signed by a Polish government deeply influenced by the Church's hierarchy.

But in fairly short order, the political situation in Poland, and along with it the political role of the Catholic Church, grew considerably more complicated. Many other institutions and movements arose to compete with the Church for influence in a much more pluralist politics. Moreover, the special place that the Church had played in the national mythology eroded rapidly. It was one thing for Poles to look to the Catholic Church for political leadership under communism, but it was apparently quite a different thing for Poles to accept political direction from the Church and its leaders after communism toppled.

Ewa Morawska argues that the Church's agenda in Poland remained basically consistent over the years (Morawska 1995: 47–75). The Church has always wanted to protect its institutional interests and impose its moral and social teachings on Polish society. That was the Church's suppressed hope before 1989, and that has been the Church's expressed intention after. What has been fundamentally *inconsistent*, Morawska maintains, is the public's response to the Church's agenda and to the Church's efforts to advance its institutional interests. While the Church's defense of itself and of its role in Polish society were not so long ago celebrated as clarion calls for national independence, very similar arguments today are widely suspected of being inappropriately sectarian and even fundamentally antidemocratic.

Morawska's argument is supported both by a careful reading of what Catholic leaders actually said and did before 1989, and by public opinion polls which show that Poles living in a new democracy are increasingly disinclined to view the Church's participation in politics as a positive phenomenon. Although Michnik had earlier grudgingly embraced the Church as a political ally in the national struggle against Soviet communism, he now characterized the Church and its social influence in the late 1980s as a potentially major obstacle to the consolidation of liberal democracy in the Republic of Poland (Michnik 1993: 244–72).[2]

---

[2] Michnik's epilogue, which was actually written in 1987 and reprinted in 1993, is not easy to characterize in simple terms. It is a complex discussion of the need for secular Polish intellectuals and their interlocutors in the Church to come to terms with the Church's "national chauvinist" past, and the implications of that past for the Church's future role in Polish society. Nevertheless, as Michnik's editor and translator, David Ost, puts it: "the essay represents a draw[ing] back from [Michnik's] previously favorable accounts of Polish Catholicism" (244).

Has the return to democracy transformed the role of the Church in Polish politics? The answer to this question depends on the answers to two closely related sets of questions. First, what approach has the Church taken to its role in Polish society. What do leaders of the Catholic Church, both inside Poland and in Rome, think that the role of the institutional Church should be in an authentically democratic Poland? What steps have those leaders taken to enshrine that role – in the Polish Constitution, in Polish law, and in the everyday processes of Polish politics? And how successful have those steps been in achieving their aims?

Second, to what degree does the new pluralist context in the Republic of Poland influence the political role of the Church and the political choices made by the Church's leadership? How has the development of a democratic party system, for example, influenced the ways in which the Catholic Church seeks to protect and advance its interests in Polish society? Similarly, how has the institution of a highly complex system of governmental checks and balances shaped the ways in which the Church advances specific policy positions such as opposition to legal abortion?

The answers to these questions have important implications for the way in which we think about the role of religious institutions in post-communist democracies. The Catholic Church is deeply enmeshed in Polish society in a million ways, and is anxious to protect its prominent role in Polish society from future encroachment through constitutional and legal protection. But democracy in Poland has brought with it a degree of political pluralism and institutional complexity that have rendered *fundamentally new* the very political terrain on which Catholic leaders seek continuity and affirmation of tradition. Morawska is right: The Church's aims are not that different now than they were before. The problem for the Church, but surely not for the hopes of genuine democracy in Poland, is that practically everything else is different.

## THE CONSTITUTION AND THE CONCORDAT

The Church's first political priority in democratic Poland has been to protect its institutional interests by assuring its long term ability to function in Polish society and public life. Some in the Church fear that the period since 1989 is a kind of interregnum, a window of opportunity during which the Church needs to act aggressively and creatively to protect itself and ensure its future as an autonomous and influential institution. To that end, the Catholic hierarchy attempted to influence the wording of the new Polish Constitution.

The Church made four basic claims about the new Constitution. First, the Constitution should explicitly recognize the Polish Christian tradition as a source of national identity. Specifically, the bishops insisted on a clear reference to God in the Preamble to the Constitution, and on prominent reference to the role of the Church in Polish history. The so-called May 3rd Constitution of 1791, Poland's first written Constitution, was cited as a potential model in this regard. Its very opening words had been: "In the name of Almighty God."

Second, Church leaders wanted the basic constitutional law to refrain from referring to itself as the highest law of the land, or some similar formulation. "Those who believe in God," wrote Bishop Tadeusz Pieronek, secretary general of the Polish bishops' conference, in an article detailing this point of view, "are convinced that the Lord God is the ultimate source of world order and of laws that govern mankind, and that some laws stemming from that source are not subject to change, which means man cannot violate them" (*FBIS-EEU–94*, August 2, 1994: 36).

Third, the bishops wanted the Constitution to fix this "existing and unchangeable law" as "the foundation of the state's order" on a number of important moral issues (36). Thus, again according to Pieronek, "the Constitution should also explicitly prohibit everything that is an obstacle to or destroys man's links to God, as well as man's links to other men, particularly in the natural forms of interaction" (37). In practice, this rather tortured formulation meant that the bishops wanted the Constitution to ban abortion from the point of conception, and to declare marriage to be open only to relationships between a man and a woman.

Finally, the episcopate expressed its opposition to any constitutional language requiring a "separation" of church and state in democratic Poland. The bishops' argument, which might well be peculiar to the post-communist context, is that any *recognition* of separation would imply a *need* for separation, that is to say a previous *lack* of separation. That, in turn, would imply that the Church, during the communist era, was "a religious association that [existed and operated] thanks to the state, that [was] ruled in line with the state's rules, and that could be dissolved because of the state's will" (38). For fairly obvious reasons, the bishops deeply resented any such rendering of recent history, however indirect that rendering might be.

The Church threw all of its institutional energy and all of its political capital into the national debate over the Constitution. But the bishops and their supporters were deeply disappointed by the Constitution that emerged.

The "reference to God" issue was settled by a statement, unacceptable to Church spokesmen, referring equally to "those who believe in God," and to "those not sharing such faith but respecting those universal values as arising from other sources"(Preamble). The bishops also failed in their effort to place natural law, or "existing and unchangeable law" above the basic law of the national Constitution. In fact, the text explicitly referred to itself as "the supreme law of the Republic of Poland" (Article 8, Para 1). On the specific *areas* of law the bishops wanted declared "existing or unchangeable," the Constitution did limit marriage to "a union of a man and a woman" and stated that "the Republic of Poland shall ensure the legal protection of the life of every human being" (Article 18 and Article 38). But the Constitution did not declare human life sacred from the moment of conception.

Though the bishops were disappointed in these outcomes and did all they could to resist ratification of the Constitution, the Church did achieve some of what it wanted in the final text. The Constitution does include several prominent references to God; its preamble does refer explicitly to the specifically "Christian heritage of the nation"; and although the Constitution does not mirror the Church's absolutist stance on abortion, it does include a reference to the "protection of life" that was later used to argue against the constitutional legitimacy of less restrictive abortion laws. Most importantly, the Constitution included one major institutional victory for the Church in that it declared that "relations between the Republic of Poland and the Roman Catholic Church shall be determined by international treaty concluded with the Holy See" (Article 25, Para 4).

This treaty between the Holy See and the Republic of Poland, commonly known as the concordat, was originally signed in 1993, at the highpoint of the Church's influence in postcommunist Poland. The agreement guarantees the Church's autonomy, particularly in terms of its own institutional structure and governance, and lays out basic parameters of the Church's public role in democratic Poland. The concordat is contentious because it appears under some interpretations to remove the Catholic Church from the constraints of the general legal and political processes of democratic Poland. Basically, the political dispute over the concordat is whether it merely *protects* the church's rights from encroachment by the state, or rather *imposes* the Church's will on the state and Polish society.

The concordat assures the Church that it can control its own internal life. It can set the boundaries of its own dioceses, for example, and control the appointment of its own bishops (Ibid.: Article 6). The document establishes national holidays, free from work, according to the Church's liturgical calendar. The list includes Christmas, of course, but more controversially it also includes the Feast of the Assumption in August, All Souls Day in November, and the days *after* Christmas and Easter (Article 9). The concordat also renders Church weddings equal to civil ceremonies, declares Catholic cemeteries inviolable, protects the right of the Church to run its own schools, *and* guarantees religious instruction in public nursery schools and kindergartens (Article 10, Article 14, and Article 24). Finally, it states ambiguously that "activities serving humanitarian, charitable, health care, research and educational purposes, pursued by legal persons of the Church, shall under law be equal with activities serving similar purposes and carried out by state institutions" (Article 22).

Opponents of the concordat charged that the agreement would allow the Church to refuse burial to non-Catholics in areas where no non-Catholic cemeteries existed; to mandate religious instruction for Poland's youngest and most impressionable children; to take control of national marriage law and ritual; and to remove any question of taxation or public funding related to the church's pastoral work from the proper channels and inevitable uncertainties of the democratic process. The leftist government that ruled Poland from 1993 to 1997 resisted the concordat in a number of ways. It called for renegotiation with the Vatican; it insisted that the Constitution be finalized first; it issued a declaration of understanding laying down its own interpretation of several disputed provisions; and it left the agreement unratified for long stretches of time.

Nevertheless, in a major victory for the Church, the concordat was ultimately endorsed by the terms of the national Constitution. President Aleksander Kwasniewski objected to some of the particulars, but argued publically that ratification was necessary to demonstrate Poland's willingness to live up to solemn agreements signed by its lawful governments. But the concordat was finally ratified by a new, much more Church-friendly government, in 1998.

The results of the Church's efforts to institutionalize and protect their status in democratic Poland through the constitutional text and the concordat can be viewed in two ways. At the most basic level, the Church did everything it could to insert its positions and its views of Polish society in the national Constitution – and it lost. Most of the issues of most interest to the Church were resolved in the final draft through compromises, but they were almost all compromises that were unacceptable to the Church's hierarchy. As a result, the Primate, Cardinal Jozef Glemp, spoke in the days leading up to the national referendum on the Constitution of the "moral doubts" raised by the draft's contents, and of the Constitution's "lack of understanding for the believing majority" (*FBIS–EEU–97*, May 6, 1997). Despite the Church's campaign, the Constitution was ratified in referendum by the voters in an election in which with only 43 percent of the electorate voted (*FBIS–EEU–97*, May 26, 1997).

Yet more fundamentally, the final results were not a defeat for the Church. Most of the Church's failures involved symbolic references to God and the Catholic national heritage. But the Church's positions on concrete matters like the concordat and specific constitutional references to marriage, religious education, and even abortion were well represented in the final draft. The problem that the bishops had with the Polish Constitution was that it was a document of compromise and accommodation. Under communism, the Church's "victories" over the regime were few and far between, but the church nevertheless enjoyed the *social and cultural* status as the unrivaled representation of authentic national consciousness. In the months and years immediately following the fall of communism, the Church and its leadership parlayed this status, and the relative weakness of all other institutions in Polish society, into a leading role in directing public policy.

However, by 1997, by the time the final draft of the Constitution was placed before the public in referendum, the Church had been joined on the public stage by an exploding number of social and cultural institutions, political parties, and interest groups. The thriving civil society that Michnik and the other dissidents had hoped for in the 1970s was at long last taking root in democratic Poland. The Catholic Church, the symbolic substitute for that civil society during the darker decades of communism, was now only one of many social forces.

The Church remained an important institution in Polish public life in the late 1990s. That position was attested to officially by the concordat, and by the protection afforded the concordat by its place in the constitution. But that position was not structurally dominant; the Church could not simply impose itself and its interests in such a pluralist environment. Instead, the Church would need to learn to advance itself through successful navigation of the myriad political processes of a thriving democratic government.

## PARTIES AND ELECTIONS IN DEMOCRATIC POLAND

The first of these political processes is the development of a working democratic party system, and the institutionalization of effective democratic elections. The leadership of Poland's Catholic Church has set its own course through electoral politics in democratic Poland, but that course has been affected by political developments outside of the Church's control. The institutional and procedural context of democratic politics has itself played a very important role in determining the political role of the Catholic Church in postcommunist Poland.

During the first democratic election in 1989, the Church was closely associated with the Solidarity Trade Union and its parliamentary candidates. Krzystof Kosela has identified fully eighteen separate ways in which the Church aided Solidarity that year, from providing Church halls for meetings and rallies, to hosting frequent public discussions between Catholic bishops and Solidarity candidates (Kosela 1990: 124–37). The Church had opposed communism for decades, and not surprisingly the Church opposed communist candidates when free elections were finally held in Poland.

Since 1989, however, partisan politics in Poland have grown considerably more fragmented, complicated, and competitive. The Church's institutional allegiance was clear in 1989, when the choice was between communism and anticommunism. But the Church's partisan interests are much less obvious when the political choice involves all brands and varieties of postcommunist parties and candidates. The Church is of course not a monolith. There are internal divisions over emphasis and tactics within the hierarchy and between the hierarchy, clergy, and organized elements of the laity (Perlez 1997: 18). But the official line of the Church, articulated by the bishops, has been to eschew endorsement of individual parties and candidates while encouraging opposition to political forces that do not share the bishops' vision of a distinctly Catholic Poland.

Before the 1991 parliamentary elections, for example, the bishops declared, collectively, that "we will not take any sides. We will not point to any ticket. We prohibit priests from waging election campaigns or allowing them to be waged in churches and chapels" (*FBIS–EEU–95*, August 30, 1995). Yet Primate Glemp stated the same year that "naturally, a Catholic can't be part of a group which objects to Christian values" (*FBIS–EEU–95*, August 30, 1995).

During the 1995 presidential campaign, the bishops' conference pointedly declined to endorse a candidate, yet the hierarchy also released a statement discouraging Catholics from supporting "candidates who participated in the exercise of power at the highest party or government levels under totalitarian rule" (*OMRI Daily Digest Vol. II*, August 29, 1995). In the final run-off between the incumbent, Lech Walesa, and challenger Aleksander Kwasniewski, the implication of this latter statement was critical, because Kwasniewski had been a minister in the last communist government.

The Polish bishops' position on electoral politics might be termed "neutral . . . but." In its latest manifestation, this position led to the following statement during the 1997 parliamentary campaign:

"As shepherds who are loyal to the teachings of the Second Vatican Council, we do not want to tie the mission of the Church to any specific political party. Nonetheless, we are not indifferent to the fact that some parties make reference in their platforms to the Catholic social teachings, whereas others reject principles of these teachings as well as Catholic values" (*FBIS–EEU–97*, February 29, 1997).

The Church's engagement with electoral politics has also been influenced by the partisan context. In this connection, two related factors are particularly important: the fragmentation of Poland's party system after communism, and the specific nature of Poland's postcommunist electoral law. The old adage that wherever there are three Poles, there will be at least four political parties has proven accurate since 1989. Poles responded to the rebirth of democracy with an explosion of party formation and party fragmentation. This was most pronounced on the center-right of the political spectrum, among the Church's old allies in the Solidarity trade union movement. The breakup of the original Solidarity movement was due to several factors: the struggle between an increasingly imperious Walesa and his erstwhile partners; deep disagreement over the uncovering and prosecuting of former supporters of the communist regime; and splits in the old opposition along secular/religious, nationalist/liberal, and politician/union leader lines, all of which had been helpfully suppressed before 1989 by the shared antipathy toward communism (Millard 1994: 295–313).

All of these factors splintered Solidarity in the early 1990's and influenced the strategies and tactics adopted by the Church during the same period. What sense would it make for the Church to tie itself and its interests to one political party when its members belonged to many different parties and movements? What would the consequences be, for example, of a close political alliance between the Church and the Christian National Movement (ZChN), a party that has strongly endorsed the Church's interests but that might in a multiparty election gain a very small percentage of the national vote or even cease exist in the longer haul? No wonder the bishops "took no sides" and "pointed to no ticket." There were too many sides to choose from, too many tickets in play. Better in the long run to remain relatively aloof from the fortunes of particular parties and focus energy instead on continuing to oppose the forces of the left in the reconstituted, so-called postcommunist parties.

The wisdom of such a course was displayed with unmistakable clarity during the 1993 parliamentary election, a campaign fought under a new electoral law passed that very year. The previous election, in 1991, was held under a system of straight proportional representation. Virtually every party that received votes received seats in the Sejm, or lower house of Parliament, and Poland's young democracy was saddled with twenty-nine parties seated in Parliament. Before the 1993 election a new electoral law was passed setting a threshold for parliamentary representation at 5 percent of the national vote for individual parties and 8 percent for

electoral coalitions. The left, composed of parties led by seasoned formerly communist politicians, played the required coalition politics masterfully through the establishment of the Democratic Left Alliance (DLA). The post-Solidarity parties on the right failed to follow suit and contested the election in fragmented, weakened isolation.

The DLA received only around 20 percent of the vote in the national election, but because of allocation distortions caused by the failure of many right-leaning parties to reach the 5 percent threshold, the former communists received fully 37.2 percent of the seats. They were then able to form a working majority coalition with the Polish Peasant Party, a group that had won only 15.4 percent of the votes but 28.7 percent of the seats (Millard 1994: 305). The government that grew out of this majority, and of the allocation distortions that made it possible, was the first stable parliamentary coalition to govern postcommunist Poland for a full four-year term.

These political dynamics meant that from 1993 to 1997 the Church had no political party or coalition to advance its interests in parliament. The Peasant Party was considerably less anticlerical that the Democratic Left Alliance, but it was a left-leaning party with close ties to the former communist government. The opposition parties that did reach the threshold – the Freedom Union and the Union of Labor – represented the segment of the old Solidarity movement that was least closely attuned to the church's interests and least amenable to the bishops' pressure. As Millard said, "this default meant that none of the parties espousing religious values and strong links with the church would be represented in the Sejm" (306).

Partisan fragmentation and the specific nature of the electoral law created a set of circumstances in 1993 wherein the Church *could not* participate in politics through political parties. The bishops were forced to adopt a relatively distant approach to particular parties because of the basic workings of Poland's early democracy. The nature of the electoral law, and of the party system it created, set a fundamental institutional context that shaped the political choices available to the church and its leadership.

In the months preceding the next parliamentary election, in 1997, the parties of the right were able to overcome their fractiousness and campaign together as the Solidarity Electoral Alliance. This newfound success at coalition building, combined with growing dissatisfaction with the left's management of the political and economic transition, led directly to the defeat of the DLA government in 1997 and to a new majority coalition of Solidarity and the Freedom Union. In this election, the Church's hierarchy was more directive in its political commentary. In a campaign pitting the former communists against a political coalition bearing the name of Solidarity, the bishops' characterizations of parties that "make reference in their platforms to the Catholic social teachings" and their denunciations of "democratic methods being used to undermine the essence of democratic order" had much clearer partisan ramifications (*FBIS–EEU–97* August 28, 1997). Once the Solidarity Alliance was formed, the communist/anticommunist political battle was joined once again, and the Church, not to mention the electorate, responded accordingly. Context still shaped the bishops' choices. But when the parties that promised to advance the Church's interests became more politically coherent, then the Church's support for those parties was able to become more coherent in turn.

## CONSTITUTIONAL CHECKS AND BALANCES IN DEMOCRATIC POLAND

In addition to a new and much more vibrant party system, the Catholic Church in Poland faces a new and much more complex set of governmental institutions. This makes it easier for the Church to influence politics and policy, for the old system was closed and monolithic. The party–state made policy, and the Church, along with the rest of society, reacted to it. The new system, by contrast, is open and pluralistic. The Church is free to contest the shape of public policy in the institutions of the state.

Yet this new set of circumstances poses a particularly daunting set of challenges to the leadership of the Catholic Church. Whereas in the past, the leaders of the Church faced a single locus of political power in the party–state, today the Church faces a complex set of governing institutions engaged in a complex web of checks and balances. If the Church is going to influence policy, it will have to learn to deal with this complexity.

Public policy on abortion can serve as a useful example in this regard. Before 1989, abortion was a leading form of birth control in Polish society. The issue was governed by a permissive 1956 law, and the Catholic hierarchy had no chance of bringing legal practice into closer conformity with Catholic teaching (Kulczycki 1995: 471–505; Jankowska 1991: 174–81). The Polish Church hierarchy acted quickly and aggressively on abortion after the communist system crumbled in 1989. The bishops not only denounced abortion and demanded criminalization, the Polish Pope also insisted that greatly restricted access to abortion was the *sine qua non* of an effectively free, and authentically Polish nation. The bishops argued that communists had imposed abortion on a reluctant Poland, but now a free Poland, a Catholic Poland, should now assert its independence by placing strict limits on its practice (Snitow 1993: 556–8).

This effort has generally been remarkably successful. Despite opinion polls that show the public deeply divided on the issue, legal abortion today is quite rare, and access to it is governed by one of the most restrictive laws in Europe. The law allows abortions only in response to rape, incest, fetal deformity, or the rare circumstance in which the woman's life or physical health would be harmed by bringing the pregnancy to term (Engelberg 1993: A7). This law was passed before the reformed communists returned to power through the 1993 election. Once in government, the DLA changed the law substantially, allowing abortions up to the twelfth week of pregnancy for women who found themselves in "major financial or personal difficulties". That legislation was then vetoed by President Lech Walesa in 1994, repassed and signed by President Kwasniewski following the 1995 presidential election, and then overturned by the Constitutional Tribunal (a close approximation to the U.S. Supreme Court) in 1997. At the moment, the restrictive 1993 law is back in effect, strongly supported by the new government and the Solidarity Electoral Alliance (Grajewski 1997).

Abortion has turned into a highly partisan political football in democratic Poland. The major contestants for power, the postcommunist coalition and the post-Solidarity coalition, hold sharply differing views on the subject and have sought to place their views into law whenever one or the other of them holds governing power. But the more salient issue is the nearly Byzantine complexity of the political and governmental processes through which this policy has been formulated, reformulated, and reformulated again.

Poland is governed by a Constitution that establishes a French-style semipresidential system with an independent judiciary added on (Duverger 1992: 142–9). This means that Poland has a hybrid institutional arrangement combining a bicameral legislature (Sejm and Senate) headed by a prime minister and cabinet, with an independently elected president holding Constitutional authority to veto legislation, all overseen by a Constitutional Tribunal vested with the power to declare acts of Parliament void if found to be inconsistent with the written Constitution (Brzezinski 1998).

Each of these institutional relationships have been involved in policy making on abortion over the last five years. The 1993 law was first passed and signed into law by the president when the early post-Solidarity leadership dominated all of the institutions of democratic Poland. When the Democratic Left Alliance took power later that year, they had enough votes in the Sejm to pass a law allowing less restrictive

access to abortion, but not enough votes to muster the two-thirds majority required by the Constitution to override President Walesa's veto.
When DLA leader Aleksander Kwasniewski replaced Walesa in 1995, the
legislative and the executive cooperated to change the law back in a less
restrictive direction. Yet the Sejm had to pass the new law twice, because
the Senate, where the DLA was weaker, had refused to go along with the
initial liberalization effort.

The issue promised to feature prominently in the 1997 parliamentary
election, but before that campaign was fully underway, the Constitutional Tribunal declared the liberalized law unconstitutional because of
its lack of clarity and because of its lack of conformity with the human
life protections of the new Constitution (Pasek 1997). Under that Constitution, the Sejm can override decisions of the Tribunal if those decisions, like this one, concern laws that were placed on the books *before*
the Constitution was ratified. In December 1997, however, the new
Solidarity government voted not to overturn the Tribunal's decision, in
effect acting to reinstate the restrictive provisions of the 1993 law.

The Catholic Church, needless to say, has been an active participant
in each and every step along this convoluted path. The Church's spokesmen emphasized opposition to abortion in their assessments of parties
during parliamentary elections, and of individual candidates during presidential campaigns. In addition, they praised President Walesa's veto in
1994, and denounced President Kwasniewski's decision to sign the liberalization two years later. Leaders of the Church also lobbied hard *for*
the restrictive law in 1993, *against* the more liberal law in 1996, and
again *for* the vote in 1997 to let the Tribunal's decision stand. The
Church's spokesmen, in fact, are the leading antiabortion figures in contemporary Poland and they make no secret of the high priority they place
on the issue.

However, as in the United States, the Polish Catholic bishops and their
supporters have had to participate in a policy-making process that is
characterized, like the American process, by a highly complex set of
interrelationships among separated institutions sharing power. The
Polish bishops don't have the added American complexity of federalism
and state initiative to deal with, but in national policy making they face
a government with remarkably diffuse institutional responsibility operating under the constraints of carefully drawn Constitutional checks and
balances. The Polish bishops have to electioneer for antiabortion candidates at both the legislative and executive level; they have to lobby (in
two houses of parliament) for legislation that restricts abortion; and they
have to support constitutional arguments that protection of human life
is at least in part insulated from electoral and legislative politics by the
Polish Constitution.

The abortion issue demonstrates the degree to which institutional policy making in the Polish government has grown more pluralist and more complicated. Contextual factors involving party formation, coalition building and the electoral law have posed significant restraints on the Church's role in Polish electoral politics. In a similar way, the development of semipresidentialism, the introduction of an independent judiciary, and the inauguration of a system of complex checks and tenuous balances have also constrained, or at least defined, the role of the Church in directing public policy.

## CONCLUSION

Under communism, the Church in Poland and throughout Central and Eastern Europe, had to fight the government for its very survival. Nothing like such a fight is necessary now, of course, the challenges facing the Catholic Church in democratic Poland are significant, more complicated, and maybe even more troubling, than the challenges posed by communism. It would be a powerful irony indeed if the end of communism, long sought by Poland's Catholic leadership, turned out in the long run to undermine the Church's leading role in Polish society.

Before 1989, the institutional Catholic Church in Poland was against communism. Following 1989, it just isn't enough for the Church to be *against* something, the Church must also be clearer about what it is *for*. Which parties and coalitions, for example, does the Church find acceptable and which does it not? Which particular public policies does the Church favor and which does it not? What future for Poland does it envision, and which variations on that vision is it willing to fight for, or to resist?

Arriving at answers to these questions could well exacerbate tensions within the Catholic hierarchy and clergy over the degree to which the Church pushes to preserve some identifiably Catholic Polish identity, and the extent to which the Church is willing to press its teachings on issues like abortion and education into national law. But it seems to me virtually certain that the process will require Polish bishops and priests to rethink their relationship with the Polish nation for which they claimed to speak for so long.

Thus far the Church in Poland has been effective in advancing its own interests within a democratic polity without either alienating its own membership, or engineering its own marginalization in the political arena. But the Church is advancing those interests within a completely new political context, one that will in time call for basic shifts in the way the Catholic clergy approaches the political process in Poland.

Democratic Poland is now home to a thriving party system and a very complex governing structure. The Catholic hierarchy, like leaders of all other organized interests, will learn that it has to be flexible, creative, and open to compromise if it wishes to be politically effective. Polish bishops will probably have to temper some of their political rhetoric, and give up some of their less subtle invocations of Catholicism as the exclusive definition of authentic Polish identity. These invocations served as an indispensable foundation for effective resistance to communism before 1989, and as an understandable basis for post revolutionary triumphalism immediately following that historic year. But they are much less viable as a platform from which to project a long-term presence in an increasingly pluralist polity and society.

In short, the Polish bishops must work toward a new relationship not only with political institutions and political process, but also with the Catholic people of the Polish nation. In the not-so-good-old days, the bishops were assumed to speak for the people. Now, the people can most definitely speak for themselves – in public opinion polls, election results, and maybe most importantly through other organized interests. A half a century ago, Stalin asked "how many divisions has the Pope?" Today, Poles are asking themselves, "how many political supporters have the Catholic bishops?" Do the people continue to identify themselves with the church politically, as well as religiously and socially? Do the bishops actually speak for a substantial segment of the population? Or are they rather a kind of institutional holdover from another time?

In asking these questions, of course, Poles are no different from Americans, Brazilians, Spaniards, or any of the other peoples around the world for whom the Catholic Church plays a significant but not necessarily defining political role. Yet the status of the Catholic Church in democratic Poland is of particular interest at the moment for a number of reasons. First, the Polish Pope looks to his native land as perhaps the most important test of his Church's ability to retain a viable public role after the fall of communism. The Polish population is overwhelmingly Catholic; the Church has occupied a central place in the life of the nation for centuries. If the Church cannot retain a significant role in Poland, where else in Europe will it be able to do so? (Byrnes 1996: 433–48) Second, Poland is about to join NATO and has started talks toward eventual integration in the European Union. This will inevitably lead it to adopt Western economic styles and Western political identities, and it will be fascinating to see whether Poland can resist adopting Western secularism.

During and immediately after communism, it was common for Poles to express their wish to live in a "normal" country. Now, more than a decade after the rebirth of democracy, that wish has become a reality.

Normalcy, meaning in this connection freedom, pluralism, and institutionalized democracy, has come back to Poles in a rush at the end of a tragic century in their national history. But for the leadership of the Catholic Church in democratic Poland, these welcome historical developments have brought with them an entirely new political context that will require the Catholic Church to play a substantially new political role. The changes in context are unavoidable; the Church's response to those changes remains uncertain.

## REFERENCES

Brzezinski, Mark. 1998. *The Struggle for Constitutionalism in Poland*. New York: St. Martin's Press.

Byrnes, Timothy A. 1996. "The Catholic Church and Poland's Return to Europe." *East European Quarterly* 30: 433–48.

Davies, Norman. 1982. *God's Playground: A History of Poland Volume II, 1795 to the Present*. New York: Columbia University Press.

Duverger, Maurice. 1992. "A New Political System Model: Semi-Presidential Government." In Arend Lijphart (ed.). *Parliamentary Versus Presidential Government*. Oxford: Oxford University Press: 142–9.

Engelberg, Stephen. 1993. "Poland Acts to Curb Abortion: Church Seeks Ban." *The New York Times*, January 8.

Grajewski, Marcin. 1997. "Polish Legislators Restore Tough Abortion Law." *Reuters*, December 17.

Jankowska, Hanna. 1991. "Abortion, Church and Politics in Poland." *Feminist Review* 39: 174–81.

Kosela, Krzysztof. 1990. "The Polish Catholic Church and the Elections of 1989." *Religion in Communist Lands* 18: 124–37.

Kubik, Jan. 1994. *The Power of Symbols Against the Symbols of Power: The Rise of Solidarity and the Fall of State Socialism in Poland*. University Park, PA.: Pennsylvania State University Press.

Kulczycki, Andrzej. 1995. "Abortion Policy in Postcommunist Europe: The Conflict in Poland." *Population and Development Review* 21: 471–505.

Michel, Patrick. 1992. "Religious Renewal or Political Deficiency: Religion and Democracy in Central Europe." *Religion, State, and Society* 20: 339–44.

Michnik, Adam, edited, translated, and with an introduction by David Ost. 1993. *The Church and the Left*. Chicago: University of Chicago Press.

Millard, Frances. 1994. "The Polish Parliamentary Elections of September 1993." *Communist and Post-Communist Studies* 27: 295–313.

Morawska, Ewa. 1987. "Civil Religion Versus State Power in Poland." pp. 221–32. In Thomas Robbins and Roland Robertson (eds.). *Church-State Relations: Tensions and Transitions*. New Brunswick, NJ: Transaction Books.

⸻ 1995. "The Polish Roman Catholic Church Unbound: Change of Face or Change of Context." pp. 47–75. In Stephen P. Hanson and Willfried Spohn (eds.). *Can Europe Work? Germany and the Reconstruction of Postcommunist Societies*. Seattle: University of Washington Press.

Osa, Maryjane. 1989. "Resistance, Persistence, and Change: The Transformation of the Catholic Church in Poland." *Eastern European Politics and Societies* 3: 268–99.

1997. "Creating Solidarity: The Religious Foundations of the Polish Social Movement." *East European Politics and Societies* 11: 339–65.

Pasek, Beata. 1997. "Abortion Law Struck Down." *Associated Press News Service*, May 28.

Perlez, Jane. 1997. "As a Priest Gives Poles Hate Radio, Rome Stirs." *The New York Times*, December 14.

Snitow, Ann. 1993. "The Church Wins, Women Lose." *The Nation*, April 26: 556–8.

Szajkowski, Bogdan. 1983. *Next to God . . . Poland: Politics and Religion in Contemporary Poland*. New York: St. Martin's Press.

Weschler, Lawrence. 1982. *Solidarity: Poland in the Season of its Passion*. New York: Simon and Schuster.

Michele Dillon's description of the role of the Irish Catholic Church in the framing of public debate in Ireland is perhaps the clearest instance in this book of a dominant religion providing a "sacred canopy" within which democratic politics can be conducted. Of all the cases considered in this book, Ireland most closely approximates a setting in which religion can perform an authentically "priestly" role. Unlike the Polish case, in which the institutional role of the Catholic Church is contested, Irish Catholicism exerts its political influence primarily through the cultural expectations of ordinary citizens. The values articulated by Catholic elites in the Republic of Ireland provide conceptual boundaries, within which civil, yet highly pluralistic, public debate can occur.

# 3

# Catholicism, Politics, and Culture in the Republic of Ireland

*Michele Dillon*

The Irish Republic is an independent, sovereign, and democratic state, and is legally, politically, and economically separate from Northern Ireland. The Republic of Ireland is a small (approximately 3.5 million people) and relatively homogeneous society (91 percent Catholic), in which Catholicism has played a historically dominant role in articulating national identity. The reach of Catholicism is well inscribed both institutionally (in law, education, social policy, etc.) and in the Irish collective memory, and its symbols and meanings provide a powerful, common-sense interpretive framework for everyday life.

## CATHOLICISM AND IRISH IDENTITY: HISTORICAL BACKGROUND

The long tradition of Catholicism in Ireland, and its historical coexistence with the struggle against British colonialism critically shaped Irish political and cultural identity. Following the arrival of the British-born missionary, Patrick, in the fifth century, Ireland developed a vibrant religious culture that included a vigorous monasticism. The monasteries were centers of religious and cultural learning, and Irish monks established many similar houses in Europe until the Golden Age of the Irish Church dissipated in the ninth century following successive Viking conquests and their targeting of the monasteries' riches. Whether or not Irish monasticism "saved civilization" as the best-selling author Thomas Cahill (1995) contends, the legacy of the monks endured in Ireland's collective memory with its self-representation as the "Island of Saints and Scholars." This identity reaffirmed for successive Irish generations that they were the inheritors and preservers of a distinct Catholic heritage that should not be compromised by the impure forces of modernity and secularism.

Following the Reformation, Ireland remained steadfastly Catholic whereas England embraced Protestantism. This division cemented the

47

distinctiveness of Irish identity and intensified the tension between Ireland and England that had begun with the English Norman invasion of Ireland in the twelfth century (1169). Ireland's persistent struggle to maintain an independent identity against foreign forces was most severely challenged by its systematic colonization by England beginning in the sixteenth century. The British colonization of Ireland occurred in the broader context of Counter Reformation politics whereby the British Crown sought to establish English Protestant settlers in Catholic Ireland. As part of Tudor plantation policy, Irish lands in the midland, northern, and southern regions of the country were confiscated and given to English settlers while the poorer-quality land in the west was left to Irish landholders. The success of England's plantation policy was demonstrated by the fact that at the end of the seventeenth century, Catholics owned only 14 percent of Irish land (see Corish 1985: 123; Hayes-McCoy 1976).

Britain's systematic policy of ensuring the economic and political dispossession of the Irish was further reflected in the Penal Laws (1695–1829) which among other provisions prohibited Catholics from buying or inheriting land previously owned by Protestants, and restricted land leasing (see Beckett 1966; Wall 1961). The Penal Laws also sought to lessen the hold of Irish Catholicism; they prohibited the celebration of the sacraments, terminated Catholic schools, and ordered the exiling of priests and bishops (Wall 1961). Despite the breadth of their intent, however, the laws were relatively ineffective in attenuating Irish Catholicism. Despite the threats against it, the Irish Catholic Church managed to organize its diocesan and parish system that had initially been drawn more closely into line with Vatican policy in the twelfth century. The Irish Catholic culture shaped during the penal era was based on the reforms institutionalized at the Council of Trent (1549–63): reforms that stressed unquestioned obedience to official church authority, and regular participation in Church rituals and devotions (Corish 1985: 130–1). Although the Penal Laws crystallize the longstanding British subjugation of the Irish people and their culture, the laws were counterproductive in that the response to them paved the way for the consolidation of the place of Catholicism in Irish society. Similar to the long-standing historical role of Catholicism in Poland as a symbol of resistance against foreign tyranny (Szajkowski 1983: 2), the economically and politically dispossessed Irish appropriated Catholicism as the marker of their resistance against English colonization. Catholicism, therefore, contrary to Marxist assumptions, served as a politically empowering rather than disempowering force as the Irish used it to distinguish themselves from Britain and from the Anglo-Irish Protestant landowners. Catholicism and Irishness thus became intertwined as synonymous, and forged for the Irish people a collective identity whose meanings and boundaries remained relatively solidified until their public contestation starting in the early 1970s.

## POLITICAL INSTITUTIONAL STRUCTURES AND PROCESSES

The cultural association between Catholicism and Irishness was institutionalized with the establishment of a politically independent Ireland following Ireland's sovereignty from the United Kingdom in 1922 as the Irish Free State.[1] The partitioning of Ireland into twenty-six counties that subsequently became the Republic of Ireland (under the Republic of Ireland Act, 1948), and six counties of Northern Ireland (which remained part of the United Kingdom) followed religious divisions to some extent. Catholics comprised 95 percent of the population in the south, and although there was a substantial number of Catholics in the North, they were clearly a minority subordinate to the Protestant majority. Following the Anglo-Irish Treaty (1922), there was a bitterly fought civil war in the twenty-six counties between Treaty supporters and their opponents who wanted a united rather than a partitioned Ireland. The Treaty supporters prevailed and their leaders formed the first postindependence government with Cumann na nGaedheal (the precursor to Fine Gael) in power, and Sinn Fein (the precursor to Fianna Fail) in opposition.

Political scientists (e.g., Garvin 1996) emphasize the stability of the democracy that was established in Ireland following independence. Despite its violent backdrop, and contrary to deterministic assumptions that economic "backwardness" (Gerschenkron 1962) undermines modernization, Ireland's transition to political and economic independence was, from a comparative perspective, remarkably smooth. Unlike other Catholic and economically underdeveloped countries, such as Italy and Spain, whose struggle for democracy was interrupted by authoritarian political regimes, the establishment of a "successful" democracy in Ireland in the early twentieth century positioned it alongside economically advanced and historically Protestant countries such as the United Kingdom, Switzerland, and Denmark (see Kennedy, Giblin, and McHugh 1988: 14–15).

Ireland has a parliamentary political system (the Oireachtas) comprised of a democratically elected lower house of representatives (the Dail) and an upper house (Seanad), whose members are either appointed

---

[1] The (British) Government of Ireland Act (1920) partitioned Ireland, and the subsequent Anglo-Irish Treaty, signed in December 1921 and accepted by the Irish parliament in January 1922, conferred dominion status on the Irish Free State (twenty-six counties). See Lee (1989: 43–55).

by the prime minister (Taoiseach) or elected by various educational, industrial, and agricultural constituencies. The office of president, which is largely ceremonial, was introduced in 1937. The parliament is the national legislative authority, but it is constitutionally prohibited from enacting laws that contravene principles affirmed in the Constitution unless those principles (e.g., a ban on divorce) are first overturned by a majority vote of the Irish electorate in a referendum on the specific constitutional article.

Distinctive to Irish politics is its system of voting: Proportional Representation (PR) by means of a Single Transferable Vote (STV) among multiple candidates in multimember constituencies. Each constituency returns a minimum of three elected members to parliament. This strongly democratic and intraparty (as well as interparty) competitive system is credited with ensuring the parliamentary participation of "minority" groups, especially women, in Irish politics. Although political party loyalty is strong in Ireland, the STV system facilitates voters' decision to give their Number One vote to a candidate from their own party, and to give their second or third, etc., preference votes to, for example, a woman from a different party thus enhancing that candidate's ability to get elected based, in part, on vote transfers. Vote transfers can siphon off support from the dominant parties and contribute to the electoral success of independent candidates or candidates from very small political parties (e.g. Democratic Left), who then, especially during periods of voter dissatisfaction with the major parties, may become important players in coalition governments despite their representation of "minority" interests.

On the other hand, the PR–STV system enhances the success of campaigns that emphasize cross-party issues, specific personalities or appeals to "vote for a woman." Especially since the early 1980s, women have successfully contested a number of national and European parliamentary seats. It is noteworthy indeed that in recent decades women have held an average of 8 percent of the seats in the national parliament, thus demonstrating a level of political participation significantly higher than that for women in other Western democracies, including the United Kingdom and the United States. Although the election of Mary Robinson (in 1989) as the first woman president of Ireland was hailed as a watershed, Irish women have in fact been active in politics for a long time, and were a visible force in the preindependence revolutionary struggle. Indicative perhaps of the normalcy of women in Irish politics, the presidential race to succeed Mary Robinson comprised four women candidates. The successful candidate was Mary McAleese, the nominee of Fianna Fail, who, unlike Mary Robinson, who campaigned during the 1970s and 1980s for social liberalism (on contraception, divorce, homosexuality), was politically active in the 1980s on behalf of social conservative causes (prolife, antidivorce).

Notwithstanding the edge given to minority parties by PR, postindependence Irish politics have been dominated by Fianna Fail, a somewhat populist, socially conservative, and economically liberal (Keynesian) party, and Fine Gael which is more liberal on social issues but more likely than Fianna Fail to emphasize fiscal restraint while embracing "just society" policies. In addition to these two dominant parties, there is the left-of-center, Labour Party; two smaller left parties, the Workers' Party (WP) and the Democratic Left (DL); and since 1989, a right-of-center, Progressive Democrats Party (PDs), founded by members who split from Fianna Fail but whose policies tend to cut into voter support for Fine Gael. Each national election also usually sees the return of from three to five independent candidates, and since the 1990s, a candidate from the environmentally focused Green Party. Although there are clear ideological differences between the parties, coalition governments are a fairly characteristic feature of Irish society, between Fine Gael and Labour, and in more recent years, between Fianna Fail and one or all of the smaller parties (PDs/Labour/WP/DL).

Compared to some other European Catholic countries (e.g., France, Italy, and Spain), anticlericalism is not a feature of Irish politics. While Fianna Fail is more closely aligned than the other political parties to traditional Catholicism and to the Church hierarchy, all politicians overtly maintain a respectful disposition toward the Church. The absence of anticlericalism is not surprising in view of the dominance of Catholicism in Irish culture and its primacy among the electorate and politicians themselves. For example, it is indicative of the political-cultural power of the Catholic Church that when the Fine Gael/Labour coalition government tried to introduce contraception legislation in the early 1970s, during the Parliament vote, the prime minister and leader of Fine Gael (Liam Cosgrave), and one of his cabinet colleagues voted against the proposal on grounds of conscience. At the same time, nevertheless, politicians also maintain the independence of their policy positions, as for example, their prohibitive laws relating to political terrorism in Northern Ireland, even when those policies are at odds with some of the more compassionate views of either the Irish Church hierarchy or the Vatican (see Fitzgerald 1991: 184–9).

It is also noteworthy that despite the dominance of Catholicism in Irish society, the religious affiliation of non-Catholic candidates does not prevent their electoral success. Non-Catholics are frequently elected to parliament and to local and municipal offices, and two of Ireland's seven presidents were Protestants (Douglas Hyde, the first president, and Erskine Childers).

Similarly, despite, or maybe because of, the cultural dominance of Catholicism, religious questions are generally not contested in Irish politics. The public referendum debates on divorce and abortion (that I will discuss in more detail later) clearly were an exception to this on account of the religiously charged nature of the specific issues. The lead-up, however, to the 1983 prolife referendum highlighted the strategic political importance that moral issues can garner in Irish society. In the early 1980s, the socially conservative prolife movement (the Pro-Life Action Campaign, PLAC), was able to exploit a period of relative instability in Irish government when two short-lived minority coalition governments collapsed (see Farrell 1987). The two major party opponents, Fianna Fail and Fine Gael, each gave a commitment to PLAC that if elected to government, they would hold a referendum designed to insert a prolife amendment into the Constitution.

In Ireland, religiosity is not a significant independent predictor of party allegiance, unlike in Italy (Wertman 1982) or Spain (see Manuel, this book), although some studies suggest that among men, frequent church attendees appear more likely to support Fianna Fail (see Nic Ghiolla Phadraig 1986: 152). Political loyalty is also relatively independent of social class (see Mair 1992), age, and gender. While there is acceptance among social scientists for the description of Irish politics as being "without social bases," it is nonetheless the case, as argued by Michael Laver (1992: 360–1), that voting behavior is structured to some extent by social background. Insofar as social class, age, and gender interact with religiosity, one can thus hypothesize, for example, that young and middle-aged professional women are more likely than their age peers who are full time homemakers to be more critical of official Church teaching on sexual morality and to vote for Fine Gael rather than for Fianna Fail. In similar fashion, young urban males who are semiskilled or unemployed are likely both to not attend Church and to vote for the Workers' Party or Labour. Religiosity, therefore, matters in Ireland, but operationalizing it and then isolating its independent contribution to voting behavior is rather difficult. These difficulties are exacerbated on account of the fact that religion as an independent variable and measures of religiosity are not generally included in Irish national opinion surveys. Further, because there is no Irish national election study, estimates of religion's impact on politics remain tentative at best.

## IRISH CATHOLIC POLITICAL CULTURE

Church and state are separate institutions in Ireland, unlike, in the United Kingdom, where the Crown is also the head of the Church of England. The Protestant Church of Ireland was disestablished in 1869. There is no formal channel of communication between the government and the Irish bishops even though there is overlap between church and state in the performance of specific civic functions such as the official registering of marriages as part of the Catholic marriage ceremony. Similar to other countries, the Vatican has a diplomatic representative (Papal Nuncio) in Ireland, and the Irish government has an ambassador to the Holy See.

Notwithstanding the official separation of church and state in Ireland, both institutions, at least up until the 1970s, affirmed an Irish national identity grounded in Catholic moral and social teaching. As interpreted by successive governments, and endorsed by successive electorates, this conservative, nationalist ideology embraced protectionist policies that aimed to build a sovereign country that was independent not only politically, but also economically and culturally. This led, for example, to agricultural policies designed to increase the number of people working and living on the land, and the veneration of the superiority of rural community life and traditional values (see, for example, Brown 1985: chapters 1–5; Lee 1989: chapters 2–4).

The culturally dominant view was that Catholic values should be the definers of Irish identity notwithstanding the existence of a substantial number (approximately 7 percent of the population) of Irish and Anglo-Irish Protestants living in the Republic (Brown 1985: 107–8). Knowing the hearts of the Irish people by looking, as he proclaimed, into his own, the long-standing Irish political leader, Eamon de Valera (Fianna Fail) saw Ireland essentially as a "Catholic nation," a worldview that he eloquently explained: "Since the coming of St. Patrick fifteen hundred years ago, Ireland has been a Christian and a Catholic nation. All the ruthless attempts made through the centuries to force her from this allegiance have not shaken her faith. She remains a Catholic nation" (quoted in Brown 1985: 151). Committed to ensuring the continuity of an Irish Catholic nation, de Valera's government prohibited the sale and importation of artificial contraceptives, regulated dance halls, and taxed foreign newspapers.

Irish Catholic identity was most clearly institutionalized with the publication of the Irish Constitution in 1937. The Constitution declared that the state would not endow or discriminate against any religion, and it recognized by name the diversity of religious congregations in Ireland. Notwithstanding this pluralistic gesture, however, the Constitution affirmed the "special position of the Holy Catholic Apostolic and Roman Church as the guardian of the Faith professed by the great majority of the citizens" (Article 44:2).

The Constitution also emphasized traditional social values specifically relating to the family and to women. It stated:

"The State recognises the Family as the natural primary and funda-mental unit group of Society, and as a moral institution possessing inalienable and imprescriptible rights, antecedent to all positive law. The State, therefore, guarantees to protect the Family . . . as the necessary basis of social order and as indispensable to the welfare of the Nation and the State. . . . The State pledges itself to guard with special care the institution of Marriage . . . and to protect it against attack. No law shall be enacted providing for the grant of a dissolution of marriage" (Article 41).

Intertwined with this natural law understanding of marriage and the family, the Constitution stressed women's unique status, recognizing "that by her life within the home, woman gives to the State a support without which the common good cannot be achieved" (Ibid.). The Con-stitution did not make any reference to contraception, abortion or homo-sexuality, in part because unlike divorce, for which there had been some limited legal provision dating back to British rule, contraception, abor-tion and homosexual behavior were already criminalized in nineteenth-century laws.

As crystallized by the Constitution, Ireland's postindependence polit-ical culture was essentially a Catholic culture. Although the clergy had a dominant presence in local parishes (and dioceses) as pastors, overseers of state-funded primary and secondary education, and as community leaders, they were not officially engaged in public policy making. But they did not need a formal political role because the worldview embraced by politicians coincided with Catholic social teaching. Thus when politi-cians proposed socio-moral legislation that reflected Catholic teaching, they were giving voice to ideas that many sincerely believed served the common good. Catholic values defined the common-sense and as such provided Irish politicians, clergy, and the people alike with a ready-made, consensual ideology. Just as national Catholicism in Franco's Spain saw secularization as a threat to both church and nation (Linz 1991: 163), the maintenance of Irish national identity was understood as being immutably linked with preserving the primacy of Catholicism. There-fore, unlike in the United States or in postcommunist Poland (see Dillon 1996), the Church hierarchy in Ireland does not need to publicly demon-strate the compatibility of Church opposition to abortion with national cultural ideals.

One government policy initiative that threatened to crack the con-sensual relation between church and state was a proposal in the late 1940s to introduce universal health care for mothers and children. The Church hierarchy objected to the proposed legislation on the grounds that it contravened Catholic teaching on subsidiarity and what it saw as unnecessary state intervention in family morals (see Whyte 1980:

120–302). The government avoided direct confrontation with the Church hierarchy over the issue by eventually reformulating the legislation such that when the scheme was enacted in 1953, the bishops had received virtually all of the concessions that they had demanded (Fanning 1985). Postindependence Ireland thus presented itself as a Catholic nation, and its clearly defined boundaries were well institutionalized in laws, public policies, and daily routines (such as the continuing practice of playing a recording of the ringing of the Angelus bell on national television and radio at 6 p.m. every evening). Given this context, it is not surprising that the fragmentation of the consensus that law and public policy should be in synchrony with Catholic moral teaching was relatively protracted in unfolding, as I will discuss in the next section.

A further difficulty in cracking this consensus was the nature of Irish Catholicism. A legalistic strand in Irish Catholicism gives short shrift to the role of personal conscience and the belief that personal morality and public law can be at odds with official Catholic teaching (see, for example, Gallagher 1981; Inglis 1987: 14–32). On the contrary, the theology presented by priests and bishops and in large part accepted by the majority of Irish Catholics, is a dogmatic overemphasis on Catholic rules, duties, and obligations. Unlike the practical understanding of Catholicism in the United States (e.g., Dillon 1999) or in traditional Catholic countries such as Italy, Spain, and Poland, many Irish Catholics find it hard to accept that one can be a "good" Catholic and yet disagree with Vatican teaching on contraception, divorce, women's ordination, etc. While some Irish Catholic theologians take a critical and "progressive" stance toward the boundaries of Catholicism (e.g., S. Freyne 1996; Lane 1985), their influence in Irish society is fairly limited. Despite being the "Island of Saints and Scholars," theology is seen as a subject suited primarily to seminarians and religious teachers and therefore, is not, for example, offered in the curriculum of the National University of Ireland.

Related to the hold of Catholicism in Irish society, is the relative absence of an easily accessible language of individual or group rights. Unlike in the United States, for example, where such discourse is commonplace (cf. Glendon 1991), Irish politics in general tends to avoid "rights talk" unless the questions at issue concern workers' rights as expressed by the trade union movement, or personal property and land rights. The communitarian emphasis in Catholicism as interpreted in Ireland tends to stress the individual's communal obligations rather than the community's obligation to be responsive to diverse individual circumstances. Irish people are well aware of and committed to international human rights issues. This consciousness is in large part due to the collective and individual initiatives of Irish bishops in advancing global economic development programs. At the same time, nevertheless, public policy issues pertaining to economic and social justice in Ireland itself seem harder to realize.

Some commentators argue that the Catholic bishops have failed to provide leadership in directing public attention to the issue of economic inequality in Ireland. Although bishops, both individually and collectively, have in the past, and continue today to speak out on problems associated with rural poverty, they appear to be far less concerned with urban poverty and the socioeconomic deprivations confronted by the working class and the unemployed (see O'Hanlon 1993). Overall, the church hierarchy has been much less active on economic issues than it has been on questions of sexuality and marriage, etc. It is not just the bishops, however, who are faulted for the failure of the Irish to develop a greater sense of socioeconomic justice. Some writers (e.g., Hamilton et al. 1992) portray politicians and the electorate in general as unwilling to make commitments in these areas, and see this status quo disposition reflecting the absence of a culture of solidarity in Ireland more generally.

## ECONOMIC AND SOCIAL MODERNIZATION

A change in the orientation of Irish economic policy in the late 1950s from agricultural protectionism to industrialization paved the way for unprecedented growth in the economy such that the 1960s and 1970s saw a transformation in Ireland's economic and social structure (see Rottman and O'Connell 1982). Agriculture's lessening economic role and its replacement with the building of a more technological and service-oriented economy became the engine for broader societal change. The main evidence of change was seen in increased urbanization, increased participation in high-school and college education, the expansion of a white-collar middle class, increased participation of women in the paid labor force, expanding consumerism resulting from the growth in personal disposable income, and, following the introduction of television in 1962, the broadening of a vibrant and cohesive mass public. These changes coincided with and to some extent were also aided by Ireland becoming a full member of the European Economic Community (EEC, now European Union, EU) in 1973.

Cultural changes also began emerging during these years. In 1972, during a period of heightened cross-border political tension due to the resurgence of conflict in Northern Ireland, 84 percent of the Irish electorate, in a pluralistic gesture, voted to delete the Constitution's acknowledgement of the "special position" of the Catholic Church. There were also practical indications that the special hold of Catholicism on Irish people's consciousness was lessening somewhat. Starting in the early 1970s, there was evidence of a steady decline in fertility rates (Sexton and Dillon 1984), a pattern that was further advanced by the legalization of contraception in 1979. In addition, public opinion polls indicated a steady increase in favorable attitudes toward divorce, from 21 percent in 1971 to 53 percent by 1983, trends that were further reflected in frequent political and mass media discussion about sexuality, contraception, and marital breakdown. The 1980s, however, saw an abrupt challenge to the march of cultural "progress." In 1983, two-thirds of the electorate endorsed a constitutional amendment prohibiting abortion, and in 1986, two-thirds of the voters rejected a proposal to introduce a fairly restrictive form of divorce. More than ten years later these decisions were reversed. Divorce was legalized in 1995 (endorsed this time by over half of the national electorate), and legal access to abortion was expanded in 1992.

The political and cultural importance of Catholicism in Irish society thus seems to be waning. In addition to the indicators discussed above, there are further signs of the church's reduced presence in daily life. Although the vast majority (91 percent) of the Irish people still identify as Catholic, there has been a decline in the number of people who attend church weekly – from 91 percent in the early 1970s (Nic Ghiolla Phadraig 1986) to 76 percent in the 1990s (Eurobarometer 1995). There has also been an increase in the proportions who disagree with various aspects of official Church teaching on divorce, celibacy, and women priests (Fagan 1998). The role of the Catholic Church in primary and second-level education has also diminished significantly. Noteworthy too, vocations to the priesthood have declined; whereas 259 Irish priests were ordained in 1970, 124 were ordained in 1994 (O'Leary 1995). It is of further significance that for a society in which the Church hierarchy has for so long authoritatively presented bishops and priests as above error, recent years have seen a succession of public confessions by Church officials of either personal (sexual) wrongdoing or that of the institutional church (e.g., regarding its condemnation of inter-religious marriages).

But although the power of Catholicism in Irish society has become less monopolistic than heretofore (see Inglis 1987), it is nonetheless the case that it continues to provide a salient interpretive framework for many people. In comparative reference, Ireland, in many respects, remains a "Catholic nation," with over three-quarters of Irish Catholics attending church regularly, compared, for example, to 67 percent in Poland, 52 percent in Italy, 48 percent in the United States, and 38 percent in Britain (Greeley 1993: 51). At the same time, nevertheless, being a Catholic society today is clearly different in practice to what it

meant in the first half of the twentieth century. The symbols and meanings associated with Catholicism now mingle with and compete against
other equally powerful secular symbols in the Irish public consumer
culture (see the essays in Peillon and Slater 1998). That the meanings of
Catholicism change in different historical and sociopolitical contexts is
evident not only in the greater autonomy between individual believers
and official Church authority noted above, but is reflected also in the
changing role of the Church hierarchy in the public sphere.

## THE CHANGING POLITICAL ROLE OF THE
## CHURCH HIERARCHY

The Church hierarchy in the 1940s and '50s was not hesitant to intervene in the political process when, in the words of Dublin archbishop
John Charles McQuaid, it perceived the state trying to intervene "in a
sphere so delicate and so intimately concerned with morals" (published
in Whyte 1980: 446–8). Church-state relations in Ireland, as elsewhere,
however, became more complex in the aftermath of the doctrinal delib-
erations by Church leaders (cardinals and bishops) at the Second Vatican
Council (1962–1965). As is well documented, Vatican II, among its
multifaceted reforms, officially affirmed the autonomy of church and
state, recognized religious pluralism, and Catholics' and other people's
freedom to follow the dictates of their conscience. Of particular relevance to Irish society in view of the dominance of Catholicism in its
culture and laws, and the special recognition given to the Catholic
Church in the Irish Constitution, Vatican II emphasized the political
obligation to recognize the rights of minority religious groups. While
Vatican II may have intended its understanding of religious freedom to
apply primarily to countries in which Catholicism was the minority religion, it was nonetheless the case that the existence of a minority Protestant population in the Republic of Ireland meant, following Vatican II,
that greater public attention had to be given to the ways in which Irish
laws, on contraception for example, might contravene Protestants'
understanding of religious freedom.

The Irish Catholic bishops responded to the changes advanced both
by Vatican II and the modernization of Irish society by adopting a less
authoritarian form of collective self-presentation and public discourse.
The first evidence of a more liberal stance by the church hierarchy on
morality and church-state relations was seen in 1973 when the Irish parliament broached the possibility of legalizing artificial contraception. For
the first time in Irish history, the bishops publicly acknowledged the distinction between civil law and Catholic morality. Stating that it did not
wish to intervene in the process of government, the church hierarchy

argued that, even though the two spheres may not always coincide, it was the duty of governments to govern and of bishops to preach. Thus on contraception, the bishops stated:

The question at issue is not whether artificial contraception is morally right or wrong. The clear teaching of the Catholic Church is that it is morally wrong. No change in the State law can make the use of contraceptives morally right, since what is wrong in itself remains wrong, regardless of what State law says. . . . It does not follow, of course, that the State is bound to prohibit the importation and sale of contraceptives. There are many things which the Catholic Church holds to be morally wrong, and no one has ever suggested, least of all the Church herself, that they should be prohibited by the State.

The bishops reiterated its position on the autonomy of law and Catholic morality in subsequent debates extending the provision of the law on contraception in 1978 and in 1985, declaring in 1978, for example, that "Those who insist on seeing the issue purely in terms of the State enforcing or not enforcing, Catholic moral teaching . . . are missing the point."

The most forceful articulation of the Irish bishops' politically noninterventionist stance occurred in 1984 on the occasion of official talks concerning the future of Northern Ireland at the New Ireland Forum. As delegates to the talks, the bishops' representatives stated:

The Catholic Church in Ireland totally rejects the concept of a confessional State. We have not sought and we do not seek a Catholic State for a Catholic people. We believe that the alliance of Church and State is harmful for the Church and harmful for the State. . . . We have repeatedly declared that we in no way seek to have the moral teaching of the Catholic Church become the criterion of constitutional change or to have the principles of Catholic faith enshrined in civil law.

As these quotations illustrate, the Church hierarchy's affirmation of the autonomy of law from Catholic morality shows the Irish bishops embracing Vatican II principles recognizing the state's, political citizens' and religious believers' freedom to interpret political and moral issues relatively independent of official church teaching. As might be expected, however, in view both of the emphasis on sexual morality in official church teaching and its accentuation by Pope John Paul II (e.g., 1995) in promulgating a universal morality, the Irish bishops do not always adhere to their self-proclaimed noninterventionist stance in public debates.

The 1983 pro-life referendum debate provided a clear indication of the limits of the church hierarchy's pluralism. Although the bishops stated that they recognized "the right of every person to vote according to conscience," at the same time they called for a pro-life vote. Such a vote, they argued, would "constitute a witness before Europe and before the whole world to the dignity and sacredness of all human life from conception to death." Individual bishops went further that the collective statement by strongly urging people to vote pro-life and omitting any reference to the relevance of personal conscience. Subsequent divorce referendum debates (in 1986 and 1995) further highlighted the ambivalence of the bishops' stance on the autonomy of civil law and Catholic doctrine. Again, while the bishops' official collective statements emphasized the noninterventionist stance articulated since the 1970s, individual bishops and priests stressed that divorce legislation had no basis in Catholic social and moral doctrine.

While the Church hierarchy presents itself as a nonpolitical actor, and clearly does not want a theocracy in Ireland, the tension in its wavering between proclaiming nonintervention while actually taking a partisan stance in public debates can be understood in part as reflective of its interpretation of its institutional role. An exchange on Irish national television at the outset of the 1986 divorce debate provides some insight into the bishops' outlook. In a television interview, the Church hierarchy's spokesman (Bishop Cassidy) emphasized that "the Church will not participate in the campaign as such because I don't particularly like the word campaign [because] it has unhappy overtones. It suggests that we will be holding public meetings and other platforms and knocking at doors." Challenged by the interviewer that "there are public meetings every Sunday at which people assemble, i.e., Mass, and the priest speaks from the pulpit," Bishop Cassidy responded that "inevitably it [divorce] would have to be part of pulpit teaching. The pulpit will be used but not abused." Therefore, while the bishops appear genuinely to believe in the separation of church and state, it is also the case that as "teachers of the faith," they experience an obligation to "teach Catholics the truth of the faith . . . and *the social and moral implications of any piece of legislation*" (emphasis mine, quoted in Dillon 1993: 95–6). What the bishops see as "teaching," many other people may well see as "campaigning" insofar as the views put forward, consonant with official Church teaching, will be unequivocally supportive of a particular stance.

### THE CHURCH HIERARCHY'S ROLE IN LEGITIMATING CRITICAL INQUIRY

More significant, however, than whether or not the bishops see themselves as politically active, is the relatively new, secular manner in which they present official church teaching on publicly contested issues. In recent decades in Ireland, the hierarchy, paralleling its emphasis on the autonomy of civil law from Catholic morality, has adopted a more empirically grounded style of argumentation. This observation is theoretically significant in view of the fact that some contemporary social theorists (e.g., Habermas 1992; Rorty 1998) dismiss the possibility of an emancipatory role for religion. Jurgen Habermas, in particular, sees religion as a premodern, undifferentiated belief system, and as such he fails to appreciate that religion has evolved in response to and incorporated Enlightenment principles of critical reason (Schussler Fiorenza 1992: 74). Consequently, for Habermas (1992; 1987: 77), religious institutions and religious discourse are impediments to emancipatory, political, and cultural changes that shed the coercive hold of tradition, dogma, and sacred authority. By contrast with this limited view of religion, other studies (e.g., Casanova 1994) show that public religion can play a prophetic and critical role in focusing attention on human rights and social justice issues.

What I would like to suggest in this chapter is that irrespective of whether one sees the Catholic Church's opposition to divorce or abortion as culturally "regressive" or "progressive," the manner in which it has presented its views on these issues in Ireland has had an unanticipated emancipatory effect. While church opposition to abortion and divorce is grounded in the Church's belief that these practices are contrary to natural and divine law, Church officials avoid such abstract and divine reasoning in public debates. Instead, they ground their claims in nondoctrinal, secular and empirical arguments (see Dillon 1993; 1996), and link their objections to a broader sociological concern for the welfare of individuals and families, and the Irish common good.

The Church hierarchy's first systematic use of secular reasoning occurred in the 1986 divorce referendum debate (though it has incorporated empirical reasoning in its doctrinal statements since the early 1970s). In the divorce debate, the bishops framed divorce principally in terms of its negative sociological consequences. Typical of the Church's arguments was the following claim by the hierarchy's spokesman:

Divorce has very serious consequences for society . . . once divorce is introduced it is very difficult to restrict it . . . Take a look at the evidence . . . Take a look at the evidence in any country in the world. In 1983, for instance, in America, there were 2.4 million marriages and there were 1.2 million divorces. That's one out of two. In Great Britain at the moment the figure is running two out of every five.

The bishops also stressed the negative consequences of divorce for women and children, arguing "children are the chief casualties and victims of divorce. There is strong evidence from the United States and other countries that children of divorced parents are prey to a cluster of psychological and emotional problems and personality disorders."

Regarding women, church officials maintained that: "There are many indicators that divorce favors men rather than women. One California study found in 1982 that men experienced a 42 percent increase in their standard of living following divorce, while women experienced a 73 percent loss." Related to these negative effects, the bishops also drew attention to the financial costs incurred by the state resulting from the increased prevalence of marital breakdown and one-parent families.

The Church hierarchy's use of secular reasoning extended the impact of the church's anti-divorce stance by presenting arguments that could, in principle, be understood by Catholics and non-Catholics alike. By taking a sociological approach, the Church managed to redirect public attention away from its fundamental, moral opposition to divorce, to a focus on its practical and empirical implications. Rather than simply declaring as it would have done in the past, that divorce is a "mortal sin," or stressing that it is contrary to God's law, the Church hierarchy sought to demonstrate empirically that divorce did not make good sociological sense.

The Church's sociological vision of a postdivorce society was clearly one that coincided with Catholic moral teaching. Importantly, however, the nontheological way in which it presented its case opened up the communicative possibilities for talking about divorce and other religious and culturally sacrosanct issues. Although historically there is a long association in Ireland between marriage and economic considerations (cf. Kennedy 1973: 139–72), the Church's explicit sociological framing of marriage during the 1986 debate gave people permission to publicly talk about marriage in a more expanded way than that validated by the categories of sacrament and sin. Its use of empirical reasoning legitimated the fact that marriage is not solely a sacramental or doctrinal question but one that can and should be evaluated in terms of its economic and other practical implications. Equally important, the Church's recourse to empirical analysis, by extension, invited counter-claims and gave other debate participants the legitimacy to use secular argumentation. The Church hierarchy's embrace of sociological rather than moral argumentation, notwithstanding the inevitability of its antidivorce conclusions, thus opened up in a relatively new way the public conversation about marriage and divorce.

When people have permission to publicly talk about morally charged issues in terms of everyday experiences rather than ideal or transcendent significance, the narratives allow people to hear about different realities and to recognize the diverse circumstances that people encounter. As emphasized by the political philosopher Iris Young, such stories can act as a bridge toward the understanding of differences: "Narrative reveals the particular experiences of those in social locations, experiences that cannot be shared by those situated differently but that they must understand in order to do justice to the others . . . narrative provides an important way to demonstrate need or entitlement" (1996: 131–2).

It is reasonable to suggest, therefore, that once the Irish people were free to talk about marriage and divorce in an empirical and critical manner, they then necessarily encountered ideas, facts, and personal experiences that provided alternative frameworks with which to, at least, *think about* the contested question. For various reasons, many people (64 percent of the electorate) rejected the 1986 prodivorce initiative. But despite the amendment's defeat, the public conversation had been opened up with counter-claims and possibilities that could be argued against, but not silenced. I am not suggesting that the debate was a model of pubic rationality; to the contrary, the weight of tradition and dogma was heavy, and there was much hyperbole and factual distortion. Nevertheless, from the perspective of cultural change, some of the new ideas and alternative scenarios that got circulated into the first divorce debate may, over time, have acquired salience for an increasing number of people. Its expansion of conceptual categories (e.g., the highlighting of the diverse marital situations encountered in Ireland, and evidence for the idea that divorce may be a necessary personal and institutional option) likely contributed to paving the way for the subsequent shift in the public's judgment about divorce (as seen in the 1995 referendum result endorsing divorce).

The power of understanding new possibilities can be far-reaching in its impact. With changes achieved in the laws on divorce and abortion, issues that are central to official church teaching, the Irish people have broken the inevitability of the link between public morality and Catholicism. As I have suggested in this chapter, the Catholic Church can take some of the credit for opening up, however unintentionally, the contours of Irish public discourse by its use of empirical and practical reasoning. In light of this, it is somewhat ironic, but not surprising, that critical inquiry may increasingly turn toward the institutional practices of the church itself. Recent years have seen greater public criticism of official church teaching on celibacy, for instance. This discussion was fueled in the summer of 1995 when some of the Irish bishops themselves, and against the position of some of their fellow-bishops, publicly called for a reconsideration of the Vatican's stance. There is also public criticism of the Vatican's continuing opposition to women priests (e.g., G. Freyne 1995), an issue that is primed to remain on the public mind in view of national survey data indicating that a substantial majority of Irish people favor women's ordination (Greeley and Hout 1996).

## CONCLUSION

The relation between religion and politics in Ireland is multilayered. For historical and cultural reasons, Catholicism has a special place in Irish society. Yet the implications of this are neither monolithic nor static. Similar to the global Catholic Church, Irish society experienced a major transformation in the early 1960s. The changes in Catholicism ushered in by Vatican II, and the economic social, and cultural changes that began to take hold in Ireland during the same period, influenced each other. One result was a shift in Irish people's practical understanding of Catholicism such that they became increasingly willing to crack the synchrony between official Church teaching and civil laws (e.g., contraception and divorce). At the same time, the Church hierarchy reinterpreted, and in the process expanded, its public role. While emphasizing the autonomy of church and state, it simultaneously participated in public debates under the rubric of "teaching the faith." Yet, it did so by embracing secular reasoning, and thus extended the salience of its discourse on the common good. It also, I suggest, indirectly facilitated cultural change by expanding the categories and targets of public discourse, including, however inadvertently, critique of the church itself.

Notwithstanding economic and social change, Catholicism continues to hold a critical place in Irish politics and culture. Yet, it seems too simple to claim, as Ronald Inglehart (1997: 99) does, that Ireland is a "hyper-Catholic" society. While the historical legacy of Catholicism in Ireland is deeply rooted, it is not deterministic. Both the church and society change, and change one another. The Irish experience shows, as do the experiences of many other different countries (e.g., United States, Spain, Poland, Latin America), that Catholicism can coexist with and adapt to diverse political and sociocultural configurations. The moral challenge for the twenty-first century is whether religion and politics can interact in ways that will facilitate the building of more egalitarian local and global communities.

### REFERENCES

Beckett, J. C. 1966. *The Making of Modern Ireland, 1603–1923*. London: Faber and Faber.

Brown, Terence. 1985. *Ireland: A Social and Cultural History, 1922–1985*. London: Fontana.

Cahill, Thomas. 1995. *How the Irish Saved Civilization: The Untold Story of Ireland's Heroic Role from the Fall of Rome to the Rise of Medieval Europe*. New York: Doubleday.

Casanova, Jose. 1994. *Public Religions in the Modern World*. Chicago: University of Chicago Press.

Corish, Patrick. 1985. *The Irish Catholic Experience: A Historical Survey.* Dublin: Gill and Macmillan.

Dillon, Michele. 1993. *Debating Divorce. Moral Conflict in Ireland.* Lexington: University Press of Kentucky.

1996. "Cultural Differences in the Abortion Discourse of the Catholic Church: Evidence from Four Countries." *Sociology of Religion* 57: 25–36.

1999. *Catholic Identity: Balancing Reason, Faith, and Power.* New York: Cambridge University Press.

Eurobarometer. 1995. *Public Opinion in the European Union.* (Spring) No. 42.

Fagan, Sean. 1998. "A Spiritual Challenge to the People of God." *Doctrine and Life* 48:4.

Fanning, Ronan. 1985. "Fianna Fail and the Bishops." *Irish Times*, Feb. 13 and 14.

Farrell, Brian. 1997. "The Context of Three Elections." In Howard Penniman and Brian Farrell (eds.). *Ireland at the Polls, 1981, 1982, and 1987. A Study of Four General Elections.* Chapel Hill, NC: Duke University Press: 1–30.

Fitzgerald, Garret. 1991. *All in a Life. An Autobiography.* Dublin: Gill and Macmillan.

Freyne, Gail Grossman. 1995. "Rite and Reason." *Irish Times* (July 4): 12.

Freyne, Sean. 1996. "Infallible?" *The Furrow* 47: 44–46.

Gallagher, Raphael. 1981. "Morality in a Changing Irish Society." *The Furrow* 32: 713–24.

Garvin, Tom. 1996. *1922: The Birth of Irish Democracy.* New York: St. Martin's Press.

Gerschenkron, Alexander. 1962. *Economic Backwardness in Historical Perspective.* Cambridge, MA: Harvard University Press.

Glendon, Mary Ann. 1991. *Rights Talk.* New York: Free Press.

Greeley, Andrew. 1993. "Religion Not Dying Out Around the World." *Origins* (June 10) 23: 49, 51–8.

Greeley, Andrew, and Michael Hout. 1996. "Survey Finds Catholics Want More Say." *National Catholic Reporter* (June 14).

Habermas, Jurgen. 1987. *The Theory of Communicative Action.* Volume Two. Boston: Beacon Press.

1992. "Transcendence from Within: Transcendence in this World." 226–250. In Don Browning and Francis Schussler Fiorenza (eds.). *Habermas, Modernity, and Public Theology.* New York: Crossroad.

Hamilton, Tim, Brian Lennon, Gerry O'Hanlon, and Brian Sammon. 1992. *Solidarity: The Missing Link in Irish Society.* Dublin: Jesuit Center for Faith and Justice.

Hayes-McCoy, G. A. 1976. "The Completion of the Tudor Conquest and the Advance of the Counter Reformation, 1571–1603." In T. W. Moody et al. (eds.). *A New History of Ireland: Early Modern Period, 1534–1691.* Oxford: Clarendon.

Inglehart, Ronald. 1997. *Modernization and Postmodernization.* Princeton: Princeton University Press.

Inglis, Tom. 1987. *Moral Monopoly: The Catholic Church in Modern Irish Society.* Dublin: Gill and Macmillan.

John Paul II. 1995. *The Gospel of Life*. New York: Random House.

Kennedy, Kieran, Thomas Giblin, and Deirdre McHugh. 1988. *The Economic Development of Ireland in the Twentieth Century*. London: Routledge.

Kennedy, Robert. 1973. *The Irish: Emigration, Marriage, and Fertility*. Berkeley: University of California Press.

Lane, Dermot. 1985. "Christian Feminism." *The Furrow* 36: 663–675.

Laver, Michael. 1992. "Are Irish Parties Peculiar?" In J. H. Goldthorpe and C. T. Whelan (eds.). *The Development of Industrial Society in Ireland*. New York: Oxford University Press: 359–81.

Lee, J. J. 1989. *Ireland, 1912–1985: Politics and Society*. Cambridge: Cambridge University Press.

Linz, Juan. 1991. "Church and State in Spain from the Civil War to the Return of Democracy." *Daedalus* 120: 159–178.

Mair, Peter. 1992. "Explaining the Absence of Class Politics in Ireland." In J. H. Goldthorpe and C. T. Whelan (eds.). *The Development of Industrial Society in Ireland*. New York: Oxford University Press: 383–410.

Nic Ghiolla Phadraig, Maire. 1986. "Religious Practice and Secularisation. In Patrick Clancy et al. (eds.). *Ireland: A Sociological Profile*. Dublin: Institute of Public Administration: 137–54.

1992. "Trends in Religious Practice in Ireland." *Doctrine and Life* 42: 3–11.

O'Hanlon, Gerry. 1993. "A Middle-class Church for a Working-class People." *The Furrow* 44: 3–11.

O'Leary, Olivia. 1995. "Many are Called but Fewer Choose to Answer." *Sunday Tribune*, June 11: 10–11.

Peillon, Michel, and Eamon Slater (eds.). 1997. *Encounters with Modern Ireland*. Dublin: Institute of Public Administration.

Rorty, Richard. 1998. *Achieving our Country: Leftist Thought in Twentieth Century America*. Cambridge, MA: Harvard University Press.

Rottman, David, and Philip O'Connell. 1982. "The Changing Social Structure of Ireland, 1957–1982." In Frank Litton (ed.). *Unequal Achievement: The Irish Experience*. Dublin: Institute of Public Administration: 63–88.

Schussler Fiorenza, Francis. 1992. "The Church as a Community of Interpretation: Political Theology between Discourse Ethics and Hermeneutical Reconstruction." In Don Browning and Francis Schussler Fiorenza (eds.). *Habermas, Modernity, and Public Theology*. New York: Crossroad: 66–91.

Sexton, J. J., and Michele Dillon. 1984. "Recent Changes in Irish Fertility." *Quarterly Economic Commentary*, May: 21–40.

Szajkowski, Bogdan. 1983. *Next to God ... Poland. Politics and Religion in Contemporary Poland*. New York: St. Martin's Press.

Wall, Maureen. 1961. *The Penal Laws, 1691–1760*. Dundalk: Dundalgan Press.

Wertman, Douglas. 1982. "The Catholic Church and Italian Politics: The Impact of Secularisation." In Suzanne Berger (ed.). *Religion in West European Politics*. London: Frank Cass & Co: 87–107.

Whyte, John. 1980. *Church and State in Modern Ireland*. Dublin: Gill and Macmillan.

Young, Iris Marion. 1996. "Communication and the Other: Beyond Deliberative Democracy." In Seyla Benhabib (ed.). *Democracy and Difference: Contesting the Boundaries of the Political*. Princeton: Princeton University Press: 120–35.

The fourth chapter examines yet another national setting in which a "Catholic monopoly" appears to present concerns in the Iberian countries of Spain and Portugal. The Iberian cases nicely illustrate the hazards of attempts by religious bodies to perform priestly political functions. They also provide an interesting example of the "lazy monopoly" hypothesis. Despite the virtual absence of serious *religious* competition, the Church does not serve as a primary source of national identity, nor is it a particularly strong competitor in the political process. Paul Manuel's account of the history of the clerical/anticlerical split in Iberian politics suggests that the political role of the contemporary Catholic Church in Spain and Portugal has been limited by the Church's historical identification with previously discredited antidemocratic regimes, and overt opposition to previous popular governments. The contemporary Church appears to have a visible, but "domesticated" political role in Iberia during the post-Vatican II era.

# 4

## Religion and Politics in Iberia

### Clericalism, Anticlericalism, and Democratization in Portugal and Spain

### Paul Christopher Manuel

#### INTRODUCTION TO RELIGION AND POLITICS IN IBERIA

In the overwhelmingly Roman Catholic "consensual" Iberian region, religion and politics has generally hinged on the issue of clericalism versus anticlericalism. The Roman Catholic Church plays a leading role in the political and social fabric of Portuguese and Spanish society, so it has quite naturally engendered both unbridled loyalty and fierce opposition among the population in each nation. The clerical/anticlerical cleavage has long been a major aspect of Iberian politics and society, but in recent years, its salience has declined under democratic rule in Portugal and in Spain.

This chapter will approach the question of religion and politics in the Iberian peninsular by examining the emergence, development and evolution of the clerical/anticlerical cleavage in both Portugal and Spain. It will first present a brief overview of the religious composition in each nation, then discuss three key phases of the religion and politics relationship in the twentieth century in each country, and conclude with some thoughts on what may account for the narrowing, or perhaps even the eclipse, of the Iberian clerical/anticlerical divide in recent years.[1]

#### A BRIEF OVERVIEW OF RELIGION AND POLITICS IN IBERIAN SOCIETY

##### The Religious Composition of Portugal

The population of Portugal (which includes those living on Portuguese territory on the European continent and in the Atlantic islands of the

[1] The author wishes to express his gratitude to Dr. Janice Farnham, R. J. M., of the Weston Jesuit School of Theology in Cambridge, Massachusetts, for her assistance with this chapter.

Azores and Madeira) numbers approximately ten million people. Some 97 percent of this population is at least nominally Roman Catholic, and most baptisms, marriages, and funerals are performed according to Roman Catholic ritual. For these reasons, the Catholic Church has come to be known as the very definition of Portuguese civil society (de Sousa Franco 1987). Thus the population of Portugal is not divided in its religious faith, but in their levels of devotion.

There are important regional variations in the practice of Catholicism. Some 70 percent of the population living in the central and northern regions, and in the islands, regularly attend Sunday Mass. In contrast, only about 30 percent of nominal Catholics routinely attend Mass in the city of Lisbon, and that percentage drops to roughly 15 percent of nominal Catholics in the scarcely populated region of the Alentejo, south of Lisbon (Wiarda 1994).

The central, northern, and island areas are rather conservative politically, and devoutly Catholic; the impoverished region of the Alentejo is both communist and anticlerical. Perhaps the most convincing explanation offered to account for these regional differences centers on patterns of land ownership: In the center and northern regions, as well as in the islands, most people own small tracts of land. These parcels barely provide subsistence for the people, but at least do give them a sense of ownership in the land. On the other hand, about 10 percent of the population lives under very different land ownership patterns in the Alentejo region. The land in this area is very flat and dry, and frequently suffers droughts. There, large tracts of land are owned by Lisbon aristocrats, who spend occasional weekends and vacations there. This population of landless peasants, who work the land and are poorly and irregularly paid, tend to be procommunist and anticlerical.[2]

British and American citizens have brought Protestantism to Portugal, but it constitutes only 1 percent of the population. Many British live in the Algarve region in the far south of Portugal, and are members of the Church of England. Several American Protestant groups, including Mormons and Pentecostals, have been active in Portugal of late. This foreign presence in Portugal represents approximately 50,000 persons. The Portuguese Jewish community is centered in Lisbon, and numbers around 1,000 persons (Wiarda 1994).

---

[2] Tom Gallagher (1996) also notes that the Roman Catholic Church's support of the right-wing Prince Miguel in the Portuguese civil war of 1832–4 hurt its standing among the population in the Alentejo, and was a key factor in the development of the strong anticlerical feelings in that region.

## The Religious Composition of Spain

The Spanish population numbers some 39 million, almost four times the size of the Portuguese population.[3] As in Portugal, approximately 97 percent of the population of Spain are Roman Catholics, and most baptisms, marriages and funerals are performed according to Roman Catholic rites (Clark 1990). And like Portugal, there is a clerical/anticlerical cleavage that is important to understanding Spanish politics.

The clerical/anticlerical cleavage in Spain has typically followed urban/rural and conservative/progressive societal cleavage patterns. Urban, well-educated, and politically progressive city dwellers have been far less likely to regularly attend Mass than people living in the country. Indeed, approximately 60 percent of nominal Catholics living in the countryside attend Mass frequently, with roughly 30 percent of them attending Mass regularly. In contrast, only about 20 percent of Catholics living in the large cities, including Madrid, attend Mass regularly (Clark 1990).

Historically, practicing Catholics in Spain have supported conservative political parties, which traditionally espoused a worldview similar to that of the Church. Anticlerical sectors have tended to support parties of the left. More recently, practicing Catholics have demonstrated a willingness to support leftist parties. For example, in what was arguably a watershed event, upwards to 25 percent of practicing Catholics voted for Felipe González's Socialist Party in the 1982 legislative elections (Pérez-Diaz, 1993). Further, it is becoming more common for educated, city people to attend Mass regularly. As we will examine later, this new and unusual pattern of behavior may be a result of the momentous internal changes experienced by both the Spanish state and the Roman Catholic Church over the past thirty years.

Finally, and similar to the Portuguese case, most Protestants in Spain are of foreign origin. Only representing 1 percent of the population, there are about 300,000 total Protestants of various denominations, including the Church of England, Jehovah's Witnesses, and Mormons. The Spanish Jewish community numbers about 13,000 people (Clark 1990).

### THE ORIGINS OF THE CLERICAL/ANTICLERICAL DIVIDE IN IBERIA

Portugal and Spain are two of the oldest nation–states in Europe, and the Roman Catholic Church has played a preeminent role in all sectors

---

[3] This includes those living on the national territory on the Iberian peninsular, the Balearic Islands in the Mediterranean, the Canary Islands in the Atlantic, and the city–states of Ceuta and Melilla in North Africa.

of society in each country since their founding almost one thousand years ago. Indeed, Rome was not only present at their founding, but had a hand in the very creation of these states (Payne 1974). In each case, the Church provided material and spiritual support to the Portuguese and Spanish kings during their battle of *reconquista* against the North African Moors. Rome's support for the national project in Spain and Portugal generated widespread elite and popular support for the Catholic Church, which, in turn, became part of the very national fabric of these two countries. As Eusébio Mujal-León (1982) observes:

Historically, the link between Catholicism and the State has been very close in Spain: the Church has an exalted role in the *reconquista* from the Moors and galvanized subsequent crusades against Jews and heretics domestically, and against Protestantism in Europe more generally. As cement for the Castellan monarchs and their successors in building the Spanish nation, Catholicism became indissolubly linked to the national identity.

Mujal-León's observation can equally be applied to Portugal. In short, the Catholic religion is an essential element of the present spiritual life, culture, and history of Portugal and Spain.

A logical corollary to the first point is that anticlericalism – the outright rejection of the church and of all religious things – has also been a pronounced feature of the political and social life of Spain and Portugal throughout their respective histories. The seeds for the clerical/anticlerical cleavage line were sown at the very birth of the Portuguese and Spanish nation–states. Absolute political power and legitimacy in Portugal and Spain until the democratic revolutions of the modern era were in the hands of the monarch, in line with the doctrine known as the divine right of kings. That doctrine postulated that monarchical power was absolute, granted to the monarch by God. The Roman Catholic Church legitimized the monarch's claim to divine authority, and, in turn, typically received royal grants of land, among other goods (Higgs 1979). In spite of the occasional conflict between the Crown and the Church (for instance, when the monarch resented the influence of a particular bishop, or of a religious order) the relationship between them was generally stable and mutually beneficial. Certainly, the imperial power of Portugal and Spain in the fifteenth and sixteenth centuries brought great riches to the monarchs, and extended the scope of the Roman Catholic Church worldwide (Boxer 1978). These successes deepened aristocratic support for this Iberian absolutist model of political development, which was predicated upon the alliance of cross and sword (Bruneau 1976).

To be expected, this system of governance posed a great challenge to Portuguese and Spanish reformers in the aftermath of the French Revolution of 1789 (see Gibson 1989 and Payne 1973). These reformers tended to be well-educated people from aristocratic families, and at least at first, members in good standing with the Church. Yet, try as they might, their efforts at reform were consistently rebuffed by the monarch, and by the Church hierarchy.

Indeed, the institutional Catholic Church stood staunchly against the democratic and liberal revolutions of the modern era, in favor instead of the existing order (Conway 1997). Pope Pius IX, who served between 1846 and 1878, was generally distrustful of liberal, republican, and socialist political movements, considering each of them to be flawed in important ways. Following the political and social upheavals associated with the revolutions of 1789 and of 1848, and the loss of papal territories during Italian unification in 1860, Pius IX viewed these new philosophies as not only a direct threat to the fabric of European society, but also as a grave danger to the papacy itself. In response, he issued the *Syllabus of Errors* in 1864, which denounced liberalism and republicanism as incompatible with Catholic and Christian views (Chadwick 1975). He felt that these modern approaches to government were too materialistic, too individualistic, and hostile to God. The *Syllabus* was followed a few years later by the doctrine of Papal infallibility, issued by the First Vatican Council in 1870. That doctrine established the papacy not only as the moral, spiritual, and institutional center of the Catholic Church, but also as the focus of Catholic opposition to modernity. Thomas Bokekenkotter (1990) remarks that these actions, considered in their entirety, resulted in "a divorce of secular culture from the Church and the state of siege mentality that characterized modern Catholicism down to our day." In short, the official Church reaction to the first wave of democratization in Continental Europe was to react against it, to oppose it, to fear it, and to condemn it.

By so strongly resisting the changes associated with the democratic and liberal revolutions of post-1789 Europe, a whirlwind of anticlerical sentiment settled in upon reform sectors throughout the continent, especially in Catholic countries. Gildea (1994) notes, for instance, that anticlerical sectors in France strongly believed that the Church represented a serious danger against reason, progress, and freedom, and, therefore needed to be removed from the political and social equation before true progress could be made.

The same was true for Iberian anticlericalism. Indeed, although long a part of Iberian history, the origins of the modern clerical/anticlerical cleavage line at the elite level can be traced to the very first encounters between the Iberian children of the Enlightenment (i.e. the university educated city dwellers), who preferred a republican form of government, and the protectors of the old Iberian order (i.e. the crown, the military, the old aristocracy, and the Roman Catholic Church). In reaction to the

1864 *Syllabus of Errors*, these reformers sought, among other objectives, to remove the Church from its dominant societal role in education. Education was a concern to republican sympathizers, because in their view, enlightened change could only emanate from people open to new ideas, philosophies, and, in particular, new approaches to knowing God (Gibson 1989).

Neither the Church nor the reformers were particularly interested in compromise, and quickly came to view each other as the enemy. In particular, Church leaders reasoned that if they were to maintain their privileged position in society, then the reformers would have to be kept out of power. Alternatively, the reformers understood that any chance they had of success required that the Church and the other elements of state power be dislodged from it (Shubert 1990). In short, the Spanish and Portuguese Republicans were often frustrated by having to deal with a powerful crown and aristocracy, who were supported by a conservative Church hierarchy (see Herr 1971 and Wheeler 1978). Mutual resentment was generated, the Republicans became staunchly anticlerical, and the clerical/anticlerical division was intensified among the political elite.

There were anticlerical sentiments at the popular level in Iberia as well. Indeed, popular anticlericalism has been a feature of Portuguese and Spanish civil society since at least the seventeenth century (Badone 1990; see Ullman 1968). In Spain, for instance, Adrian Shubert (1990) notes that a 1627 collection of Spanish proverbs contained hostile feelings against the clergy. Among the complaints voiced at the popular level were rent disputes with the land-owning Church, as well as a generalized view of the clergy as "greedy, oppressive and immoral." Ruth Behar (1990) observes that those espousing an anticlerical worldview consider priests to be mere equals, "functionaries of the church and of the state," who have no special powers to "hear confessionals, provide Communion, and give the sacraments." Likewise, Caroline Brettell (1990), following Joyce Riegelhaupt (1984), notes that popular anticlericalism in Portugal characteristically views the parish priest, as well as the church hierarchy itself, to be impediments to knowing God.[4] Such popular sentiments of anticlericalism have, of course, many causes; arguably, the Church's close relationship with the monarchy, its fear of modernity, and its neglect of the general population in Iberia, helped to generate those feelings (Burns 1992).

---

[4] Although there were cases of popular anticlericalism in Portugal, it should be noted that the anticlericalism under the First Portuguese Republic was found primarily among the political elite. Unlike Spain, there were no cases of church burning in Portugal (Gallagher 1996).

## CRITICAL PHASES BETWEEN RELIGION AND POLITICS IN PORTUGAL AND SPAIN DURING THE TWENTIETH CENTURY

Both Portugal and Spain went through three distinct phases of relations between religion and politics during the twentieth century. First, the population of each country lived under anticlerical Republican regimes at the beginning of this century. Second, both adopted proclerical fascist and corporatist regimes in the 1930s. Third, they each made successful transitions to democracy in the 1970s and 1980s, and these new democracies each adopted constitutional provisions guaranteeing the freedom of religion.

There is one important differences between their national political experiences during this time as well: Spain suffered through a divisive civil war in which religion played a very contentious role from 1936 to 1939. During the Spanish Civil War there were brutal acts perpetrated by anticlerical Republican forces against members of the clergy, including the murder of priests, nuns, and monks, as well as the burning of churches and convents (McLeod 1997). These frightful acts, in a real sense, dismembered Spanish civil society, and subsequent efforts to bridge this cleavage in Spain became momentously difficult.

There were also two distinct phases in the politics of the Roman Catholic Church in the twentieth century. From the turn of the century until the Second Vatican Council in 1962, the Church was an antimodern, antidemocratic, antiliberal institution. After Vatican II, the Church fully embraced the idea of reconciling itself to the modern, liberal and democratic world. Indeed, it is no exaggeration to say that a new kind of official Roman Catholic Church was born after the 1965 issuance of both *Gaudim et Specs* and *Dignitatis Humanae*. It is important to note, however, that Vatican II did not just happen; it was the end-point of what had been a complex and long-evolving debate among theologians within the Church, some of whom had argued since the First Vatican Council for the need to adapt Catholicism to modernity (Bokenkotter 1990). The Church's adoption of that view at Vatican II had profound implications for Portuguese and Spanish Catholicism. We will return to this point shortly.

### PHASE ONE: ANTICLERICAL REPUBLICAN REGIMES IN THE IBERIAN PENINSULAR (CIRCA 1900s TO 1930s)

Iberian democratic reformers finally managed to seize power in the nineteenth and twentieth centuries. Once in power, the First Portuguese Republic (1910–26), and the Second Spanish Republic (1931–6), attempted to exclude the Roman Catholic Church from state power and curtail its influence in civil society. Let us look at each case in some detail.

## The Portuguese First Republic and the Church (1910–26)

The overthrow of King Manuel II by young Republicans in 1910 paved the way for the inauguration of Portugal's First Republic. This was an elite, anticlerical and Lisbon-based regime. (Payne 1980). This regime was a "republic" in name only, it did not allow many groups in the society to participate politically and discouraged the creation of organizations in civil society (Robinson 1979).

The First Republic was particularly successful in blocking the Church from any influence in the state. In that regard, Prime Minister Afonso Costa steered a number of the most restrictive anticlerical laws in Portuguese history through the National Assembly, including the *Lei de Separação* of 1911. Following the 1905 French law of separation, this new Portuguese law not only separated church and state, but it also placed the Church under the control of the state, and closed the theology program at the University of Coimbra (Gallagher 1996). It provided for the closing of many seminaries, the elimination of the national observance of holy days, the secularization of cemeteries, and the nationalization of some Church property. Even some of the eighteenth-century anticlerical laws, which dated back to Marques de Pombal's expulsion of the Jesuits from Portugal, were brought back into effect. In sum, the Portuguese First Republic created a strong, centralized, secular, and administrative state in Lisbon, which, combined with the widespread anticlerical feeling among civil servants, kept the institution away from state power during the life of the First Republic (Linz 1977, Opello 1991). And yet, this effort to contain Church influence was not very successful. Richard Robinson (1979) has noted that:

[these laws] proved counterproductive in as much as it further stimulated a revival of religious feeling and brought about an increased sense of urgency among Catholics concerning the problems of building up the organizational structure of religion. Far from bringing greater unity, it divided society by reinforcing political and ideological divisions.

In fact, these legislative measures prompted the formation of Catholic groups throughout the country by people who were deeply troubled by the official anticlericalism of the Lisbon regime. One of these groups, the *Centro Academica da Democraçia Cristão* (CADC, the Christian Democracy Academic Center), was founded by students at the University of Coimbra in 1912. Two of its student members later played critical political roles: One of them, Manuel Gonçalves Cerejeira, became the cardinal of Lisbon and the other, Antonio de Oliveira Salazar, became the country's dictator (Gallagher 1996).

Ultimately, the First Republic was overthrown by a military coup on 28 May 1926. The regime's effort to limit Church influence was but one of several factors in its eventual downfall, which also included political instability and a bad economy. To address the economic situation, the military asked Antonio de Oliveira Salazar, who was by then a professor of economics at the University of Coimbra, to become the minister of finance. He accepted, and by 1929 had successfully brought order to the national economy. When the military decided to return to the barracks in 1933, they offered to support him as the new premier. Salazar accepted, and established a new order, called the *Estado Novo*, or New State, in 1933 (Linz 1977). Among other goals for this new regime, Salazar sought close ties with the Church.

### The Spanish Second Republic and the Church (1931–6)

The same general pattern between church and state existed in Spain in the early portion of the twentieth century. Although the First Spanish Republic (1810–1923) had managed to coexist with the Catholic Church, the Second Republic (1931–6) was overtly hostile to it (Callahan 1984). Anticlericalism became a pronounced feature in the 1930s, when some of the most drastic anticlerical laws in Spanish history were adopted (Payne 1984).

Following the seven-year military dictatorship (1923–30) of Primo de Rivera, who had overthrown the First Republic with the promise to restore order, a new Republican regime was created following gains made by Republican forces in the 1931 municipal elections. King Alfonso XIII abdicated the Spanish throne, and the Second Spanish Republic was formed. One of the goals of the well-educated, secular and urban-based leaders of the Second Republic, led by Prime Minister Manuel Azaña of the anticlerical Radical Party, was to undermine the power and influence of the Catholic Church in Spanish politics and society (Pérez-Diaz 1993). To that end, they included several anticlerical legal provisions in the Constitution of 1931. Among other measures, these constitutional provisions disestablished the Church, cut off all state subsidies to religious organizations, and secularized cemeteries. There were also stipulations for the legalization of divorce, a secular education system, and the confiscation of Jesuit properties. Further, public religious displays were disallowed, and some religious orders were expelled (Andrés-Gallego and Pazos 1998).

Despite this hostile tone against the Catholic Church, Pope Pius was ready to work with the Republic even as late as 1935 (Bokenkotter 1990). But the Republicans were not interested in developing a working relationship with the Church. Moreover, the anticlerical tone of the new Republic ignited a somewhat dormant anticlericalism among the population (O'Connell 1971). In May of 1931, for example, angry crowds in Madrid, Barcelona, Seville, and in other large cities burned churches, and

destroyed over twenty convents (Payne 1984). This hostile anticlericalism in the early years of the Second Republic did not bode well for the
development of a societal consensus on the role of religion and politics
later on.

Conservative Catholics were greatly concerned with these attacks on
the church. They were represented in Parliament by the so-called Spanish
Confederation of the Autonomous Right (*Confederación Española de
Derechas Autónomas*, or CEDA), which was led by the devout Catholic
law professor, José María Gil Robles (Vincent 1996b) The CEDA sought
to carve out space for the Catholic Church in the Second Republic, and
its political position was considerably strengthened when it emerged as
Spain's largest political party after the 1933 legislative elections. In return
for his party's strong showing, Gil Robles was given a cabinet position
(Shubert 1989). And yet, no real accommodation among the opposing
sides was ever reached.

Catholics were particularly alarmed when the anticlerical socialist and
communist alliance, known as the Popular Front, gained a plurality in
the 1936 legislative elections (Hermet 1980). When the new leftist government announced that it planned to pursue massive nationalizations,
militant Spanish nationalists and fascists, inspired by the emergence of
fascist governments in Germany, Italy, and Portugal, argued that the time
was ripe for the Second Republic to be overthrown. Shortly thereafter,
on July 7, 1936, a national insurrection broke out. Spain divided into
pro-Republican and pro-Nationalist zones, and both sides committed
horrible atrocities in what became a fratricidal civil war (see Sanchez
1964).

In reaction to the anticlerical tone of the Second Republic, the Spanish
bishops proclaimed their support for General Francisco Franco in 1937,
opting for fascism over the modern political ideologies of republicanism,
socialism, and communism (Andrés-Gallego and Pazos 1998). That
decision particularly enraged the Republican side, and, in response, many
of its political activists decided to attack the Catholic Church itself.
Although churches were generally respected in the Nationalist zone, they
came under attack in the Republican zone. There, anticlerical radicals
killed some 4,184 priests, 2,365 monks, and 283 nuns. They also burned
churches, abbeys, and convents (Shubert, 1989). This cemented the cler-
ical/anticlerical cleavage, and made any eventual societal healing rather
problematic (Edles 1998).

### PHASE TWO: PROCLERICAL CORPORATIST REGIMES IN IBERIA (CIRCA 1930S TO 1970S)

In the aftermath of these anticlerical Republics, right-wing fascist regimes
were put into power by the military in Portugal and Spain. Once in

power, both Salazar in Portugal and Franco in Spain built proclerical, antimodern, antirational, antiliberal, anticommunist corporatist states, in direct opposition to the anticlerical Republican regimes. In addition, each leader reached formal agreements, or Concordats, with the Vatican, to demonstrate to their respective populations that the Pope himself supported their new political regimes (Brassloff 1998).

## Salazar's Portugal and the Church

Portuguese dictator Antonio Salazar designed a corporative system of government in 1933, calling it a New State, or *Estado Novo* (Robinson 1979 and Whitehead 1986). With the blessing of the Portuguese Church, Salazar used the ideology of corporatism to oppose democratic philosophies that dominated political discourse in Continental Europe and in the Anglo-American world (Linz 1965).

In particular, Salazar was influenced by two Papal encyclicals: *Rerum Novarum: The Condition of Labor* in 1891, authored by Pope Leo XIII,[5] and by Pope Pius XI's 1931 encyclical, *Quadragesimo Anno: After Forty Years* (see Hollenbach 1979). Salazar sought to create a corporative system of government and societal organization in Portugal that he believed represented a third way from the models of democratic liberal capitalism and state-run communism. Corporatism, he argued, would avoid the excesses of individualism and materialism, and result in the common good. Article 5 of the *Estado Novo* Constitution, adopted in 1933, declared Portugal to be a corporative and unitary Republic, in which the family and the Church played leading roles (Gallagher 1983). The Constitution also recognized Catholicism to be Portugal's official religion (de Sousa Franco 1987).

The cardinal of Lisbon from 1930 to 1971 was Manuel Gonçalves Cerejeira, who had been a member of CADC with Salazar at the University of Coimbra (Gallagher 1996 and Georgel 1985). Working with him, Salazar helped the Catholic Church in a number of ways. He shepherded various statutes through the newly created Corporative National Assembly, including the creation of the Church radio station, known as *Radio Renscença*, the creation of Catholic University in Lisbon, and legislation against Protestant missionary activities. The Concordat of 1940 signed between Salazar's Portugal and the Vatican further cemented this relationship. This agreement provided for the recognition of the Holy See by Portugal, prohibited government officials from interfering with Vatican correspondences with the Portuguese Church, and granted the Church the right to establish its own education system, which would

[5] Pope Leo XIII served from 1878 to 1903.

function alongside the state system. It also ascribed civil status to Catholic marriages, and forbade divorce (Bruneau 1976).

In spite of his general proclerical stance, Salazar never actually allowed the Church much influence on political matters. This point is well illustrated by Salazar's troubles with Oporto's bishop Antonio Ferreira Gomes in 1958. At that time (which was before both the start of the colonial war and Vatican II) the bishop wrote a poignant letter to Salazar, which criticized the *Estado Novo's* record on human rights in Portugal and in the African colonies. Salazar's response to this overt act of defiance was to first, not to allow Ferreira Gomes back into Portugal following a 1959 trip abroad, and, second, demand that the Vatican name a new bishop of Oporto. The Pope refused Salazar's request, and a stalemate ensued: Ferreira Gomes was not allowed to return to Portugal for ten years (Gallagher 1996). Salazar took advantage of this situation to warn other clergy that he would not tolerate any further dissent among Catholics, and took steps to keep power away from Church officials.

Salazar sought to concentrate actual power in his own hands, and was wary about sharing it. Although he was more than happy to appear with the Cardinal of Lisbon and other Church officials in photo-ops, and to support proclerical legislation, the *Estado Novo* ultimately belonged to Salazar, and to no one else. In this regard, the Portuguese historian A. H. Oliveira Marques (1976) reminds us that:

The Catholic feature of the New State must be emphasized but not exaggerated, for Salazar's regime (unlike Franco's) never posed as an "apostolic" system engaged in some kind of crusade against anti-Catholic elements. The Premier's few public remarks on Catholicism and religion in general were always strikingly moderate and tolerant, in contrast to his strong beliefs and extremist attitudes on other subjects. His speech of 1940, when the Concordat with Rome was signed, showed a remarkably middle-of-the-way position, uncommitted to any all-pervasive Church influence and definitely opposed to Church meddling in politics. Thus no attempt was made to reunite Church and State.

Salazar did grant the Church a privileged position in his *Estado Novo*, and simultaneously, kept it at arm's length from actual political power.

## Franco's Spain and the Church

In Spain, many Catholics, reacting against the radical anticlericalism of the Republican period, supported Franco. Once in power, Franco abolished all anticlerical legislation adopted during the Republic, and in 1941 reached an important agreement with the Spanish Church. That agreement provided that Catholicism would be named as Spain's official religion, granted the Church freedom to operate without state limits, and provided for state funding for the Church, among other measures (O'Brien and Shannon 1997).

In spite of these apparent good relations, the Catholic Church was very wary about the actual political direction Franco would follow in the late 1930s and early 1940s. At that time the Spanish Church was a profoundly conservative and antimodern institution, and it distrusted the radicalism and dynamism of one of Franco's biggest supporters, the Falange fascist movement. Certainly, the Church and the Falange were tactical allies during the Civil War, but a future collaboration between them after Franco's victory was unlikely (Payne 1984).

The defeat of the Axis powers by the Allied Forces in World War II ended any chance of a powerful state role for the Falange in Spain, and paved the way for improved ties between Franco and the Church (Mujal-León 1982). That relationship was codified with the August 27, 1953 signing of the Concordat between the Vatican and the Spanish state, which provided that Catholicism would continue its status as Spain's official religion. In addition, the Concordat exempted the clergy from state taxation, permitted Church documents to be published without prior censorship, granted a state subsidy to religious personnel, and gave the Church the right to supervise religious education in schools. In return, the Vatican recognized Franco's state, and agreed to permit it some say in the appointment of Spanish bishops.[6] Franco's rule was never seriously challenged from within Spain, and the support he received from the Church was an important element of his legitimacy. Surprisingly, the first significant winds of political change to reach Franco's Spain actually emanated from the Vatican.

### The Impact of the Second Vatican Council on Iberian Religion and Politics

By the 1960s the Vatican began to move away from its former "third way" of fascism-corporatism social organization, even though this system was still being used by Portugal and Spain (Dorr 1992). The new realities of the Cold War, and the threat of the spread of atheistic communism worldwide, greatly concerned both Pope John XXIII and his successor Pope Paul VI, who wanted to carve out a new place for the Roman Catholic Church in the modern world (Hastings 1991).

John XXIII, who was the Pope from 1958 to 1963, wrote two significant encyclicals, *Mater et Magistra* (1961) and *Pacem in Terris*

---

[6] When the economy was sputtering in the 1950s, Franco turned for help to the technocratic ministers affiliated with the Catholic lay order Opus Dei. They were permitted to run the economy, and by opening the protected economy to the world, fundamentally changed the course of economic policy. Opus Dei had a significant hand in what became known as the so-called Spanish economic miracle in the 1960s and after.

(1963), which focused the attention of the Church squarely on the key social and political justice issues of the modern and industrializing world. Although this body of work manifests the traditional Catholic wariness of the Lockean emphasis on individualism and views of private property, it also seeks to reconcile Catholic concerns for the dignity of human life with the modern demands for political freedom and economic equality (see Seidler and Meyer 1989).[7] In other words, under Pope John's leadership, the Church began the process of reconciling itself, at least partially, with liberal, representative democracy.

One of the key issues Pope John XXIII wanted explored as he convened the Second Vatican Council in 1962 was the role of the Roman Catholic Church in the modern world. After three years of discussion and debate, the Second Vatican Council, with the approval of Pope Paul VI, released *Gaudium et Spes: Pastoral Constitution on the Church in the Modern World* and *Dignitatis Humanae: Declaration on Religious Freedom* in 1965.[8] In what was arguably a watershed event in the life of the modern Church, these two documents attack any and all political regimes that do not guarantee and protect human rights and religious freedom. They also assert that governments should protect the rights of free assembly, of common action, of expressing personal opinions, and of professing a religion both privately and publicly.

*Gaudium et Spes* manifests the Vatican's interest in breaking its alliance with the dictators in Portugal and Spain. It declares that the Church "stands ready to renounce the exercise of certain legitimately acquired rights if it becomes clear that their use raises doubt about the sincerity of her witness or that new conditions of life demand some other arrangement." Similarly, *Dignitatis Humanae* proclaims religious freedom to be a basic human right, and calls upon all governments to protect that right, claiming that "a wrong is done when government imposes upon its people, by force or fear or other means, the profession or repudiation of any religion, or when it hinders men from joining or leaving a religious community." These documents made it crystal clear that the Vatican had come to view the continuance of its close relationship with the reactionary Iberian regimes as harmful for the Church, as well as for Iberian society, and wanted to change course.

---

[7] Pope John XXIII, who served between 1958 and 1963, made a number of key contributions to Catholic social justice teaching. In 1961, he issued *Mater et Magistra*, which deals with the question of social justice. In that encyclical, he emphasizes that the state has the moral duty to intervene in the marketplace to ensure that property be used for the common good. Two years later he authored the watershed encyclical *Pacem in Terris*, which endorses the "welfare state" model of capitalism. In particular, it supports the rights to life, food, clothing, shelter, medical care, culture, and education of all people.

[8] Pope Paul VI served from 1963 to 1978.

In their totality, *Gaudium et Spes* and *Dignitatis Humanae* identified a new and proper role for the Church in the modern world. Rather than maintaining a sixteenth-century theocratic state model, which was characteristic of the pre-Vatican II Church in Portugal and Spain, the post-Vatican II Church saw itself as an essential and dynamic player in both political and civil society. Within that context, it sought to maintain its traditional role in education and health care, as well as use its influence to sway larger societal debates on abortion, contraception, divorce, welfare, and other human rights issues to its point of view (see Hanson 1987). As such, the Catholic Church not only reconciled itself to the modern, democratic, and liberal world, but it also attempted to carve out a "moral space" within it where it could play a critical role. The Church changed after Vatican II, and that change influenced the course of Iberian Catholicism.

## Vatican II and Portugal

Vatican II took place as Portugal was waging its colonial war in Africa. The Vatican was not at all happy about the Portuguese regime's failure to reach a political settlement with the African nationalists, and made its displeasure known. To that end, Pope Paul VI, who had visited Fátima in 1967, infuriated Salazar's successor, Marcello Caetano, when he received the leaders of the liberation movements from Angola, Mozambique, Guinea-Bissau, and Cape Verde at the Vatican in 1970 (Gallagher 1996).[9]

Bishops in Portugal and Spain became more public in their criticisms of their respective regimes, encouraged by the teaching of Vatican II. In Portugal, for example, the bishops of Beira and of Oporto publicly questioned the ethics of continuing the colonial war. A Catholic intellectual movement was founded at that time, which was rather critical of the regime, and its journal, *O Tempo e o Modo*, became an influential source of ideas in the anti-Salazar movement. These developments assuaged concerns held by many devout Catholics, who feared that the Church's official association with the regime might cause the growth of anticlericalism in civil society (de Sousa Franco 1987).

The fact that some Portuguese bishops were openly critical of the regime and of the colonial war prevented a close working relationship between the Church and state in the 1960s and beyond. And yet, as long as the conservative Manuel Gonçalves Cerejeira remained Cardinal of Lisbon, the Portuguese Church officially remained loyal to Salazar. Cerejeira took great steps to limit and control the implementation of the

---

[9] Caetano became Portuguese Premier in 1968.

changes adopted at the Second Vatican Council in Portugal, and managed, at best, to hold off the winds of change for a few years.

## Vatican II and Spain

Vatican II started something of a *problematique* within the Spanish Church, which was experiencing great internal changes in the 1960s and 1970s (Cooper 1975). On the one hand, the older Spanish clergy were opposed to *Gaudium et Specs* and *Dignitatis Humanae*. Some 90 percent of the Spanish bishops, most of whom had lived through the Spanish Civil War, were against the new teachings (Edles 1998). On the other hand, younger priests were very supportive of Vatican II. According to the findings of a 1970 poll, 62 percent of the Spanish clergy actually opposed the Church's close relationship with Franco's regime. That number jumped to a 86 percent disapproval rating when just considering the responses of priests under thirty years old (Shubert 1989). In addition, the first Joint Assembly of Bishops and Priests held in 1971 declared that since the special relationship between Franco and the Church was born out of the fratricidal civil war, it was, almost by definition, shameful, and should be ended.

Vatican II played a critical role by providing large sectors of the clergy both the justification, and institutional support, to break with Franco's regime (Brassloff 1998). There were efforts at increased ecumenical dialogue to discuss how the Spanish Church should integrate the new teachings. Among the important Catholic journals at the time were *Aún*, published by the Jesuits, and *Cuadernos para el Diálogo*, founded in 1963 by Joaquín Ruíz Giménez. These journals were leading the way to a generalized philosophical and spiritual reawakening in Spain (Vincent 1996a).

Pope Paul VI wanted to end the close association of the Church with the Franco regime. The key instrument at his disposal was the naming of new bishops in Spain. After Vatican II, the Pope began to reject candidates recommended by Franco for positions in the Spanish Church, avoiding direct conflict by making "interim" appointments. Over Franco's objections, Paul VI named Vincente Enrique y Tarancón as Archbishop of Toledo and Primate of Spain in 1969, and later named him Archbishop of Madrid. Under Tarancón's leadership, the Spanish Church started to implement the teachings of Vatican II, and adopted a more politically moderate tone (Pérez-Diaz 1993). In spite of his disagreements with the Pope, Franco remained loyal to his faith to the end. His death on November 25, 1975 ended an era, and set up both the possibility for a peaceful transition to democracy, as well as the normalization of church-state relations in Spain.

Both Salazar and Franco had build conservative antimodern regimes in the 1930s, which were in harmony with the then constituted Catholic Church. However, when the Church changed after Vatican II, both of these regimes lost a vital part of their raison d'être. In the end, neither of these regimes managed to last much time beyond Vatican II, nor, perhaps more importantly, beyond the deaths of their founders.

## PHASE THREE: THE NEW DEMOCRATIC REGIMES IN THE IBERIAN PENINSULAR (1970s TO PRESENT)

Quite unexpectedly, Portugal and Spain adopted democratic regimes in the 1970s. The two nations followed very different paths to democracy: There was revolutionary upheaval in Portugal, and an evolutionary process of change in Spain. And in each case, the new regimes sought to concurrently limit the influence of the Roman Catholic Church while maintaining good relations with it. Of note, the post-Vatican II Church strongly supported the efforts in each country to build democratic regimes.

### The Church and Portugal's Transition to Democracy

By the early 1970s, the Portuguese regime was in crisis. Portugal's thirteen year (1961–1974) colonial war in Africa had eroded its legitimacy in the eyes of not only elements of the Church, but also among junior military officers. These officers formed themselves into an opposition group called the Armed Forces Movement (MFA), and overthrew the regime on April 25, 1974. That military action plunged the country into a two-year period of turmoil and agitation (see Manuel 1995).

Once in power, a key problem for the MFA was that it was ideologically fragmented, and was not sure in what direction to take the country. Factions of various political ideologies appeared among MFA soldiers, including moderate, socialist, and communist groups. They battled each other in an effort to gain control of the levers of governmental power from 1974 to 1976. During that larger political struggle, many MFA members displayed strongly anticlerical feelings. Holding the Church responsible for its collaboration with for the long-lasting Salazar dictatorship, there were many MFA-inspired attacks against the Church during the transition.

Antonio de Ribeiro, the new bishop of Lisbon (Cardinal Cerejeira had stepped down in 1969) was extremely careful in his statements during this time, taking great pains not to incite anticlerical movements, and to limit attacks against the Church. Communist-leaning MFA Prime Minister Vasco Gonçalves, had the opposite fear. He understood the power and authority of the Church, and feared a religious backlash against the

MFA. Throughout his rule in 1974 and 1975 he worked hard not to offend the conservative clergy, and to find common ground with progressive Catholics. Further, Gonçalves tried to stop radical anticlerical activities engineered by MFA member.

The anticlerical situation, however, quickly spiraled out of the control of both Ribeiro and Gonçalves, as evidenced by the *Radio Renascença* case. During the so-called "hot summer" of 1975, communist workers took over the Church-run *Radio Renascença*, and broadcasted anticlerical propaganda. They held the station for over a year, and were only removed in the fall of 1976 by MFA commandos, who were by then under the control of political moderates (Manuel 1995).

There were other incidents. The MFA's radical anticlerical 5th Division Cultural Dynamism squad, for example, sought to reeducate the people about the virtues of communism. Upon entering a village, these officers would sometimes take down crucifixes on chapels and churches, and require the village people to listen to their interminable lectures on why all religions, and especially Catholicism, were bad. As Gonçalves had feared, these activities induced an impassioned reaction against the communists and other leftist groups by the country people in the deeply religious northern areas and in the Islands.

Indeed, these anticlerical actions revived an allegiance to the Church by many Portuguese, who felt that the leftist MFA threatened their very way of life. During that time, the supposed Marian apparitions at Fátima took on powerful symbolism for many people. According to devout Catholics, the Virgin Mary appeared to three country children of Fátima in May of 1917 and asked them to pray for the conversion of Russia from the coming evils of communism. In 1975, the possibility of a communist regime in Lisbon led many people to believe that they had not been praying hard enough. So, believers prayed for the conversion of Russia, as well as for that of Portugal.

The Catholic Church spoke out during this time as well. For example, prior to the April 25, 1975 elections for a Constituent Assembly, Portuguese bishops asked all Catholics to vote for any party that would guarantee the values of family, education, and liberty, and warned the people not to accept at face value the easy promises of any party which pledges the creation of a "utopia-on-earth" program (Manuel 1995). In addition, Antonio Ribeiro, the cardinal of Lisbon, addressed the MFA's anticlericalism in his homily at Sunday Mass on March 27, 1975:

For a little while now we have been aware that anti-clericalism in Portugal, an old sin, an inheritance from another era, has sprung back to life at this time with vigor and strength. But, it has also occurred to us that [anti-clericalism] has as an obstacle the civil and common sense of the Portuguese people. . . . The shameless and insolence of some of the political activists has been greeted with the reproach and disapproval of the Portuguese people, even non-Catholics.

The moderate results of the April 25, 1975 election combined with the politico-military victory of the moderate "Group of Nine" MFA officers in November 1975 was warmly greeted by Church officials. The Church also supported the democratic Constitution of 1976, which provided for freedom of religion as well as a separation of Church and state (Manuel 1996). In the years since the adoption of the new democratic constitution the Party of the Democratic Center (CDS) has been likened to a Christian Democratic type party, but there has been no successful explicitly Catholic political movement in Portugal.[10]

### The Church and Spain's Transition to Democracy

Unlike the Portuguese case, the Spanish transition was a negotiated and gradual process of political opening which took place under the close guidance of Franco's successor, King Juan Carlos. Both sides of the Spanish Civil War had reason not to work with the other side after Franco's death. The Republicans could fault the Church for its staunch support of a brutal dictator; the Church could accuse the Republicans of atrocities committed against priests and nuns in the 1930s (Hanson 1987). And yet, both sides agreed that it would be best to set these vindications and revindication aside, and try to build a new and peaceful order.

Franco's chosen successor, King Juan Carlos, was in essential agreement as to the Church-state relations in the post-Franco era with Cardinal Enrique y Tarancón. The Concordat of 1953 would be scrapped, and a new relationship would have to be negotiated. In 1976, however, the matter was not just up to the two of them – the political parties also had a say in the new Church-state relationship. Representatives from the traditionally anticlerical Spanish Socialist Workers' Party (PSOE) and the Spanish Communist Party (PCE), negotiated with the pro-Church conservative forces of the Alianza Popular (AP) and the Union of Christian Democrats (UCD) in 1977 and 1978. These were hard and important

[10] The failure of Catholicism to become a significant political force under democracy in Portugal may be seen as a legacy of the treatment of the Church by the *Estado Novo*. Tom Gallagher (1996) has astutely noted that "If democracy's chance had come in the late 1950s or 1960s, rather than in 1974, Catholics could have played an important role in defining the shape of the new politics. The Church and its lay offshoots had many public-spirited individuals within its ranks at that time whose dedication to the cause of political and economic justice was shaped by profound religious convictions. But most of them would subsequently channel their energies in other directions as the space in which to express political and social concerns within the church became increasingly circumscribed."

negotiations. Ultimately, a set of compromises were reached by the parties on the so-called "*night of Jose Luis*," which took place on May 22, 1978, named after the restaurant where the negotiations took place (Edles 1998). Although the socialists and communists went into the negotiations with the goal to disestablish the Church once and for all, they finally agreed to a compromise with the conservative forces in the name of political stability and societal peace.

The terms of this compromise essentially achieved two objectives: to please the anticlerics, it created a free and open religious space for all religions, and allowed for state-run schools; to please the clerics, it recognized the indispensable role of the Catholic Church in the life of the nation. In particular, all sides agreed to Article 16 of the Constitution of 1978, which reads: "The public powers will take into account the religious beliefs of Spanish society and will maintain the consequent relations with the Catholic Church and other confessions." Their agreement also led to the elaboration of Article 27 of the Constitution, which separates private and public education, and Article 32, which provides for civil divorce procedures. Although some remaining pro-Franco members of the Spanish clergy, including Cardinal Primate Marcelo González Martín, denounced these agreements, the Constitution received the endorsement of the Spanish Bishops' Conference (Hastings 1991). The compromises reached on "*the night of Jose Luis*" granted stakes in the new democratic system to both clerical and anticlerical elements, improving the new regime's chances for durability.

The Spanish Constitution of 1978 formed the basis of a new Concordat signed between the Vatican and the Spanish state on 3 January 1979. By the terms of this new agreement, the king gave up all of the rights accorded to the Spanish state from the Concordat of 1953. For its part, the Church also relinquished its special rights, including the ability to block civil divorce proceeding. This new Concordat managed to amicably settle the new terms of the religion and politics relationship in Spain, all the while avoiding the divisive anticlericalism of the Second Republic (Hanson 1987).

## CONCLUSION: HAS THE CLERICAL/ANTICLERICAL CLEAVAGE BEEN TRANSCENDED IN IBERIA?

The historical terms of the clerical/anticlerical divide in Iberia have been finally settled, and the relationship between religion and politics in Portugal and Spain has entered into a new phase. Two key factors are responsible for this transformation.

First, the governments of Spain and Portugal have significantly changed over the past thirty years. After the successful wave of democratization in the 1970s, they are each currently enjoying stable, democratic rule for the very first time in their respective histories. Further, the new opportunities presented to each of them by membership in the European Union has tended to shift the attention of the political elite away from purely parochial concerns to the larger issues affecting Europe. The Church certainly plays an important role in each country, but there are no longer any legal restrictions on other religions: The 1976 Portuguese Constitution, and the 1978 Spanish Constitution, each provide for a separation of Church and state. This is not at all to say that religion has become politically irrelevant in contemporary Portugal and Spain, but to point out that there has been a significant shift from the close Church-state relationship in the 1940s and 1950s to the present situation in which religious issues are discussed in an open democratic forum, and processed through the party system.

In addition, the Roman Catholic Church has also changed significantly in the years since Vatican II. Having reconciled itself to the modern world, the Church accepted the transition to a liberal democracy in each country. It now understands that it will have to fight for its views on moral issues in the imperfect forum of democracy, and that it will sometimes lose legislative battles. Functioning under a democratic regime and with a free press, many internal problems of the Church have become well known to the citizenry of Portugal and Spain in recent times as well, including the decreasing number of priests and nuns. The Church has been unable to stop legislation legalizing divorce, and continues its struggle against the legalization of abortion in both Portugal and Spain. The generally moderate behavior of the post-Vatican II Church, combined with an awareness among the population of the Church's internal problems, have tended to assuage the fears of the anticlerical factions in each country that the Church would regain its former position as a hegemonic power in Iberian society.

Of course, people still disagree about religion and politics, but it no longer represents the flashpoint it once did. In many ways, then, the present terms of the church-state relationship in Portugal and in Spain under democracy are more tenable and, perhaps, even more durable, than when the Church enjoyed "special rights" under corporatism. As such, an unexpected result of the democratization of Portugal and Spain in the 1970s may be seen to be the eclipse of the traditional clerical/anticlerical divide in Iberia in the 1980s and 1990s.

What role will religion play in the politics of the future for Portugal and Spain? That is an open question, but it is certainly safe to assume that religion will continue to be an important force in Portugal and Spain under the new democratic regimes. Even after all of the changes brought on by democratization, Portugal and Spain remain Catholic countries, and the attitudes of the clergy can and will continue to influence the attitudes of their numerous flock. In this regard, Ronald Inglehart, in his recent study of forty-three nations entitled *Modernization and Post-modernization*, has placed Portugal and Spain in a category known as "Catholic Europe," along with Belgium, France, and Italy. Inglehart's findings suggest that even though the direct influence of the Catholic Church has dropped off in recent years, these populations continue to demonstrate more traditional, so-called survival values than the populations of the Protestant nations of Northern Europe. These survival values include preferences for law and order, strong political leaders, jobs and economic growth, a hierarchical religious structure, and a social structure predicated on a two-parent heterosexual family unit. Inglehart notes that these are the dominant values of not only Catholic Europe, but are shared with the Roman Catholic countries of Latin America and East Europe as well.

At the very least, we can take from Inglehart's findings that even as the Roman Catholic Church recedes from its former powerful position in the two Iberian nation-states, indications are that it will continue to influence the morality and values of this population. As we reach the end of the twentieth century, Portugal and Spain may be presently classified as modern, democratic, stable, European, and Catholic counties.

### REFERENCES

Andrés-Gallego, José and Anton Pazos. 1998. *Histoire Religieuse de l'Espagne*. Paris: Les Editions du Cerf.

Antunes, Manuel Luís. 1982. "Notas sobre a organização e os meios de intervenção da Igreja Católica em Portugal: 1950–1980." *Análise Social* 72/73/74. 1141–54.

Aubert, Roger. 1981. "The Continuation of the Old Regime in Southern Europe." In Hubert Jedin (ed.). Volume VII. *History of the Church: The Church Between Revolution and Restoration*. Burns and Oates: London.

Badone, Ellen. (ed.). 1990. *Religious Orthodoxy and Popular Faith in European Society*. Princeton: Princeton University Press.

Behar, Ruth. 1990. "The Struggle for the Church: Popular Anti-clericalism and Religiosity in Post-Franco Spain." In Ellen Badone (ed.). *Religious Orthodoxy and Popular Faith in European Society*. Princeton: Princeton University Press. 76–112.

Birmingham, David. 1993. *A Concise History of Portugal*. Cambridge, U.K.: Cambridge University Press.

Bokenkotter, Thomas. 1990. *A Concise History of the Catholic Church*. New York: Image Books.

Boxer, Charles R. 1978. *The Church Militant and Iberian Expansion 1440–1770*. Baltimore: Johns Hopkins University Press.

Brassloff, Audrey. 1998. *Religion and Politics in Spain: The Spanish Church in Transition. 1962–96.* New York: St. Martins Press.

Brettell, Caroline. 1990. "The Priest and His People: The Contractual Basis for Religious Practice in Rural Portugal," In Ellen Badone (ed.) *Religious Orthodoxy and Popular Faith in European Society.* Princeton: Princeton University Press. 55–75.

Bruneau, Thomas. 1976. "Church and State in Portugal: Crisis of Cross and Sword." *Journal of Church and State*, 18, 3, Autumn. 463–90.

Buchanan, Tom and Martin Conway. 1996. *Political Catholicism in Europe, 1918–1965.* Oxford: Clarendon Press.

Burns, Gene. 1992. *The Frontiers of Catholicism: The Politics of Ideology in a Liberal World.* Berkeley: University of California Press.

Callahan, William J. 1984. *Church, Politics and Society in Spain, 1750–1874.* Cambridge, MA: Harvard University Press.

Canico, João, S. J. 1981. "The Church in Portugal." *Pro Mundi Vita Dossiers: Europe/North America.* Dossier No 14: July. 1–32.

Cardoso, Manuel P. 1993. "The Churches in Portugal." *Expository Times* 104, August. 323–8.

Chadwick, Owen. 1975. *The Secularization of the European Mind in the Nineteenth Century.* Cambridge, U.K.: Cambridge University Press.

Clark, Robert P. 1990. "The Society and Its Environment." In Eric Solsten (ed.). *Spain: A Country Study* (2nd ed.). Washington, D.C.: U.S. Government Printing Office. 69–134.

Conway, Martin. 1997. *Catholic Politics in Europe, 1918–1945.* New York: Routledge.

Cooper, Norman B. 1975. *Catholicism and the Franco Regime.* Beverly Hills, CA: Sage.

Cruz, Manuel Braga da. 1996–1997. "A Igreja na Transição Democrática Portuguesa." *Lusitania Sacra*, 8/9. 519–36.

de Sousa Franco, A. 1987. "A Igreja e o Poder em Portugal, 1974–1987." In Mario Baptista Coelho (ed.). *Portugal: O Sistema Político e Constitucional, 1974–1987.* Lisbon: Instituto de Ciencias Socias, Universidade de Lisboa.

Documentos Pastorais, 1967–1977. 1977. Lisbon: Conferençia Episcopal Portuguesa.

Dorr, Donald. 1992. *Option for the Poor: A Hundred Years of Catholic Social Teaching.* Maryknoll, NY: Orbis.

Edles, Laura Desfor. 1998. *Symbol and Ritual in the New Spain: The Transition to Democracy After Franco.* Cambridge, U.K.: Cambridge University Press.

*Eleições em Abril: Diário de Campanha.* 1975. Lisbon: Libir Editions.

Felicidade, José da. Editor. 1969. *Católicos e Política de Humberto Delgado a Marcelo Caetano.* Lisbon: Edição do autor.

Figueirdeo, Antonio de. 1976. *Portugal: Fifty Years of Dictatorship.* New York: Holmes and Meier Publishers.

Franca, Luis de. 1981. *Comportamento Religoso da População Portuguesa.* Lisbon: Moraes Editors.

Freire, José Geraldes. 1976. *Resistência Católica ao Salazarismo-Marcelismo.* Oporto: Telos.

94        *Paul Christopher Manuel*

Gallagher, Thomas. 1996. "Portugal." In Tom Buchanan and Martin Conway (eds.) *Political Catholicism in Europe, 1918–1965*. Oxford: Clarendon Press. 129–55.

   1983. *Portugal: A Twentieth Century Interpretation*. Manchester, U.K.: University of Manchester Press.

Georgel, Jacques. *O Salazarismo*. 1985. Lisbon: Publicações Dom Quixote.

Gildea, Robert. 1994. *The Past in French History*. New Haven: Yale University Press.

Gibson, Ralph. 1989. *A Social History of French Catholicism, 1789–1914*. London: Routledge.

Hanson Eric O. 1987. *The Catholic Church in World Politics*. Princeton: Princeton University Press.

Hastings, Adrian. 1991. *Modern Catholicism: Vatican II and After*. New York: Oxford University Press.

Hermet, Guy. 1980. *Les Catholiques dans l'Espagne Franquiste*. 2 vols. Paris: Presses Universitaires de France.

   1986. *L'Espagne au XX Siecle*. Paris: Presses Universitaires de France.

Herr, Richard. 1971. *Historical Essay on Modern Spain*. Berkeley: University of California Press.

Higgs, David. 1979. "The Portuguese Church." In William J. Callahan and David Higgs (eds.) *Church and Society in Catholic Europe of the Eighteenth Century*. Cambridge, U.K.: Cambridge University Press.

Hollenbach, David, S. J. 1979. *Claims in Conflict: Retrieving and Renewing the Catholic Human Rights Tradition*. New York: Paulist Press.

Huntington, Samuel. 1968. *Political Order in Changing Societies*. New Haven: Yale University Press.

*IDOC Bulletin*. "The Church and Revolution: Portugal" No. 28 Fall 1975: 13–15.

Inglehart, Ronald. 1997. *Modernization and Postmodernization*. Princeton: Princeton University Press.

Kay, Hugo. 1970. *Salazar and Modern Portugal*. London: Eyre and Spottiswoode.

Lannon, Frances. 1982. "Modern Spain: The Project of a National Catholicism." In Stuart Mews (ed.). *Religion and National Identity*. Oxford: Basil Blackwell. 567–90.

Latourette, Kenneth Scott. 1958. *The Nineteenth Century in Europe: Background and the Roman Catholic Phase*. Vol. 1. New York: HarperCollins.

Leal, A. B. 1968. "Catholics, the Church and the Dictatorship," *Portuguese Colonial Bulletin* January 7. 398–401.

Lewy, Guenter. 1965. "The Uses of Insurrection: The Church and Franco's War." *Continuum*, 3 Autumn. 267–90.

Linz, Juan J. 1991. "Church and State in Spain from the Civil War to the Return of Democracy," *Daedalus* 120, 3 Summer. 159–79.

   1977. "Spain and Portugal: Critical Choices." In David S. Landes (ed.) *Western Europe: The Trials of Partnership*. Lexington, MA: Lexington Books. 241.

1965. "Totalitarian and Authoritarian Systems." In Nelson Polsby et al. (eds.) *Handbook of Social Sciences*. Vol. 3, Reading, MA: Addison Wesley.

Manuel, Paul Christopher. 1995. *Uncertain Outcome: The Politics of the Portuguese Transition to Democracy*. Landover: University Press of America.

1996. *The Challenges of Democratic Consolidation in Portugal: Political, Economic and Military Issues*. Westport: Praeger.

Marques, A. H. de Oliveira. 1976. *History of Portugal*. 2nd ed. New York: Columbia University Press.

Martins, Oliveira. 1969. *A History of Iberian Civilization*. New York: Cooper Square Publishers.

McLeod, Hugh. 1997. *Religion and the People of Western Europe, 1789–1989*. Oxford: Oxford University Press.

Mujal-León, Eusébio. 1982. "The Left and the Catholic Question in Spain." In Suzanne Berger (ed.). *Religion in West European Politics*. London: Frank Cass. 32–54.

Nevins, Lawrence. 1976. "Old Wine in New Bottles: How Fascists Become Militants of the Left." *Worldview* 19 May. 12–14.

O'Brien, David J., and Thomas A. Shannon (eds.). 1997. *Catholic Social Thought: The Documentary Heritage*. Maryknoll, NY: Orbis.

O'Connell, James R. 1971. "The Spanish Republic: Further Reflections on its Anticlerical Policies." *The Catholic Historical Review* 57: 2. 275–89.

Opello, Walter C., Jr. 1991. *Portugal: From Monarchy to Pluralist Democracy*. Boulder, CO: Westview Press.

Payne, Stanley G. 1987. *The Franco Regime, 1936–1975*. Madison, WI: University of Wisconsin Press.

1984. *Spanish Catholicism*. Madison, WI: University of Wisconsin Press.

1980. *Fascism*. Madison, WI: University of Wisconsin Press.

1973. *A History of Spain and Portugal*, 2 vol. Madison, WI: University of Wisconsin Press.

1961. *Falange: A History of Spanish Fascism*. Stanford, CA: Stanford University Press.

Pérez-Diaz, Víctor. 1993. *The Return of Civil Society: The Emergence of Democratic Spain*. Cambridge, MA: Harvard University Press.

Pinto, Antonio Costa. "On Liberalism and the Emergence of Civil Society in Portugal." *Working Papers No. 2*, Instituto de Sociological Historica, Universidade Nova de Lisboa.

Riberio, Antonio Cardinal. 1976. Remarks in *Os Bíspos e a Revolução de Abril*. Lisbon: Ispagal.

Riding, Alan. 1991. "Pope Visits Fátima to Tender Thanks: Credits the Virgin Mary With Freeing East Europe and Saving His Life in '81." *The New York Times* 14 May.

Riegelhaupt, Joyce. 1973. "Festas and Padres: The Organization of Religious Action in a Portuguese Parish." *American Anthropologist*, 75. 835–52.

1982. "O Significado Religioso do Anticlericalismo Popular." *Análise Social* 72/73/74. 1213–29.

1984. "Popular Anti-clericalism and Religiosity in pre-1974 Portugal." In Eric R. Wolf (ed.). *Religion, Power and Protest in Local Communities: The Northern Shore of the Mediterranean.* Berlin: Mouton. 93–114.

Robinson, Richard. 1979. *Contemporary Portugal: A History.* London: Allen and Unwin.

Sanchez, José M. 1964. *Reform and Reaction: The Politico-Religious Background of the Spanish Civil War.* Chapel Hill, NC: University of North Carolina Press.

Seidler, John, and Katherine Meyer. 1989. *Conflict and Change in the Catholic Church.* New Brunswick, NJ: Rutgers University Press.

Shubert, Adrian. 1990. *A Social History of Modern Spain.* London: Unwin Hyman.

Soares, Mario. 1989. "Speech on Portuguese Anti-Semitism." *Christian Jewish Relations*, 22: Spring, 37–8.

Solsten, Eric. (ed.) 1994. *Portugal: A Country Study.* 2nd ed. Federal Research Division: Library of Congress.

Stobel, Lester. 1973. *Facts on File: 1973.* New York: Facts on File.

Ullman, Joan Connelly. 1968. *The Tragic Week: A Study of Anti-clericalism in Spain 1875–1912.* Cambridge, MA: Harvard University Press.

Vincent, Mary. 1996a. "Spain." In Tom Buchanan and Martin Conway (eds.) *Political Catholicism in Europe, 1918–1965.* Oxford: Clarendon Press. 97–128.

1996b. Catholicism in the Second Spanish Republic: Religion and Politics in Salamanca, 1930–1936. Oxford: Clarendon Press.

Wasserstein, David. 1992. "Jews, Christians and Muslims in Medieval Spain." *Journal of Jewish Studies* 43 Autumn. 175–86.

Wheeler, Douglas. 1978. *Republican Portugal, A Political History.* Madison, WI: University of Wisconsin Press.

Whitehead, Laurence. 1986. "International Aspects of Democratization." In Guillermo O'Donnell, Philippe C. Schmitter, and Lawrence Whitehead (eds.) *Transitions from Authoritarian Rule: Comparative Perspectives.* Baltimore: Johns Hopkins University Press.

Wiarda, Howard J. 1993. *Politics in Iberia: The Politics Systems of Spain and Portugal.* New York. HarperCollins, 1993: 24–96.

1994. "The Society and Its Environment." In Eric Solsten (ed.). *Portugal: A Country Study.* 2nd ed. Washington, D.C.: U.S. Government Printing Office. 63–112.

Williams, H. Fulford. 1953. "The Diocesan Rite of the Archdiocese of Braga, Portugal." *Journal of Ecclesiastical History*, October 4. 123–38.

Of all the case studies in which a single religious tradition appears dominant, Israel would seem most likely to constitute an instance in which religion is a source of national identity and cohesion. Not only does an historically shared Jewish identity provide the very rationale for the state of Israel, but the nation is often threatened by aggressive neighbors who cast their opposition to Zionism (at least partially) in religious terms. However, Israeli Judaism does not provide a consensual "sacred canopy," but rather serves generally critical, prophetic, functions. Religion provides a fertile source of conflict in Israeli politics, in which two principal cleavages are salient. Kenneth Wald describes the issues raised by the Ultraorthodox haredim as approximating the "culture wars" which have characterized several Western societies. Further, the forces of Modern Orthodoxy have brought issues of territorial acquisition and retention to the center of Israeli political debate, and have occasionally been associated with violent and antidemocratic activities. Wald suggests that the political power and theological assertiveness of Modern Orthodoxy may well limit the ability of the Israeli state to reach accommodation with its neighbors.

# 5

# The Religious Dimension of Israeli Political Life

*Kenneth D. Wald*

> Was Israel established by King David or Theodore Herzl?
>
> Bishara Azmi, 1997

As the world's only Jewish state – Jewish both by design and population – Israel presents a unique set of questions to students of religion and politics. How large a role does Judaism play in the politics of contemporary Israel? How does the political system balance the imperatives of Jewish law and the demands of governing a modern state? How are conflicts between religious groups moderated? In what ways does Judaism influence the nature and conduct of political life? Does Judaism reinforce or undermine the maintenance of a democratic regime? Do the distinctive qualities of Judaism promote a different style of politics from that associated with states dominated by Christian or Muslim populations? How does the fact of Jewish dominance influence the treatment of non-Jewish minorities who live in the state? How does the character of the state influence Jewish religious groups themselves?

The breadth of questions precludes definitive answers in a single chapter. Indeed, entire volumes have been devoted to each of the questions raised in the preceding paragraph (Abramov 1976; Dowty 1998; Liebman and Don-Yehiya 1984). The central focus of this chapter is Israel's identification as a Jewish state. That is the quality that sets Israel apart from the other nations covered in this volume and, indeed, the trait that distinguishes Israel from all other states that have existed in the modern world. Following a brief overview of Israel's religious heritage and the position of its non-Jewish inhabitants, the chapter focuses on the two major political cleavages that incorporate a religious dimension – relations between religious and secular Israeli Jews and the tension between religious nationalists and the advocates of territorial compromise.

## BACKGROUND

Along with the United States and Russia, Israel is one of the three major population centers of world Jewry (Cashman 1995). More than 80 percent of Israel's approximately 5.5 million citizens are adherents of Judaism (Central Bureau of Statistics 1998). Surveys suggest that about 20 percent of Israeli Jews are highly observant, another 20 percent are wholly nonobservant, and the remaining 60 percent, usually described as "traditional," follow a mix of religious and secular customs.[1] According to the most recent census data, the non-Jewish inhabitants of Israel comprise approximately 800,000 Muslim Arabs (mostly Sunni), 150,000 Christian Arabs (mostly Greek Catholic and Greek Orthodox), 80,000 Druze Arabs and a sprinkling of smaller faiths (Ministry of Foreign Affairs 1998).[2]

This population distribution reflects both the ideological heritage of the Israeli state and long-term historical forces. The state of Israel celebrated its fiftieth birthday in 1998, but the modern nation is the embodiment of a much older impulse. The area known today as Israel was part of the ancient homeland of the Jewish people until they were expelled by the Romans in 66 A.D. During the long period of exile that followed, Jews continued to look to this land as their home, and prayers for a return to Jerusalem were incorporated into the liturgy of Sabbath worship. In one sense, the Jewish people never accepted their banishment as a permanent condition but as an "unnatural" exile to be ended when God restored them to their rightful home in Zion. In the interim, however, the Jews spread across the globe and established durable diaspora communities in many regions. The longing for Zion did not disappear over the centuries but, like the appearance of the Messiah, was postponed until the dim and distant future. Though some Jews made their way back to the ancient homeland, living as aliens under foreign rulers, most lived

---

[1] In Judaism, religious intensity is measured by adherence to prescribed ritual behavior rather than acceptance of specified religious belief. Thus, the world "Orthodoxy" is used to describe Jews who follow a rigorous prayer regimen, engage in certain rituals, adhere to strict dietary guidelines, observe laws and customs relating to family purity, and otherwise comply with guidelines set down by Jewish tradition. Surveys of Israeli religious practice classify respondents into religious categories based either on their reported religious behavior or their self-description. For specifics, see Kedem (1991).

[2] The international community does not recognize Israel's sovereignty over several geographical areas it acquired during the Six Day War of 1967. Israel customarily excludes from its population data the Arabs who reside in the areas known as the West Bank and the Gaza Strip but includes Arabs who live in East Jerusalem and the Golan Heights, even though the latter do not regard themselves as Israeli citizens. The majority of Israel's Arab citizens live within the pre-1967 borders of the state and do accept Israeli citizenship. They may distinguish between a Palestinian identity and Israeli citizenship.

and died elsewhere. By the early nineteenth century, Jews could be found virtually everywhere but the major centers of Jewish settlement were in Asia (the Arab Middle East), northern Africa and eastern Europe. The conditions of these Jewish communities varied widely depending on the attitude of local rulers and the extent of religious tolerance.

What we might call theological Zionism, the identification of Jerusalem as the lodestar of Jewish civilization, trusted to God to bring about the end of exile. The longing for a return to the ancient homeland took more concrete shape in the late nineteenth-century movement known as political Zionism, founded by Theodore Herzl (Vital 1982). The Zionist movement called for immediate reestablishment of a Jewish homeland in the Middle East and, in the interim before that goal could be recognized, promoted the immigration of Jews to the area then known as Palestine. The appearance of Zionism at that time was the product of complex forces – the contagious growth of nationalism among European minority groups, the prevalence of virulent anti-Semitism in many "enlightened" states, the continuing misery of Jews in areas that had not yet transcended feudal conditions, and the erosion of Jewish identity in places where assimilation had become possible. Together, these conditions fueled the expansion of Zionism until the goal of creating a Jewish state in the Middle East was formally endorsed by Great Britain in the 1917 Balfour Declaration.

Stimulated by Zionism, Jews made their way to Palestine by hook or by crook throughout the nineteenth and twentieth centuries, settling in cities and the country-side, building up a functioning Jewish community with a wide range of social, cultural, religious, and political institutions, and developing a modern Hebrew language (Horowitz and Lissak 1978). To the indigenous Arab population of Palestine, predominantly a village society, the large-scale Jewish immigration from Europe represented an alien intrusion and was resisted with both active and passive means. Following years of political maneuvering, furious diplomatic efforts, the horrors of the Nazi Holocaust in Europe, and open confrontation with the British authorities who ruled Palestine from 1918 to 1947, the creation of a new Jewish homeland was finally approved by the United Nations in 1948. At the moment of independence, the new state was home to perhaps 650,000 Jews and an estimated 700,000 Arabs.[3]

The events that followed independence dramatically enhanced the Jewish character of the Israeli population. In a savage war with the surrounding Arab nations whose armies had invaded the infant Israeli state,

---

[3] For a useful summary of the debate over the size of Israel's Arab sector at independence, see Appendix I in Morris (1987).

most Arab residents of Palestine fled or were expelled beyond the borders
of Israel. The approximately six thousand Jews killed in the fighting were
soon replaced by the immigration of most of what remained of European Jewry after the Holocaust. At the same time, as the rising tide
of Arab nationalism in the Middle East and North Africa made life
extremely uncomfortable for the large Jewish communities in those
areas, most of the population left en masse for Israel. New communist
regimes in Eastern Europe completed the work of the Holocaust by
driving out most of their surviving Jewish communities who also fled to
Israel. Just six years after independence, then, the population had
returned to prewar levels but the Jewish share had climbed to around 90
percent (Mahler 1990, 38). Although the remaining Arab population
within Israel grew steadily due to high levels of fertility, Jewish pre-
dominance was reinforced over the following decades by additional
waves of immigrants from around the globe.[4] As late as the 1980s and
1990s, Israel continued to draw large cohorts of Jewish immigrants from
the Soviet Union and its successor states and, in a series of dramatic air-
lifts amid the chaos of civil war, to transplant to Israel virtually the entire
ancient Jewish community of Ethiopia.

If measured solely by the sheer force of numbers, then, Israel is a state
of the Jews. But to Zionists, Israel's Jewishness was not incidental but
its very purpose. Israel was conceived as a haven for Jews, a sanctuary
where they could escape the ever-present threat of persecution that had
accompanied life in exile. In the proclamation of independence issued on
May 15, 1948, the founders declared Israel's central purpose to "open
the gates of the homeland wide to every Jew and confer upon the Jewish
people the status of a fully privileged member of the community of
nations." The massacre of millions of European Jews in the Holocaust
had made that task even more urgent.

Defined in that way, it is clear that Judaism occupies a special place
in Israeli political culture and it is fair to say that it has achieved the
status of a de facto established religion. Describing Judaism as the "de
facto" established religion recognizes that it is privileged in ways that
make Jews more than first among equals. Apart from defining the very
purpose of the state, Judaism supplies the state with its dominant language of Hebrew, its weekly and annual calendar, and many of its state
ceremonies, symbols, and traditions. In an otherwise open political
system, Israel bars ballot access to political parties that deny the Zionist

---

[4] In the immediate aftermath of the War of Independence (known as The Great Catastro-
phe to Palestinians), Arabs who remained, thought to be a security risk, were placed
under a military regime that severely curtailed such basic rights as travel, land ownership, communication, and political organizing (Lustick 1980).

character of the state. Israeli citizenship is available to non-Jews but Jews are favored by immigration policy and in terms of many social benefits. Taken together, these policies and practices have persuaded some scholars that Israel should not be regarded as a liberal democracy that takes no notice of the religious character of its citizens. Rather, they contend, Israel is better understood as an "ethnic democracy" that respects the civil rights of non-Jewish citizens but does not grant them full equality with Jews and rejects their claims to internal sovereignty.

But Israel's proclamation of independence also promised "freedom of religion, conscience, language, education, and culture," pledged to "ensure complete equality of social and political rights to all its inhabitants irrespective of religion," and committed to "safeguard the Holy Places of all religions." As a parliamentary democracy rather than a theocracy, Israel does in fact provide the free and unfettered religious worship guaranteed by its Independence proclamation. Israeli citizenship is not limited to Jews. Perpetuating the "millet" system inherited from Ottoman rule and maintained by the British during their period of sovereignty, the modern Israeli state provides public funding for the religious needs of non-Jewish communities, permits them to choose their legally mandated day of rest, leaves questions of family law to the religious courts of each religious tradition, and allocates money for educational institutions under Christian and Muslim control. The same electoral regulations that bar anti-Zionist parties also deny legal recognition to movements that promote racial or religious incitement against minorities. Given these qualities, Israel does not promote theocracy, the fusion of religion and state found in Iran, nor the rigid separation between the two domains as in the secular state established in the United States. Like most democratic states, Israel follows a middle way between these extremes (Monsma and Soper 1997).

Because of the substantial autonomy granted to minority – meaning non-Jewish – religious communities, religious freedom is not a significant factor in the ongoing conflict between Jews and Arabs. This does not mean that religion is absent from the conflict. Indeed, the verbal battle between the two sides is laced with religious language, symbols, and imagery (Shipler 1986). Jewish Israelis often attribute Arab hostility not to pragmatism or nationalism but to a deep-seated anti-Semitism rooted in centuries of religious conflict between Islam and Judaism. Much of the hostility of the Arab nations toward Israel is in fact expressed as opposition to its "Zionist" character. That sentiment sometimes leads to calls for Jihad, or a holy war, to excise the "cancer" of a Jewish state from the Muslim Middle East. Among Palestinians, the term favored by Arab residents of Israel and the refugees who left during the War of Independence, religious themes may also be invoked in public discourse.[5] The most violent wing of Palestinian nationalism, the Hamas organization, portrays itself as a grassroots Muslim movement and recruits its terrorists with explicitly religious appeals. The intense violence that broke out in the fall of 2000 was described by Palestinians as the "Al-Aqsa Intifada," referring to a mosque on the Temple Mount in the Old City of Jerusalem. Nonetheless, I would argue, the root of Arab-Jewish tension is conflict over land and self-determination, resources that are only incidentally related to religion. To the Palestinian community, the paramount issue has been the loss of territory and sovereignty that accompanied Jewish migration to Palestine and the establishment of a Jewish state. For Arabs outside Palestine, Israel was detested as "a bridgehead planted in their midst by Western powers determined to keep Arabs divided and to frustrate their national ambitions" (Shlaim 1995, 25). One should not mistake the idiom of the conflict – religious language, symbols, and imagery – for the substance of the conflict. There is more than enough religiously based political conflict in Israel without having to impose that framework on what is essentially a nationalist struggle!

## RELIGION AS A POLITICAL FORCE

Among Israeli Jews, the vast majority of the population in the state of Israel, religion has increasingly emerged as a source of division and struggle. Such a claim may seem bizarre given the widespread tendency to assume that common religious identity promotes national cohesion, or a sacred canopy. If religion bequeaths to people a sense that their fates are linked, forged in the "primordial" mists of time and reinforced constantly by common experience and interaction, then surely a shared religion should enhance the development of a sense of peoplehood (Gutmann 1979, 31). These assumptions are true for most religions, and they hold even more strongly for Jews. After all, Judaism was long

---

[5] The flashpoint usually involves the Temple Mount, the highest point in the Old City of Jerusalem and site of the first and second Temples of the ancient Hebrew kingdoms (Halevi 1996). Since the seventh century, it has housed the Dome of the Rock, holy to Islam as the site where Mohammed began his night journey to heaven, and the sacred Al-Aqsa mosque. Upon Israel's conquest of the Old City in 1967, the government reaffirmed exclusive Muslim rights to the site while claiming for Israel the supporting Western Wall beneath it. Periodic attempts by Jewish extremists to reclaim the Mount have inflamed Muslims and led to violent clashes with police. While I would not discount the religious feelings involved on both sides, I think this conflict has less to do with the intrinsic religious values attached to the Temple Mount than to the manner in which it symbolizes national autonomy. This is certainly true on the Jewish side, where Orthodox authorities have long prohibited Jews from walking on the Mount lest they inadvertently step on consecrated ground from the Temple period.

thought to be the glue that held the Jewish people together during their centuries of exile and it remains the agent that binds the dispersed Jewish people to the state of Israel. Nonetheless, while it may promote national integration on some levels, religion also has the capacity to divide people into competing camps. In contemporary Israel, Judaism has increasingly played a divisive role.

To judge by the increasingly harsh rhetoric that pervades public discourse, Jewish Israel is polarized between its religious and secular communities. This description overlooks a more complicated reality. In fact, as I shall argue, there are two different religious cleavages that animate much of Israeli political debate. In the first of Israeli Judaism's two major fractures, the division runs between an Ultraorthodox minority and the less observant sectors of the Jewish population. The power of this tension indicates the unresolved nature of the Zionist debate over whether Israel was to be a Jewish state or a state of the Jews. Some observers regard this line of cleavage as the major domestic challenge to the survival of the state (Chafets 1996; Schmemann 1998). The other form of intra-Jewish conflict, the second cleavage examined in this chapter, is built upon the aspirations of Israel's religious Zionists, a community embedded primarily within the realm of modern Jewish orthodoxy. In a sense, this division represents the other side of the Palestinian-Israeli conflict because it too constitutes a form of territorial nationalism. Less known outside Israel than the religious-secular debate, this particular line of conflict poses the most potent long-term threat to the stability and viability of the Israeli polity.

## THE THEOCRATIC CHALLENGE OF ULTRAORTHODOXY

Some years ago, when I asked an Israel friend why he planned to move from his comfortable home in a Jerusalem suburb, he told me that he was leaving because "the blacks" were moving into the neighborhood. The shock must have registered on my face because my friend quickly added that he was not referring to Israelis of African origin but rather to the community of religious Jews whose men dress in black hats and coats. This community, known variously as the Ultraorthodox, or *Haredim*, is the offshoot of a eighteenth-century revivalist movement that swept across Jewish settlements in eastern Europe.[6] The descendants and converts to this movement are now found around the world, but approximately half of them live in Israel, where they are estimated to constitute about 10 percent of the entire Jewish population and half of the "religious" population (Heilman 1992, 12). In an attempt to

---

[6] I will italicize the Hebrew word on first usage and use normal fonts in subsequent references.

minimize contact with other communities, they cluster in dense "urban villages," where the streets "throb with pious Jews in black garb, bearded, bespectacled, chattering in Yiddish, tumultuous, in a hurry, scented with the heavy aroma" of eastern European cuisine (Oz 1983, 3). In religious practice, the Ultraorthodox are known for maintaining the strictest standards of religious observance and for refusing to make accommodations to secular society. Although the use of the term is controversial, they are sometimes described as "fundamentalist" and equated with similar "extreme" wings of Islam, Christianity, and Buddhism. Like fundamentalist movements elsewhere, they are notoriously schismatic and organized in rival sects that often bear only slightly less hostility to one another than they do toward the secular culture of modernity.[7] Despite the powerful differences between various wings of the Ultraorthodox movement, this discussion focuses on their shared traits.

Israel poses a theological problem for the Ultraorthodox (Ravitzky 1996, ch. 4). Owing to a history of disastrous episodes led by false messiahs, Jewish tradition had long warned against attempting to bring a Jewish state into being by the actions of humanity. That was God's task. In addition to the sin of trying to "hasten redemption," Ultraorthodoxy charged Zionism with heresy for claiming to have created a Jewish state without a foundation in Torah, the Jewish sacred tradition. For the Haredim, Israel will deserve to be considered a "Jewish state" only when the government enforces the biblical prescriptions that collectively make up the core of "halacha," or Jewish law. This theocratic option was explicitly rejected by the Zionist founders of Israel, who were steeped in European socialism and known for their irreligious if not antireligious sentiments.

The leaders of the new state nonetheless pledged to the Ultraorthodox that Israel would maintain what has become known as the Status Quo regarding religion (Shimshoni 1982, 478). Under this agreement, the state would maintain a Jewish character in several respects. Jews would be accorded their traditional day of rest on Saturday, Jewish dietary laws would be followed in the kitchens of all state institutions, and the state would fund a religious school system to which observant parents could send their children. The religious affairs of the Jewish community were entrusted to a chief rabbinate with authority to fund local religious services, control Jewish holy places, certify dietary practices in

---

[7] To secular eyes, the qualities that unite the Ultraorthodox world are more compelling than the issues that divide them. Signifying that perception, casual observers sometimes equate subgroups of Haredim, such as the Hasidic sects, with the whole. In practice, the Haredim are divided over a wide range of religious questions, over the degree to which they should engage the outside world, and by severe ethnic cleavages.

the food industry, and maintain legal control over all aspects of Jewish personal status – marriage, divorce, adoption, burial, conversion, etc. Jewish men engaged in full-time religious study were exempted from military service and observant women were either exempted or given the option of alternative national service. The enforcement of religious custom, such as the prohibition upon labor and motorized transport on Saturdays, was to be contingent upon the religious composition of local communities. This produced the strange norm that public transport would run at full strength on the Sabbath in largely secular Haifa, operate in reduced mode in the more religiously mixed area of Tel Aviv, and remain at a standstill in Jerusalem, the holiest city to observant Jews. In an even finer gradation within cities, the state would close roads in religious neighborhoods on the Sabbath while permitting traffic elsewhere.

These concessions were not made to placate a powerful enemy. At the time of statehood, Israel was home to a mere ten thousand Haredim, less than 2 percent of the population. Indeed, it was probably the weakness of this community that inspired the secular David Ben-Gurion to guarantee the Jewish character of the state. Ben Gurion and many of the founding Zionists saw Ultraorthodoxy as doomed by modernity and unlikely to pose a long-term problem for the emerging Israeli state. Under these conditions, a generous policy toward Ultraorthodoxy would secure the community's allegiance to the state at small cost. The Status Quo would permit devout Jews to participate in the life of the nation without seriously disadvantaging the nonorthodox majority. Although there were tensions and conflicts over the content of Status Quo in the early years, the policy largely held. The Ultraorthodox acquiesced in the state, withholding their deepest affection but nonetheless participating to the extent of paying taxes, obeying the law, and confining their demands to such apparently peripheral issues as prohibiting autopsies, archaeological digs that disturbed Jewish graves, Sabbath desecration, and other practices that insulted Judaism.

Ben Gurion's prophecies of Ultraorthodox extinction proved to be spectacularly off the mark. Far from contracting, the Haredim grew at a rapid pace. Their population was augmented by extremely high rates of fertility, immigration of traditionalist communities, and the development of an Ultraorthodox subcommunity among Israel's large population of Sephardic Jews from the Arab states of the Middle East and North Africa. The current estimates put the Haredi population of Israel between 250 and 300 thousand, a number equivalent to 10 percent of the Jewish population and half of the religious sector. The largest concentrations are still found in Jerusalem, where the Ultraorthodox are nearing majority status, and in certain Tel Aviv suburbs, but the Ultraorthodox have spread out to formerly secular areas in towns, cities, and rural areas. Wherever they live, the Haredim continue to form enclaves that are defended against the larger culture. The change in numbers has been accompanied by a change in culture and lifestyle. What was once something of a folk religion, relying on informal transmission of tradition and custom, has become highly institutionalized. Leadership has passed from rabbis and community elders to Torah scholars who head the great and influential academies of Jewish learning known as *yeshivot* (singular *yeshivah*). Although these islands of traditionalism still venerate faith over science, they have appropriated many modern forms of technology such as computers, the VCR, and tape recorders as tools to spread the message of traditionalism.

The numerical success of the Haredim has also been underwritten by the generous financial subsidies provided under the Status Quo policy. The relative handful of Torah scholars whom Ben Gurion casually exempted from conscription has swollen into an army of nearly thirty thousand full-time yeshivah students (Hirschberg 1998, 10). Many are thought to be registered in name only so they can draw state grants while simultaneously holding down "secular" employment. In addition to exemptions, they receive stipends worth several times the funding allocated to university students. Ultraorthodox women have largely forsworn the national service envisioned as an alternative to compulsory military enlistment. The web of institutions controlled by the Ultraorthodox, vast networks of day care centers, state religious schools, adult care facilities, language training classes, etc., also draw state subsidies valued at $250 million per year (Halevi 1992, 7). These benefits are jealously guarded by the Ultraorthodox political parties that emerged as major players in the 1980s. Once content to entrust their representation to others, the Haredim now vote at high levels, serve in government ministries, and extract financial rewards for supporting governing coalitions. In the current Knesset, for example, Haredi parties hold twenty-three of the seventy-one seats commanded by the governing majority and fill nearly a fourth of cabinet positions. While Israel's government changed hands in 1999, the religious parties switched allegiance and maintained almost exactly the same leverage as they had under the Netanyahu administration. By threatening to withdraw support, they have an effective veto power over many government decisions.

Numbers and political power may have encouraged the Haredim to assert their claims more boldly. In terms of public policy, their spokesmen now clamor for the state to be more fastidious in its Jewish character. Claiming that God will delay redemption as retaliation for the sins of Jews, they demand, among other priorities, that the state severely restrict abortion, cease all transportation on the Sabbath and holidays (including flights by the Jewish airline, El Al), ban the growth or importation of nonkosher meat, impose severe standards of modesty on public displays, and use their control over certificates of *kashrut* (signifying compliance with kosher dietary practices) to impose other forms of religious observance on hotels, restaurants, and other public places. They remain insistent that the chief rabbinate, increasingly Ultraorthodox in tone, maintain sole authority over marriage, divorce, burial, and other matters of personal status. They refuse to allow the other streams of Judaism – the nonorthodox varieties that are preponderant in the diaspora – any form of legal recognition. They have called on the state to limit immigration to Jews who conform to the classic halachic definition, permitting entry to only those non-Jewish dependents and relatives who convert to Judaism under orthodox auspices. In well-publicized incidents, Ultraorthodox crusades have sometimes utilized violence, riots, civil disobedience, and other forms of disruptive behavior. Within their enclaves, for example, extremists have burned down newsstands that sell "secular" publications, disrupted public worship services by nonorthodox groups, beaten women who appear immodestly clothed in public, and stoned private automobiles that drove near Haredi neighborhoods on the Sabbath.

Outside their own community, the Haredim are a controversial and often despised sector of Israeli society. Survey data from 1991 show that they tied for last among nine groups whom the public was asked to rate on a scale running from "very positive" to "very negative" (Levy, Levinsohn, and Katz 1993, B-12). The Haredim were assigned a positive ranking by 41 percent of Israeli Jews, a figure that is easier to interpret when one recognizes that exactly the same percentage of Israeli Jews responded positively to Arabs! The enmity has several sources. Israelis who serve in the military, spend long years in the reserve, and pay some of the highest taxes in the world often denounce the Haredim as parasites, who consume but do not produce. Secular Israelis are particularly infuriated by the willingness of the Haredim to draw benefits from a society that they so openly and provocatively disdain. On Israeli holidays celebrating national independence, for example, the news media routinely carry stories about ritual burnings of the Israeli flag on the streets of Ultraorthodox enclaves and broadcast pictures of ordinary Haredim going about their business while the rest of Israel observes a solemn moment of silence as a tribute to those who fell in battle.

Despite these provocative images, one should not exaggerate the tension between secular and religious Israeli Jews. Many Israelis outside the religious sector grudgingly respect the Ultraorthodox for their fidelity to tradition and veneration of Jewish learning. Even Jews who dislike the messenger of traditional Judaism believe the state should retain a

Jewish character and do not personally suffer from many of the Status Quo provisions enacted to placate the Haredim. Indeed, substantial majorities endorse such Status Quo policies as kosher kitchens in public institutions, closing roads in religious neighborhoods on the Sabbath, and maintaining the prohibition on civil marriage. But the Israeli public is equally strongly committed to ending what it sees as Ultraorthodox privilege by requiring all young men and women to perform military service and to accord equal public status to nonorthodox streams of Judaism (Levy, Levinsohn, and Katz 1993).

For their part, the Haredim have a very different image of their goals and aspirations. Far from picturing their community as a juggernaut out to impose theocracy, they regard their community as small, vulnerable, and besieged (" 'Black' Power" 1990). With so many men outside the workforce and women confined to jobs that pay low wages, they find it a constant struggle to feed, clothe, and house their large families. The Ultraorthodox life is difficult to sustain in the face of modernity as the allures of contemporary civilization – materialism and sensuality – seem constantly poised to invade the insular precincts of traditional Judaism. Far from consuming resources to which they are not entitled, the Ultra-orthodox spokesmen contend, they generally receive from the state far less in services and subsidies than they contribute by taxation. On the vexing question of military service, the Haredim point to the difficulty of reconciling the demands of Ultraorthodox observance and military service and the special dangers this could pose for unworldly young women. In less practical terms, they argue that Israel is defended both by its soldiers, and by God, who appreciates the religious fidelity of yeshivah students. On the larger criticism of their anti-Zionism, the Haredim insist they are more sinned against than sinners. They point to a strain of virulent antiorthodoxy in Zionism, accusing the Israeli "veterans" (Socialist pioneers) of showing contempt toward the religious immigrants who arrived after statehood and continuing to show their disregard for sacred Jewish traditions by going to the beach rather than fasting on the Day of Atonement. Haredi spokesmen justify their refusal to celebrate Israeli holidays or participate in public mourning for fallen soldiers by claiming that such ceremonies are not part of the Jewish tradition.

Whatever the validity of their claims, the Haredim have been able to sustain their power through a remarkably high degree of political cohesion that translates into an effective legislative presence. Though initially reluctant to legitimize the Israeli state by participating in its institutions, several Haredi political parties have emerged in the recent past. With their hierarchical tradition of authority, the religious communities have voted with almost 100 percent solidarity for the candidates favored by their rabbinical authorities and, taking advantage of Israel's almost pure system of proportional representation, have catapulted the religious parties to legislative significance. The "western" Haredim have a number of distinct parties that have run on a common electoral list under the "Torah Flag" banner. The haredim from the east broke from their European brethren to form a Sephardi party, known as Shas, that rose to third largest in the Knesset elected in 1999. Unlike the Ashkenazi wing of this movement, the Ultraorthodox from eastern countries have moved beyond Knesset membership to occupy top governmental positions in such critical ministries as education, interior, and immigrant absorption. As long as neither of Israel's two largest parties comes close to holding a legislative majority, the haredi parties will be attractive coalition partners and will exact a price for their support of "secular" political initiatives.

For all their growth and power, the Haredim remain a small subpopulation whose power has been exercised on issues that are not central to Israeli political debate. The maintenance of Orthodox authority on religious matters, a subject of strong feelings in the Diaspora, is less salient to Israelis because most were raised in Arab states or eastern Europe where nonorthodox Judaism was simply unknown. Where issues do impinge on the prerogatives of the nonorthodox majority, they are often resolved by granting symbolic victories to the Haredim but negotiating accommodations that retain the status quo (Don-Yehiya 1986; Sharkansky 1996). The Israeli national airline may have been grounded on the Sabbath at the insistence of the Haredi political parties but landing rights could be reallocated to foreign airlines, preserving travel opportunities on Saturday. The no traffic zone might be enlarged around Ultraorthodox islands on the Sabbath, but alternative roads could be built to funnel secular travelers to the stores, bars, restaurants and other public entertainments that have expanded operating hours on the weekend. Jews who want to marry or non-Jews who wish to convert outside the Orthodox rabbinate can do so abroad and the state will recognize these actions. If all else fails and the demands of the Ultraorthodox cannot be accommodated, the Ultraorthodox political parties usually prove more concerned with maintaining state subsidies for their institutions than in forcing secular Israelis or the state into a halachic mode. On these occasions, they may be persuaded to forego their religious objective in exchange for additional state funding.

Thus in sum, the conflict between the Ultraorthodox and other Israelis seldom touches on vital questions that might endanger the preservation of the state. That is not the case for the other major intra-Jewish cleavage to which we now turn our attention, the conflict over territorial nationalism.

## TERRITORIAL NATIONALISM AND THE
## MODERN ORTHODOX

Since the Six Day War of 1967, when Israel acquired huge new tracts of land via military conquest from its attackers, the Israeli public has been polarized about what to do with the new territory. In the first stages of victory, when there was hope for reconciliation with the Arab states, the Labor government treated the lands as bargaining chips to be exchanged for peace treaties. The failure of the Arab states to play along led to a hardening of Israeli attitudes, helping stimulate a political movement that regarded the territories as vital to Israeli security in the next war. Ten years after the war, the Likud party came to power on a platform of territorial maximalism. Unlike Labor, which had signaled a willingness to exchange land for peace, Likud took the position that Israel had the right to maintain those territories located in the ancient Hebrew kingdoms of the Middle East. That issue continues to define the principal axis of political conflict in contemporary Israel.

To a considerable degree, the Modern Orthodox community has provided the core constituency for territorial nationalism (Peres 1995, 104). The community of Modern Orthodoxy constitutes about 10 percent of the Jewish population of Israel and makes up half of the religious sector. Like their Ultraorthodox contemporaries, the Modern Orthodox community is defined religiously by its professed adherence to the commandments enshrined in halacha. As the adjective suggests, this segment of the religious sector differs from the Ultraorthodox in having made peace with many aspects of contemporary society. Because they are committed to living in greater harmony with modern culture rather than resisting it at all costs, Modern Orthodoxy does not insist on segregating itself in virtual ghettos. The Modern Orthodox attempt to follow Jewish law, but to do so while participating fully in society. Except for the cloth head coverings worn by men and the longer skirts of women, adherents of this religious tradition do not differ much in appearance from nonreligious Israelis. Although they usually attend different schools and participate in different youth groups, the Modern Orthodox often share with their secular counterparts a lifestyle that incorporates respect for secular education, commitment to material comfort, and openness to Western traditions in music, theater and art. They converse in modern Hebrew rather than the Yiddish still favored by many of the Ultraorthodox.

This commitment to social integration is not accidental but part of the historical context that produced this stream of contemporary Jewry. The ancestors of today's Modern Orthodox are the Religious Zionists who embraced both Judaism and Zionism in the late nineteenth century and who worked with the socialist advocates of a Jewish state (Luz 1988). They stood apart from the mass of Ultraorthodox who, as previously noted, rejected Zionism both because it arrogated the task of redemption to humankind and because its most passionate advocates were nonreligious socialists. Yet the Religious Zionists parted company with their socialist fellow travelers by insisting that the new Jewish state must carve out an important role for religious institutions and values. The partnership could be justified because the religious authorities of the community argued that antireligious Zionists were inadvertently doing the holy work of God even as they fulminated against traditional Judaism (Ravitzsky 1996, ch. 3). Because what they shared was more significant than their differences, the Religious Zionists managed to work relatively peacefully with secular Zionists in laying the foundations for modern Israel. They did so by creating a set of religious institutions – labor unions, schools, banks, youth groups – that paralleled the "official" Zionist entities but retained an express commitment to traditional Judaism.

Because they were Zionists, the Modern Orthodox enthusiastically embraced the Jewish state that emerged in 1948. Indeed, they are commonly described with the label "National Religious". From the beginning, they served in the military and participated fully in the responsibilities of citizenship. While the Haredim withdrew from even the religious stream of state education and trusted their own rabbis over the State Rabbinate which was "tainted" due to its complicity with Zionism, the Modern Orthodox put their stamp of approval on the "official" religious institutions of Israel. The Modern Orthodox also participated in the Israeli political process, giving much of their support to the National Religious party (NRP). The party was not reluctant to join the governing coalition and usually supported Labor's foreign policy line. Owing to the Ultraorthodox boycott on serving in official positions, the Modern Orthodox were quick to seize control of the various religious ministries and funneled state resources through their own institutions. In matters of religion and state, they largely accepted the Status Quo. Although they usually sided with the Ultraorthodox when religion and state collided, the Modern Orthodox seldom initiated these conflicts. Until the Six Day War, the Religious Zionists were probably the strongest evidence for the integrationist role of Judaism in Israeli society.

Of all the sectors in Israeli society, the Modern Orthodox were the most affected by Israel's stunning military success in 1967. In the months before the war, as Arab leaders spoke openly of driving Israel into the sea and Holocaust memories were rekindled, Israel's plight seemed desperate. The decisive victories over the Arab armies, the conquest of parts of the ancient holy land, the reunification of Jerusalem under Israeli authority – all these events seemed not simply remarkable but divinely ordained. A movement that can perhaps best be described as revivalist swept over the some of the leading Orthodox *yeshivot* (Don-Yehiya 1996). To the enthusiasts of this movement, Israel's miraculous success indicated that the redemption of the world was at hand. The victory was taken as a sign that God intended the Jews to reclaim all of their original homeland. The best way to hasten the Messianic age was to reenact the original Zionist mission by settling the land – in this case, the land that Israel acquired by military means in 1967. The Modern Orthodox were the leaders of the initial movement to settle in what Israel called the administered territories (Lustick 1988; Sprinzak 1991, ch. 5). At first, the settlements were dictated by strategic considerations and the Labor Government understood them to be beachheads chosen to defend Israel proper. But for the most enthusiastic of the settlers, mere questions of strategic advantage were secondary to the larger task of reclaiming Israel's patrimony. The Religious Zionist movement began a systematic campaign to plant settlements in holy areas whether or not the Government approved. When Likud came to power in 1977, it enthusiastically embraced the settlement cause and provided generous subsidies to encourage further activity.

The secular parties that dominated rival governments may have assumed they were using the settlers for their own purposes, Labor to frighten Arab states into peace negotiations, Likud to so colonize the territories that they could never be returned in the event of peace negotiations. But both parties failed to understand the religious passion that fueled the settlement movement. Eventually, these differences produced a significant gulf between the settlers and the major parties. Labor's professed willingness to return the captured lands in the event of peace obviously put the Religious Zionists at odds with the dovish Labor party. But even Likud, which shared the Land of Israel vision, eventually found itself at odds with Religious Zionism. Concerned principally with questions of security, the Likud's goal was to preserve the additional territorial buffer provided by the West Bank, formerly controlled by Jordan, and the Golan Heights of the north, taken from Syria in fierce fighting. The Gaza Strip and Egypt's Sinai Desert, Israel's other conquests in 1967, were of lesser value because they provided minimal military benefits. When Egypt's Anwar Sadat made clear his willingness to offer peace terms to Israel in the 1970s, Likud seized the opportunity provided by the Camp David Agreement to remove one of Israel's most dangerous enemies from the strategic equation. Sadat's price included return of the Sinai and the evacuation of the Israeli settlements planted there. Although Likud acquiesced, the religious settlers in particular were bitterly disappointed that a party sharing its philosophy of territorial nationalism should so callously expel Jews from their ancient homeland. In the eyes of some of the religious settlers, Likud's "betrayal" took on cosmic dimensions because it so obviously violated the will of God (Sprinzak 1991, ch. 4).

The opposition to the Camp David Agreements by many Religious Zionists illustrated the degree to which the movement, once part of the mainstream Zionist consensus, had moved to the extremes of the Israeli political spectrum. That position was maintained over the years as the settler movement became the major opponent of Israeli concessions on matters of Palestinian autonomy or sovereignty. Even among Religious Zionists who did not settle in the West Bank – the vast majority of the community – its retention became part and parcel of what Charles Liebman and Eliezer Don-Yehiya (1983) described as a new Israeli civil religion. In this faith, replete with symbols, holidays, mechanisms of socialization and other aspects of a distinctive religious faith, the land itself acquired sacred status. Land was not merely the means to an end – security for the Jews, a haven, an opportunity for "normal" existence – but rather an end in itself. To return the land to "foreign control" was not merely bad policy but a betrayal of God's will.

The debate over the land polarized Israeli public life. Although heated ideological rhetoric was not new to Israel and was indulged in by partisans on both sides, critics suggested that religious sentiment inflamed the advocates of territorial nationalism. The traditional distrust of Gentiles fused with Biblical imagery to produce a portrait of Israel's Arab antagonists that deemphasized their humanity. In a particularly vicious example of this stereotyping, the Palestinians were portrayed as a modern incarnation of the Amelekites, sworn enemies of the ancient Hebrew tribes whom the Bible had commanded Jews to exterminate.[8] The negative imagery extended beyond the Palestinians, who were in fact competitors for land, to those Israeli Jews who most ardently spoke out in favor of Palestinian rights and territorial compromise. Because most "doves" were grounded in Western liberal values, invoking human rights, civil liberties, and democracy, they too were portrayed as apologists for a perspective alien to traditional Judaism. "In the eyes of the

---

[8] There is a less violent version of this argument, expressed by Pinchas Hayman (1995) in the pages of the *Jerusalem Post*. According to Hayman, who teaches at the Orthodox Bar-Ilan University, the concept of a Jewish nation means that Israeli citizenship is the exclusive preserve of Jews and hence that "we have every right to exclude non-Jews from the body politic (while seeing to their social, medical, educational, and other needs)." Such a perspective, while distant from the crude calls for genocide against the Palestinians, clearly warrants treating them as subjects with lesser rights than Jews. For a balanced discussion of the constitutional dilemmas posed by Israel's Jewish self-identification, see Peled (1992).

orthodox," wrote Israel's most distinguished anthropologist, "the positions of the doves and hawks are associated with diffuse cultural differences. It is part of the great clash between those faithful to the heritage of Jewry on the one hand, and the rootless on the other hand, between 'Guardians of the Torah' and detractors of the Torah, between goodness and corruption" (Deshen 1995, 118). This style of religiously informed discourse, treating one side of a political debate as the fount of virtue and the opposition as an incarnation of the devil, often leads to brutality.

Fueled by these visions, the extreme wings of Religious Zionism eventually gave way to acts of violence and savagery. A Jewish terror underground emerged on the West Bank in the early 1980s, assassinating Arab political leaders, bombing an Islamic college campus, and planting explosives on buses carrying Arab passengers. An observant Jew and respected physician in the Territories, Baruch Goldstein, reacted to the murder of a friend by a Palestinian with a murderous onslaught of his own, machine-gunning to death twenty-nine Muslims as they prayed in 1994. Within the pre-1967 borders of Israel, other Religious Zionists were found to have fomented violence and brutality against Arabs and, on occasion, against the Jewish left that supported Palestinian statehood. Although these acts of terror were routinely denounced by the National Religious party and by many religious leaders of Religious Zionism, there were other voices that provided religious sanction for such acts. Sometimes, the sanction was implicit as when the Chief Rabbi of Israel gave a eulogy at the funeral of Meir Kahane, founder of the extreme *Kach* movement, who spoke of Palestinians as animals and advocated their forcible expulsion from all of Israel. Religious justification could also be explicit. When Israel began to move toward a comprehensive settlement with the Palestinians, raising the possibility of evacuating Jewish settlements in the Territories, some rabbis from the movement publicly urged observant soldiers to refrain from carrying out orders that violated God's intent. In a country where the nonpolitical stance of the army had become almost a religious article of faith, such an extreme statement signaled the destabilizing capacity of the conflict over the land.

The apotheosis of religious violence was reached on November 4, 1995, when Israel's prime minister, Yitzhak Rabin, was assassinated by Yigal Amir. Far from being a loner or social outcast like many assassins, Amir was a product of the Religious Zionist youth movement, a part-time student in a Modern Orthodox yeshivah and a law student at Israel's orthodox university, Bar-Ilan. His rationale for killing Rabin was simple and chilling. Rabin was a traitor, endangering Jewish lives by returning sacred land for an evanescent peace. Under Jewish law, Amir claimed, Rabin was a tyrant who deserved murder. In a chilling display of the logic of religious violence, he cited rabbinical warrant for his reasoning (Golinkin 1996).

Israelis debated and continue to debate whether Amir was simply a deluded ultranationalist or if his actions in some way implicated Modern Orthodoxy. Did the assassination reveal that something was fundamentally wrong with Religious Zionism in the 1990s? Certainly, the sentiments that Amir articulated were not unique to the Modern Orthodox and were heard outside Religious Zionist circles. Many blamed Amir for the act but held Likud responsible for its incitement and extreme attacks upon the Labor-led peace process. But the stories reported by journalists also underlined the degree to which religion and land had become entangled in Orthodox discourse and suggested that Amir's actions were in some significant way the logical outgrowth of exposure to the growing extremism found in Religious Zionist circles (Horovitz 1995). Despite calls for a candid reassessment of their political values and the need to educate Modern Orthodoxy about democratic values, the Rabin assassination seems only to have hardened views on both sides (Halevi 1998). To much of the nonorthodox Israeli public, who once viewed Religious Zionism as an ally in the Zionist enterprise, the nonharedi Orthodox have now become a major threat to the preservation of Israeli democracy.

The Rabin assassination underlines the fundamental danger to Israeli democracy of religious extremism. Ironically, the carrier of that sentiment was not the Ultraorthodox theocrats about whom so much has been written, but the seemingly well-integrated and adjusted Modern Orthodox community. It is crucial to emphasize that this generalization is just that and should not be taken for an iron law. There are Ultraorthodox Jews who have joined the camp of territorial nationalism, and many Religious Zionists have rejected the sacralization of land that has emerged within their community. But in the main, it is correct to identify territorial maximalism with the contemporary Religious Zionist movement and to note its limited appeal among the Ultraorthodox. The most widely respected sage among Haredim from North Africa issued a ruling at the time of Camp David that the government was justified in exchanging territory for peace if doing so would save Jewish lives – the overriding value in halacha. In large measure because they do not venerate the state, the Haredim have been much less agitated about questions of land and borders. This has led the Ultraorthodox parties – unlike the National Religious party that still speaks for the territorial nationalism of Religious Zionism – to an essentially pragmatic position in foreign policy debates. If Israel is meant to occupy the whole of the ancient kingdom, God will see to it. If not, it is not a matter to occupy religious authority. With such an attitude, the Haredi parties have shown less concern for the global issues of war and peace that consume most other Israeli political movements. Although they have made comfortable alliances with the advocates of religious nationalism, these coalitions, have been driven less by ideology than by practical considerations, which are subject to negotiation (Shragai, 2001). There are no principled reasons for the Haredim to join the ultranationalist camp.

## CONCLUSION

This chapter has reviewed the two major Israeli cleavages associated with religion and the question of Israel's Jewish character. The conflict over religion and state, associated largely with the Ultraorthodox community, is not generally likely to threaten the survival of the state. The debate over the sacred status of land, associated primarily with a wing of Modern Orthodoxy, has already shown itself much more portentous for the future of Israeli democracy.[9]

These findings also speak to larger questions about the role of religion in political life. At the very least, the patterns apparent in the Israeli context suggest the need to distinguish carefully among varieties of what is usually called religious fundamentalism. In public discourse, "fundamentalism" is a unitary concept, a term that seems to describe high levels of religious enthusiasm or, in darker form, to denote a style of religious extremism that rejects compromise and accommodation with modernity. In this sense, argues Samuel Heilman (1994, 173), fundamentalists are defined at base by Atheir believers' conviction (correct or not) that their religion as they practice it is part of an unbroken tradition beginning with the earliest prophets and practitioners of the faith and continuing into the contemporary present, linking all those who came before as well as those who shall come after and who remain true to the faith, in one great chain of religious being.

The Israeli case underlines the need to recognize the diversity within fundamentalism. When the construct of fundamentalism is applied to Israel, it usually denotes the first of the two cleavages we reviewed, the clash between the allegedly theocratic Ultraorthodox, or Haredim, and the rest of the Israeli population. Consider that five of the six Jewish case studies in an authoritative volume devoted to global fundamentalism focused exclusively on the Ultraorthodox (Marty and Appleby 1994). When American Jewry discusses the issue of religious coercion in Israel,

---

[9] Some scholars have argued that the distinction between the two wings of Orthodoxy is breaking down. On the religious front, the tendency for the National Religious to become ever more rigid is described ominously as the "Haredization" of the Modern Orthodox. At the same time, there are signs that some of the Ultraorthodox are converging with the Religious Nationalists on a position of territorial maximalism.

the images that recur are the "black hats" that symbolize the Haredim. On some counts, the Haredim certainly appear to fit the fundamentalist category. Most importantly, they claim to practice a pure form of Judaism, uncorrupted and eternal. However, if we understand fundamentalism to include the requirement that groups must in some way challenge and attempt to conquer their societies, then it seems less likely that the Haredim fit the mold. In general, they have not confronted society unless it impinged on them. The customary response has been to retreat from Israeli society by forming insular enclaves.

Based on external appearances, the carriers of the second cleavage discussed above do not so readily seem to fit in the fundamentalist category. The Religious Zionists who have embraced territorial nationalism do not emulate the Ultraorthodox by attempting to seal themselves off from modernity. Rather, they seek to participate fully in contemporary society. Yet if they are not separatists who disdain modern culture, an implicit criteria of fundamentalism, they surely do meet the criteria in terms of their desire to remake Israel in a religious mold. They regard Israeli ownership of the entire land of Israel not in self-interested terms, as a resource to be exploited, but as a precondition for the return of Israel to the ways of God. In that sense, they are much more likely than the Haredim to act in the manner that we associate with fundamentalism.

This suggests that the fundamentalist label may be less useful than it first seems for characterizing important subgroups within Judaism. As Heilman suggests (1994, 176), the characteristic mode of behavior by the Ultraorthodox, cultural isolation, might better be described as a form of religious traditionalism. The Haredim attempt to preserve the past (as they understand it) by warding off the forces of change. This strategy maximizes the social distance between the Ultraorthodox and the less religious or irreligious sectors of the Israeli population. It is only when people "create the conditions to resist alternatives to [the past]," when they enter the activist stage of confrontation, that they warrant being described as fundamentalists. Despite their superficial similarities to those outside Orthodoxy, the Religious Zionists surely meet that standard more than the Haredim. With that definition, we reinforce the conclusion that Israel faces two different types of religious challenges and that the movement for religious nationalism is by far the more daunting of the two cleavages.

Owing to the dynamism of life in the Middle East, few observers would confidently predict the future of religious conflict in Israel. Recent events suggest that religiously based political conflict is most intense when the question of security assumes a lower profile on the public agenda but recedes somewhat from public consciousness when security concerns are most salient. After Israel signed onto the Oslo peace process, many Israelis began to foresee a day when questions of national survival would become moot. As religious nationalists slowly came to terms with the probable loss of Israeli sovereignty over biblical lands, what they perceived as Israel's birthright, the credibility of territorial maximalism was on the wane. With that issue appearing to be on the way to solution or at least less urgent, both advocates of a halachic state and the supporters of secularism became more active. In the 1999 elections, both the overtly religious parties and their most determined opponents – an openly secular party and the largely nonreligious parties supported by Russian immigrants – made sizable gains at the expense of the major parties. With the outbreak of the Al-Aqsa intifada and the apparent repudiation of Oslo by Ariel Sharon, Israel's new prime minister elected in 2001, most analysts foresee a period of heightened tension and Arab-Jewish violence. Under those conditions, it seems, concerns about religious coercion or a halachic state will resonate less deeply among the Jewish electorate. As Israelis grapple with their doubts about the Palestinian commitment to a negotiated settlement, less energy is likely to be devoted to debating the religious character of the Jewish state. Given the depth of the conflict, however, no one should mistake the suspension of overt conflict for a permanent solution to the festering religious cleavages.

### REFERENCES

Abramov, S. Zalman. 1976. *Perpetual Dilemma: Jewish Religion in the Jewish State*. Rutherford, NJ: Farleigh Dickinson University Press.
Azmi, Bishara. 1997. Remarks to the Conference, "The Impact of Religion on Politics at the End of the Twentieth Century." Jerusalem: November 12.
" 'Black' Power: Myth and Reality." *Jerusalem Report* (November 22): 12–15.
Cashman, Greer Fay. 1995. "Jews in Diaspora on the Decline; Worldwide Number is 13 Million." *Jerusalem Post* (10 April): 3.
Central Bureau of Statistics [State of Israel]. 1998. *Israel in Figures* [On-line]. Available HTTP: http://www.cbs.gov.il/israel_in_figures/population.htm#a.
Chafets, Ze'ev. 1996. "A Two-State Solution." *Jerusalem Report* (November 28): 22.
Deshen, Shlomo. 1995. "Religion in the Israeli Discourse on the Arab-Jewish Conflict." In *Israeli Judaism*. Shlomo Deshen, Charles S. Liebman, and Moshe Shokeid (eds.). New Brunswick, NJ: Transaction: 107–23.
Don-Yehiya, Eliezer. 1986. "The Resolution of Religious Conflicts in Israel." In Stuart A. Cohen and Eliezer Don-Yehiya (eds.). *Conflict and Consensus in Jewish Political Life*. Tel Aviv, Israel: Bar-Ilan University Press: 203–18.
1994. "The Book and the Sword: The Nationalist Yeshivot and Political Radicalism in Israel." In *Accounting for Fundamentalism: The Dynamic Character of Movements*. Martin E. Marty and R. Scott Appleby (eds.). Chicago: University of Chicago Press: 264–302.

Dowty, Alan. 1998. *The Jewish State – A Century Later.* Berkeley, CA: University of California Press.

Golinkin, David. 1996. "Responsa." *Moment* (February): 24–5.

Gutman, Emanuel. 1979. "Religion and Its Role in National Integration in Israel." *Middle East Review* 12: 31–6.

Halevi, Yossi Klein. 1992. "An Uneasy Alliance." *Jerusalem Report* (January 16): 7–12.

1996. "The Battle for the Temple Mount." *Jerusalem Report* (October 3): 18–20.

1998. "Democracy or Theocracy?" *Jerusalem Report* (March 19): 22–6.

Hayman, Pinchas. 1995. "A Very Visible Illness." *Jerusalem Post* (May 7): 6.

Heilman, Samuel. 1992. *Defenders of the Faith: Inside Ultra-Orthodox Jewry.* New York: Schocken Books.

1994. "Quiescent and Active Fundamentalisms: The Jewish Cases." In *Accounting for Fundamentalism: The Dynamic Character of Movements.* Martin E. Marty and R. Scott Appleby (eds.). Chicago: University of Chicago Press: 173–96.

Hirschberg, Peter. 1996. "Mixed Reception for Ultra-Orthodox Draft Plan." *Jerusalem Report* (February 19): 10.

Horowitz, Dan, and Moshe Lissak. 1978. *Origins of the Israeli Polity.* Chicago: University of Chicago Press.

Horovitz, David. 1995. "Israel Fights for its Soul." *Jerusalem Report* (December 14): 14–20.

Kedem, Peri. 1991. "Dimensions of Jewish Religiosity in Israel." In *Tradition, Innovation, Conflict: Jewishness and Judaism in Contemporary Israel.* Albany: State University of New York Press: 251–77.

Levy, Shlomit, Hanna Levinsohn and Elihu Katz. 1993. *Beliefs, Observances and Social Integration among Israeli Jews.* Jerusalem: Louis Guttmann Israel Institute of Applied Social Research.

Liebman, Charles S., and Eliezer Don-Yehiya. 1983. *Civil Religion in Israel.* Berkeley: University of California Press.

1984. *Religion and Politics in Israel.* Bloomington, IN: Indiana University Press.

Lustick, Ian. 1980. *Arabs in the Jewish State: Israel's Control of a National Minority.* Austin: University of Texas Press.

1988. *For the Lord and the Land: Jewish Fundamentalism in Israel.* New York: Council on Foreign Relations.

Luz, Ehud. 1978. *Parallels Meet: Religion and Nationalism in the Early Zionist Movement.* Philadelphia: Jewish Publication Society.

Mahler, Gregory S. 1990. *Israel: Government and Politics in a Maturing State.* San Diego: Harcourt, Brace, Jovanovich.

Ministry of Foreign Affairs [State of Israel]. 1998. *Facts About Israel* [On-line]. Available HTTP: http://www.israel.org/facts/soc/fsoc3.html.

Monsma, Steven V. and J. Christopher Soper. 1997. *The Challenge of Pluralism: Church and State in Five Democracies.* Lanham, MD: Rowman & Littlefield.

Morris, Benny. 1987. *The Birth of the Palestinian Refugee Problem, 1947–1949.* New York: Cambridge University Press.

Oz, Amos. 1983. *In the Land of Israel*. London: Flamingo.

Peled, Yoav. 1992. "Ethnic Democracy and the Legal Construction of Citizenship: Arab Citizens of the Jewish State." *American Political Science Review* 86: 432–43.

Peres, Yochanan. 1995. "Religious Adherence and Political Attitudes." In *Israeli Judaism*. Shlomo Deshen, Charles S. Liebman and Moshe Shokeid (eds.). New Brunswick, NJ: Transaction, 87–106.

Ravitzky, Aviezer. 1996. *Messianism, Zionism, and Jewish Religious Radicalism*. Chicago: University of Chicago Press.

Schmemann, Serge. 1998. "In Israel's Bitter Culture War, Civility is a Casualty." *New York Times* (21 July).

Sharkansky, Ira. 1996. *Rituals of Conflict: Religion, Politics and Public Policy in Israel*. Boulder, CO: Lynne Rienner.

Shimshoni, Daniel. 1982. *Israeli Democracy: The Middle of the Journey*. New York: Free Press.

Shipler, David K. 1986. *Arab and Jew: Wounded Spirits in a Promised Land*. New York: Penguin Books.

Shlaim, Avi. 1995. *War and Peace in the Middle East: A Concise History*. Rev. ed. New York: Penguin Books.

Shragai, Nadav. 2001. "Religious, Right-Wing and Realistic." *Haaretz* (15 February).

Sprinzak, Ehud. 1991. *The Ascendance of Israel's Radical Right*. New York: Oxford University Press.

Vital, David. 1982. *Zionism: The Crucial Years*. Oxford: Oxford University Press.

Sussan Siavoshi account of religious politics in Iran provides another interesting illustration of the prophetic/priestly distinction. Clearly, the Iranian revolution in 1979 is a classic example of a religious tradition and a religious leader providing critical, prophetic opposition to a secular regime, and, indeed, of the sacred supplanting a formidable secular opponent. However, despite the prominent role of Islam in creating the contemporary Iranian regime, and of providing legitimacy for the revolution, the priestly role of Islam in contemporary Iran is now the subject of some debate. Despite the lack of visible religious opposition to Iranian Islam, the clerical regime established by the Ayatollah Khomeini has encountered opposition from Islamic and secular sources with respect to earlier attempts to establish a theocratic "Islamic republic." The Iranian case is perhaps the clearest example of the difficulties with religion serving as a legitimating "sacred canopy."

# 6

## Between Heaven and Earth

### *The Dilemma of the Islamic Republic of Iran*

#### *Sussan Siavoshi*

The Iranian revolution of 1979 replaced the monarchial regime of the Pahlavi dynasty with an Islamic republic. The charismatic leader of the revolution, Ayatollah Ruhollah Musavi Khomeini, sought to create a theocratic state to preside over a religiously guided polity. At the helm of this state he envisioned a wise and pious Islamic jurist, the custodian of a true and sacred worldview, leading the faithful and supportive community toward salvation. This vision of a religious polity has been increasingly challenged since Khomeini's death in 1989, and especially since the election of Mohammed Khatami to the presidency. The challenges comes from both without and within the system, and although the most outspoken challengers couched their views in religious terms, their argument denies religion a presiding place in politics, and almost relegates it to the periphery.

There is a struggle underway in Iran that involves competing visions of public life. It involves institutional as well as behavioral, philosophical as well as prosaic, educational as well as judicial realms. The opposing forces have focused most intensely on the constitution of the Islamic republic. The tension that exists between the republican aspects of the constitution and the power given to the religious elite, particularly to the office of the *velayat-e faqih* (the leadership of the jurisprudent, or supreme leadership), has created the most obvious ground to debate the proper relations between politics and religion. This chapter will shed light on the problematic of the relationship between religion and politics in postrevolutionary Iran by concentrating on the constitution as one of its most important contested areas. Iran is in transition, and the interpretation of the constitution is now the most salient issue for all political forces. The outcome of debates over the interpretation of the constitution will affect all policy areas, including the rights of women, religious minorities, and the press. After a brief historical background, I will first elaborate on Khomeini's position on Islamic governance and its

125

impact on the character of the constitution. I will then focus on the challengers and how their diverse views on religion and its relations to politics shape the political debate in Iran.

## HISTORICAL BACKGROUND

Iran is a country of over 60 million people, nearly 90 percent of who are Shii'a Muslims.[1] Another 10 percent are Sunnis while Zoroastrians, Christians, Jews, and the adherents of the outlawed Bahai faith constitute only around 1 percent. This overwhelming Muslim majority did not always translate into dominant Islamic influence in politics in the twentieth century. During the rule of the Pahlavi dynasty, the state forcefully challenged the religious establishment, and removed its traditional control from many public areas including the judicial and educational systems.

After declaring himself king, Reza Shah (r: 1926–41), the founder of the Pahlavi dynasty, embarked on a program for the modernization of Iran. His vision of a modern Iran was modeled after his perception of the modernizing experience of the West, although such modernization could not interfere with his despotic power. He believed that modernization required secularization of the polity and reduction of the clergy's influence in politics.

During the late nineteenth and early twentieth century, many Muslim clerics played a leading role in fighting the dictatorship of the Qajar dynasty and the corresponding foreign influence. The clergy was particularly active in the tobacco movement (1891–2), a protest against a concession that granted a British tobacco company monopoly over the production, sale, and export of tobacco. The clergy also provided sanctuary, organization, and leadership to the constitutional revolution (1905–11), a movement that forced the Shah to allow a represented assembly and to grant a constitution.

Reza Shah sought to prevent such activism. He imprisoned and later killed the most influential politically active clergyman, Sayyed Hasan Modarres. To reduce the prominence of Islamic law (Shari'a) he adopted French codes of law in commercial, criminal, and civil domains. During

[1] Shi'ism is one of the two main sects of Islam, the minority sect. The difference between the Sunnis and Shi'ites was over the issue of succession to the Prophet Mohammed. According to the Sunnis, Ali, the son-in-law and the cousin of Mohammed was only the fourth rightful caliph (successor) in the line of caliphs who were both the spiritual and temporal authority of the Islamic community. The Shi'ites believe that Ali was not only the first rightful temporal ruler but was the Imam, the sole authoritative interpreter of Quran and phrophet's tradition (Hadith) and that he was without sin. As far as the future leaders of the community are concerned the Shi'ites believe that the office of Imam would pass to the other members of Ali, and the Prophet's family by designation.

his rule, the secular educational system expanded drastically at the expense of religious education. These changes limited the employment prospects for those with religious educations, which led many religious citizens (including the clergy) to send their children to secular educational schools. Reza Shah also mandated the partial emancipation of women through relaxation of some social restrictions such as veiling, a move that angered many traditional Muslims.

Reza Shah was forced by the Allied powers to abdicate in 1941, and was replaced by his son, Mohammed Reza Shah. Over the next several years, a movement arose to protest British control over Iran's oil, and this developed into an independence movement. It drew support from large segments of the society, and eventually coalesced into the National Front. Several prominent religious leaders were active in the movement, but secular and liberal activists dominated the group, especially the charismatic Mohammed Mosaddeq, a French-educated aristocrat. Mosaddeq sought to establish a democratic polity in Iran. Mossadeq symbolized the call for the nationalization of the oil industry in 1950, and was chosen by the parliament as prime minister in 1951.

Mohammed Reza Shah sought to remove Mossaddeq as prime minister and failed, and the Shah fled the country. A CIA-backed coup d'état toppled Mossaddeq in 1953 and restored the Shah. The strong opposition of Western nations toward Mosaddeq and his movement disillusioned many Iranians with the West, and led them to begin to develop indigenous ideas about government and politics, including Islamic approaches.

In the early 1960s, a little-known cleric named Ayatollah Khomeini led a movement of opposition to the Pahlavi regime. The revolt was violently crushed in 1963, and Mohammed Reza Shah consolidated his power and followed his father's plans for modernization. In pursuing his plans Mohammed Reza Shah did not allow any group, including the clergy, to influence the course of policies. He particularly and harshly oppressed the secular opposition to his rule. The despotic and arbitrary character of the regime led to widespread dissatisfaction. The Shah relaxed his grip in the 1970s under pressure from the Carter administration, at a time when he was terminally ill. Calls for reform from secular liberal intellectuals soon grew to demands for the end of the Pahlavi dynasty. The leadership of this movement did not remain with the secular intellectuals, however, but was captured by Ayatollah Khomeini from exile.

The participants in the 1978–9 Iranian revolution constituted a broad-based coalition of left, right, liberal, radical, moderate, and militant groups, each with secular and religious adherents. The religiously oriented liberation movement favored political liberalism and capitalism.

Another religious group, the Mujaheddin Khalq, was radical, militant, and had leftist economic preferences. The secular National Front had moderate, liberal sympathies and an evolutionary view of change, while the communist Tudeh party was more radical and militant.

Khomeini, the popular leader of the revolution, had sympathy for neither liberal nor secular ideas. Once the revolution triumphed, it devoured most of its children; the ousting of coalition partners happened in phases. Liberals and moderates, both religious and secular, were the first losers. The takeover of the American embassy and the ensuing hostage crisis greatly helped the militant and radical forces to discredit and expel the moderate forces from power. The secular radical/militant forces were the next to go. By the early 1980s, power was concentrated in the hands of the militant clergy. Khomeini successfully mobilized support for his Islamic regime through the use of religious symbols and construction of a national identity based on religion. A religious national community was now ready to accept his vision of the proper form of government and its relations with religion.

## KHOMEINI'S VISION

Ayatollah Khomeini had long aspired to a polity modeled after his vision of the first Islamic religious-political order led by the prophet Mohammed. Khomeini argued that Mohammed both brought divine laws and executed them.[2] Khomeini argued that Islamic government should not determine its laws by the wishes of the majority, but through religious insights from the Quran. There was no need therefore for a national legislature; instead he called for a "planning assembly" to design guidelines compatible with Islamic rules. These guidelines would be employed by the executive branch to provide for the welfare of the society.[3]

Khomeini argued that Islamic government is not despotic because its leader doesn't rule in an arbitrary manner.[4] The ruler of the Islamic government is limited by God's laws as revealed in the Quran, and indicated in the Hadith. To ensure that the ruler will actually observe the laws of God, he must satisfy certain conditions. The *vali* (leader) must be wise, just, and knowledgeable of divine laws. Khomeini's ideas on leadership of the Islamic jurist were first published in 1970 while he was in exile in Iraq.

Khomeini's thoughts on leadership of the Islamic community evolved after the establishment of the Islamic republic in 1979. He initially argued that the supreme leader must observe all the rules and laws of

---

[2] Imam Khomeini (S), *Velayat-e Faqih* (Rule of Jurisprudent), 5th ed. Tehran, 1997, p. 15.
[3] Ibid., pp. 33–4.    [4] Ibid., pp. 32–3.

Islam as documented in the Holy Book and the Prophet's Hadith. Later he held that the just leader should be able to break both the Islamic laws and the religious-legal contract that he made with people if the wellbeing of the Islamic system demands it.[5] Likewise, man-made laws, including the constitution should not deter the leader from ruling the way he sees fit, and if his rulings are in apparent conflict with the laws, the former will have priority over the latter.[6] Through these statements Khomeini gave life to the novel idea of *velayat-e motlaqe-ye faqih* (the absolute leadership of the Jurisprudent) that became the blueprint for a model Islamic republic.

### THE BIRTH OF THE ISLAMIC REPUBLIC AND ITS CONSTITUTION

A vibrant and pluralistic political and ideological atmosphere existed in the first few months after the triumph of the revolution, but the first referendum in April 1979 provided the people with an option between only two forms of state: a monarchy and a Islamic republic. The overwhelming majority of the Iranians opted for the latter.

The next step for the revolutionary leaders was to give the Islamic republic its institutional form. A heated debate over who should be in charge of writing the constitution resulted in the defeat of the secular participants who sought a large constitutional assembly. On August 3, 1980, Iranians elected a seventy-two member Assembly of Experts, consisting mainly of clergy, which was charged with the task of writing the constitution of the Islamic republic. The Assembly was to decide the extent of religious control over politics, and whether to include the institution of *velayat-e faqih* in the Constitution.

Despite the opposition of some of the revolutionary forces, the majority within the Assembly of Experts created the office of *velayat-e faqih*, and gave it sweeping power. The framers of the new constitution devoted articles 107 to 111 to the institution of *velayat-e faqih*, based on Khomeini's ideas on leadership. Article 110 gave the supreme leader the power to appoint and/or remove high officials of the executive and judiciary branches and the military high command. The supreme leader also had the power to declare war and peace. The constitution was approved through a popular referendum in December 1979.

The first supreme leader, Khomeini, was chosen directly by the people, but the Constitution provided that future leaders were to be elected by the Assembly of Experts. The Assembly of Experts, through its own bylaws, decided to limit its membership to those learned in religious

[5] Mohsen Kadivar, *Nazariyeha-ye Dowlat dar Fiqh-e Shi'e*. Tehran, 1997, p. 108.
[6] Kadivar, p. 109.

knowledge. In addition to choosing the supreme leader, the Assembly has the responsibility to oversee his performance. Article 111 provides for the possibility of the removal of an incompetent or unjust supreme leader by the Assembly of Experts.

The constitution has also provided for a twelve-member Guardian Council that has the responsibility to investigate the compatibility of parliamentary legislations with the constitution and with Islamic law. Since 1991, this body has assumed also the power to approve or reject the candidacy of any individual for the parliament, the presidency, and the Assembly of Experts. Half of the members of the Guardian Council are from the clergy and are appointed by the leader. The rest of the members are jurists who are selected by the head of judiciary and approved by the parliament.

These institutional arrangements gave religious authorities overwhelming control over politics. But secular and religious liberals did manage to include provisions in the constitution that could be used to challenge both the influence of the clergy over politics and the authoritarian aspects of the new political system. Most important is the definition of the role and rights of the people. Article 58 asserts that God, who has absolute authority over the universe, has made human beings master of their destiny and no one may take this authority from them. Article 3 provides for the participation of people in determining their political, economic, social, and cultural destiny, and Article 6 calls for the elections of public officials such as the president, representatives of the parliament, and the members of the local councils, and for referenda. There are also articles regarding the legitimate rights and freedoms of the people. The last part of Article 9 states that, in the name of protecting the sovereignty and independence of the country, no authority may take away the legitimate freedom of the people. Articles 23 to 27 also address rights such as freedom of thought, of expression, and of association.

In 1989, the Constitution was amended, primarily in an effort to concentrate power. The power of the supreme leader was vastly expanded to include the right to determine both the general course of policies and to supervise their implementation. Article 57 was amended to include the adjective *absolute* to describe the authority of the *vali-e faqih*.

This expansion in power disturbed both secular and religious citizens. For the seculars the disturbing aspect of this office was twofold: its authoritarian nature and the interference of religion into politics at the highest level. Religious liberals were more concerned with the extent and form of the influence of religion on politics. Traditionally in the Shiite Islam there had been no single authority for interpretation of religious dogmas or for setting rules of conduct. Citizens could choose which religious leaders to emulate, and this gave a pluralistic and somewhat democratic character to organization of the religion. The office of *velayat-e faqih* clashed with this tradition, especially in the realm of politics.

The amended constitution therefore contained many authoritarian aspects, but retained language inserted by liberals that could be interpreted in democratic ways. When Ayatollah Khomeini, the first supreme leader, was alive, the tension between the democratic and theocratic aspects was not a source of widespread public debate. After Khomeini's passing the inherent tension between the two sides of the constitution inevitably led to controversy.

## POLITICAL FORCES AND THE CHARACTER OF THE STATE

The controversy over the proper relations between politics and religion centers on the function of government. Is government an agency for preparing people for salvation, which implies control over all aspects of the lives of its subjects, or is government an entity that should seek to satisfy the temporal needs of those who are subject to its authority? Related to this is the question of leadership: who should be the leader/s and on what basis? In the case of the office of *velayat-e faqih*, the question was whether the office should remain dominant in the political system, be modified, or perhaps even eliminated.

Two general and competing views on the nature of government and its proper relations with religion have emerged among religious intellectuals. I will briefly focus on the views expressed by three religious intellectuals who seem to have effectively captured the essence of the debate. The first view is expressed in "the trusteeship of the private owners of the commons," the political treatise of Ayatollah Mehdi Ha'eri Yazdi. According to Hae'ri, governing is the technique of administering the internal and external affairs of a country. People living in close proximity form a government to secure their well-being, and choose a person or a group to be their trustee. The trustee performs the task of government, but can be removed by the people because the relationship between government and the people is based on a contract.[7]

Hae'ri asserts that the domain of morality is an unchanging and abstract domain, while the domain of politics is fluid and changing. Therefore, religious expertise should not mix with politics. He concludes his argument by seeking support from the Qoranic verse *Va Amrahom Showry Beynahom*, meaning that the temporal affairs of the people (including politics) should be left to the people to resolve through deliberation, not through divine revelation.[8]

In an indirect response to Hae'ri, Hasan Rahimpour argued for the mixing of religion and politics on three grounds. First, *sa'adat bashari*

---

[7] Ibid., p. 182.    [8] Ibid., pp. 183–4.

(human felicity or blissfulness) is connected to politics, to methods of creating social life, and to the behavior of the state. Second, areas that interfere in human felicity or human wretchedness are part of the domain of religion. Third, religion must deal with areas concerning social relations and issues of governing, by taking positions and setting limits.[9] Based on these three premises, Rahimpour defends the institution of *velayat-e faqih*, arguing that God has defined the conditions of leadership, including knowledge of religious laws. He concludes that *velayat-e faqih* is the most suitable institution for governing an Islamic society.[10]

Others take a position between these minimalist and maximalist views. One of its most prestigious and influential spokesmen is Ayatollah Ali Montazeri, the former heir apparent of Ayatollah Khomeini. Montazeri was one of the members of the original Assembly of Experts, and supported the inclusion of the office of *velayat-I faqih* in the constitution. He argues, however, that the supreme leader should watch over the country by stopping the officials, such as the president or his ministers, from committing illegal actions. But interference in the affairs of the government is not part of the responsibility/right of the supreme leader. Montazeri argues that government, which is based on the constitution and elected by the people, must administer the affairs of the country independent of the supreme authority. He implicitly advocates the removal of the added powers given to the supreme authority in the amended version of Article 110 of the constitution. Emphasizing the political sovereignty of the people, he concludes that in the contemporary world a system that is based on the absolute rule of a few individuals, with no meaningful participation of the people, is doomed to failure.[11]

Each of these three positions has support among some Iranian political forces, and the eventual winner is not yet clear. The greatest challenge to the existing set up has come from factions within the political elite: much of the recent openness of the system has been due to elite politics. The Iranian state is in transition – a temporary moment with serious elite conflict over authoritarian and democratic impulses. Among the Iranian elite there are those who ardently support comprehensive control of politics by religion, manifested in the idea of *velayat-e motlaqeh-e faqih*, and others who forcefully challenge both authoritarianism and clerical control of political office. Recent political change has occurred because of elite negotiation, confrontation, competition, and cooperation. Therefore it is important to understand the factions within

---

[9] Hasan Rahimpour, published in the quarterly, *Ketab-e Naqd* (the Book of Critique), No. 4. Fall 1997, p. 373.
[10] Ibid., pp. 388–9.   [11] See *Arzeshha*, Op. Cit., p. 47.

the elite, and their positions in this debate about the relationship between religion and politics.

## FACTIONAL POLITICS

Despite all the rhetoric about unity among Muslim revolutionaries, political factions have existed since the Islamic revolutionary forces consolidated their power.[12] Differences in religious worldviews and differences on social, economic, political, and cultural issues led to the dissolution of the only sanctioned political party, the Islamic Republic party, which was supposed to represent Islamic unity, in June of 1987. Many members of the defunct party belonged to the religious organization of *Jame'y-e Rohaniyat-e Mobarez*, The Society of Militant Clergy (SMC) which itself became subject to internal tension. The source of the tension was two different interpretations of Islam. Some members of the SMC believed in a conservative or static interpretation of Islam while the others promoted a more dynamic interpretation of religion that could address the specific characteristics of the contemporary world.

In 1988, on the eve of the elections of the third session of the parliament, twenty three members of SMC, including the current president of Iran Mohammed Khatami, left the SMC and formed the rival organization of *Majma'e Ruhaniyoun-e Mobarez*, the Association of Militant Ulama (AMU). In many ways Khomeini was closer to the AMU, which had the reputation of being a radical and leftist organization, than to the SMU, a more conservative group. Neither group was monolithic or well organized. There were also other organizations or associations, most of them related to one or another profession, that clustered around these two primary organizations.

As time passed further splits occurred within the ranks of both the "left" and the "right" factions and led to the emergence of at least four general political tendencies: the traditional right, the modern right, the traditional left, and the modern left. Each one of these tendencies has some institutional manifestations, supporting groups and publications. The traditional right favors free-market economics, restrictions on culture and lifestyles, and authoritarian political structures. The top

---

[12] See Sussan Siavoshi, "Cultural Politics and the Islamic Republic: Cinema and Book Publication," *International Journal of Middle East Studies*, Vol 29, 1997, pp. 511–12. For a more detailed account of factional politics and their development in the Islamic republic, see Ahmad Ashraf, "Charisma, Theocracy, and Men in Power in post-Revolutionary Iran," in *Politics of Social Transformation in Afghanistan, Iran, and Pakistan*. Myron Weiner and Ali Banuazizi, Sussan Siavoshi (eds.). "Factionalism and the Iranian Politics: The Post-Khomeini Experience," *The Journal of the Society for Iranian Studies*, Vol 25, 1992, pp. 27–49; and Shahrough Akhavi, "Elite Factionalism in the Islamic Republic of Iran," *The Middle East Journal*, Vol 41, 1987, pp. 181–201.

echelons of the judicial branch, most of the members of the Guardian Council and the Assembly of Experts, and the head of state-controlled television and radio are part of this faction. The SMC is its most prominent organization, surrounded by a cluster of economic and professional groupings. The traditional bazaar bourgeoisie – the merchants – constitute the most influential social base of the traditional right.

The modern right faction also supports free markets, but is more tolerant of cultural openness. Its political stand is mixed: Some of its adherents are politically authoritarian while others are democratic. To aid political coalition building, its adherents publicly take democratic stands. Some of the members of Khatami's cabinet, a large number of the governmental managers, and a large minority of the members of the parliament are members of this faction. The newly formed party of *Kargozaran-e Sazandegi Iran*, Managers of Construction of Iran Party, is the most visible organizational manifestation of the modern right. In the absence of survey data it is not easy to determine with accuracy the social base for this tendency. However, it is likely that support comes from well-educated, professional, and bourgeois Iranians.

The traditional left supports state regulation of the economy and puts its emphasis on social justice rather than economic growth. It is restrictive in its cultural outlook, and has authoritarian views on politics. Its supporters are not well represented in the high echelons of the state apparatus, but are represented in the lower ranks of the government and the army. Most vigilante activities, including burning of bookstores and attacking demonstrators and liberal political figures are attributed to the supporters of this point of view. *Ansar-e Hezbollah* and the *Basij-e Daneshgahi* (a minority university student organization), are two groups that support the ideas of the traditional left. The social base of the traditional left consists of the economically disadvantaged, young people, and a large segment of the *Sepah-e Basij* (Basij army).

The modern left is skeptical of or ambivalent about privatization of the economy, more tolerant on cultural issues, and supportive of political pluralism. This tendency is represented by President Khatami, and by some of his cabinet members. In coalition with the modern right, the modern left has a large working majority in parliament. Organizationally, this tendency is represented by many members of the AMU; and *Sazman-e Mojahedin-e Enqelab-e Eslami*; the Organization of Warriors of the Islamic Revolution (OWIR); and the newly formed party of *Jebhey-e Mosharekat Iran- Eslami* (the Islamic Iran's Front for Participation). The social base of this faction is mostly young and educated people, including many university students.

By elections for the fifth parliament in 1996, loose coalitions of factions had formed over issues of culture and political openness. The modern right and the modern left joined forces into what we might call the reformist camp, and the traditional left and traditional right have joined into a conservative/authoritarian camp. Political and cultural issues were more salient to elites than economics in the 1996 election, and have remained so afterward. Mohammed Khatami won the election, and his campaign advocated freedom, rule of law, and the sovereignty of people. His candidacy and victory helped to solidify this coalitional structure: No matter what any group or individual thought about economics, the defining line was their adherence to authoritarianism or democracy.

Most of the adherents to the conservative/authoritarian camp support the expanded power of the *velayat-e faqih*. They believe in the traditional, patrimonial, and religious base for legitimation: The legitimate state should be led by the old, wise, and devout father of the nation, the *vali faqih*, who has the best interest of his children at heart. The leader is appointed by God, who is the source of his legitimacy.[13] The leader must obey the laws of god but not those made by humans.[14] The leader is not the trustee of the people, and can rule as he sees fit; the relationship between the people and the leader is one of command and obedience.[15] Many supporters of this theocratic/authoritarian view consider anybody who deviates even slightly from this interpretation of the system and its requirement as *anti-velayat-e faqih*.

Within the reformist camp, there is a diversity of views both on the relationship between religion and government, and on the method of achieving popular sovereignty. Some push for rapid, radical reform to actualize the republican aspects of the constitution, including the elimination of *velayat-e faqih*. Other reformers seek more gradual change through negotiation and compromise with the authoritarian camp.

The president of Iran, many of his ministers and advisers, grand ayatollahs such as Montazeri or Yusef Sane'i, support this second position. Khatami, for example, has become the greatest champion of the rule of law, and of upholding of people's legitimate rights and freedom. He has frequently stated that government is the servant of the people and not their master. He has also warned against the battle between religion and freedom, arguing that history has shown that religion will loose if it fights freedom.[16] The grand ayatollah Yusef Sane'i, in his *dars-e kharej-e fiqh* (the advanced courses of *fiqh*), has put a great amount of emphasis on

---

[13] See Mesbah Yazdi's statement published in daily *Jama'e*, July 20, 1998, p. 4.
[14] See Hojjat-ol Eslam Ferdosipour's speech published in daily *Salaam*, July 4, 1998, p. 2.
[15] Ibid.
[16] See the text of Khatami's speech during the first anniversary of his election to presidency, *Hamshahri*, May 24, 1998, Internet Edition.

the importance of the people in the constitution and has defended their freedom to choose.[17]

At the same time all the adherents of gradual reform option publicly support the institution of *velayat-e faqih*. What many mean by this support however, is for the supreme leader to become a supreme moral *guide* with responsibility to supervise and advise rather than to make policies.[18] Such an institution can either be directly elected or can be chosen by the true representatives of the people. There can be periodic elections or there can be a watchdog body to make the supreme guide accountable.

The struggle between these factions will determine the relationship between religion and politics in Iran in the future. Will religion retain its central place in determining policies and defining the character of the Iranian state or will be relegated to the periphery? Will Iran be a theocratic state or will it move toward secular republicanism? Do moderate forces have a real chance of gradually reforming the system? The answer of course largely depends on the relative power of each position.

## THE FUTURE OF THE ISLAMIC REPUBLIC

For years, those who took the authoritarian/theocratic position controlled most positions of power in Iran, especially after the death of Ayatollah Khomeini. Secular liberals were basically suppressed and or demoralized, and moderate reformers had little power. This changed with the election of Mohammed Khatami as president of Iran in 1997. The result of the 1997 presidential elections was a surprise to nearly all students of Iranian politics. In an election with an unprecedented 90 percent turnout, Khatami won an astonishing 70 percent of the vote, despite his lack of support of the supreme leader, the power establishment, and the state-owned radio and television. Ever since his election, his campaign slogans about rule of law, freedom, civil society, and political development have become the dominant concepts in Iranian political discourse. The 1999 nationwide town and village council elections, in which the supporters of Khatami won with an impressive margin demonstrated once again the popular support for his message of reform.[19] The February 2000 parliamentary elections were overwhelmingly won by proponents of reform. Even some spokespersons for the authoritarian camp have begun to adopt the discourse on freedom and the rule of law. Of cause, Khatami himself was easily reelected in 2001.

---

[17] Published in the weekly *Payam-e Azadi*, June 27, 1998, p. 3.
[18] See for example Montazeri's speech in *Arzeshha*, op. cit.
[19] For example in Tehran alone, all the fifteen elected members to the city council were part of the modern left and right coalition.

University students have also been mobilized in support of the rule of law, freedom of the press and meaningful popular participation. In June 1999, Iran witnessed one of the biggest student demonstrations in opposition to authoritarianism since the time of Mohammed Reza Shah. Many demonstrators have been attacked verbally and physically, and many leaders have been jailed, but influential political figures including the supreme leader Ayatollah Khamenei and the head of the council of guardian Ayatollah Kashani, have felt compelled to go to the university and answer the probings of the students. The openness that followed Khatami's assumption of presidency has reinvigorated secular liberals as well. A series of daring articles, essays, and commentaries has appeared in the secular press. It seems that Iran has embarked on a course of further and faster transformation. There are genuine signs of political openness and pluralistic politics.

However, it is not yet certain that Khatami's supporters can implement a smooth transformation toward less authoritarian government. Popular support is the greatest resource of moderate reformers, and that support may not be reliable in the longer term. Many of Khatami's strongest supporters are impatient for change, and want him to adopt a more assertive posture relative to the authoritarians, but Khatami continues to patiently work behind the scene. It is possible that some of these supporters may withdraw their support and choose a more confrontational posture. The student protests in early summer suggest a growing demand for more rapid change.

It is my contention that the seculars, if they insist upon a rigid interpretation of humanist republicanism, may be doomed to failure. If there is any hope for them it is through slower reform of the system, mostly through the adherence to the ideas of the reformist faction. The greatest hope for the reformist elite is if its leaders such as Khatami can avoid polarization and therefore are able to reduce the insecurity and mistrust that exist among the conservative and authoritarian elements. This will require delicate and careful political action.

The conservative/authoritarian forces still have control over the instruments of force, and they have significant financial resources. There are still bans on many publications by moderates and secular activists. The Council of Guardians rejected the candidacy of many secular and moderate activists, so the third session of the Assembly of Experts, elected in October 1998, is now dominated by the conservative/authoritarians. Outspoken members of the reformist elite have been jailed. The eruption of a foreign policy crisis might give the adherents of authoritarian position a rationale to emphasize unity and national security, therefore legitimizing the existence of an absolutist leadership.

Yet one should not underestimate the long-run potential influence of those who are pushing for gradual change toward a more open polity.

They consist mostly of young and educated segments of the society, armed with both motivation and expertise. Most look at government as predominantly an instrument to satisfy the worldly needs of the people. Among the religious reformers, many believe that it must be the decision of the people, with their diverse views of Islam, that will determine the extent of religion's influence on politics, not one authoritarian figure chosen by "the religious elders" of the society. No rational political actor, religious, secular, authoritarian or liberal, can ignore this potentially powerful social force in the long run. There is a struggle going on within Iran about the character of its polity and about who should control that polity. Part of Iran is still looking towards heaven and part is searching on earth for the best possible fate. Who would prevail? In this era of transition, the winners might be those who are trying to bring heaven and earth closer together.

This chapter provides a transition between systems with dominant religious traditions and the analyses of more competitive systems that follow. The political role of a recently reawakened public Islam is a fact of life in the countries under consideration, but in none of the cases does Islam provide anything approaching a "sacred canopy." Rather, the various manifestations of Middle Eastern Islam tend to provide a transcendent perspective from which politics can be criticized, and in which Islam fills a highly visible prophetic role. Mehran Tamadonfar's comparative analysis of Islamic politics in Egypt, Algeria, and Lebanon illustrates the idea that a common religious viewpoint can have radically different political manifestations, regardless of the presence or absence of serious *religious* competition. Tamadonfar's account of "Islamism" suggests that a thoroughgoing, noncompartmentalized theology will occasion the rise of serious opposition from a variety of religious and secular sources, which would seem to limit the potential for Islam to provide a priestly source of political and social cohesion. Further, the analysis presented in this chapter suggests that the specific form of religious politics manifested in a particular country is likely to be shaped by external forces. The legacy of French colonialism in Algeria and the reality of foreign powers competing within Lebanon each provide contexts in which Islam assumes a political stance.

# 7

# Islamism in Contemporary Arab Politics

*Lessons in Authoritarianism and Democratization*

*Mehran Tamadonfar*

Islam plays a pivotal role in all aspects of Muslim societies. Arab leaders have had to contend with Islam as a political and ideological force ever since Mohammad's temporal rule. The demands and requirements of Islam and Islamism have always shaped Arab political systems, processes, and policies, regardless of the type of regime in power. Islam has historically been subject to a cyclical pattern of political quietism and activism. The periods of activism have been marked by intense and often violent struggles for political dominance of Islam, whereas the quietist periods were marked by retreat and subjugation to the established orders. Given the significance of Islam in Arab societies, however, even during the periods of quietism Islam has played a determining role in Arab politics.

The current Islamist activism has brought a worldwide attention to Islam as a sociopolitical force. Samuel Huntington's concern about the "clash of civilizations" in this century focuses in part on danger to the West from the Muslim world (Baker, p. 118). Islam will remain a dominant force in Arab political life, but it is not so monolithic as many observers believe.

## ISLAMISM IN ARAB POLITICS

Students of the Middle East and Islamic politics have long struggled over the proper terms to describe the movement of Islamic activists, using terms such as Islamic fundamentalism, Islamic revivalism, and Islamism. The term Islamic fundamentalism gained a great deal of popularity in the United States after the Iranian revolution. If fundamentalism is a reference to devotion to the basic and original precepts of Islam, then all Muslims are fundamentalists because they all believe in the Oneness of Allah (*Tawhid*), accept the Quran as God's divine ordinance, and fulfill their duties in accordance with the Quran and other Islamic sources.

141

Those who use the term Islamic fundamentalism are usually drawing attention to perceived similarities between Islamic activists and those who are active in orthodox American Protestantism. Yet not all Islamic activists are antimodern, nor are they necessarily antiliberal. Most accept change within the confines of Islam. In Arabic there is no equivalent to fundamentalism, and those engaged in the Islamic movements prefer to be referred to as Muslims or Islamists (*Islamiyyun*).[1] The term has come to mean primarily those Islamic activists who do not seek pluralistic democratic governments but instead seek governments that would give authoritative rulings in accord with the teachings of the Quran.

Islamist groups use Islam as a political force to mobilize the public, gain control of the political authority, and enforce their Islamic agenda on the society. They do not normally seek to modernize Islam or to pursue theological reformation. Instead, they appropriate Islam as an ideology for social and political change in accordance with their particular understandings of the religious texts and practices. Their ultimate objective is to pattern rule after that of the Muhammad's era (*Salaf*). Thus, they glorify and idealize the past, vilify the present, and seek political activism that is often manifested in political militancy in their search for an Islamic order (Faksh, p. xv).

Islamism is rooted in the Islamic history and culture. Unlike the Shi'i Muslims who developed a doctrinal justification for their activism and quietism (*Taqiyya*), the predominantly Sunni Arabs practiced both quietism and activism without a doctrinal justification. Instead, they legitimized their quietism by arguing for the preservation of the Islamic community (*Ummah*), and explained their activism in the need for justice and primacy of Islamic values. Historically, periods of decline and crisis have been followed by a rise of Islamism with the hope of reinvigorating the faith and establishing the true Islamic order.

Since the early nineteenth century, the Arab world has witnessed three periods of Islamic activism largely in response to intense crises arising from internal weakness and foreign hegemony. The leaders of these

---

[1] As the western observers grew intent on using the label of Islamic fundamentalist as a reference to the reactionary fanatic terrorists who seek to bring about change violently, the term became increasingly less relevant to these movements that embrace a wide range of strategies including democratization and the use of peaceful and constitutional means to bring about change (Moten, pp. 126–7). Muslims also reject the term revivalism because they contend that political quietism is not the abandonment of Islam, and thus political activism is not Islamic revival. Others reject "Islamism" as a "clumsy neologism" (Henry Munson, Jr., p. 4). However, many Muslim activists refer to themselves as Islamists (*Islamiyyun*). Islamism not only underscores the ideological nature of the movement it is also devoid of erroneous assumptions in "Islamic fundamentalism" and "Islamic revivalism."

mostly violent revolts blamed the societal deterioration on the alienation from Islam, and called for return to Islam as the only salvation. The Wahhabis in Arabia, the Mahdis in the Sudan, the Sanusis in North Africa, and the Islamic reform in Egypt exemplified the nineteenth-century Islamism in the Arab world. The second period of activism climaxed in the 1940s with the rise of the Muslim Brotherhood (*al-Ikhwan al-Muslimoun*) in Egypt.

The current, longest period began in the aftermath of the Arab defeat in the 1967 war by Israel and intensified with the growing social and economic dislocations, widening gaps between classes, and rising authoritarianism. The Iranian revolution of 1978–9 transformed the current Islamist movement into a global force that spread its influence throughout the Arab and non-Arab Muslim world. The Gulf war and the consequent anti-Western sentiments offered a new life to the Islamist movements and reinforced their demands for the destruction of the current Arab regimes and the establishment of an Islamic state. Referring to the Gulf war as "a blessing in disguise," Hasan al-Turabi, a leading Islamist theoretician and the head of the ruling National Islamic Front in the Sudan, suggested that the war popularized Islamism and undermined non-Islamic governments. He concluded "There is a course of history that makes the establishment of Islamic states almost inevitable" (*Middle East Policy, 1.3. p. 55*).

Islamism of the 1980s and 1990s is an indigenous popular response to a wide range of social, economic and political problems in the Arab world. Social and economic modernization of the Arab societies during the past fifty years widened the economic and social gaps between the elites and nonelites and the secular and traditional elements. Economic modernization and the consequent urbanization have resulted in social and economic dislocations, mass impoverishment, and cultural and spiritual disturbances. These developments have coincided with the growth of the centralized and authoritarian states that have become the protectors of the secular westernized elites. Thus, the traditional and lower classes have become alienated and radicalized. The growth of the urban and modern classes has economically marginalized and alienated the traditional classes (Bagader, p. 118). The inability of secular nationalists to respond to these crises not only jeopardized the legitimacy of the current regimes, it enabled the Islamists to offer an Islamic alternative.[2]

According to R. Hrair Dekmejian, today's Arab Islamism is pervasive, polycentric, and persistent. This movement is not limited to a certain

---

[2] For a detailed discussion of the impact of modernization on the rise of Islamic militancy refer to: Oliver Roy, *The Failures of Political Islam*. Cambridge, MA: Harvard University Press: 1994.

segment of the population or certain communities. The movement is increasingly embraced by the upper and middle as well as the lower strata in practically every Muslim community regardless of the size or political, cultural, and economic settings. It lacks a hierarchical organization or centralized leadership. Thus, while it has gained a transnational appeal, it generally remains localized in character. Furthermore, despite major setbacks, the movement remains unusually persistent in its commitment to its goals and strategies (Dekmejian, pp. 3–4).

The Islamists are critical of what they see as an erosion of the role of religion in public life, and call for the restructuring of the Arab society and state in the image of Islam. They reject secularism in all of its manifestations. To the Islamists, secularism has improperly relegated Islam to the private realm and, thus, has transformed the politically dynamic Islam of Muhammd into an establishment Islam preoccupied with rituals and devoid of any dynamism. According to the Islamists, the steady decline of the Muslim world and the gradual hegemony of the West should be attributed to this secular trend. To end this decline, Islamists contend, the only solution is the return to Islam. Arab and non-Arab Islamist thinkers like Sayyid Qutb, Abu Al Mawdudi, and Khomeini generally agree that the establishment of an Islamic state is the prerequisite to the actualization of Muslim life. In an Islamic state, political control would be coextensive with the totality of Muslim life, suggested Al Mawdudi (Faksh, p. 5). Similarly, Qutb and Khomeini reject any separation of politics and religion in Islam.

Of course, the nature and scope of the Islamic order has long been a subject of debate among Islamic scholars. There is no disagreement, however, that this order reflects the sovereignty of God, but there is widespread disagreement on the role of the clergy in the Islamic polity. To Khomeini and his Arab Islamist supporters, the clergy, as the viceregents of God, are the only legitimate leaders of the community. Arab Islamists, however, generally reject this notion and even criticize the traditional ulama for their inability and unwillingness to resist the current un-Islamic regimes and to further the authentic Islamic values.

A major demand of the Islamists is the rejection of the Western cultural heritage and the restoration and the reassertion of the Islamic value. To them, Western culture is "a paradigm of moral decay and the consequent defilement of society"(Faksh, p. 8). To Qutb and other Islamist thinkers, the West represents the new *Jahiliyyah,* which in the Arab and Islamic perspectives means pagan ignorance, largely referring to the conditions of pre-Islamic Arabia that exhibited godlessness, moral laxity, corruption, and oppression. Islamists call for the eradication of this *Jahiliyyah,* because they believe its consequences and implications are more sinister and pervasive than the pre-Islamic *Jahiliyyah.* Qutb said that the Western hegemony allows the "White man's civilization" – materialism, hedonism, and consumerism – to erode the moral and spiritual basis of Muslim societies (Faksh, p. 9).

In light of this argument, Islamists reject all imported ideologies including socialism, liberalism, and Islamic reformism, Nasserism, and other secular nationalist orientations (Aziz al-Azmeh, p. 64). These ideologies, Islamists suggest, advance Western domination and prevent the realization of true Islam. Although this perspective might reflect a desire to return to a "primitivist utopia" (Azmeh, p. 64), the Islamist ideology is clearly more dynamic and modern. Socialism is rejected for its preoccupation with materialism. Islamists have rejected the Western liberal ideas for their reliance on the concept of popular sovereignty, because the ultimate sovereignty in Islam belongs to God.

Some Islamists, however, have embraced a limited notion of democratic-liberal participation, and have continued to participate in democratic elections. Ideologically, however, the Islamists' advocacy for liberal practices is a matter of strategy rather than a genuine commitment to democracy. As Azmeh astutely observes, for the Islamists, "democracy becomes a totalitarian passion whereby the Islamist party substitutes itself for the body politic, conceived as a social protoplasm which remains formless until it is endowed with an Islamic order" (Azmeh, p. 70).

Islamists also reject nationalism because Islam is a universalistic ideology that underscores the unity of the community of believers (*Umma*). Islamists have consistently rejected any form of ethno-racial (*Qawmiyyah*) or national (*Wataniyyah*) particularism, because these forms of particularism breed secularism and result in the erosion of Islam.

Contrary to the traditional Sunni doctrine of obedience to authority, a principle that has often been emphatically supported by the Sunni clerics and practiced in Arab societies, many Islamists find the holy war (Jihad) as the only answer to the current crisis. These Islamists are ready and willing to challenge the existing regimes by force, if necessary. Like many other theoretical innovations by the Islamists, this strategy also redefines the concept of Jihad in the Sunni worldview. Unlike Shi'ism, the Sunni political theory lacks an explicit doctrine of revolution (Dekmejian, p. 86). Except in rare instances, the Sunni ulama have sought obedience to the political authority and have limited Jihad to fighting non-Muslim foes.

In the Islamist perspective, Jihad is no longer a war against non-Muslim pagans, it is a form of political struggle and even rebellion against those (including Muslims) who prevent the reassertion and restoration of Islam in the form of an Islamic government. Many Islamist scholars agree on this strategy. Qutb and Al-Mawdudi consider Jihad against the tyrannical non-Islamic regime a religious obligation for all Muslims. Qutb, like many other Islamists, sees Jihad as a tool for com-batting the duality of Good (Islam) and Evil (*Jahiliyyah*), and the final victory of Islam and the destruction of the *Jahiliyyah*. This struggle ultimately liberates humankind from oppression and slavery (Faksh, pp. 13–14).

As the Islamists challenge the existing Arab regimes and their secular and nationalist supporters, the regimes' responses have ranged from accommodation and co-optation to confrontation and repression. Both conservative and secular-nationalist regimes use these measures to control the Islamists and to contain their appeal. The choice of a certain strategy by a regime reflects not only each country's historical and con-textual circumstances, but also the organizational and ideological characteristics of the specific Islamist movement they are facing.

## ISLAMISM AND AUTHORITARIANISM IN EGYPT

Islam and Islamism are deeply rooted in the history and politics of Egypt, but in the twentieth century, Egyptian Islamism has had to face the growing role of secular-nationalism, limited liberalism, and socialism that have been supported by the authoritarian Egyptian state. The state, particularly the postmonarchic regimes, has resorted to a variety of ideologies including Pan-Arabism, Nasserist Socialism, populism, and secular-liberalism to gain legitimacy and popular support for modernizing policies, and to contain challenges by the Islamists. Today, these ideologies play a counterbalancing role to Islamism in the Egyptian political life.

The origins of the current Islamism in Egypt date back to the last part of the nineteenth and early decades of the twentieth centuries. Dissatisfied with the monarchy and critical of the Egyptian society and culture, Hasan al-Banna, a school teacher, founded the Society of Muslim Brotherhood (*Jama 'at al-Ikhwan al-Muslimoun*) in 1928 as a young Muslim men's association to promote personal piety and religious activity (Andersen, p. 149).[3] Frustrated with the state's unwillingness to underscore the Islamic values in the society and by the growing influence of the secular elements, the Brotherhood gradually turned to radicalism and employed violence against the regime. It found salvation in return to Islam and adopted the credo that: "God is our goal, the prophet is our leader. The Quran is our constitution, struggle is our way. Death in the

---

[3] For elaborate discussions of the history of the Brotherhood refer to: Richard P. Mitchell, *The Society of Muslim Brotherhood*. Ann Arbor: University of Michigan Press, 1970, and Ishaq Musa Husaini, *The Muslim Bretheren*, Beirut: Khayat's, 1956.

service of God is the loftiest of our wishes. God is great, God is Great" (Quoted in: Mitchell, pp. 193–4).

As the "Supreme Guide" of the movement, Banna dominated the Brotherhood until his assassination in 1949 by the government in retaliation for the assassination of the prime minister, Fahmi al-Nuqrashi, by the Brotherhood a year earlier. A largely religious reformer, Banna sought the reassertion of Islam to the Egyptian life and the end of foreign cultural and political influence (Lippman, pp. 36–7). By emphasizing moderate reform and building an extensive institutional infrastructure under Banna's leadership, the Brotherhood grew into a populist transnational Pan-Islamic movement with followers all over the Muslim world (Faksh, p. 43). In Egypt, it began an effective campaign against the forces of change and modernity, government corruption social and economic injustice, and foreign influence.

The Brotherhood's success in the 1940s to attract a massive following was largely due to the Brotherhood's ability to build an extensive network of social, educational, religious and charitable organizations across Egypt. The Brotherhood gradually institutionalized its roles in the social and economic lives of the young and disinherited Egyptian lower and middle class, and drew massive support among the traditional elements of the society. The young and educated Brotherhood leaders and their followers were not only critical of the government but also of the traditional clerics who continued to preach subjugation to authority and to neglect societal degradation. The anticlericalism of the Brotherhood is largely explained by their view that traditional clerics have contributed to the ossification of Islam by relying on irrelevant and antiquated religious formalism, and by refusing to underscore the politically dynamic role of Islam (Faksh, p. 44).

The Brotherhood welcomed the officers' coup of 1952, but Nasser's secular-nationalism and socialism were irreconcilable with their goal of reestablishing an Islamic order. Although Nasser reintroduced Islam into Egypt's political rhetoric by helping Al-Azhar to grow and by allowing Islamic publications, his radical economic policies and Pan-Arab strategies pushed Islam to the sidelines in the Egypt of the 1960s and 1970s. As a secular-nationalist, Nasser viewed organized religion as the major obstacle to the socioeconomic and political order, and he made a concerted effort to distance Islam from political life and to relegate it to the private realm.

Nasser decimated the Brotherhood through such repressive measures as imprisonment, torture, and execution of its leaders. But as Nasser and his supporters failed to fulfill the demands of the lower and traditional classes, the Islamists with their extensive social and economic role offered an alternative to the state. Moreover, Nassar's repressive policies radicalized the Brotherhood that had kept a semblance of cooperation with the regime.

It was the young Sayyid Qutb who, in response to Nasser's policies and ideologies, developed the radical and confrontational Brotherhood ideology that still inspires the Islamists, even outside Egypt. Qutb's *Signposts* (*Ma'alim fi'l Tariq*), that has become the manifesto of many Islamist groups, rejected all contemporary states including Nasser's Egyptian state by calling them a *Jahiliyyah*, and recommended that the only solution is action (*Harakah*) rather than discourse (*Bayan*). While he did not explicitly call for the use of weapons against the state, his emphasis on the need for action indicates his commitment to violent confrontation with the state (Kepel, pp. 27–55). Qutb undoubtedly radicalized the Brotherhood, and Nasser's policies helped the emergence of radical Islamist groups in Egypt. Nasser's defeat in the 1967 war shook the foundations of secular-nationalism and socialism in Egypt. The radical Islamists were ready to wage a war against the state.

To eliminate the Nasserists and socialists and to improve the chances of his pro-western foreign policy and market-oriented economy, Sadat tried to make Islam the key cultural-organizational-ideological pillars of the post-Nasserist order. Wrapping himself in the Islamic symbolism and projecting himself as the believer-president (*al-ra'is al Mou'min*) (Hanafi, p. 63), Sadat tried to create his own version of Islam in a way which reflected the perception of the ruling strata and the traditional clerics. He reinforced the *Shari'ah* basis of the Egyptian law by declaring the *Shari'ah* a principal source of legislation in Egypt in the 1971 Constitution, and allowed a more expansive role for the Brotherhood in social welfare policies. He allowed the creation of "Islamized spaces" around the mosques, schools, and neighborhoods, which helped to spread their political influence.

Yet Sadat also banned religious political parties by adopting the Political Parties Law 40 of 1977. This law successfully thwarted the political ambitions of the Brotherhood, which never gained a legal status in Egypt, and even after seventeen years of legal wrangling in 1993 the courts found the law constitutionally sound (Fluehr-Lobban, p. 92). Most Islamists, especially the most radical elements, rejected Sadat's government and sought a genuine Islamic order.

Sadat's policy of rapprochement with the Israelis, as manifested in the Camp David Accords of 1979, and market economic policies that widened the gap between the rich and poor and heightened corruption, led to a deteriorating relationship with even the traditional clerics. Increased poverty and unemployment, deteriorating social services, increased repression and purges, and declining confidence in the state brought the Islamists to the forefront of political action. The Brotherhood's compromising and moderate policies were no longer acceptable to the radical groups who were convinced that confrontation is the only viable strategy.

In this atmosphere, a large number of highly divergent groups emerged in Egypt. All were militant, but they differed in their organization, leadership style, ideology, and strategy (Ibrahim, p. 127). Some, like the Technical Military Academy Group (also known as the Islamic Liberation party) established democratic procedures for leadership and decision making. Others, like the Apostasy and Flight Group (*Jama'at al-Takfir wa al-Hijra*) were extremely autocratic. Because of these differences, the groups did not cooperate in their efforts to overthrow the state. However, they all embraced violence in their effort to reassert Islam and rejected the moderation of the Brotherhood.

The Islamists successfully recruited university students, and the *Jama'at Islamiyya* – the student Islamist movement – was the most dominant and genuine mass movement in Sadat's Egypt. The *Takfir* group never had the broad appeal that the Brotherhood had. While its membership did not exceed 4000 (Lippman, p. 40), it had a more diverse group of followers, including women and children, who opted for removing themselves from the *Jahili* society. Providing a powerful imagery of Muhammad's flight from Mecca to Medina in 622 A.D. and his triumphant return eight years later, they presented a very powerful symbolic-ideological message: "A message that included the image of the just community withdrawing from the world, fleeing the domain of the unjust and hypocrites to take refuge and spiritual discipline in seclusion and asceticism" (Gilesnan, p. 187).[4]

This organization's violence against the regime culminated in the assassination of the Minister of Endowments, and subsequently the regime destroyed the organization by an effective campaign of arrests and executions of the organization's members and leaders in 1977. The Islamists' violence against Sadat climaxed in his assassination in 1981 by a militant faction called Islamic holy war (*Jihad I-Islami*).

A small extremist splinter group, the Jihad, followed a lesser-known Islamist thinker, Abd al-Salam Faraj. Faraj's tract, *The Hidden Imperative*, preached violence as the only solution for the removal of the infidels from power. *The Hidden Imperative* was nothing but a Jihad against the state and those who compromise with the infidel state. Faraj said, "In the Islamic countries, the enemy is at home; indeed, it is he who is in command. He is represented by those governments that have seized power over the Muslims, and that is why Jihad is an imperative for every

---

[4] *Takfir*'s strategies are discussed in Tareq Ismael and Jacqueline S. Ismael, *Government and Politics in Islam*, New York: St. Martin's Press, 1985, p. 117.

individual" (Quoted in Kepel, p. 202). This is how Jihad justified the assassination of Sadat, even though there are Islamic prohibitions against political assassination. The group that assassinated Sadat was an alliance of the civilian, military and religious personalities; the cleric Shaykh Abd-al Rahman issued religious decrees which provided legitimacy for the action (Esposito, 1984, pp. 208–9).

Not all Islamists favored violent confrontation with the state and the assassination of Sadat. The Brotherhood remained fairly moderate, and the *Jama'at-I-Islamiyyah* focused on the immoral conduct of the population and resisted confrontation with the state. Young activists supported the more radical groups who were seeking a rapid solution through confrontation with the state. These young radicals often came from rural areas or small towns, and from the lower or lower-middle class, but they had high levels of education. According to Esposito, they could be considered "model young Egyptians" who were alienated from the urban environments to which they had migrated. Islamism provided them with a family and an ideology that not only criticized the existing rules, but also provided them with an agenda for radical change, an agenda that was rooted in their traditional religious worldview (Esposito, 1984, pp. 203–4).

The assassination of Sadat shook the Egyptian state. The radical Islamists continued their violence not only against the state but also against the Coptic Christians, a religious minority who were viewed as aliens serving the interests of the West. In an effort to paralyze the regime and reject the west and its ways, the radical Islamists like the New Jihad targeted Egyptian tourism costing the state billions of dollars in foreign currency revenues.[5]

The Mubarak regime continued some of Sadat's policies designed to co-opt the traditional clerics and moderate Islamists, but adopted a fiercely repressive strategy against the radicals. Like Sadat, Mubarak uses Islamic symbolism and relies on state-sponsored Islam and the traditionalists who reject militancy as "un-Islamic" and inconsistent with the Sunni moderation. He reaffirmed the *Shari'ah* as the principal source of Egyptian law, resulting in the 1985 amendments to the 1979 Personal Status Law that limit women's rights in divorce, child custody and alimony. These amendments made it once again difficult for women to initiate divorce or gain custody (Najjar, pp. 62–3).

Mubarak has allowed further expansion of "Islamized spaces" or "zones." These neighborhoods or villages that are controlled by the Islamists are like "puritan enclaves representative of the future ideal society" (Faksh, p. 50). They provide services and implement their own

---

[5] The loss of tourism, which is worth $3 billion in hard currency annually, cost Egypt between $700 million to $1 billion in 1992 due to the terrorism of the radicals.

rules and Islamic laws in these zones. The Islamists also exercise a great deal of influence in the educational institutions, professional associations, unions, and local councils.

At the same time the government has clashed with radical Islamists in an effort to restore the state's hegemony. The government has arrested many for violating antiterrorist laws, and the subsequent trials in military courts have drawn strong criticism from international human rights groups. The High Constitutional Court has ruled these military trials as constitutional. Criticizing the human rights organizations as functionaries of the Nasserists and Islamists, Mubarak has emphatically said: "I refuse to allow human rights to become a slogan to protect terrorists" (Ajami, 1986, p. 26).

Furthermore, Mubarak has tried to discredit the Islamists and their foreign backers and to promote regional cooperation with Tunisia, Algeria, Saudi Arabia, and Pakistan. He even pushed for the adoption of a resolution equating terrorism with international organized crime and called for a concerted international effort to combat it at the 1995 International Conference on the Prevention of Crime and the Treatment of Offenders (Cordahi, p. 12). Mubarak has even become more confrontational with such moderate Islamists as the Brotherhood. He is curbing their social functions and limiting their role in elections.

Religious parties are illegal, but in the 1980s the regime tolerated the Islamists' participation in elections. Generally, these parties have done well in any election with some fairness and freedom. In the 1984 parliamentary elections, the Islamists won eight seats working in alliance with the New Wafd Party, and in 1987 the Brotherhood won thirty-seven seats while running in alliance with other parties (Ghadbian, pp. 51–2). Frightened by the Islamists' electoral successes, the government passed legislation to change election procedures of the councils, unions, and other professional associations, intending to facilitate control of these bodies by the ruling National Democratic Party. To curb the Islamists' influence in the civic organizations, the law requires that all organizations be registered and licensed by the government. The Islamists and their supporters in the New Wafd boycotted the 1995 parliamentary elections and accused the government of fraud. Many Islamists and their leaders were arrested, and only one Islamist gained a seat in the parliament as an independent (Ghadbian, p. 52). In the parliamentary elections of 2000, the Islamists fielded seventy-five candidates as independents. Despite serious restrictions and electoral irregularities, two of the Islamist-backed independents won parliamentary seats in the first round of elections.

While secular liberals are concerned about these anti-democratic measures by the government, they along with the Christian Copts do not trust the Islamists and their true commitment to democracy and do not seriously challenge these measures. Ironically, in today's Egypt, despite apparent retrogression in democratization the liberals "have no choice but to take cover under a disliked state apparatus to escape the menace of fundamentalism"(Faksh, p. 56).

Islamists do not pose a serious threat to the state and the secular-liberal rule in the Egypt. Undoubtedly, they will remain a major political force in Egyptian life in the near term. In the long run, the influence of the radical and moderate Islamists will depend upon the degree to which the state can address the enormous social, economic, and political problems. For now, the regime relies on the support of elites and the military for its survival. However, as the Iranian revolution demonstrated, no regime can maintain legitimacy in a Muslim society in the face of such intense opposition from the Islamists unless it broadens its own base of support by pursuing constructive economic and social policies and political liberalization.

### DEMOCRATIZATION AND ISLAMISM IN ALGERIA

Although Algerians are predominantly Arab Muslims, Islamism does not have a long history in Algerian politics. The absence of Islam from political life in Algeria can be largely attributed to French colonialism (1831–1962) and the French cultural penetration of Algeria. This form of cultural imperialism not only diluted the Arab-Algerian cultural and national identity, it resulted in sociopolitical schisms among the Algerian Arabs, Francophones, and Berbers.

With French colonialism, secularism dominated Algeria and Islam was marginalized. Islamic activities were primarily limited to religious, social and moral issues advanced by the rural Sufi orders and the few urban-based ulama organizations. During this period, the only dynamic Islamist movement was the Association of the Algerian Muslim Ulama founded by Sheikh Abdul Hamid Ben Badis in 1931. Invoking the Muslim ancestral heritage, this association intended to pattern the Islamic reform after the early Islamic traditions. They rejected the ritualistic Islam of the rural "Holy Men" and emphasized an Arab-Islamic national identity by encouraging education and the use of Arabic language instead of French. While the association remained largely religious, social and nonpolitical, its reformism and commitment to an Algerian national identity stimulated the 1954 revolution, which initiated the war of independence (1954–62) against France (Faksh, pp. 65–6).

The independence movement, however, was dominated by the secular-nationalists that marginalized the Islamists but used them to mobilize the masses in support of anti-colonialism and nationalism. Although the Algerian revolution rejected all manifestations of colonialism, after the successful revolutionary war, the National Liberation Front founded the Algerian state according to the well-known French Jacobin model of centralized state (Arkoun, p. 176). The state Constitution adopted some formal democratic institutions and procedures, but the regime has been dominated by a secular-bureaucratic-military alliance ever since. This alliance under the leadership of Algeria's charismatic war hero, Houari Boumedienne, steered the country in a socialist path to development and treated Islam as a cultural element of the Algerian identity (Deeb, p. 6).

While the regime paid lip service to Islam as an instrument of legitimizing its radical socialist policies, it made every effort to control the religious establishment and the interpretation of Islam. To this end, in 1966, the government established a Higher Islamic Council as the sole authoritative body to issue religious legal decrees (*Fatwa*), and subsequently nationalized Islam by incorporating the religious establishments into the bureaucracy under the supervision of the Ministry of Religious Affairs. Almost two decades of secularism, the marginalization of Islam and Arabism, and the increasingly ineffective and counterproductive Socialist-Marxist policies alienated the younger and dissatisfied Muslims and resulted in the emergence of moderate and radical Islamist groups.

In 1964, the Association of Islamic Resurrection was the first Islamist group created with the goal of restoring true Islamic values by rejecting foreign cultural penetration, modernism, and state-sponsored clericalism. Although the regime suppressed this movement in 1966 and finally banned it in 1970, the Islamists' opposition did not completely disappear. Despite serious and widespread opposition to the undemocratic nature of the regime and its inegalitarian policies that had resulted in the widening gap between the poor and undereducated Arabists (Arab-educated) and the well-to-do Francophones, the Boumedienne government maintained its legitimacy by implementing social welfare policies and by relying on the revolutionary mythology that linked the leaders to the independence movement.

The fragile nature of this legitimacy made it susceptible to crisis after Boumedienne's death in 1978, when the Islamist opposition reemerged forcefully. The League of the Islamic Call led Islamist opposition in the early 1980s in response to the unraveling social, economic and political conditions. The Benjedid's government in the early 1980s experienced an acute agricultural crisis related to the mismanagement of the land reform policies, uncontrolled urbanization, growing unemployment, high inflation, shortages in housing and basic goods, declining oil and gas revenues, growing foreign debts, and widening inequalities (Dekmejian, p. 205). Gradually, Algeria's problems came to resemble those of Sadat's Egypt.

To alleviate the economic problems, Benjedid adopted economic liberalization similar to Sadat's *Infitah*. In a sharp contrast to Sadat's purges and repressive policies, Benjedid also pursued political liberalization, despite opposition from the hard-liners within the military-secular-bureaucratic alliance. Like *Infitah*, Benjedid's economic liberalization aggravated the economic difficulties by creating a "new class" of elite entrepreneurs and deteriorating the conditions of the masses.

Furthermore, political liberalization strengthened the Islamists and alienated the Berbers, the military and the secular elites. The Islamic opposition reached its apex with the birth and growth of the Islamic Salvation Front (FIS) in 1989. Initially Benjedid did not view the FIS as a threat because they were neither overtly politically active nor were they popular outside the "Islamic spaces." Trying to both accommodate the Islamists and to use them as a counterbalance against the leftists, Boumedienne hardliners, Berberist forces, and feminists, Benjedid tolerated the Islamists' efforts in building independent mosques and spreading their influence through social welfare and educational activities.

Until the October 1988 riots, the government effectively controlled the Islamists' political activities and prevented them from becoming a mass movement. The upheaval, however, weakened the government, discredited Benjedid's policies, and gave a boost to the FIS (Faksh, pp. 70–1). The government was forced to initiate genuine democratic reforms. In February 1989, the regime adopted a new constitution that revoked the FLN's monopoly of power, and accounted for free political parties and elections and freedom of speech and press. It also contained an escape clause that, like Egypt, banned religious political parties. However, Benjedid chose not to invoke this clause (Viorst, p. 244). Benjedid established a multiparty parliamentary democracy, the first of its kind in the Arab world. Although the opposition by the military and the Berber socialists and nationalists who worried about the Islamists' domination overshadowed the euphoria, within a year more than fifty political parties emerged in the Algerian political scene.

The FIS was officially recognized in August 1989, despite the ban on religious parties, and gradually became the principal Islamist movement opposing the regime. Although a diverse movement with moderate and radical tendencies, the FIS was committed to the establishment of an Islamic order and could not reconcile its ideology with that of the ruling party and the regime. Like the Brotherhood in Egypt, it actively sought the elimination of the secular state and the establishment of a *Shari'a*-based Islamic system by establishing an extensive support infrastructure. However, "with two diametrically opposed visions of society – secular versus Islamic – the fault lines in the Algerian struggle are deeper by far and more potentially destabilizing than their equivalent in Egypt."

(Faksh, p. 71). Drawing its support primarily from lower-class, less educated Arabophone city dwellers lacking in economic opportunity (Dekmejian, p. 205), the FIS was now ready to destroy the state either by electoral contestation or violent confrontation.

In the first free elections in twenty-eight years in Algeria, the FIS won stunning victories in the June1990 local and December 1991 national elections. In the local elections, the FIS captured 55.5 percent of the municipal councils and two thirds of the provincial assemblies (I'brahim, 1990). These results demonstrated the end of one-party rule in Algeria and the beginning of true pluralism. Some even believed that Algeria after these elections "emerged as the most liberal political system in the Arab world" (Hudson, p. 417). More than fifty political parties campaigned in the first round of national elections. In this round, the FIS won 188 seats, only 28 seats short of a majority in a 430-seat National Assembly. Much to the regime's dismay, the FLN was third with 15 seats and the Socialist Forces Front came second with 25 seats (Wright, 1992, pp. 134–5). The FIS was expected to win at least 150 of the remaining 199 seats to be decided in the second round of the elections (Najib Ghadbian, p. 56).

Empowered by the magnitude of its victory, the FIS openly called for the end of the regime. They proclaimed that "Islam is the solution," and suggested that the FIS represented God and any vote against the party was a vote against God. It became abundantly clear that the FIS was interested in power not in democracy (Faksh, p. 72), although the Islamists continued to pretend their willingness to function democratically in the mosques and participate in democratic elections (Dekmejian, p. 208).

Similar to the Iranian revolution, however, electoral support for the FIS was largely a protest against the ruling FLN rather than support for an Islamic state. Unlike Iran and Egypt, the Algerian military has a long-standing political role and has, since the revolutionary war, acted as the guardian of the secular state. In this role, the military had generally opposed Benjedid's democratization efforts and was even unwilling to share power with the FIS. Supported by the Berbers and the secular forces, the military stepped in after the FIS objected to the changes in election laws that favored the FLN candidates. In the May–June 1991 clashes between the military and the Islamists many were arrested and killed, martial law was declared for four months, and the second round of the elections was postponed. The ensuing chaos proliferated the radicalization of the FIS, despite defections by some moderate groups such as the Movement for Islamic Society and the Islamic Renaissance. Increased violence resulted in the ousting of Benjedid in January 1992, the invalidation of the election results, and the cancellation of the second round of the elections by the military. Some Islamists left the FIS and created radical rebellious groups such as the Islamic Group, the Algerian Afghans (the veterans of the Afghan war against the Soviet Union), the Apostasy and Flight Organization (unrelated to its Egyptian counterpart), and the *al-Jaz'ara* (an initially moderate faction turned radical in response to the repression). These groups later coalesced to form two major militant rebellion groupings: The Armed Islamic Group (GIA for its French acronym) and the military wing of the FIS called the Islamic Salvation Army (Faksh, p. 74). These two groups continue their Jihad against the military by terrorism, bombings, and assassinations.

After the coup and ousting of Benjedid, the military suspended the democratic process altogether, and established a five-member civilian High State Council (or Presidential Council). This Council rejected accommodation with the Islamists, illegalized the FIS, and pursued a confrontational strategy against the opposition. Justifying these policies in the name of democracy, Ali Haroun, a respected member of this council suggested: "The FIS has had the honesty to declare that it is not democratic, that it is against democracy . . . that when it takes over there will be no more elections, there will be the *shura*, the religious men who meet together and decide in your behalf. The FIS says it would use elections to gain power; afterwards, there would be no more elections" (Virost, p. 249).

The head of the Council was assassinated in 1992, and the reign of terror by the Islamists targeted not only the political establishment but also the anti-Islamist journalists, intellectuals, judges, and academicians. The new president Liamine Zeroual, a reputed moderate army officer who replaced the High State Council in 1994, pursued a two-pronged strategy of economic reform and political dialogue coupled with repression. These economic reforms intended to lower subsidies and facilitate assistance from international financial institutions. Since the political dialogue with the moderates did not resolve the outstanding issues, the government pushed for more repressive policies.

Unable to achieve its goals either through violence or direct negotiations with the military, the FIS joined all parties who had received 80 percent of the votes in the 1992 elections at a meeting in Sant 'Egidio under the sponsorship of the Vatican. The government did not support this effort, but the meeting was a great success for the FIS even though it had to make important concessions. In mid-January 1995, the group reached a National Pact that emphasized the goals of democratic-pluralism, freedom, multi-culturalism, and the legalization of the FIS. The FIS agreed to end violence against the "innocent people." It also agreed to accept peaceful transition of power, if voted out of office. The

FIS, in return for recognition, did not assert its right to rule based on the 1992 election results.

The radical Islamists rejected the National Pact for its failure to call for an Islamic state. The military rejected the Pact because it called for "the nonintervention of the army in political affairs." This was a radical change that nullified the Algerian military's long-standing supremacy in the political system (Virost, p. 270). While the military showed some flexibility later by allowing a rally, with the FIS participation, calling for an end to emergency rule and a return to democracy, its goal of preserving the secular state was diametrically different from that of the Islamists.

The opposition boycotted the presidential elections of November 1995 and the parliamentary elections of 1997, but over 75 percent of the population ignored the boycott, and Zeroual won the election with 61 percent of the popular vote. Only Hamas, a moderate Islamist group, was allowed to run an Islamist candidate in this election and he came second to the president with 25.3 percent of the popular vote (Ghadbian, p. 56). The military saw the election results an endorsement of eliminating the FIS and Islamists as the major political force (Faksh, p. 80). As a surprise move, Zeroual called for early presidential elections in April 1999, suggesting that the election was a step toward democracy (Chalala, p. 5).

The new president, Abdelaziz Bouteflika, has continued his predecessor's confrontational policies against the Islamists. By some estimates, to date some 70,000 to 80,000 people have been killed in the clashes between the military and its supporters with the opposition. The November 22, 1999 assassination of Abdelqader Hachani, the moderate leader of the FIS who has sought peaceful coexistence with the government, exemplifies the complexity of the current violence in Algeria. While the government blames the radicals, especially the GIA, for the reign of terror, and vows to eradicate them, there seem to be abundant evidence pointing to the military's and their supporters' culpability. Amnesty International and a number of observers of Algeria have suggested that by founding the Patriots battalion and arming 100,000 volunteers as a part of a "self-defense force," targeting the FIS and their supporters, and refusing to assist the victims of violence, the government is openly and directly inciting violence. It has even been suggested that there is a link between these massacres and the sale of agricultural lands. In a sinister move, some contend, economic and political leaders are exploiting the violence to eliminate the small farmers and even their potential heirs to the land by killing their youngest children (Chalada, p. 6).

The Islamists' failure to counter the military and to achieve its objectives is largely due to the opposition from a wide-range of secular, nationalist, and socialist elements to the establishment of an Islamic state similar to the one in Iran. This fear is reinforced by the enactment of such policies as closing movie theatres, school gender segregation, banning alcohol, and adopting dress codes by Islamist-controlled town councils (Roy, 1994, pp. 80–5). Furthermore, the Berbers, who compose about twenty percent of the population, are culturally against Arabization and favor the French colonial legacy. In sharp contrast to the Islamists, the Berber-led Socialist Forces Front (FFS) and the Rally for Culture and Democracy (RCD) also advocate a society that is secular, democratic, pluralist, and multicultural (Faksh, p. 76).

## ISLAMISM IN THE LEBANESE CONFESSIONAL POLITICS

The Lebanese civil war that began in the mid-1970s and lasted for a decade and a half is explained by the failures of the Lebanese confessional political system to adapt to the changing dynamics of the Lebanese society. The system was designed to accommodate the interests of various ethno-religious groupings, but as the Shi'i population grew in number, and the social and economic gaps between Muslims and non-Muslims widened, the system gradually lost its legitimacy. By 1975, the Shi'is composed about thirty percent of the Lebanese population due to their growth and the declining Christian population as a result of migration. In fact, by that time the Shi'is had become the largest single confessional community, surpassing the Maronite Christians and Sunni Muslims (Kramer, 1996, p. 211). Despite this demographic growth, the Shi'is could not close the social and economic gap with the Christians and the Sunnis, and began challenging the confessional system and its policies.

These domestic conditions and a series of regional and global developments explain the rise of Islamism in Lebanon and its ultimate domination of the Lebanese civil war. The Palestinian intrusion in Lebanon and the subsequent Israeli invasion, the continued Syrian-Israeli hostilities, the establishment of the Islamic republic in Iran and the clerics' commitment to a world-wide Islamic revolution, and the heightened Western, especially American, hegemony in the region contributed to a growing Muslim fear that they are no longer in charge of their own destiny in the Lebanese political system. These fears radicalized the Lebanese Muslims and led to the emergence of Islamist groups along sectarian lines. The Lebanese Islamism thus was divided into the Shi'i and Sunni groups and the Druze remained outside the Islamist movement.

The Sunni Islamism manifested itself in a number of groups that ideologically ranged from radical to moderate. The Islamic Association has been active since 1948, and has called for the establishment of an Islamic state as a means to reverse the spiritual and political decline of the Muslim world. Their leader, Fathi Yakan, rejected any foreign ideologies as alien to Islam (Yakan, 1984, pp. 87, 109–10). Largely urban based, this organization has shown affinity towards the Brotherhoods, Iran, and the Hizbollah, and has rejected the Lebanese confessionalism without directly confronting the Syrians (Dekmejian, p. 163).

Two distinctly different Sunni Islamist groups rival this organization: The Unicity Movement (*Harakat al-Tawhid al-Islami*) and the Islamic Society of the Philanthropic Projects. The *Tawhid* was founded in 1982, and pursued a confrontational policy with the Lebanese state and Israel. While combining Islamic militancy with a degree of pragmatism and realism, this organization rejected any secular state and sought the establishment of an Islamic order. However, in order to neutralize the Sunni sentiments and to avoid confrontation with Syria, it did not call for a republic patterned after the Iranian Shi'i regime.

At the climax of the civil war in the 1980s, this organization became a state within a state in Tripoli by carrying out trials and public executions of both civil and Islamic laws and by fighting the pro-Syrian militias. *Tawhid* maintained good ties to Iran and rejected sectarianism and called for Islamic unity (Wright, 1988, pp. 59–60). Directly connected to *Tawhid* was the Islamic Liberation Organization which indirectly attacked the Syrian interests by kidnapping the Russians.

The Islamic Society of Philanthropic Projects was founded in 1930 as a moderate organization. However, due to major theological differences with the *Jama'at*, the Philanthropists turned radical and fought the *Jama'at* in 1988–9. Following spiritual revivalism of the Sufis, the Philanthropists reject sectarian disunity and advocate pluralism and tolerance. Thus, they have gained a great deal of following among the urban middle class Sunnis and have currently become a key player in the Lebanese confessional politics (Dekmejian, p. 165).

Traditionally, the Shi'is were the most underrated political force in Lebanon. Ideologically committed to justice and resistance to oppression, they responded to their deteriorating social, economic, and political conditions with greater radicalism and militancy than the Sunnis. From the outset, the Shi'i movement was disharmonious and reflected the ideological conflicts and personal rivalries among the Lebanese clerics in the 1970s. Many of these clerics were the products of the Shi'i clerical learning centers in Najaf (a city in southern Iraq), where they were exposed to radical Shi'i ideas similar to Khomeini's and had build personal connections with and loyalties to clerics throughout the Middle East. These ideological differences and personal loyalties resulted in the rise of such diverse leaders as Abu Musa al-Sadr whose Amal organization

emphasized Lebanese identity and Shaikh Muhammad Hussain Fadlallah of the Hizbollah who advocated the Shi'i transnational activism.

The Lebanese Shi'i Islamist movements gradually revolved around two
major organizations: The Hope (Amal), and the Party of God (Hizbollah). An Iranian-born Lebanese, Imam Musa al-Sadr, founded Amal as
"the Movement of the Disinherited" in the late 1960s. While generally
moderate, the organization reacted to the civil war by calling for armed
struggle in the interest of equality within a multiconfessional Lebanese
state. Recognizing the nature of Lebanese society, al-Sadr did not call for
the establishment of an Islamic state (Wright, 1988, p. 63). Nabih Berri,
a secular and moderate pro-Syrian, became the organization's secretary
general after al-Sadr's disappearance in 1975. He followed the Syrian
line and opted for a "peaceful solution" to the Lebanese civil war. Berri's
secularism and moderation factionalized the Amal and the younger and
more militant Shi'is created the Islamic Amal and Hizbollah with outside
support.

As the most militant Shi'i organization, the Hizbollah emerged in June
of 1982 as the result of coalescence among several Shi'i groups including the Lebanese branch of the Call (*Al-Dawa*), the Islamic Amal, and
the Hussain Suicide Squad. Loosely organized, the Hizbollah acted as an
umbrella organization covering such organizations or cells as the Revolutionary Justice Organization and the Organization of the Oppressed of
the Earth that carried out many terrorist activities. Influenced by Iran,
the Hizbollah is ideologically patterned after the Islamic Republic of
Iran, with emphasis on the leadership role of the clerics (Doctrine of
*Vilayat-e Faqih*). However, the influence of Iran over the Hizbollah has
often been exaggerated. While Iran did play a critical role in the formation and the ideological and political development of the Hizbollah, it
did not control the organization, and the organization did often act independently of the Iranians (Ranstrop, 1997, p. 33). The leaders of the
organization were strong antinationalist and Pan-Islamist visionaries
who did not just seek an Islamic republic in Lebanon, rather they advocated a world-wide Islamic revolution.

In his book, *Islam and the Logic of Force*, Fadlallah called upon all
Muslims to organize against imperialism and secular politics and to safeguard the survival of Islamic values and movements (Fadlallah, 1981, p.
246). He, like other leaders, called for an Islamic state based on the
Quran and the Twelver Shi'a thought.[6] In pursuit of these objectives, the

---

[6] For a more elaborate discussion of Hizbollah's ideology see Martin Kramer, "Redeem-
ing Jerusalem: The Pan-Islamic premise of Hizb'allah." In David Menasheri (ed.). *The
Iranian Revolution and the Muslim World*. Boulder, CO: Westview Press, 1990, pp.
105–30.

Hizbollah resorted to such extremist policies as hostage taking, bombing and political assassination.

Operating in three areas in Lebanon – The Biq'a, Beirut, and Southern Lebanon – the organization gradually established an extensive decision-making and operational infrastructure. The supreme decision-making bodies were the Consultative Council, which was headed by twelve senior clerical members who supervised and coordinated overall activities of the organization, and the Deciding Assembly, which was headed by Fadlallah and consisted of eleven other clerics responsible for all strategic matters. Within the Consultative Council, there existed seven specialized committees dealing with ideological, financial, military, political, judicial, informational, and social matters. Similar organizational structures existed in each of the three regions with accountability to the central Consultative Council. Iran was officially represented on the Consultative Council by Iranian military and diplomatic representatives. After 1989, Hizbollah was reorganized into five major components headed by a secretary general: *Majlis al-Shura, Majlis al-Karar*, the Political bureau *(Maktab al-Siyasis)*, Special Security Apparatus, and the Islamic Resistance (the military wing). There seems to be great organizational linkage between the Hizbollah and Iran.

Khomeini's death and Iran's growing foreign policy moderation, and Syrian rapprochement to the West after the Gulf war and her determination to control Lebanon eroded Iran's influence in Hizbollah and gradually allowed them to act more independently of Iran towards the end of the 1980s (Ranstrop, 1997, p. 45). The Hizbollah agreed to the Syriansponsored 1989 Ta'if agreement and sharply readjusted its strategy by agreeing to participate in the modified confessional Lebanese political system. This strategy forced Hizbollah to abandon the ideal of Pan-Islamism and the desire for an Islamic state in practice. Fadlallah tried to justify the need for moderation by saying: "Like all revolutions, including the French revolution, the Islamic revolution did not have a realistic line at first. . . . At that time it served to create a state, it produced a mobilization, a new religious way of thinking and living, with the aim of winning Muslim autonomy and independence from the superpowers." But, he added, "the new phase which should now be reached is the normalization of relations with the rest of the world" (Quoted in Kramer, 1996, p. 226).

Still, some of the leading clerics continue to argue that Hizbollah is committed to the destruction of the Lebanese state from "within" (Ranstrop, p. 58). These developments factionalized the leading clerics on such major issues as participation in the 1992 parliamentary elections. Although the radicals continued to object, the moderates like Shaikh Nasserallah suggested, "Our entry to the ranks of parliamentary representatives gives us the opportunity to defend our resistance on the political plane" (Ranstrop, 1997, p. 77). Similar to the Islamists in Egypt, Jordan, and Algeria, now Hizbollah had abandoned the revolutionary slogan and had substituted it with the call for democracy. To that end, the organization was transformed from a revolutionary one into a political party committed to grassroots social activism. Today, the Hizbollah pursues a two-prong strategy within the framework of the Ta'if agreements: participation in democratic elections, and continued resistance to Israel and determination to liberate Jerusalem.

In the 1992 parliamentary elections, the first in twenty years, the sixty seats that were allocated to Muslims were contested by Sunnis and Shi'is. Hizbollah's popularity was reaffirmed by its ability to win twelve seats compared to five for the Sunnis (Ghadbian, p. 53). The Hizbollah representatives have pursued three objectives in the Lebanese parliament: to pressure the government to follow an anti-Israeli foreign policy, to oppose any negotiation with Israel, and to support the policies designed to help the needy and poor, especially in the war-stricken areas. Given the fact that Hizbollah remains armed and continues its link to the Syrians and the Iranians, the future of the organization's policies will depend upon domestic developments in Lebanon and the wishes of Iran and Syria.

Undoubtedly, Hizbollah's moderation was facilitated by the Syrian move towards the west, Iran's moderation, and the end of Iranian-Syrian cooperation in Lebanon. Any future deterioration of the Syrian-Iranian relationship and move toward radicalism could easily turn the tide in Hizbollah. Clearly, there continues to be a struggle between the Hizbollah radicals and moderates over the organization's agenda. As a clear victor in the Lebanese civil war, Hizbollah continues to exhibit a great deal of commitment to the modified fragile Lebanese political institutions. This has resulted in support and respect for the organization. The Syrians, however, continue to allow and even encourage Hizbollah's confrontational policies towards Israel. In turn, by violent retaliations, the Israelis are intent not to be defeated by the Islamists (Shehadi, 1999, pp. 20–1).

## CONCLUSIONS

The political role of Islam is subject to a cyclical pattern of activism and quietism. Islamists are Muslim activists who have historically pursued the goal of establishing an Islamic order by employing wide-ranging strategies including democratic participation in as well as violent opposition to the existing regimes. In the contemporary Muslim world, the rise of Islamism is due to the continued authoritarianism of the secular regimes, the growing social and economic deterioration of their societies and the consequent mass frustration, and the increasingly open Western hegemony that jeopardizes the dignity and integrity of Muslims who are ideologically committed to justice and equality. With the exception of the Sudan, which is run by a military-based Islamic system, the current Arab Islamic activism has failed to realize the goal of an Islamic order. Mubarak's intensified authoritarianism targeting mainly the Islamists, the erasing of the Islamists' electoral successes by the Algerian military regime, and Hizbollah's rejection of revolutionary war and resort to reformism have made some to conclude that today's Islamism has failed.

This failure, according to some, is largely due to the movement's lack of organizational cohesion and centralized authority; its radically ideological and nonpragmatic nature; its programmatic inadequacy to address the domestic, regional, and global issues; and its unchanging commitment to a form of religious exclusivism and nationalism that disregards multiculturalism, pluralism, and secularism (Faksh, 1997, pp. 110–12).

The Islamists' commitment to gain power, by eradicating the existing regimes and establishing Islamic states, has resulted in strange and tenuous alliances even among the authoritarian elites, the military, and the Muslim and non-Muslim secular and liberal forces in the contemporary Arab societies. As the 1990s came to a close, it became increasingly apparent that internal and external oppositions to Islamism are too strong to allow the violent overthrow of the existing regimes and their replacement by Islamic alternatives. It is, however, premature to conclude that the current reversals in strategy are indications of the end of Islamism. If the long and tumultuous history of Islamic activism is any guide, the move towards moderation by the Egyptian Brotherhood, the Algerian FIS, the Lebanese Hizbollah, and other Islamists is simply a change of strategy in response to the existing realities rather than the abandonment of their goal. The Islamists have and will always be committed to the Islamic order and will pursue all viable avenues in achieving that goal. The current change is neither a failure nor a retreat, it is simply a pragmatic response to the social, economic, and political realities of the end of the twentieth century.

### REFERENCES

Ajami, Fouad. 1986. "The Impossible Life of Muslim Liberalism." *The New Republic*, June 2.

Al-Azmeh, Aziz. 1996. *Islams and Modernities*, 2nd ed. London and New York: Verso.

Al-Banna, Hasan. 1974. *What is Our Message?* Lahore, Pakistan: Islamic Publications.

Anderson, Roy R., Robert F. Seibert, and Jon G. Wagner. 1993. *Politics and Change in the Middle East, Sources of Conflict and Accommodation*, 4th ed. Englewood Cliffs, NJ: Prentice Hall.

Arkoun, Mohammad. 1988. "Algeria." In Shireen T. Hunter (ed.). *The Politics of Islamic Revivalism, Diversity and Unity.* Bloomington and Indianapolis: Indiana University Press: pp. 171–86.

Bagader, Abubaker A. 1994. "Contemporary Islamic movements in the Arab world." In Akbar S. Ahmed and Hastings Donnan (eds.). *Islam, Globalization and Postmodernity.* London and New York: Routledge: pp. 114–26.

Baker, Raymond William, "Invidious Comparisons: Realism, Postmodern Globalism, and Centrist Islamic Movements in Egypt." In John Espositio (ed.). *Political Islam, Revolution, Radicalism, Or Reform?* pp. 115–33.

Chalala, Elie. 1999. "In Algeria's Killing Fields, A Hidden Government Role?" *Humanist*, vol. 59, No. 2, March/April.

Cordahi, Cherif. 1995. "Egypt: Facilitating Extradition." *Middle East International*, 12 May: pp. 8–16.

Deeb, Mary Jane. 1989. "Algeria" In Stewart Mews (ed.), *Religion and Politics, A World Guide.* Essex, UK: Longman Group.

Dekmejian, R. Hrair. 1995. *Islam in Revolution, Fundamentalism in the Arab World*, 2nd. ed. Syracuse NY: Syracuse University Press.

Esposito, John L. 1984. *Islam and Politics.* Syracuse, NY: Syracuse University Press.

Fadlallah, Myhammad Husayn. 1981. *Al-Islam wa-Mantiq al-Quwwa*, 2nd ed. Beirut.

Faksh, Mahmud A. 1997. *The Future of Islam in the Middle East, Fundamentalism in Egypt, Algeria, and Saudi Arabia.* Westport, CT: Praeger.

Fluehr-Lobban, Carolyn (ed.). 1998. *Against Islamic Extremism, The Writings of Muhammad Sa'id al-Ashmawy.* Gainesville, FL: University of Florida Press.

Ghadbian, Najib. 1997. *Democratization and the Islamic Challenge in the Arab World.* Boulder, CO: Westview Press.

Gilsenan, Michael. 1988. "Popular Islam and the State in Contemporary Egypt." In Fred Halliday and Hamza Alavi (eds.). *State and Ideology in the Middle East and Pakistan*, New York: Monthly Review Press.

Hanafi, Hasan. 1982. "The Relevance of the Islamic Alternative in Egypt." *Arab Studies Quarterly*, Vol. 4, No. 3, Spring: pp. 60–71.

Hudson, Michael. 1991. "After the Gulf War: Prospects for Democratization in the Arab World." *Middle East Journal*, Vol. 45, No. 3, Summer: pp. 407–26.

Ibrahim, Saad Eddin. 1980. "Anatomy of Egypt's Militant Islamic Groups: Methodological Notes and Preliminary Findings." *International Journal of Middle East Studies*, 12, No. 4, Dec.: pp. 436–39.

   1982. "Islamic Militancy As a Social Movement: The Case of Two Groups in Egypt." In Ali E. Hillal Dessouki (ed.). *Islamic Resurgence in the Arab World.* New York: Praeger: pp. 117–37.

   1990. "Islamic Party in Algeria Defeats Ruling Group in Local Elections." *New York Times*, June 14.

Ismael, Tareq Y. and Jacqueline S. Ismael 1985. *Government and Politics in Islam*. New York: St. Martin's Press.

Kepel, Gilles (trans. Jon Rothschild). 1986. *Muslim Extremism in Egypt, the Prophet and Pharaoh*. Berkeley and Los Angeles: University of California Press.

Kramer, Martin. 1996. *Arab Awakening & Islamic Revival, The Politics of Ideas in the Middle East*. New Brunswick and London: Transaction Publishers.

Lippman, Thomas W. 1982. *Islam, Politics and Religion in the Muslim World*. New York: Foreign Policy Association Headline Series, No. 258, March/April.

Mitchell, Richard P. 1969. *The Society of the Muslim Brothers*. London: Oxford University Press.

Mortimer, Robert. 1991. "Islam and Multiparty Politics in Algeria." *Middle East Journal,* Vol. 45, no. 4, Autumn: pp. 575–93.

Moten, Abdu Rashid. 1996. *Political Science: An Islamic Perspective*. New York: St. Martin's Press.

Munson, Henry Jr. 1988. *Islam and Revolution in the Middle East*. New Haven and London: Yale University Press.

Najjar, Fauzi M. 1992. "The Application of Shari'a Laws in Egypt." *Middle East Policy*, Vol. 1, No. 3: pp. 62–73.

Ranstrop, Magnus. 1997. *Hizb'allah in Lebanon, The Politics of Western Hostage Crisis*. New York: St. Martin's Press.

Roy, Oliver. 1994. *The Failure of Political Islam*. Cambridge, MA: Harvard University Press.

Shehadi, Nadim. 1999. "Violent Dialogue." *The World Today*, Vol. 55, Nos. 8–9. August-September. pp. 20–1.

Viorst, Milton. 1998. *In the Shadow of the Prophet, The Struggle for the Soul of Islam*. New York: Anchor Books.

Wright, Robin. 1988. "Lebanon." In Shireen T. Hunter (ed.). *The Politics of Islamic Revivalism, Diversity and Unity*. Bloomington and Indianapolis: Indiana University Press: pp. 57–70.

1992. "Islam, Democracy, and the West." *Foreign Affairs,* 71 no. 3, Summer: pp. 131–45.

Yakan, Fathi. 1984. *Islamic Movement: Problems and Perspectives*. Indianapolis: American Trust Publications.

Christopher Soper and Joel Fetzer's analysis of religious politics in France, Germany, and England provides some important insights into the possible political roles of religion. First, despite strong evidence of persistent secularization of European mass publics, religion remains a source of possible political mobilization, given the appropriate issue agenda. Second, the interaction of the religious composition of the population and government policies toward religion has profound effects on the politics of immigration and globalization. The case of France illustrates that a de facto religious monopoly, combined with Catholic opposition to the French Revolution and its aftermath, creates a situation in which religious membership occasions anti-Islamic prejudice, but religious activity may have the opposite effect. By contrast, the religious pluralism which characterizes Germany creates opportunities for greater religious tolerance, and the nonassertive state church in Great Britain has served to sever the religious basis of attitudes toward immigration and Islam. Finally, despite twentieth-century trends toward secularization, religious affiliation and participation retain their effects on the party system in all three nations.

# 8

# Religion and Politics in a Secular Europe

## *Cutting against the Grain*

### *J. Christopher Soper and Joel Fetzer*

Religious conflict is not the primary feature of the political life in Western European nations. With the exceptions of Ireland and Northern Ireland, Western Europe has the highest level of secularization in the world, with declining church membership and the retrenchment of religious belief into the private sphere. Secularization has pushed religion toward the margins of political and social life. There has been a loss of religious influence in public institutions, and the state has gradually dispossessed the Church of some of its traditional political functions. Secular forces have, without question, weakened the political impact of religion in Western Europe.

Yet religion is more significant for the politics of Western Europe than classical secularization theory would have predicted. Religion is important for the politics of specific issues, particularly immigration and education. It continues to affect the structure and content of politics for each nation, remaining an important component of party coalitions and in voter choice in virtually every Western European country. Religious influence may have dissipated in recent decades, but it certainly has not disappeared.

Religious disputes are most likely to arise in politics when outside values threaten a religious community. Lipset (1981) argued that status distinctions based on religion are often the basis of the political divisions of a society. Majority religions, often with the support of the state, subject minority religions to various types of social and political discrimination. Minority groups respond by forming movements of religious defense, thereby bringing religious cleavages to the center of political debate (Lipset 1981).

Many of these religious disputes were settled, or at least minimized, in the middle part of this century as European states extended benefits to most "outside" religious groups. As the state began to treat religious groups more or less equally, it minimized the political basis for religious controversies. However, the latter part of the century has brought to religious communities two new challenges that are spilling over into politics: religious pluralism and secularism. The immigration of large numbers of non-Christians in recent decades has both strengthened and refocused the majority-minority cleavage in European politics. Muslims are the largest group of recent immigrants in Europe, and in every state they face prejudice and varying amounts of political discrimination. Muslim rights have become a central political question in every European nation, dividing religionists into majority and minority camps.

Secularism has also reignited religiously based political conflict. Religious groups view secularism as a political and ideological threat to their interests. Secularism undermines the social place of religion in society, and also poses a political challenge to the idea that the state should grant to certain religious communities material or political benefits, as all European states do. Where the state has proposed limiting those privileges, religious groups have mobilized to reaffirm their position in society.

In this study, we will focus our attention on the politics of three countries: France, England, and Germany. These nations represent the three dominant patterns of religious politics that are found in the region. The distinctions that we have in mind are twofold. The first is among Catholic-dominated countries (France), Protestant-dominated countries (England), and religiously mixed countries (Germany). The second distinction is among nations with a tradition of anticlericalism and strict church-state separation (France), those with a state church (England), and those where the state accommodates more than one religious tradition (Germany).

We will begin our analysis by looking at the demographic data on church membership and involvement in the three countries to determine the extent to which secularism has undermined traditional religious practice. We turn next to the institutional context that shapes how religious politics occurs in each nation. The religious makeup of each nation and the resolution of church-state issues centuries ago provide the framework through which religious issues become politicized and resolved in contemporary politics. Our third section focuses on two contemporary issues, immigration and education, which demonstrate both the relevance of religion in politics and the significance of contrasting patterns of church-state relations. The immigration of Muslims and other religious minorities has threatened inherited church-state practices and made religion more relevant, not less, to the political debate in each nation. The conflict over state support for religious schools and religious instruction in state-run schools, on the other hand, exposes most clearly the secular challenges to religion.

## CHURCH MEMBERSHIP IN ENGLAND, FRANCE, AND GERMANY

Each of the countries we examine has its own particular blend of majority and minority religions. Catholics make up about 62% of the population of France, and the nonreligious constitute almost 34%. French sources posit around 5% Muslims, 1% Protestants, and 1% Jews (Frémy and Frémy 1987: 13, 571; Hargreaves 1995: 119).[1]

England presents a more Protestant face, with about 39% of its population identifying with the Church of England and almost 41% nonreligious. Brierley (1997: 2.8, 2.10, 4.3 & 10.12–10.14) estimates roughly 2% of English citizens are free-church Protestants (e.g., Methodists and Baptists), 1% Muslims, .7% Sikhs, .5% Eastern-Orthodox Christians, .3% Hindus, and .2% Jews.

In the former West Germany, Catholics and *Evangelische* (members of the principal Protestant denominations in Germany; generally Lutherans) are evenly balanced at about 39% each. Nonreligious Western Germans constitute almost 15% of the "old Federal states'" population, members of non-Christian religions (primarily Muslims but also including a much smaller Jewish community) about 4%, "other Christians" (e.g., Eastern Orthodox) over 2%, and free-church Protestants (i.e., U.S.-style "evangelicals") a little over 1%. In the former German Democratic Republic, almost 67% of the residents are not religious, 26% are *Evangelische*, a little over 5% Catholic, and roughly 1% free-church Protestants. Other religious communities are vanishingly small (Schafers 1997).

Recent immigration from Africa, Asia, and the Middle East has fueled much of the growth in non-Christian religions in Western Europe. With a foreign-born population of around 9.4%, France is home to large communities of ethnic Algerians, Moroccans, Tunisians, sub-Saharan Africans, and Indochinese. Roughly 6.2% of England's population is "ethnic," originating mainly in India, Pakistan, Nigeria, Hong Kong, and the West Indies. United Germany contains around 8.8% "foreigners," many of whom were nonetheless born on German soil. Principal countries of origin include Turkey, the ex-Yugoslavia, and Italy (Segal 1993: 111; Wollenschläger 1994; Dupâquier 1995: 461; Brierley 1997: 4.4; Schäfers 1997: 25, 98).

Western Europeans have continued to distance themselves from traditional religion (Inglehart 1990: 185–211; Michelat et al. 1991; Ashford and Timms 1992: 33–47; Lambert 1993; Dogan 1995). Data from the

---

[1] Because of rounding and different methods of estimation, not all proportions add up to 100 percent.

last twenty-five years show an unmistakable decline in religious commitment and practice. Comparison of the 1973 European Communities Study with the 1994 Eurobarometer 41.1 shows that the proportion of French who identify with no religion has risen from 10.8% to 33.7% in only twenty-one years. The trends for England and the former West Germany parallel these French results, increasing from 27.4% to 41.0% and from 4.9% to 17.5%, respectively. At the opposite end of the religiosity scale, the percentage of West Europeans claiming to attend church at least weekly declined markedly from 1973 to 1994. While 13.9% of all valid French respondents reported at least weekly church attendance in 1973, only 6.8% could say as much twenty-one years later. The corresponding figures for the other countries are 16.4% versus 10.4% (England) and 21.7% versus 11.5% (West Germany).

Yet recent secularization has not loosened all ties between religion and political behavior (Dalton 1996: 182–5). The relationship between church attendance and partisan affiliation remains as robust now as in the early 1970s. In 1973, according to the European Communities Study, French respondents who attended church more than once a week were 3.9 times more likely to identify with a right-leaning party than were those who never attended church.[2] By 1994, Eurobarometer 41.1 suggests the equivalent figure was still 3.1 times more likely. In England in 1973, more-than-weekly attendees were 1.4 times more likely to identify with such parties, but by 1994 this probability had climbed to 2.0. The odds of very frequent attendees identifying with the right also rose in West Germany, increasing from 2.4 times more likely in 1973 to 2.6 times more likely twenty-one years later.

### INSTITUTIONAL CONTEXT OF RELIGION AND POLITICS

Seymour Martin Lipset and Stein Rokkan showed that religion was a significant factor in the foundation of the European party system through such key events as the Reformation and the French Revolution (Lipset and Rokkan 1967). They argued that in the early twentieth century a freezing of the party system occurred which extended the early impact of religion into the contemporary political era. A useful starting point for our discussion is their hypothesis about the importance of the preconditions for religious politics in Western Europe. We contend that inherited institutions do matter for the emergence of religious politics in Western Europe, and that the key factors for modern politics include the relationship among confessional groups and the legal status between the institutions of the church and the state in each country.

[2] In 1973, "right-leaning parties" included the Reformists and Gaullists (France), the Conservatives, Liberals, and Nationalists (England), and CDU/CSU and Free Democrats (West Germany). For the equivalent list for 1994, see the note to Table 8.1.

There are few nations in the world that have formalized as strict a separation of church and state as has France. French constitutional and legal sources firmly establish that no religion is to receive any legal establishment, that the state must be neutral in regard to religion, and that churches are part of the private sector and may not receive any direct state funding.[3] These legal provisions were accompanied by a head-on attack on the Roman Catholic Church (Basdevant-Gaudemet 1996).

This separation can be traced to the French Revolution which pitted the state against the Catholic Church in a conflict for control over the social and political order. The Church became identified with the traditional order and a revival of the *Ancien Régime*; it opposed the secularization, democratization, and political liberalism of the French Revolution.

The state, on the other hand, became an implacable opponent of the Church and even tried to destroy it with a series of radical reforms in the early years of the Revolution, including changing the calendar to coincide with the start of the French Republic rather than the birth of Jesus and introducing a series of pseudoreligious ceremonies celebrating the ideals of the Revolution. This dechristianizing campaign failed, but the revolutionaries did establish a regime of church-state separation that helped to fuel a lasting animosity between the partisans of the Church and of the Revolution. A politics of antagonism between clerical and anticlerical forces developed that infused French politics for the next two centuries (Frigulietti 1991; Gibson 1991; Meyer and Corvisier 1991).

The state periodically sought to use its mandate of separatism to curb the power of the Church, which in turn allied itself with conservative political forces that defended its social and political position in society. The role of the Church in the modern state became a primary line of cleavage for the political parties that formed in the late nineteenth century; Roman Catholics supported the conservative party, while minority faiths and nonpracticing Catholics supported left-of-center parties. Politics became an arena of conflict where the parties aggressively opposed or defended separatism, or *laïcité*.

The institutional structure of religion and politics in England is quite different. England has an established church, the Church of England, which enjoys certain benefits from the state.[4] The monarch is the head of the church, and the church carries out the coronation and all other

---

[3] The law does not apply in three *départements* in eastern France, Haut-Rhin, Bas-Rhin, and Moselle.

[4] The Church of England is the established church in England only; the Church of Scotland is the established church in Scotland; Wales and Northern Ireland do not have an established church.

state functions where prayer or religious exercises may be required. In addition, the Church of England has reserved seats in the House of Lords, which ensures a formal role for the church in legislation that affects it. Finally, the Church of England enjoys a level of social and political influence that its legal privileges alone cannot explain. Membership in the church is concentrated in the middle and upper classes, and the church has come to have significant representation in the upper echelons of the nation's political, legal, and cultural institutions (Medhurst and Moyser 1988; McClean 1996).

There was a strong rivalry between the Church of England and dissenting churches that spilled over into party politics in the late nineteenth century. The Conservative party defended the established church and attracted most Anglican votes, while the left-of-center Liberal party consolidated the support of religious minorities (Wald 1983). This competition was short-lived, for by the turn of the century, the state had begun to accommodate minority religions in educational policy. It took some time and political effort for dissenting churches to secure equal funding for their schools and win other concessions from the state, but the Church of England gradually came to see its role as working with Roman Catholics, Protestant nonconformists, and even Jews to promote consensual religious values.

At the start of the twentieth century there was, ironically, less political conflict around religion in England, which had an officially established church, than in France, where the state was ostensibly "neutral" toward religion. The left-of-center parties, Liberal and then Labour, opposed the political privileges enjoyed by the Church of England, but they were not secular or anticlerical and they did not advocate a separation of church and state. Consequently, there was no need for the formation of a party of religious defense because the state retained a formal role for it in public life. As Michael Fogarty notes, British churches did not face a direct challenge "in the form of state supremacy over the churches . . . or of sectarian liberalism" (Fogarty 1992: 302). Religion remained a significant factor in party voting for the next several decades, but the political impact of religion waned.

The institutional structure of religion and politics in Germany is a hybrid of the French and English models. The Basic Law affirms that there is to be a separation of church and state; the state may not favor or establish any particular religion. On the other hand, the constitution links the church and state in certain endeavors. The state levies a church tax (8–9 percent of income tax), or *Kirchensteuer*, on members of the recognized Catholic and *Evangelische* churches and of Jewish congregations that provides for a majority of the churches' budget and helps finance many of their social, health, and cultural activities (Robbers

1996). The religious makeup and history of Germany go a long way toward explaining this unusual system.

Germany has been a religiously mixed country since the Peace of Westphalia affirmed the practice of *cuius regio, eius religio* (the religion of the ruler is the religion of the state). Given Germany's multitude of states, principalities, and free cities this norm created areas dominated by one Christian tradition or another. The unification of Germany under Bismarck in 1871 brought these disparate traditions together into one multiconfessional nation–state. The leadership of the new German state was conservative and overwhelmingly Protestant. The state allied itself with the Protestant *Evangelische* churches, and Bismarck launched his famous *Kulturkampf* to establish state supremacy over the Catholic Church, including control over primary education and suppression of the Church's political role. As in France, the political threat from the state led to the formation of a Catholic party of religious defense, the *Zentrum*, which lasted until the end of the Weimar Republic (Spotts 1973). The difference with France was that the political division in Germany was between Catholics and Protestants, rather than Catholics and secular liberals.

The end of the Second World War brought significant constitutional and political changes to the relations between church and state. First, Protestants and Catholics put aside their historical animosity and formed the interconfessional Christian Democratic Union.[5] The party committed itself to promoting nonsectarian Christian values, although it quickly developed into a catchall conservative party advocating policies that benefited both churches. Second, the new West German constitution adopted the principle of church-state separation (first articulated during the Weimar era), which means that the state may not favor any particular religion. On the other hand, the Basic Law formalized the church tax system (Kommers 1997).

Despite the decline in church membership and practice in the three countries, public-opinion surveys confirm that the historical patterns of church-state relations remain significant in contemporary European politics. The data in Table 8.1 on West European partisanship generally support Lipset's theory. In countries with a majority religion, right-leaning parties and the dominant religion often join forces to defend their status-quo privileges and prestige against attacks by religious and other minorities. In such an environment, religious minorities usually support left-leaning, or anti-status-quo parties. French Catholics are substantially more likely to identify with such right-leaning French parties as the RPR

---

[5] In the southern German state (or *Land*) of Bavaria, the Christian-Democrat affiliate is known as the Christian Social Union.

Table 8.1. Religion and Support for Right-Leaning Parties

|  | France | England | W. Germany | E. Germany |
|---|---|---|---|---|
| Catholic |  |  |  | 2.104*** |
|  |  |  |  | (.412) |
| Active | 2.621*** | .093 | 1.269*** |  |
|  | (.359) | (.445) | (.324) |  |
| Nominal | 1.307*** | .957** | .556** |  |
|  | (.223) | (.393) | (.256) |  |
| Main Protestant |  | 1.505*** | .555 | 1.739*** |
| Active |  | (.389) | (.568) | (.471) |
| Nominal |  | 1.020*** | .340 | .914*** |
|  |  | (.224) | (.244) | (.192) |
| Other religion | .407 | .252 | −1.322 |  |
|  | (.498) | (.356) | (1.063) |  |
| N | 822 | 593 | 840 | 776 |

$p < .10$ ** $p < .05$ *** $p < .01$.

*Note*: Estimates are dichotomous logistic-regression coefficients. Standard errors in parentheses. Cases with missing data deleted list-wise. Although only religious variables shown, models also controlled for income, gender, age, employment status, occupation, and education. Base category for religious variables is nonreligious. Active affiliates attend church at least once a week. Main Protestant group is Church of England (England) and *Evangelische* (Germany). Other religion includes, among other affiliations, free-church Protestants in France, England, and western Germany. Right-leaning parties include: all UDF factions, RPR, Centre national des indépendants, Union pour la France, Chasse, Pêche et Nature, and Front National (France); Conservatives and Liberal Democrats (England); CDU/CSU, FDP, National Demokratische Partei, and Republikaner (western Germany); and CDU, FDP, Deutsche Soziale Union, and Republikaner (eastern Germany).
*Source*: 1994 Eurobarometer 41.1.

or UDF.[6] Secular citizens, Jews, Protestants, and Muslims are more likely to support such left-of-center parties as the socialists or communists.

In England, the state's more accommodating treatment of religious minorities appears to have reduced such partisanship effects slightly, yet the underlying majority/minority cleavage remains. Members of the Anglican Church are significantly more likely to support a right-leaning

---

[6] Neofascist, anti-immigrant parties such as the French Front National and the German Republikaner certainly occupy the far right of the political spectrum. Increased religious practice generally *reduces* support for this far-right fringe (Falter 1994: 82–7; Boy and Mayer 1997: 103–8), however. One therefore should not interpret table 8.1 as indicating that belonging to the religious majority boosts support for the far-right as well as for mainstream conservative parties.

party (usually the Tories) whereas "dissenting" Protestants, Jews, practicing Catholics, Muslims, and nonbelievers are more likely to support a left-of-center party (generally Labour).

The German data tell a different story. In the former West Germany, neither Catholics nor *Evangelische* hold a clear majority. The partisan effects of religious affiliation thus become more muddled, arguably reflecting the historic Lipset/Rokkan-type affinities between certain religious groups and their related political parties. Though the CDU/CSU is multiconfessional, its constituency may still mildly reflect its historic links to the pre-WWII Catholic *Zentrum* party. Even in 1994, Catholics were modestly more likely to support a right-leaning German party (largely the Christian Democrats); *Evangelische*, free-church Protestants, and nonbelievers were more likely to support parties of the left (generally the Social Democrats or Greens).

The former German Democratic Republic is arguably the exception that proves the rule. The East German state once suppressed religion, and the clear majority of respondents there today claim no religious affiliation. In this formerly East Bloc region once ruled by the Stalinist SED, the left – not the right – probably represents the political "status-quo." The religious, whether Protestant or Catholic, are more likely to support the right and liberalization, and members of the nonreligious majority are more likely to support the arguably pro-status-quo but *left-of-center* parties (i.e., the SPD and PDS).

In France and England, those who actively practice the majority faith are more likely to support the right than are nominal affiliates. This link between religion and partisanship probably does not result from partisan cues emanating from the pulpit. With the exception of priests who preach against voting for neofascist parties such as the National Front (Tincq 1996), most clergy in these countries avoid explicit public endorsements of a particular party. Rather, we suspect that such phenomena originate more in family socialization or laity-based social learning than in partisan sermons. One might grow up in an upper class, devoutly Anglican, strongly Tory household and thus simultaneously acquire one's life-long religious practices and political views. Alternatively, one might regularly attend an Anglican Church which is disproportionately composed of upper-class Tories. Though one might have joined the church for purely religious reasons, continued interaction with fellow parishioners might push one's politics in a conservative direction.

## CONTEMPORARY ISSUES IN RELIGION AND POLITICS

Two contemporary issues that have infused the political debate surrounding religion are the immigration of non-Christians and the rise of secularism. Both phenomena have posed a serious test for the traditional arrangement between church and state. What makes immigration particularly controversial is that the largest numbers of non-European immigrants are Muslims, whose presence threatens the inherited relationship between the Christian churches and the state in each country. The state does not automatically extend to Muslims and other religious minorities the rights and privileges that the main Christian churches have gradually secured for themselves, and the place of Muslims in Western European societies has become a politically significant issue.[7]

Muslims are the third largest religious group in Germany, for example, but they have yet to attain the public corporation status that is the major requirement of being included within the church tax system. German officials claim that the absence of a coherent organizational form for Muslims makes it difficult for the state to cooperate with them, but this attitude also suggests that church-state law in Germany was written with Catholic and *Evangelische* churches in mind. What this policy means in practical terms is that Muslims have not been fully incorporated into the well-developed system of partnership between church and state (Karakasogula 1996). The state has also been less than accommodating to other religious minorities. The German government has declared that the 30,000-member Church of Scientology is a commercial enterprise and has denied it the rights afforded other religious groups. The state of Bavaria has even refused to hire Scientologists for civil service jobs (Monsma and Soper 1997).

In England, there is no statutory protection against religious discrimination, but it is generally Muslims and other newer religious minorities, rather than Christians, for whom discrimination is an issue (Barker 1987). Biased media images depicting British Muslims as religious fundamentalists do not lessen anti-Islamic prejudice. The attack on Salman Rushdie's *Satanic Verses* by some leaders of the British Islamic community, their failure to dissociate themselves from the Ayatollah's *fatwa*, and subsequent street demonstrations against the book in Bradford only reinforced a cultural stereotype of Muslims as an "illiberal" religious group that could not comfortably fit within British society (Modood 1990).

The political controversy over Muslim rights is stronger still in France, where the right-wing National Front political party has challenged the expansiveness of French law that allows for the naturalization of Islamic

---

[7] Religion and immigration politics also intersect in religiously motivated civil disobedience to West European immigration laws. German clergy have developed a *Kirchenasyl* ("church asylum") network patterned after the U.S. Sanctuary Movement (Just 1993), and French Catholics have also "illegally" sheltered immigrants threatened with deportation (Tincq 1998).

immigrants. The nationalists have attacked *jus soli* – the right to French nationality by being born on French soil – on the ground that even second-generation Muslims immigrants have not sufficiently assimilated French social and cultural norms and cannot possibly be good citizens. The Front has even suggested denaturalizing and deporting North-African-born French nationals in order to prevent France from becoming "an Islamic Republic" and to protect the French "species" from "cross-breeding." Mainstream conservative parties, recognizing the political appeal of the National Front, have called for raising barriers to naturalization and cracking down on "clandestine immigration" (Brubaker 1992; Simmons 1996).

Educational policy exposes the degree of French hostility toward Islamic immigrants. Muslims in France make up close to 10 percent of the school population, but there are no state-financed Islamic schools, and the state has been implacable in its opposition to supporting them. Public schools have often been unwilling to accommodate Islamic cultural practices. The famous *affaire des foulards* exemplified the French attitude toward Muslim immigrants. In September of 1989 the principal of a public high school in Creil suspended three Muslim girls because they insisted on wearing the chador, or Muslim headscarf, in class. The principal, Martinique-native Ernest Chenière, claimed that wearing the chador violated the French laws on *laïcité* that required a formal separation of the state from religion. "I completely support the separatist ideal," he affirmed. "It's *laïcité* that has allowed the public school to be the melting pot in which, through the alchemy of education, differences vanish so the nation can emerge" (Cody 1989; Gonod 1989; Gaspard and Khosrokhavar 1995; Prost 1998).[8]

The debate that ensued also illustrates how the institutional context of religious politics in France exacerbated the conflict. French supporters of the ban could make a "principled" appeal to the separationist impulses of the Constitution to support their position, an argument that left-wing secularists shared with right-wing nationalists. On the left, Socialist politician Kofi Yamgnane maintained that "Islam must accept the Republican pact. That is to say, accept the separation of church and state [and] renounce . . . the wearing of headscarves in school." For their part, the National Front saw the incident less about "neutrality in the school" than about "the colonization of France" by Muslims. Yet other right-wing opponents of immigration, such as former Interior Minister Charles Pasqua, viewed the chador as a "mark of difference" which is "not acceptable" in the "secular school."

---

[8] The year before the scarf affair, the same headmaster had also made sure that several Jewish students in the school attended classes during *Shabbat*.

For Muslims, however, *laïcité* is not ideologically neutral, but is used by the state to deny them recognition as a religious group and to assimilate them into irreligious values. As then Minister of Education Lionel Jospin, himself a Protestant, argued during the scarf affair, "*laïcite* must not appear to be another form of fundamentalism." As in the past, the state's commitment to a "separation" of church and state has not minimized the politicization of religious disputes, but actually encouraged it. The state's secularist ideology does not easily accommodate religious groups, whether they are Catholic, Jewish, or Muslim, that wish to retain their distinctive religious and cultural identity (Halstead 1993).

Educational policy toward Muslims has not been as discriminatory in England or Germany as it has been in France (Rex 1994). Since 1944, the government in England has funded Protestant, Catholic, and Jewish schools. For the past thirteen years, however, it refused to finance Muslim schools despite consistent appeals from Islamic authorities. The government claimed that separate Islamic schools threatened the comprehensive state school model with its liberal assumptions about the role of education and religion in a democracy. Muslims who wanted to retain their distinctive religious and cultural values questioned the assimilationist purpose of the current system (Ashraf 1988). In 1997, however, the newly elected Labour government finally approved applications for state financing of two Muslim schools.

The inherited institutional structures in Germany and England have also made it easier than in France to accommodate religious minorities on such issues as religious dress in school and the content of religious education. While almost all of the religion classes in the German public schools are in the Catholic or *Evangelische* traditions, there has been little principled opposition by state authorities to incorporating Muslim instruction in public schools. In an exhaustive study of a school system in one large English city, James Beckford found that Hindus, Muslims, and Sikhs were able to bring their distinctive religious values to bear on debates over educational policy (Beckford 1998).

Survey data confirm that the different state responses toward Islamic immigration in these countries have had a spillover effect on politics. Where the most prominent groups of immigrants belong to religions other than that of the native-born religious majority, Lipset's theory might suggest that members of the dominant religion will disproportionately oppose immigration (Fetzer 1998).

The data in Table 8.2 partly support this prediction. In France, Catholics are more likely to endorse nativism than are Protestants, Jews, or the nonreligious. In England, religious affiliation does not influence attitudes on immigration, probably because the English state has been

Table 8.2. Religion and Opposition to Immigration

|  | France | England | W. Germany | E. Germany |
|---|---|---|---|---|
| Catholic |  |  |  | −.139 |
|  |  |  |  | (.204) |
| Active | .426*** | .174 | −.153 |  |
|  | (.158) | (.230) | (.156) |  |
| Nominal | .714*** | −.064 | .115 |  |
|  | (.083) | (.197) | (.115) |  |
| Main Protestant |  | −.008 | −.685** | −.305 |
| Active |  | (.183) | (.289) | (.253) |
| Nominal |  | .092 | .162 | −.216** |
|  |  | (.107) | (.106) | (.092) |
| Other religion | .072 | −.070 | −.432 |  |
|  | (.185) | (.165) | (.289) |  |
| N | 827 | 578 | 854 | 786 |
| $R^2$ | .203 | .246 | .181 | .095 |

$p < .10$ ** $p < .05$ *** $p < .01$.

*Note*: Estimates are ordinary least-squares coefficients. Standard errors in parentheses. Cases with missing data deleted list-wise. Although only religious variables shown, models also controlled for income, gender, age, employment status, occupation, and education. Base category for religious variables is nonreligious. Active affiliates attend church at least once a week. Main Protestant group is Church of England (England) and *Evangelische* (Germany). Other religion includes, among other affiliations, free-church Protestants in France, England, and western Germany. Opposition to immigration measured by items on whether "too many" foreigners live in the given country and whether their rights should be restricted or extended. Dependent variable ranges from 2 to 6.

*Source*: 1994 Eurobarometer 41.1.

more accommodating to religious minorities than has the French government. In West Germany, religious differences are also small, and in East Germany only the nominally *Evangelische* are distinctively opposed to immigration. Whether the East German effect for *Evangelische* confirms or disconfirms Lipset's theory may depend on whether such East German Protestants view themselves as a religious minority in a predominantly secular region or as the new religious majority in United Germany.

Among French Catholics and German *Evangelische*, those who attend church at least once a week are significantly less nativist. Since right-leaning political parties have usually opposed immigration, this finding may appear paradoxical when compared to the effect of church attendance on partisanship (see Table 8.1). We would argue, however, that Western Europeans' views on immigration reflect a different process of attitude formation from that of partisanship. Family socialization is a major source of party loyalties, but we think it is less likely that families influence immigration-related attitudes. Even today, European parents are probably much less likely to instill their immigration-related views in their children than American parents of the 1950s were to transmit their racial attitudes to their offspring.

Many religious elites in these three countries do not hesitate to speak out against xenophobia and religious intolerance (Associated Press 1984; Just 1990: 1–5; Tincq 1996). These cues from the pulpit, we would submit, produce the pro-immigration effect of church attendance.[9] Nominal affiliates are not exposed to these pro-tolerance cues, and may see their religion as merely cultural (Allport 1979: 446–57). A nominal French Catholic or German Lutheran might treat Christianity not as a rationale for Sermon-on-the-Mount-style humanitarianism but more as an ethno-cultural identity which she or he must defend, Crusader-like, against the Muslim, Middle Eastern "invaders." Or as William James (1902: 331) remarked, "Piety is the mask, the inner force is tribal instinct."

Methodological considerations make any cross-national findings about the causes of opposition to Islam (see Table 8.3) tentative at best.[10] The French data seem to confirm Lipset's theory about religious minorities. Nominal Catholics are particularly hostile to Islam and to permitting mosques in France. The nonreligious, members of minority faiths, and active Catholics are less opposed to Islam. As religious minorities themselves, Jews, Protestants, Buddhists, and the nonreligious have less of a stake in maintaining the supremacy of Catholicism in France. Active French Catholics, meanwhile, may be absorbing protolerance cues from the Church hierarchy.

---

[9] As Jelen and Wilcox (1998) suggest, such cues might prove even more influential if they were to come from clergy belonging to a religious minority.

[10] Ideally, we would have liked to have had a three-country survey asking whether Islamic practices or religious instruction should be permitted in state-funded schools. Unfortunately, however, few European data measuring attitudes toward Islam exist. After repeated inquiries at data archives and polling firms in all three countries, the best measures we found were: an item about one's general feelings toward Islam and a question on whether it was "normal" for Muslims in France to have their own mosques (France; 1995 SOFRES French National Election Study); an item on whether the respondent was "prejudiced" against "Muslim people" (England; 1993–4 Fourth National Survey of Ethnic Minorities); and a question about whether Islam should be taught in state schools just as Christianity currently is (Germany; 1996 ALLBUS). Obviously, these measures of "opposition to Islam" are only very roughly equivalent, making rigorous cross-national comparisons problematic.

### Table 8.3. Religion and Opposition to Islam

| | France | England | W. Germany | E. Germany |
|---|---|---|---|---|
| Catholic | | | | −.893 |
| | | | | (.589) |
| Active | −.148 | −.282 | .415 | |
| | (.122) | (.906) | (.283) | |
| Nominal | .271*** | −.650 | .259 | |
| | (.070) | (.890) | (.216) | |
| Mainline Protestant | | | | −.120 |
| | | | | (.302) |
| Active | | −.813 | .813* | |
| | | (.919) | (.489) | |
| Nominal | | −.101 | .461** | |
| | | (.870) | (.214) | |
| Free-Church Protestant | −.101 | | 1.052* | |
| | (.186) | | (.591) | |
| Active | | −.569 | | |
| | | (.954) | | |
| Nominal | | .279 | | |
| | | (.891) | | |
| Other Christian | | −1.171 | 1.038** | |
| | | (.986) | (.460) | |
| Jewish | −.909** | | | |
| | (.441) | | | |
| Muslim | −2.470*** | | | |
| | (.297) | | | |
| Other religion | −.456* | −.744 | −1.608*** | |
| | (.241) | (1.116) | (.519) | |
| N | 3,165 | 1,596 | 1,305 | 299 |
| R² | .114 | | | |

* *p* < .10 ** *p* < .05 *** *p* < .01.
*Note*: Estimates are ordinary least-squares coefficients for France, otherwise dichotomous logit coefficients. Standard errors in parentheses. Cases with missing data deleted list-wise. Although only religious variables shown, models also controlled for income, gender, age, employment status, occupation, and education. Base category for religious variables is nonreligious. Active affiliates attend church at least once a week. Main Protestant group is Church of England (England) and *Evangelische* (Germany). Other religion category includes respondents who have some religious affiliation but are not included in the groupings represented by the other religious regressors for a given country (e.g., Hindus in France). Only white respondents included in English sample. Measures of opposition to Islam vary and might not be strictly comparable across countries; see text for details. Dependent variables range from 2 to 8 for France, 0 to 1 elsewhere.
*Sources*: 1995 SOFRES French National Election Study (France), 1993–4 Fourth National Survey of Ethnic Minorities (England), and 1996 ALLBUS (Germany).

Religious differences do not help explain English attitudes toward Islam. This may reflect the English state's greater willingness to accommodate religious minorities.[11]

The predominantly nonreligious eastern German sample probably does not permit useful results for the Islam question.[12] In West Germany, however, Catholics, the nonreligious, and members of "other" religious faiths are less likely to oppose the teaching of Islam in public schools. *Evangelische* (especially the most religiously active), free-church Protestants, and "other Christians" are more likely to oppose teaching Islam.

Secularism poses a different kind of challenge to religious groups, but it can still inspire political mobilization among religionists in ways consistent with Lipset's theory. In each of the three countries religious groups have fought the imposition of a "secular" educational philosophy that would exclude or minimize religion from the state-run school, and they have argued against efforts to restrict state support for private, religious schools.

The French public school system has often been the locus for this kind of conflict between the state and the Catholic Church. The French state secularized public education in the early part of the twentieth century to inculcate common values in all of its citizens. Public schools could offer moral, but not religious education, and the only legitimate values for the public schools were those shared by the entire nation.

The intent of public education was the assimilation of separate religious, ethnic, and linguistic communities, many of them recent immigrants. The Catholic Church responded to this threat in a predictable way: it created private schools under Catholic control that instilled a religious view of the world to its adherents. A primary reason for the church-state conflict on education, therefore, was that the Church perceived the state's commitment to a "secular" education as a direct challenge to religion (Berger 1985).

Despite the French government's pledge to secularize education, the state and the Church reached a compromise that allowed state funds to go directly to Catholic schools in return for a commitment by those schools to cover the national syllabus. At present, 13 percent of primary

[11] Alternatively, nonrandom measurement error in the dependent variable might mask any religious anti-Islamic sentiment. Asking respondents how "prejudiced" they are might not constitute an accurate measure of this sensitive, quasiracial attitude.

[12] The results for eastern Germany are something of a wash because most respondents are opposed to all religious instruction in state schools and hence were removed from the analysis. (The question asks whether Islam and Christianity, Christianity, or no religion at all should be taught.) Achieving statistical significance becomes difficult with the resulting small sample (299 respondents). At any rate, neither being Catholic nor being *Evangelische* had any statistically significant effect in the former DDR.

school and 20 percent of secondary school children are educated in state-funded private schools. This arrangement reduced, but did not eliminate the conflict over education. While church and state reached an agreement on education, there remained tension between the two institutions. In 1984, the Socialist Mauroy government proposed to tighten state supervision over private schools. In the face of this "secular" challenge, and fearing a loss over the content of private education, Catholics helped mobilize the largest mass protests against the government since 1968. The government eventually retreated in defeat.[13]

The church-state issue that stirred up the most controversy in Germany in recent years concerned a Bavarian law that required every public-school classroom to display a crucifix (Caygill and Scott 1996). In 1995 the Constitutional Court ruled that if any student objected to having a crucifix in the classroom, it would have to be removed. The major religious groups opposed the decision, as did Chancellor Kohl and other political leaders. The Court did not threaten the partnership between church and state on education in Germany, however. The Basic Law states that religious instruction shall be a part of the curriculum in state-run schools. Religious bodies control the content of what is taught in those courses, and parents select for their children the type of instruction that they are to receive. Religious instruction must be voluntary, however. The Court ruled that requiring a crucifix in every classroom violated the principle of state neutrality toward religion, but the justices did not threaten the practice of voluntary religious instruction and worship in state-run schools.

The unification of Germany in 1990 also brought some political tension to church-state issues. Residents of the former German Democratic Republic, who are far less likely than their West German counterparts to be religious, have suddenly been subjected to a church tax, religion in public schools, and a more conservative policy on abortion (Mushaben 1997). There has been an increase in formal church leaving in East Germany, which is the only way to avoid paying the church tax, and the Party of Democratic Socialism, the old East-German Communist party, has come out against the church tax system. Neither of the nation's two largest parties – the CDU/CSU and SPD – opposes it, however, and the church tax has not become a major political issue.

In England, the Education Reform Act of 1988 reaffirmed the state's commitment to having religion as a part of the daily curriculum of state-supported schools. In the Act, the government included requirements for

---

[13] Of course, as Gaspard and Khosrokhvar note (1995: 186–7) some secularist French parents send their children to private Catholic schools for the allegedly superior academics, not for the religious instruction.

religious instruction and a daily act of collective worship, both of which were to "reflect the fact that the religious traditions in Great Britain are in the main Christian while taking account of the teaching and practice of the other principal religions represented in Great Britain" (Gower 1990). The Act demonstrated that Christian religious groups have significant political power when they form a political coalition to defend their common interests.

The newly elected Labour government discovered this when it proposed in 1997 to increase the state's role over admissions and curriculum in the publicly funded church schools. Thirty-five percent of all primary schools and 16 percent of secondary schools are church-related, and they receive varying levels of state support. The Labour government proposed tightening its regulation of these religious schools, but it quietly backed away from its plan when Catholic, Anglican, and Methodist church leaders strongly opposed the new regulations (Judd 1997).

There is no mystery why religious groups with a large stake in education fought the government's proposal; what is surprising is that Muslims have not favored a system of church-state separation on education or most other religious-political issues. As Tariq Modood notes: "the openness of the Anglican establishment to other denominations and faiths seeking public space, and the fact that its very existence is an ongoing acknowledgment of the public character of religion are reasons why it is less intimidating to the minority faiths than a triumphal secularism" (Modood 1994: 72).

Modood's comment indicates that a multiconfessional party of religious defense could form in Britain around issues of common interest to religionists. If religious groups perceive secularism as a political threat they may work together to preserve a public political role for religion and religiously based values in public policy. This is most likely to occur on such lifestyle issues as abortion, education, and pornography. Ironically, the secular effort to "privatize" religious faith and practice could create the conditions necessary for political cooperation among confessional groups in nations where they have historically been divided.

## CONCLUSION: THE FUTURE OF RELIGION AND POLITICS IN WESTERN EUROPE

Our findings suggest that religion will continue to have a paradoxical influence in Western Europe. On the one hand, there is no reason to believe that the historically dominant Christian churches will stem the secular tide; involvement in mainstream religion has declined significantly. It is also unlikely that the churches will recover the political power and cultural prominence that they once enjoyed; secularization has spurred a separation of religion from the state in Western Europe and politically marginalized the churches.

On the other hand, religion remains important in political party coalitions in ways that secularization theory could not have predicted, and political-religious conflicts have not disappeared from contemporary politics. This is particularly true for immigration. Despite the admittedly substantial Muslim immigration into Western Europe, we think the fear that Europe will become an "Islamic Republic" where non-Muslims are reduced to modern-day *dhimmitude* is based more on hysteria than fact (see Ye'or 1995). The Muslim proportion of the West European population remains less than 5%. Most second- and third-generation "Muslim" immigrants, moreover, are far from orthodox, practicing Muslims (Hargreaves 1995: 119–22; Tribalat 1995: 16–98). In France, for example, most will probably become nonbelievers or merely nominal Muslims just as most "old-stock" French are either nonreligious or only nominally Catholic.

A more likely possibility than an Islamic takeover is that continued west European repression of its Muslim minorities, often for religious reasons, will radicalize a few members of the younger generations the way continued U.S. repression of young working-class African Americans has persuaded some of them to adopt violence (Tribalat 1995: 98). Such a scenario seems most plausible in France, where structural racism and religious hatred have produced American-style ghettoes and riots. The short and tragic life of Khaled Kelkal provides a case study of how societal rejection of Muslim immigrants can lead to lethal retaliation. An Algerian immigrant who grew up in the slums of Lyon, Kelkal reacted to French xenophobia by embracing fundamentalist Islam, participating in an insurrection, and blowing up a Parisian commuter train. After a nation-wide manhunt, French paratroopers shot him to death in September of 1995 (Loch 1995; Gattegno and Inciyan 1996).

The experience of the three countries also suggests that religion will remain politically important whenever the state tries to remove the benefits enjoyed by the churches, particularly in education. Churches recognize the importance of using the schools to socialize children into the faith, and will therefore aggressively fight any effort to reduce state funding for church schools or to increase government regulation of them. Finally, it is possible, but far from certain, that attempts by the state to privatize faith, or actively to remove it from the public square on social and moral issues of importance to religious groups, will lead to the formation of a multiconfessional party, or coalition, of religious defense.

When political disputes over religion arise, they will inevitably be played out through church-state patterns inherited from the past. In France, this history will encourage a politics of hostility as the state's commitment to "secularism" becomes a key point of departure for those who wish to oppose the introduction of Islamic cultural practices into public institutions, or who seek to overturn the state's commitment to funding Catholic schools. In England and Germany, by contrast, the state has preserved more of a policy role for the churches and those same issues have been organized more through a model of political accommodation and compromise that has minimized the political conflict over religious issues.

## REFERENCES

Allport, Gordon W. 1979. *The Nature of Prejudice.* 25th Anniversary Edition. Reading, MA: Addison-Wesley.

Ashford, Sheena, and Noel Timms. 1992. *What Europe Thinks: A Study of Western European Values.* Aldershot, UK: Dartmouth.

Ashraf, Syed Ali. 1988. "A View of Education – An Islamic Perspective." In Bernadette O'Keeffe (ed.). *Schools for Tomorrow: Building Walls or Building Bridges.* London: The Falmer Press.

Associated Press. 1984. "Church Reports Fault Government Racial Policies." Wire-service report. Dateline London. February 3.

Barker, Eileen. 1987. "The British Right to Discriminate." In Thomas Robbins and Roland Roberston (eds.). *Church-State Relations: Tensions and Transitions.* New Brunswick, NJ: Transaction Books.

Basdevant-Gaudemet, Brigitte. 1996. "State and Church in France." In Gerhard Robbers (ed.). *State and Church in the European Union.* Baden-Baden: Nomos Verlagsgesellschaft.

Beckford, James A. 1998. "Three Paradoxes in the Relations Between Religion and Politics in an English City." *Review of Religious Research* 39: 344–59.

Berger, Suzanne. 1985. "Religious Transformation and the Future of Politics." *European Sociological Review* 1: 23–45.

Boy, Daniel, and Nonna Mayer. 1997. *L'électeur a ses raisons.* Paris: Presses de Sciences Po.

Brierley, Peter. 1997. *UK Christian Handbook: Religious Trends 1998/99 No. 1.* London: Christian Research.

Brubaker, Roger. 1992. *Citizenship and Nationhood in France and Germany.* Cambridge, MA: Harvard University Press.

Caygill, Howard and Alan Scott. 1996. "The Basic Law versus the Basic Norm? The Case of the Bavarian Crucifix Order." *Political Studies* 44: 505–16.

Cody, Edward. 1989. "France Rules on Moslem Scarf Issue: Local Authorities to be Allowed to Decide on Case-by-Case Basis." *Washington Post*, November 28: A29

Dalton, Russell J. 1996. *Citizen Politics: Public Opinion and Political Parties in Advanced Western Democracies.* 2nd ed. Chatham, NJ: Chatham House.

De Galembert, Claire. 1997. "L'état et les religions des immigrés en France et en Allemagne." In Bernard Falga, Catherine Wihtol de Wenden, and Claus

Leggewie (eds.). *Au miroir de l'autre: De l'immigration à l'intégration en France et en Allemagne*. Paris: Éditions du Cerf.

Dogan, Mattei. 1995. "The decline of religious beliefs in Western Europe." *International Social Science Journal* 47: 405–17.

Dupâquier, Jacques. 1995. *Histoire de la population française, 4: De 1914 à nos jours*. Paris: Presses Universitaires de France.

Falter, Jürgen W. 1994. *Wer wählt rechts? Die Wähler und Anhänger rechtsextremistischer Parteien im vereinigten Deutschland*. Munich: Beck.

Fetzer, Joel S. 1998. "Religious Minorities and Support for Immigrant Rights in the United States, France, and Germany." *Journal for the Scientific Study of Religion* 37: 41–9.

Fogarty, Michael. 1992. "The Churches and Public Policy in Britain." *The Political Quarterly* 63 (July–September): 301–16

Frémy, Dominique, and Michèle Frémy. 1987. *Quid 1988*. Paris: Robert Laffont.

Frigulietti, James. 1991. "Gilbert Romme and the Making of the French Republican Calendar." In David G. Troyanksky, Alfred Cismaru, and Norwood Andrews (eds.). *The French Revolution in Culture and Society*. Westport, CT: Greenwood Press.

Gaspard, Françoise and Farhad Khosrokhavar. 1995. *Le foulard et la République*. Paris: La Découverte.

Gattegno, Hervé, and Erich Inciyan. 1996. "La piste islamiste est privilégiée après l'attentat du RER Port-Royal." *Le Monde*, December 5.

Gibson, Ralph. 1991. "Why Republicans and Catholics Can't Stand Each Other in the Nineteenth Century." In Frank Tallet and Nickolas Atkin (eds.). *Religion and Politics in France Since 1789*. London: The Hambledon Press.

Gonod, Michel. 1989. "La riposte: Pourquoi ce principal de collège s'oppose à l'offensive des religieux." *Paris-Match*, November 9: 60–3.

Gower, Ralph. 1990. *Religious Education at the Primary Stage*. Oxford: Lion Educational Trust.

Halstead, Mark. 1993. "Educating Muslim Minorities: Some Western European Approaches." In Witold Tulasiewicz and Cho-Yee To (ed.). *World Religions and Educational Practices*. London: Cassell.

Hargreaves, Alec G. 1995. *Immigration, 'Race' and Ethnicity in Contemporary France*. London: Routledge.

Inglehart, Ronald. 1990. *Culture Shift in Advanced Industrial Society*. Princeton: Princeton University Press.

James, William. 1902. *The Varieties of Religious Experience: A Study in Human Nature*. New York: Random House.

Jelen, Ted G., and Clyde Wilcox. 1998. "Context and Conscience: The Catholic Church as an Agent of Political Socialization in Western Europe." *Journal for the Scientific Study of Religion* 37: 28–40.

Judd, Judith. 1997. "Bishops Force Retreat over Church Schools." *The Independent*, October 23, 1997: 10.

Just, Wolf-Dieter. 1990. *Kirchen und Ausländerpolitik seit 1871: Theologische Voraussetzungen und Begründungen des Engagements*. Mülheim: Evangelische Akademie Mülheim/Ruhr.

1993 (ed.). *Asyl von unten: Kirchenasyl und ziviler Ungehorsam – Ein Ratgeber.* Reinbek bei Hamburg: Rowohlt.

Karakasoglu, Yasemin. 1996. "Turkish Cultural Orientations in Germany and the Role of Islam." In David Horrocks and Eva Kolinsky (eds.). *Turkish Culture in German Society Today.* Providence, RI: Berghahn.

Kommers, Donald P. 1997. *The Constitutional Jurisprudence of the Federal Republic of Germany,* 2nd ed. Durham, NC: Duke University Press.

Lambert, Yves. 1993. "Ages, générations et christianisme en France et en Europe." *Revue française de sociologie* 34: 525–55.

Lipset, Seymour Martin. 1981. *Political Man: The Social Bases of Politics,* Expanded Edition. Baltimore: Johns Hopkins University Press.

Lipset, Seymour Martin, and Stein Rokkan. 1967. "Cleavage Structures, Party Systems and Voter Alignments." In Seymour Martin Lipset and Stein Rokkan (eds.). *Party Structures and Voter Alignments.* New York: The Free Press.

Loch, Dietmar. 1995. "Moi, Khaled Kelkal." *Le Monde,* October 7, pp. 10–12.

McClean, David. 1996. "State and Church in the United Kingdom." In Gerhard Robbers (ed.). *State and Church in the European Union.* Baden-Baden: Nomos Verlagsgesellschaft.

Medhurst, Kenneth and George Moyser 1988. *Church and Politics in a Secular Age.* Oxford: Clarendon Press.

Meyer, Jean, and Andre Corvisier. 1991. *La Révolution française.* Paris: Presses Universitaires de France.

Michelat, Guy, Julien Potel, Jacques Sutter, and Jacques Maître. 1991. *Les Français sont-ils encore catholiques? Analyse d'un sondage d'opinion.* Paris: Les Éditions du Cerf.

Modood, Tariq. 1990. "British Muslims and the Rushdie Affair." *The Political Quarterly* (61): 143–60.

1994. "Establishment, Multiculturalism and British Citizenship." *The Political Quarterly* 65: 53–73.

Monsma, Stephen V., and J. Christopher Soper. 1997. *The Challenge of Pluralism: Church and State in Five Western Democracies.* Lanham, MD: Rowman and Littlefield Press.

Mushaben, Joyce Marie. 1997. "Concession or Compromise: The Politics of Abortion in United Germany." *German Politics* 6: 70–88.

Prost, Antoine, 1998. "Immigration, Particularism and Republican Education." *French Politics and Society* 16: 13–22.

Rex, John. 1994. "The Political Sociology of Multiculturalism and the Place of Muslims in West European Societies." *Social Compass* 41: 79–92.

Robbers, Gerhard. 1996. "State and Church in Germany." In Gerhard Robbers (ed.). *State and Church in the European Union.* Baden-Baden: Nomos Verlagsgesellschaft.

Schäfers, Bernhard. 1997. *Politischer Atlas Deutschland: Gesellschaft, Wirtschaft, Staat.* Bonn: Dietz.

Segal, Aaron. 1993. *An Atlas of International Migration.* London: Hans Zell.

Simmons, Harvey G. *The French National Front: The Extremist Challenge to Democracy.* 1996. Boulder, CO: Westview Press.

Spotts, Frederick. 1973. *The Churches and Politics in Germany*. Middletown, CT: Wesleyan University Press.

Tincq, Henri. 1996. "Le cardinal Lustiger dénonce le danger des discours de M. Le Pen." *Le Monde*, September 19.

———. 1998. "Débat entre prophétiques et pragmatiques parmi les évêques." *Le Monde*, April 10.

Tribalat, Michèle. 1995. *Faire France: Une enquête sur les immigrés et leurs enfants*. Paris: La Découverte.

Wald, Kenneth D. 1983. *Crosses on the Ballot*. Princeton: Princeton University Press.

Wollenschläger, Michael. 1994. "Migrationspolitik und Zuwanderungsrecht, Illegalität und Legalisierung, Integration und Staatsangehörigkeitsrecht." In Klaus J. Bade (ed.). *Das Manifest der 60: Deutschland und die Einwanderung*. Munich: Beck.

Ye'or, Bat. 1985. *The Dhimmi: Jews and Christians Under Islam*. Rutherford, NJ: Farleigh Dickinson University Press.

Anthony Gill's analysis of religious politics in South America brings together several themes raised in earlier chapters. Like their religious antecedents on the Iberian peninsula, national Catholic churches in South America have traditionally attempted to exercise a priestly function of regime legitimation, and have consequently been associated with discredited, anti-democratic regimes. Unlike the Iberian churches, however, South American Catholic elites were instrumental in affecting the transformation of many regimes into their contemporary democratic forms. In a manner analogous to the Catholic Church in Poland, the prophetic success of South American churches appears to have brought about conditions that occasioned the Church's demise as a dominant religious and political actor. Unlike the Polish case, however, the public space vacated by a formerly hegemonic Catholicism was filled by a specifically religious alternative: evangelical Protestantism. Gill suggests that the resulting religious competition has revitalized the religious component of South American Catholicism, while moderating its political agenda. Further, the rise in aggregate religious participation in the region may provide an increase in "social capital," which in turn might have a positive impact on democratic consolidation.

# 9

# Religion and Democracy in South America

## Challenges and Opportunities

### Anthony Gill

## INTRODUCTION[1]

From the 1960s through the early 1980s, the Latin American Catholic Church earned a reputation as a dynamic, progressive institution that stood in courageous opposition to repressive military regimes and socio-economic injustice. Although scholars have exaggerated the extensiveness of progressive Catholicism,[2] Catholic clergy and lay agents played an important but not decisive role in restoring democratic rule to the South American continent.[3] Catholic bishops in Brazil and Chile steadfastly criticized the practices and raison d'être of dictatorships while helping to mediate the reinstatement of civilian rule (Fleet and Smith 1997; Cavendish 1995; Mainwaring 1986). In other countries – even those with pro-authoritarian episcopacies such as Argentina – grassroots Catholic communities kept pressure on dictators by exposing human rights abuses, calling attention to the needs of the poor and sheltering political dissidents (cf. Keogh 1990).[4] For their part, grassroots religious

---

[1] Helpful comments on this chapter were provided by Margaret Crahan, Joel Fetzer, Anne Hallum, Ted Jelen, and Clyde Wilcox. Franklin Donahoe provided excellent and timely research assistance. I retain responsibility for all errors.

[2] Daudelin and Hewitt (1995) argue that scholars in the 1970s and 1980s were overly optimistic in their assessments of progressive Catholicism. Similarly, Levine asserts that "[e]xcessive attention has gone to extreme cases, such as El Salvador or Nicaragua" (1995, 21) while ignoring the continuation of "traditional" status quo tendencies even within the seemingly radical Nicaraguan church (cf. Levine 1990). See Gill (1994) for a similar argument.

[3] For an excellent discussion of the causes of political liberalization in Latin America, consult Haggard and Kaufman (1995).

[4] Even in Colombia and Venezuela, two countries that avoided the authoritarian wave of the 1960s and 1970s, there was moderate pressure from grassroots Catholic activists to open the political process to previously excluded sectors of the population, namely the poor and indigenous communities (Levine 1992).

communities helped pave the way for greater levels of popular participation in government following the restoration of civilian rule.

The end to authoritarian rule during the 1980s dramatically changed
the sociopolitical landscape. Catholic clergy and lay activists now face
new challenges to the traditional role of religion in society, and enjoy
increased opportunities for strengthening democratic civil society. The
biggest challenge facing the Catholic Church in the new democratic era
is the political, social and religious pluralism that has accompanied
increased political liberalization. For most of its history, the Catholic
Church has been the hegemonic cultural institution in the region. Today
Church officials find themselves in public competition with a variety of
interest groups that do not necessarily share their policy preferences.

The rapid increase in religious pluralism may also greatly affect the
politics of the region. Evangelical Protestants have demonstrated increasing political activism as their percentage of the population has grown
(Miguéz Bonino 1999).[5] In fact, scholars now recognize that *evangélicos*,
as they are called in Latin America, acted as decisive swing voters during
recent presidential elections in Peru and Colombia. *Evangélicos* are also
making their presence felt by winning political offices at the local and
national levels. The Church's struggle to remain socially influential in
this rapidly changing environment has shaped how bishops, clergy and
lay activists behave in the political arena.

The Catholic Church has responded to this new religious pluralism
in two ways. First, it has sought to better meet the spiritual needs of
nominal Catholics, to prevent their conversion to Protestantism. Second,
it has promoted a variety of legislation that would make it more difficult for evangelical Protestants to convert Catholics. This has required
the Church to act more as a specialized interest group, and in doing so
Church leaders have sought to unify the voice of the Catholic Church
behind a more moderate political message.

This does not mean that Church officials have stopped speaking out
on general issues of moral relevance to Catholicism, such as poverty and
divorce, or on political issues such as human rights. Rather it implies

---

[5] Evangelical Protestantism is a broad-based term that encompasses a variety of different
organizations and theologies. I use this term for rhetorical simplicity recognizing the var-
iegated nature of the movements. European and African spiritist movements have also
made significant inroads in Brazil, often blending with folk Catholicism to form syncretic
religions. When discussing non-Catholic religious movements, this chapter will concentrate on Protestant movements and use the terms "Protestant" and "*evangélico*" to refer
broadly to Pentecostals, Mormons, Jehovah's Witnesses, and nondenominational Protestant churches. In Latin America, the term "*evangélico*" is commonly used as a descrip-
tive label for all these groups. On a related rhetorical issue, Church (capital C) will refer
here to the Roman Catholic Church, while church (small c) designates any Christian
religious organization.

only that the Catholic hierarchy will be more strategically cautious in their political activity in order to promote the missionary (and doctrinal) goals of Catholicism. To counter Catholic moves aimed at limiting religious competition, evangelical Protestant groups have become more involved in politics in an effort to defend their institutional interests. Church-state relations and religious liberty have therefore emerged as hotly contested political issues following the return of democracy.

Scholars have offered widely different predictions about the impact of the growing evangelical presence in the region. Martin (1990) foresees a "Latin Protestant ethic" (à la Max Weber) that will promote and stabilize liberal democratic capitalism. Deiros (1992) asserts that evangelical Protestantism produces greater political apathy, and more political conservatism. There is little evidence to support either claim. Survey data show that South American Protestants and Catholics share roughly similar political attitudes, controlling for class and other demographic variables, though Catholics are slightly more politically active. Regular churchgoers, both Catholic and Protestant, hold different political attitudes from nonchurchgoers. As increasing religious competition provides incentives for religious institutions to pay closer attention to membership, the ranks of regular churchgoers should swell. Given the relationship between such active participation and the influence spiritual values play in social behavior, religion will shape political attitudes *in the long run*.

Moreover, the community skill and norms of trust and compromise necessary for a well-functioning democracy will emanate from ongoing personal interactions in thriving religious communities, both Catholic *and* Protestant. Over time, increased religious participation helps lay the foundation for a strong civil society. To illustrate these points, I use evidence culled mostly from the experiences of Argentina, Brazil, and Chile with references to other South American countries where appropriate.

## HISTORICAL AND SOCIAL BACKGROUND

Since the Iberian Conquest of South America in the sixteenth century, the region has been overwhelmingly Catholic. The Catholic Church received exclusive dominion over the continent during the colonial period (c. 1500–1820) and this cultural hegemony lingered well into the twentieth century. Shortly after Independence in the 1820s, Liberal political parties throughout the region expropriated Church landholdings, assets and revenue-producing activities (e.g., funeral services) to finance cash-strapped governments and pay off foreign loans.[6] During the latter half of the nineteenth century most governments officially disestablished

---

[6] See Gill (1998a, 30–31) and Keshavarzian and Gill (1997) for an economic interpretation of church-state conflict during this period.

Catholicism and implemented freedom of worship in an attempt to facilitate trade with Protestant Europe. The Catholic clergy confronted a new
challenge at the turn of the century – radical labor movements such as
socialism, anarchism, and syndicalism. These movements threatened to
steal the loyalty that industrial and rural workers owed to the Catholic
Church (Stewart-Gambino 1992a: 44 and 83–4).

The Church experienced a severe shortage of priests and other personnel during this period, which limited the ability of Church officials
to build strong organizational loyalty among many of their parishioners
(Hurtado 1992 [1941]: 99–112; Poblete 1965). Clergy were frequently
assigned to middle- and upper-class parishes since this was the Church's
main financial constituency (Gill 1999). The Church did not adequately
staff poor rural villages and urban barrios, and it was precisely in these
regions that evangelical growth has been the most rapid.

In response to radical movements, the Bishops began to increase the
Catholicism's organizational presence through the creation of more
parishes, additional personnel (clergy and lay catechists) and the development of Catholic Action. Catholic Action was originally designed by
Pope Pius XI in the 1920s to deal with similar ideological threats in
Europe (Kalyvas 1996, 183) and was then transferred to Latin America
a decade later (Levine 1981: 31–2).[7] Catholic Action targeted those most
vulnerable to the callings of radical political movements – university students and urban workers, and sought to influence the values of political
elites in order to have influence over future policymakers. This strategy
worked. The Christian Democratic parties that exert a strong influence
over politics in Chile, Venezuela, and El Salvador are outgrowths of this
movement.

The 1960s and 1970s were an era of tremendous religious ferment in
Latin America. It was during this time that "progressive" Catholicism
emerged as a dynamic socio-political movement in a number of countries. Progressive Catholicism rejected the Church's traditional strategy
of elite politics and defense of the status quo, and instead adopted a
"preferential option for the poor." The intellectual engine behind this
movement was liberation theology, which combined a biblical concern
for social justice with radical, social scientific critiques of Latin American reality (cf. Gutiérrez 1973).

The liberation theology movement traces its origins back to a number
of relatively separate trends occurring in the mid-1950s.[8] First, in Europe

[7] It should be noted that before this, a number of national Catholic Churches began to
organize Catholic unions for workers, known as *círculos obreros*, as early as the 1910s.
[8] Depending upon one's historical perspective, it could also be argued that liberation theology dates back even further, perhaps to the writings of Chilean priest Alberto Hurtado

a number of theologians (e.g., Emile Houtart, Johann Baptist Metz, and Karl Rahner) began incorporating insights from Marxist and existential analysis into Catholic theology.[9] A number of important Latin American theologians, including Gustavo Gutiérrez, received their training in Belgium and France during this time and were influenced heavily by these scholars. When Gutiérrez returned to his homeland of Peru in the 1960s, he applied this critical theology in light of the immense poverty many in his country were experiencing.

Second, during this same period, a number of Catholic priests who were involved in grassroots programs designed to help the poor began to rethink the Church's more charity-based approach to alleviating poverty. Among the most notable of these individuals was Brazilian Paulo Freire who developed an educational program known as "conscientization" (consciousness-raising). This program was designed to teach the lower classes that their impoverished situation was the result of social structures that could be changed. By the late 1960s, these two strands had come together in a recognizable and uniquely Latin American "theology of liberation" that emphasized both intellectual reflection and praxis (i.e., learning through active involvement in the world).

Progressive Catholicism manifested itself organizationally in Christian base communities. These communities were typically composed of lower-class, lay activists led by a priest or catechist, and combined Bible readings with concrete political involvement, e.g., lobbying for expanded land rights (see Hewitt 1991). These groups were where the Latin American Church's "preferential option for the poor" was played out. While liberation theologians, with their emphasis on praxis, have become closely associated with the base community movement, it should be noted that not all base communities were liberationist in their theology. Many of the clergy and laity involved in these groups were unaware of the more philosophical writings of liberation theology, even though their intent to improve the lives of the poor was shared with these theologians. The final manifestation of progressive Catholicism came at the national level, where it took the form of formal opposition to authoritarianism and socio-economic injustice in Brazil, Chile, and Ecuador. National

---

(1930s) or even as far back as coloinial bishop Bartolomé de las Casas (early 1500s). See Sigmund (1990) for an excellent introduction to the history and content of liberation theology.

[9] Catholics were not the only ones to influence the development of liberation theology. Protestants such as Juergen Moltmann (Germany) and Rubem Alves (Brazil) also contributed to the liberationist dialogue. The latter completed his dissertation at Princeton in 1968 entitled "Towards A Theology of Liberation." This was the same year that Gutiérrez organized a conference with the same name in Chimbote, Peru.

bishops conferences took the lead in issuing pastoral statements
denouncing the economic and social policies of these dictatorial regimes
and setting up organizations that monitored human rights abuses and
oftentimes lobbying for the release of political prisoners.

Progressive Catholicism arose at a time of increasing poverty and
repressive military rule, and also of increased religious competition for
the loyalties of the poor. The liberalizing ideas of Vatican Council II
(1962–5) provided an added impetus for progressive, grassroots reforms
already taking place throughout the region. Not all countries developed
strong progressive movements in South America – clergy in Argentina
and Colombia remained the most resistant to change, while episcopacies
and clergies in Paraguay and Uruguay remained largely silent on the
political and economic issues galvanizing the progressive movement.[10]
Nonetheless, the progressive movement did play an important political
role in the region, invigorating a cultural institution that previously stood
firmly on the side of the political and economic elite. Even in the countries with more conservative Catholic cultures, bishops could not
completely ignore poverty and repression, and would occasionally issue
pastoral letters critical of the social situation.

By the mid 1980s, the Vatican began censuring the writings and activities of several liberation theologians. In Brazil and Chile, base communities fell under tighter ecclesiastic supervision and failed to expand the
way many scholars and activists had expected (Daudelin and Hewitt,
1995). Church leaders also began taking more conciliatory stands
toward national governments and controversial socioeconomic policies.
This change was readily apparent at the Fourth General Conference of
the Latin American Bishops in Santo Domingo (1992). The two previous meetings – in Medellín (1968) and Puebla (1979) – had focused
heavily on the region's socioeconomic problems. The final document
produced at Santo Domingo, by contrast, centered more heavily on
spiritual matters (cf. Hennelly 1993) as witnessed by the conference
theme – "new evangelization." A chapter of the conference proceedings
that dealt with "human development" retained concern for the social
and political situation in the region, but the proposed solutions took a
much less radical tone than those of the past. The Church continues to
be concerned for the plight of the poor, but the greater attention placed
on spiritual matters in recent years gives a somewhat exaggerated
appearance of increased political conservatism. Instead of seeing a "conservative retrenchment" within Catholicism, it may be more accurate to

---

[10] See Gill (1998a) for a comparison of progressive and conservative episcopacies during
this period.

characterize the current state of affairs as a *"spiritual* retrenchment" in the face of stiff religious competition.

This spiritual retrenchment occurred for several reasons (cf. Gill 1995). First, Pope John Paul II has appointed theological conservatives to positions of leadership, and strongly opposed communism in his native Poland and elsewhere. John Paul II's also sought to consolidate the Church's financial and theological control over an increasingly splintered Church.[11] Finally, the emergence of democratic governments in the 1980s removed the repressive despots who had been the focus of their opposition.

Perhaps the greater effect of political liberalization was the exodus of social activists from Church-sponsored groups as soon as secular associations gained political space to organize. Many of the grassroots Catholic organizations that arose during the 1960s and 1970s could not continue without lay activists. Recent political liberalization also has promoted the growth of a diverse civil society. Environmental groups, labor unions, ethnic and racial organizations and myriad other associations now compete for the attention and assistance of local and national policy makers. As this diversity increases and strengthens, the Catholic Church can no longer rely on a privileged cultural status to guarantee political victories.

Conceivably, the most important religious phenomenon affecting South America has been the explosive growth of evangelical Protestantism since the 1930s. Sporadic attempts by mainline Protestants (e.g., Anglicans, Presbyterians, and Lutherans) to missionize the middle and upper classes in parts of the continent during the late 1800s were largely unsuccessful since these social sectors were closely linked to the institutional Church (Vallier 1963). Once evangelicals began to proselytize among the rural and urban poor, they grew rapidly. By the 1930s Protestants were increasing significantly in Brazil and Chile (Willems 1967); by the 1960s evangelical growth had spread to most other countries. Argentina and Colombia did not see significant numbers of evangelical Protestants until the 1980s. Some authors link this phenomenon to the social anomie produced by industrialization and rapid urban-to-rural migration (Martin 1990; Lalive d'Epinay 1969; Willems 1967). Recent research shows that much of the cross-national variation in Protestant growth rates can be attributed to government regulations such as restrictive registration requirements, zoning laws and limits on media access

---

[11] Della Cava (1993) argues convincingly that John Paul II's drive to consolidate power in the Catholic Church resulted from the serious financial difficulties the Vatican found itself in during the 1970s.

that make it difficult for new religious organizations to expand (Gill 1998c).

Current estimates of the Protestant population in South America vary widely.[12] Table 9.1 provides estimates of proselytizing non-Catholic religions (including evangelical Protestantism and Spiritism) from a number of sources. While specific country estimates vary by source, there is a general consensus that Brazil and Chile experienced the greatest penetration of non-Catholic religions. Argentina, Colombia, Uruguay, and Venezuela have been relatively immune from such growth until recently.

The greatest denominational growth among Protestants has been among independent Pentecostal churches, accounting for at least two-thirds of all Protestants in the region (Stoll 1993, 3). While these churches had their origins in North American missionary denominations (e.g., Methodists and Assemblies of God), Pentecostalism is currently an indigenous phenomenon with few links to foreign missions. Foreign missionary groups, namely Mormons and Jehovah's Witnesses, are also making rapid gains regionally. Table 9.1 reports figures for Jehovah's Witnesses, which keeps extremely accurate records of their active members, known as "publishers" (Stark and Iannaccone 1997). Ethnic Protestants (e.g., British Anglicans, German Lutherans) and Jews account for a significant portion of the non-Catholic population in Argentina and Brazil, though these groups have seen little, if any, significant growth.

As we approach the dawning of the twenty-first century, the Church faces new challenges that stem increasing political and religious pluralism. The unprecedented political pluralism resulting from the expansion of democracy forces the Church to compete with secular political actors to achieve its policy preferences. The Church must also compete with other religious groups for adherents. Both forms of competition require immense amount of physical, human and intellectual resources. These resources are scarce, and constrain the political and pastoral strategies of the bishops. Moreover, religious pluralism potentially introduces an

---

[12] Measuring religious affiliation in Latin America is a difficult endeavor. Survey research has developed only recently as a social scientific tool of investigating national populations due to infrastructure limitations. Moreover, the difficulty in surveying marginalized individuals (often a significant portion of the population) leads to serious problems of bias in national surveys. Data reported from denominations are frequently unreliable or inconsistent. Census data offer the best insight into national religious affiliations, but even there, the measurement instruments are subject to high degrees of bias. For instance, in Mexico, pre-1990 census questions asked respondents if they were "Christian, Protestant or other" with that assumption that Christian equals Catholic. See Hallum (1996: 35–8) for a discussion of the methodological difficulties in assessing religious affiliation in Latin America.

Table 9.1. Estimates of Denominational Affiliation (various sources and dates)

| Source | Catholic estimates % Catholic | | Protestant estimates % Protestant | | | Survey reporting % of respondents | | Jehovah's Witnesses Inhabitants per publisher | | |
|---|---|---|---|---|---|---|---|---|---|---|
| | Catholic Almanac | | Barrett | | Johnstone | 1990 World Value Survey | | Jehovah's Witnesses Yearbook | | |
| | 1981 | 1992 | 1970 | 1980 | 1986 | Catholic | Protestant | 1986 | 1994 | % Growth |
| Argentina | 92.1 | 91.1 | 3.7 | 4.6 | 6.6 | 92.1 | 7.9 | 505 | 314 | 37.8 |
| Bolivia | 93.7 | 91.6 | 4.2 | 4.8 | 8.3 | na | na | 1,455 | 675 | 53.6 |
| Brazil | 90.1 | 88.0 | 15.8 | 18.8 | 17.9 | 80.2 | 19.8 | 748 | 404 | 46.0 |
| Chile | 85.5 | 80.4 | 16.8 | 19.2 | 24.5 | 83.7 | 16.3 | 445 | 292 | 34.4 |
| Colombia | 95.5 | 93.1 | 1.8 | 2.2 | 4.2 | na | na | 1,010 | 549 | 45.6 |
| Ecuador | 90.2 | na | 2.9 | 3.6 | 4.3 | na | na | 909 | 411 | 54.8 |
| Paraguay | 91.2 | na | 2.1 | 2.1 | 4.3 | na | na | 1,496 | 928 | 38.0 |
| Peru | 92.1 | na | 2.8 | 3.3 | 4.7 | na | na | 931 | 482 | 48.2 |
| Uruguay | 78.6 | 78.3 | 2.8 | 2.9 | 5.3 | na | na | 522 | 325 | 37.7 |
| Venezuela | 92.2 | 92.7 | 2.5 | 2.9 | 3.3 | na | na | 584 | 335 | 42.6 |

*Sources*: Consult bibliography of Chapter 9.

entirely different worldview and new set of policy preferences into the region that could alter the direction of politics. We now turn attention to the institutional (church-state) and ideational (religion-politics) issues that have emerged under a new democratic environment in recent years.

## INSTITUTIONAL CONCERNS:
### CHURCH AND STATE UNDER DEMOCRACY

While most Catholic bishops and clergy cheered the return of civilian rule in South America, the respect for pluralism that accompanies democracy has presented Catholic leaders with significant challenges. Foremost among their concerns has been the expansion of evangelical Protestantism. Pope John Paul II, addressing the general conference of Latin American bishops in 1992, referred to evangelicals as "rapacious wolves" and there is constant talk in Catholic circles about how to deal with the "invasion of the sects" (Gill 1998b). Although *evangélicos* have challenged Catholic hegemony for several decades in Brazil and Chile, the expansion of religious civil liberties in other countries such as Argentina, Bolivia, Colombia, Ecuador, and Paraguay has fueled the growth of minority religions there (Moreno 1996: 205–56).

Colombia serves as a case in point.[13] Before the 1991 constitutional reform, religious activity in the country was governed largely by the dictates of a concordat signed with the Vatican in 1887 (revised in 1953 and 1973). This legal agreement forbade non-Catholic religions from proselytizing in roughly 75 percent of the country's territory, required children to show a Catholic baptismal certificate in order to enter public schools, and required those same students to participate in Catholic Mass. The state only recognized civil or Catholic marriages, so non-Catholics who wanted a religious ceremony would have to pay for services twice (Brusco 1995, 32–5; Moreno 1996, 227–8). These restrictions served to make conversion to Protestantism a less attractive option. In 1991, under growing international and domestic pressure from Protestant groups, new constitutional legislation eliminated these restrictions and since then eyewitness accounts note that evangelical growth has taken off.[14]

---

[13] Colombia has technically been a democracy since 1957 following a brutal, decade-long civil war known as *La Violencia*. Nonetheless, the negotiated settlement of the civil war involved a formalized power-sharing arrangement between the two dominant parties, Liberals and Conservatives. Real electoral competition did not become a reality until the early 1970s. Ongoing struggles with various guerrilla bands meant that civil liberties were often curtailed and parts of the country placed under martial law. Only since the late 1980s has there been a significant movement towards genuine (not merely electoral) political liberalization.

[14] Another factor contributing to the rapid growth of evangelicals may related to their strict behavioral codes (e.g., no drinking, no smoking, etc.). Many scholars examining

With *evangélicos* making rapid headway in the region, the Catholic Church has devoted considerable energy to countering the evangelical growth (Gill 1998b). The most effective method of stopping the outflow from Catholicism has been to increase the institutional contact between the Church and its parishioners; people actively engaged in religion on an ongoing basis are less likely to convert (Iannaccone 1990). Data from the 1990 *World Values Survey* indicate that while roughly 58 percent of Protestants in South America attend services at least once a week, the figure is only 30% for Catholics.[15]

In response, Catholic bishops have made a concerted effort to reach more nominal Catholics by increasing the number of dioceses, parishes and seminarians. Tables 9.2 and 9.3 show that although the Church is still losing ground in terms of the actual number of priests available to minister to the population,[16] it has made impressive strides in attracting more seminarians. It has also expanded its bureaucratic reach by upping the number of bishoprics (typically associated with the creation of new dioceses) and parishes.

A strong effort to entice South Americans into the priesthood beginning in the early 1980s has paid off for the Catholic Church. Since the beginning of John Paul II's papacy in late 1978, the number of seminarians has more than tripled. The replacement ratio in Table 9.2 shows that in 1995, roughly 46 percent of the region's current priests could be replaced by the seminarian population. Assuming an average retirement age of sixty-five for priests, and adjusting for population growth, the number of priests per capita should begin to trend significantly upwards in the next few decades. Already, the Church's ability to increase the number of parishes and slow the decline in the priest/parishioner ratio (see Table 9.2) can be attributed to this expansion in the number of young clergy. The continued reliance on lay leaders (e.g., deacons) and foreign clergy has also helped.

religion have observed that strict religions (e.g., Mormons, Jehovah's Witnesses, Pentecostals) tend to grow faster than those with lax behavioral restrictions. Iannaccone (1994) explains that this phenomenon is related to the ability of strict religions to solve collective action problems and prevent free riding.

[15] Figures based on calculations performed by the author and available for Argentina, Brazil, and Chile only. Since church attendance was self-reported, it can be anticipated that the figures are somewhat inflated. Casual observers put the regular attendance figures for Catholics at about 10 to 15 percent (based on personal interviews). Nonetheless, the gap between Catholic and Protestant regular attendance is remarkably high and likely is due to a more favorable minister/parishioner ratio for Protestants. Berryman (1994) notes that although self-reporting Catholics far outnumber Protestants, Brazil has more Protestant ministers than Catholic priests.

[16] For comparison purposes, the priest/parishioner ratio in the United States (circa 1970) was 9.8 priests per 10,000 Catholics. See Gill (1998a: 86–7) for additional figures for other countries.

Table 9.2. Catholic Personnel in South America

| Country | Priest per 10,000 population | | | | | Seminarians per 10,000 population | | | | | Replacement ratio | | | | |
|---|---|---|---|---|---|---|---|---|---|---|---|---|---|---|---|
| | 1975 | 1980 | 1985 | 1990 | 1995 | 1975 | 1980 | 1985 | 1990 | 1995 | 1975 | 1980 | 1985 | 1990 | 1995 |
| Argentina | 1.93 | 1.84 | 1.85 | 1.76 | 1.73 | 0.13 | 0.34 | 0.65 | 0.69 | 0.59 | 0.07 | 0.18 | 0.35 | 0.39 | 0.34 |
| Bolivia | 1.45 | 1.33 | 1.36 | 1.29 | 1.48 | 0.14 | 0.15 | 0.29 | 0.53 | 0.74 | 0.09 | 0.11 | 0.21 | 0.41 | 0.50 |
| Brazil | 1.16 | 1.21 | 1.03 | 0.94 | 1.00 | 0.09 | 0.34 | 0.44 | 0.41 | 0.44 | 0.08 | 0.28 | 0.42 | 0.43 | 0.44 |
| Chile | 1.96 | 1.74 | 1.85 | 2.08 | 1.65 | 0.15 | 0.37 | 0.86 | 0.64 | 0.54 | 0.08 | 0.21 | 0.46 | 0.31 | 0.33 |
| Colombia | 2.02 | 1.92 | 1.95 | 1.93 | 1.97 | 0.40 | 0.43 | 0.89 | 1.18 | 1.24 | 0.20 | 0.22 | 0.46 | 0.61 | 0.63 |
| Ecuador | 1.88 | 1.72 | 1.66 | 1.51 | 1.53 | 0.11 | 0.11 | 0.32 | 0.52 | 0.66 | 0.06 | 0.07 | 0.19 | 0.34 | 0.43 |
| Paraguay | 1.76 | 1.60 | 1.54 | 1.36 | 1.35 | 0.22 | 0.26 | 0.72 | 0.78 | 0.64 | 0.13 | 0.16 | 0.46 | 0.57 | 0.47 |
| Peru | 1.42 | 1.36 | 1.21 | 1.12 | 1.08 | 0.15 | 0.33 | 0.48 | 0.51 | 0.59 | 0.10 | 0.24 | 0.40 | 0.45 | 0.54 |
| Uruguay | 2.00 | 1.95 | 1.86 | 2.35 | 1.72 | 0.10 | 0.15 | 0.42 | 0.35 | 0.22 | 0.05 | 0.08 | 0.22 | 0.15 | 0.13 |
| Venezuela | 1.68 | 1.40 | 1.21 | 1.06 | 1.01 | 0.13 | 0.16 | 0.30 | 0.45 | 0.45 | 0.08 | 0.11 | 0.25 | 0.43 | 0.45 |
| South America | 1.49 | 1.45 | 1.33 | 1.26 | 1.27 | 0.15 | 0.32 | 0.52 | 0.56 | 0.58 | 0.10 | 0.22 | 0.39 | 0.44 | 0.46 |

Note: Replacement ratio = (seminarians per 10,000) / (priests per 10,000). Interpret as percentage of existing priests that can be replaced by seminarians. Figures for South America represent weighted averages.

Source: Catholic Almanac (various years). Data presented in Catholic Almanac are lagged by two years, thus figures for 1995 appear in the 1997 edition of the Catholic Almanac.

Table 9.3. Catholic Bishoprics and Parishes in South America

| Country | Bishops | | | | | Parishes | | | | |
|---|---|---|---|---|---|---|---|---|---|---|
| | 1975 | 1980 | 1985 | 1990 | 1995 | 1975 | 1980 | 1985 | 1990 | 1995 |
| Argentina | 56 | 67 | 69 | 77 | 83 | 1,979 | 2,148 | 2,234 | 2,427 | 2,466 |
| Bolivia | 16 | 19 | 20 | 25 | 30 | 434 | NA | 443 | 486 | 516 |
| Brazil | 228 | 239 | 305 | 313 | 308 | 6,033 | 6,423 | 6,872 | 7,605 | 7,966 |
| Chile | 24 | 23 | 29 | 35 | 32 | 784 | 803 | 815 | 849 | 919 |
| Colombia | 43 | 45 | 57 | 65 | 74 | 1,972 | 2,216 | 2,367 | 2,813 | 3,094 |
| Ecuador | 21 | 22 | 24 | 22 | 30 | 635 | 700 | 820 | 974 | 1,041 |
| Paraguay | 9 | 14 | 15 | 15 | 17 | 236 | 260 | 282 | 324 | 325 |
| Peru | 36 | 40 | 44 | 63 | 47 | 1,160 | 1,144 | 1,250 | 1,306 | 1,407 |
| Uruguay | 10 | 10 | 11 | 12 | 13 | NA | 224 | 222 | 226 | 233 |
| Venezuela | 28 | 28 | 33 | 34 | 34 | 915 | 967 | 1,002 | 1,064 | 1,080 |
| Latin America | 471 | 507 | 607 | 661 | 668 | 14,148 | 14,885 | 16,307 | 18,074 | 19,047 |

Source: Catholic Almanac (various years) for bishop and parish data. Data presented in Catholic Almanac are lagged by two years, thus figures for 1995 appear in the 1997 edition of the Catholic Almanac.

Nonetheless, the Church in all countries continues to lack the financial and human resources required to minister to a majority of the population. Evangelical churches have the advantage of lower overhead costs (e.g., building maintenance, bureaucratic staffing, clergy salaries) and higher average contributions from their members (Conferencia Episcopal Latinoamericano 1984: 35 and 148; Berryman 1994: 9). The Catholic Church in contrast must support a large national (and international) bureaucracy, clearly a major competitive disadvantage when facing small, upstart denominations that operate out of storefronts.

Institutional restructuring has had little impact on slowing Protestant conversions in the region; Catholic episcopacies have turned toward seeking government protection from competition. The Church has sought policies that make proselytizing activities less costly for the Church (via public subsidies) and more costly for *evangélicos* (via restrictions on religious liberty). In virtually all South American countries, bishops have pushed for subsidized private education and the ability to teach religion in public schools (e.g., Moreno 1996: 240). Socializing children to a faith is one of the most effective ways of guaranteeing loyal adherents in the future (Iannaccone 1990). Likewise, bishops have sought funds for various Catholic charities and construction projects that would ease their financial disadvantages relative to evangelicals (Serbin 1999; Gill 1998b; Moreno 1996, passim).

On the other front, Church officials have attempted to make proselytizing more costly for *evangélicos* by imposing greater regulatory restrictions on them. The Chilean Catholic Church supported legislation in the early 1990s that would prohibit legal registration of churches with less than two hundred members, outlaw street preaching and monitor noise levels outside of religious buildings (Moreno 1996: 225). This legislation, had it passed, would have impinged seriously on the activities of small Pentecostal churches (many with less than two hundred parishioners) that engage in boisterous outdoor celebrations as a means of attracting passersby. The Argentine Catholic hierarchy backed legislation recently that would have made legal registration more difficult for small churches and would have limited the use of spiritual healing (Gill 1998b; Moreno 1996: 208). As in Chile, this would have had a disproportionate impact on the most rapidly growing denominations – Pentecostals. In 1994 Bolivian evangelical ministers were prohibited from evangelizing to military personnel and a national senator requested a government investigation into the activities of non-Catholic denominations for suspicion of conducting clandestine activities (Moreno 1996: 216–17).

The South American Catholic Church must also now compete with more non-religious civic associations that seek scarce public resources and specific policies. Many of these groups seek policies that conflict with official moral proclamations of the church on issues such as contraception, abortion, divorce, and education. As these associations build constituencies and develop organizational skills, the Church can no longer count on its traditional hegemonic cultural position to guarantee victory.

The result of this increasing religious and secular pluralism is that the Church must now act more like a specialized interest group. To win policy and resource battles it must be able to mobilize constituents and deliver votes. This requires a relatively unified leadership and constituency that links their membership in the Church directly to their voting behavior. The Church's constituency cuts across socio-economic groups, and creating voting unity is not easy. Understanding that the effectiveness of interest groups is closely linked to the group's cohesiveness helps, in part, to explain why Church leaders have moved to silence internal dissent within the clergy in recent years. A divided Church will be less effective in critical policy battles, and less capable of mobilizing collective action, under a pluralistic environment. Thus, the "conservative retrenchment" that has been noted by several scholars in recent years (Daudelin and Hewitt 1995; Stewart-Gambino 1992b) is not merely ideological, it is also a function of the strategic interests of the institutional Church (Gill 1995). Episcopal conferences will attempt to be the sole voice of the Church as bishops urge the clergy to avoid independent political activity. The paradoxical conclusion here is that as society becomes more pluralistic, the Catholic Church must become less so to be politically effective. Yet, this conflicts with its pastoral mission of being a spiritual force for all individuals regardless of politics.

To date, Catholic efforts to enact legislation to restrict religious competition have not met with much success in national legislatures, in part because of effective Protestant mobilization to oppose these policies. In response to proposed legislation in Chile mentioned above, "more than 10,000 evangelicals marched in Santiago to protest ... a municipal ordinance that restricted the 'emission of annoying sounds' in the city" (Moreno 1996: 225). Three Argentine evangelical organizations recently banded together in a political alliance – the National Council of Evangelical Christians (*Consejo Nacional Cristiano Evangélico*) – to protect non-Catholic denominations from discriminatory legislation.[17] Just like the Catholic Church, Protestants readily mobilize to protect their institutional interests (Lehmann 1996: 215–16).

Evangelical political efforts have met with surprising success. Peruvian *evangélicos* provided key organizational support for Alberto

---

[17] Personal interview with the organizers Eduardo Recio, Juan Passuelo, Emilio Monti, and Norberto Burton in Buenos Aires (November 19, 1996).

Fujimori's victory in the 1990 presidential primaries and general election (Fleet and Smith 1997: 251–2). Evangelicals also provided important swing votes for Colombian presidents César Gaviria and Ernesto Samper who returned the favor with legislation ensuring greater religious liberty and equal protection. In Brazil, Protestants are finding their way into elected local and national offices (Freston 1993). With free and competitive elections becoming the norm in South America, politicians are becoming more reluctant to alienate an evangelical constituency that has demonstrated an astounding ability to mobilize and vote in unified blocs despite their organizationally fragmented nature. All of this bodes well for the implementation and consolidation of religious freedom, which in turn reinforces the interest group proclivities of religious groups. In sum, one of the critical battlegrounds of religion and politics in South America in the coming years will be church-state issues with the likely outcome being movement towards greater separation of church and state.

## IDEATIONAL CONCERNS:
## A LATIN AMERICAN PROTESTANT ETHIC?

The increasing number of evangelicals in South America could have a long-term impact on the values and politics of the region. A number of scholars have observed that Latin American *evangélicos* tend to promote a theology of laissez-faire individualism and political conservatism or, at a minimum, apoliticism (Fleet and Smith 1997: 177; Deiros 1992). Given intensified political participation and competition among parties, such assertions – if correct – could imply a significant shift in the South American political landscape. The pro-authoritarian values that some scholars assert emanate from the millenarian tendencies in Pentecostal theologies might also provide an opening for renewed dictatorship. To what extent are such assertions supported by empirical evidence?

Whereas survey evidence is notoriously difficult to obtain in Latin America, and often unreliable, a few methodologically sound studies have been conducted in the past several years that provide insight into the political views of Protestants. Relying on two national surveys of El Salvador in 1988–9, Coleman, et al. conclude: "Salvadoran Protestants are distinguished primarily by their lack of political uniqueness. They are not political apologists for the right. Nor are they supporters of the insurrectionary left. They vote more frequently than some but less frequently than others. Their votes in 1989 seemed to be neither highly distinct from nor more conservative than those of Catholics" (1993: 133). Hallum (1996) supports this general conclusion in her examination of the election of Guatemalan president Jorge Serrano Elías in 1990. Looking at election returns across Guatemala's twenty-two departments, she finds that "Serrano's victory was fairly uniform across the country and was not concentrated in the most Protestant departments" leading to the conclusion that "[h]e could not rely on an evangelical voting bloc" (1996: 108). Hallum also finds that contrary to the conventional wisdom, evangelicals are becoming more active in politics in terms of campaigning, lobbying and defending human rights (1996: 111–25). Case study evidence from Brazil (Burdick 1993; Freston 1993), Colombia (Brusco 1995) and Venezuela (Froehle 1995) support the conclusion that evangelical Protestants are an ideologically diverse lot.

The 1990 *World Values Survey* provides further indications of these trends based on data from Argentina, Brazil, and Chile.[18] Table 9.4 presents a comparative statistical analysis of political attitudes for Catholics versus Protestants, frequent versus infrequent churchgoers,[19] and frequent Catholic churchgoers versus frequent Protestant churchgoers. The frequency of attendance at religious services was considered important since we would expect regular churchgoers to be influenced more by religious values than infrequent attendees (cf. Iannaccone 1990). As noted in Table 9.1 above, Protestants have a greater propensity for regular attendance. Several interesting patterns can be seen in Table 9.4.

Catholics and Protestants share an equal interest in politics and consider politics to be relatively important (see Appendix for specific variable definitions and coding). Protestants are more reluctant to discuss politics than their Catholic counterparts. Protestants who attend services at least once a week are more averse to political discussion and tend to see politics as less important and less interesting.[20] These results support the notion that fervent Protestants tend to be more withdrawn from political life.

Catholics and Protestants place themselves at similar points of the ideological spectrum, slightly right of center. Protestants have a higher spread (standard deviation) of ideological identifications, suggesting that Protestants are a significantly more diverse group ideologically. Based upon the coding in the *World Values Survey*, we can see that Protestants – both general and frequent churchgoers – place higher levels of trust in

---

[18] To keep sample sizes high for statistical purposes, data were pooled for the three countries examined here. Separate tests were run for each individual country and generally reflect the pooled results. Results available upon request from author.

[19] Frequent churchgoers were categorized as those reporting attending religious services at least once a week. Infrequency was defined as once a month or less as per the categories in the *World Values Survey*.

[20] Analysis of other variables in the *World Values Survey* indicate that Catholics and Protestants are equally likely to become involved in political parties and organizations, though the percentages of those actually doing so are small.

Table 9.4. Comparisons of Religious Affiliation and Participation With Political Variables

| | Denominational affiliation | | Church attendance | | Frequent attendance by denomination | |
|---|---|---|---|---|---|---|
| Sample Size | Catholic (2428–3021) | Protestant (447–570) | Weekly or more (928–1224) | Less than weekly (2513–3055) | Catholic weekly + (672–856) | Protestant weekly + (151–212) |
| Politics important | 2.87 (1.08) | 2.84 (1.14) | 2.82 (1.11) | 2.86 (1.09) | 2.79* (1.10) | 2.98 (1.13) |
| Interested in politics | 2.92 (1.05) | 2.92 (1.06) | 2.93 (1.05) | 2.88 (1.07) | 2.90** (1.05) | 3.13 (0.99) |
| Discuss politics | 2.19*** (0.76) | 2.31 (0.74) | 2.26 (0.76) | 2.16*** (0.76) | 2.20*** (0.78) | 2.50 (0.64) |
| Church speak on gov't policy | 0.36 (0.48) | 0.32 (0.47) | 0.38* (0.48) | 0.34 (0.47) | 0.41** (0.49) | 0.30 (0.46) |
| Ideology | 5.45 (2.37) | 5.44 (2.61) | 5.73*** (2.43) | 5.15 (2.38) | 5.74 (2.32) | 5.77 (2.71) |
| Confidence in . . . church | 1.88 (0.93) | 1.84 (1.05) | 1.53*** (0.81) | 2.21 (1.02) | 1.50 (0.75) | 1.36* (0.75) |
| Military | 2.42 (1.00) | 2.40 (1.06) | 2.28*** (1.01) | 2.58 (1.02) | 2.24 (0.97) | 2.18 (1.04) |
| Legal system | 2.65 (1.00) | 2.53* (1.07) | 2.52*** (1.02) | 2.72 (1.00) | 2.56 (1.00) | 2.30*** (1.09) |
| Unions | 2.76 (0.99) | 2.66* (1.03) | 2.66*** (1.01) | 2.79 (0.99) | 2.66 (1.01) | 2.55 (1.03) |
| Legislature | 2.84 (1.02) | 2.79 (1.03) | 2.74*** (1.03) | 2.88 (1.01) | 2.75 (1.03) | 2.54** (1.04) |
| Civil service | 2.73 (0.96) | 2.53*** (1.00) | 2.59*** (0.98) | 2.77 (0.96) | 2.64 (0.96) | 2.33*** (1.03) |

* Significant at 0.05 level. ** Significant at 0.01 level. *** Significant at 0.001 level. Sample standard deviation given in parentheses.

Coding:

"Don't know" and nonresponses were deleted from analysis.

Politics important: 1 = very important; 2 = quite; 3 = not important; 4 = not at all.

Interested in politics: 1 = very interested; 2 = somewhat; 3 = not very; 4 = not at all.

Discuss politics: 1 = frequently; 2 = occasionally; 3 = never.

Proper for you church to speak out on government policy: 1 = yes; 0 = no.

Confidence measures for church, military, legal system, unions, legislature, and civil service coded as follows: 1 = great deal; 2 = quite a lot; 3 = not very much; 4 = none at all.

Note: Higher numbers imply "less importance," "less interest," or "less confidence." Higher numbers for "Ideology" imply greater conservatism. Figures for "Church speak on government policy" indicate proportion believing their church should speak out on government policy.

Sources: 1990 World Values Survey (see Inglehart 1998). Data for Argentina, Brazil, and Chile.

212

certain governmental institutions, namely the legal system and civil service. This is an interesting result that does not suggest any immediate explanation, though it is one worth looking into since public confidence in governmental institutions is critical for the consolidation of democracy. Future research on religion and politics should examine how and why religious adherents place greater trust in civic institutions than secular actors.

Perhaps the most important finding from Table 9.4 is that the largest significant differences in political attitudes are not between Catholics and Protestants, but frequent and infrequent churchgoers, irrespective of denomination.[21] Those who attend services on a weekly (or greater) basis are those most likely to be strongly socialized to religious ways of thinking about the world. As we can see, frequent churchgoers are significantly more politically conservative and have much greater confidence in all the social and governmental institutions mentioned. If strong trust in social institutions is a prerequisite for functioning democracies, it would appear that active participation in religious organizations enhances the long-term prospects for the survivability of civilian rule. In explaining why this might be the case, Froehle argues that "Symbolically, religious communities . . . are built on notions of a transcendent common good as well as individual free choice and self-expression. In secular form, these symbols and discourses allow for politicians and ordinary citizens alike to envision a grand, alternative future while patiently working toward its slow, yet incomplete realization" (1995: 42). In less symbolic terms, participation in religious communities allows citizens to develop trusting relationships with a wider circle of people and often provides the empowering ability to develop leadership and organizational skills necessary for democratic participation (cf. Verba et al. 1996). The historically state-centric organization of South American society has provided, until recently, little space for independent civil society associations to flourish. Religious organizations offer a natural birthplace for such organizations. On a related front, Brusco (1995) discovers that evangelical Protestantism has also had a limited empowering effect on women. Strengthening the socioeconomic role of women in a society that has long held to the tenets of "machismo" bodes well for democracy as well.

---

[21] While one could claim these results are biased based upon the correlation between being Protestant and frequently attending church (see Table 9.1), the high absolute number of Catholics included in "frequent churchgoer" sub-sample (upwards of 850 Catholics versus 212 Protestants) washes out any confounding effect Protestants may introduce. Also, the comparison of frequent Catholic and Protestant churchgoers would make any strong bias visible.

To further test whether Protestants are more conservative and supportive of laissez-faire capitalism, I estimated several regression equations that included controls for age, gender, and income (see Table 9.5). If commonly accepted stereotypes of evangélicos are correct, we should see Protestants as more ideologically conservative, more willing to endorse laissez-faire economics and less supportive of democratic rule. Results suggest otherwise. The best predictors of these attitudes are the demographic, not religious, variables – age, gender, and income. The only religious variable moderately significant is "frequency of church attendance" which indicates that regular churchgoers are more conservative and slightly more supportive of economic individualism than casual church attendees. There is not a significant denominational effect on socioeconomic and political attitudes. The one exception here is that Protestants tend to favor greater degrees of political liberalization, most likely associated with their desire to obtain greater religious freedom.[22]

Thus Protestants are not more conservative than Catholics who share their social location. Moreover, there is great ideological diversity among Protestant voters in South America. These voters can be mobilized to vote as a bloc if their religious liberty is threatened, but in other elections they are unlikely to constitute a distinctive group of voters.

## CONCLUSION

Putting together our two findings – institutional and ideational – it is safe to say that religion will play an important and positive role in the gradual consolidation of democracy in South America. Increasing pluralism has challenged the cultural hegemony of the Catholic Church, but it has also provided the incentive clergy need to activate their once nominal parishioners in the faith. From this, the Church will emerge organizationally stronger, and more people will receive the spiritual attention they desire – a win-win situation for both priest and parishioner. Although radical base communities are unlikely to be the foundation for this increased Catholic participation (as scholars had earlier imagined), the increasing engagement of the population in religious life has laid the foundation for a stronger civil society. Religious pluralism combined with the greater assertiveness of Protestant groups in defending their right to worship also has prompted politicians to expand civil liberties for minority religious groups, another hopeful sign for the eventual consolidation of democratic rule. A strong civil society built from the grassroots, something that has been missing for most of South America's

---

[22] In all three countries – Argentina, Brazil, and Chile – legislation relating to the rights of religious minorities were being debated at the time of the survey (see Moreno 1996).

Table 9.5. Regression Analysis

| Dependent Variable | Ideology | | Income equality | | Economic freedom | | Liberalize government | |
|---|---|---|---|---|---|---|---|---|
| Model | I | II | III | IV | V | VI | VII | VIII |
| Constant | 4.92*** | 5.79*** | 5.05*** | 4.75*** | 2.03*** | 1.75*** | 1.11*** | 1.08*** |
| | (0.18) | (0.36) | (0.22) | (0.43) | (0.09) | (0.17) | (0.06) | (0.10) |
| Protestant | -0.15 | | 0.11 | | -0.08 | | -0.13**** | |
| | (0.13) | | (0.16) | | (0.07) | | (0.04) | |
| Frequent attendance | 0.25* | | -0.08 | | -0.12* | | -0.00 | |
| | (0.10) | | (0.13) | | (0.05) | | (0.03) | |
| Prot. freq attendance | | 0.06 | | 0.02 | | 0.03 | | 0.03 |
| | | (0.23) | | (0.26) | | (0.11) | | (0.06) |
| Raised religious | 0.15 | -0.18 | 0.26 | 0.45 | -0.04 | 0.13 | 0.00 | -0.07 |
| | (0.12) | (0.25) | (0.14) | (0.29) | (0.06) | (0.12) | (0.04) | (0.07) |
| Gender | -0.32*** | -0.36* | -0.03 | 0.03 | -0.07 | -0.03 | -0.10** | -0.08 |
| | (0.09) | (0.18) | (0.11) | (0.22) | (0.05) | (0.09) | (0.05) | (0.05) |
| Age | 0.02*** | 0.01 | 0.01 | 0.01 | 0.00 | 0.00 | 0.00*** | 0.00** |
| | (0.00) | (0.01) | (0.00) | (0.01) | (0.00) | (0.00) | (0.00) | (0.00) |
| Income | -0.05* | -0.04 | 0.17*** | 0.15** | 0.10*** | 0.12*** | 0.07*** | 0.08*** |
| | (0.02) | (0.04) | (0.02) | (0.05) | (0.01) | (0.02) | (0.01) | (0.01) |
| Adjusted $R^2$ | 0.02 | 0.00 | 0.02 | 0.01 | 0.04 | 0.04 | 0.05 | 0.05 |
| F-ratio | 11.06*** | 1.68 | 9.59*** | 3.05* | 20.30*** | 8.87*** | 31.02*** | 11.20*** |
| N | 2,665 | 758 | 3,192 | 945 | 3,122 | 917 | 3,192 | 948 |

* Significant at 0.05 level. ** Significant at 0.01 level. *** Significant at 0.001 level. Two-tailed tests. Standard errors in parentheses.

(continued)

215

## Notes to Table 9.5 (continued)

*Coding:*

*Independent variables:*

Protestant: 1 = Protestant; 0 = Catholic.

Frequent attendance: 1 = weekly attendance or more; 0 = monthly attendance or less.

Protestant Frequency Attendance: 1 = Protestants attending weekly or more; 0 = Catholics attending weekly or more.

Was respondent raised religious?: 1 = yes; 0 = no. (Recoded from original WVS).

Gender: 1 = male; 0 = female.

Age: Actual age of respondent in years.

Income: 10 categories based upon country-specific per capita income data. Higher numbers represent higher income categories.

*Dependent variables:*

Ideology: 10 categories with 1 = left and 10 = right.

Income equality: 1 = supports freedom over equality; 2 = supports neither freedom nor equality over the other; 3 = supports equality over freedom.

Economic freedom: 5 categories based upon whether person agrees with following statement: "We are more likely to have a healthy economy if the government allows more freedom for individuals to do as they wish." 1 = agree completely; 2 = agree somewhat; 3 = neutral; 4 = disagree somewhat; 5 = disagree completely.

Liberalize government: Same 5 categories as Economic freedom and based on following statement: "Our government should be made much more open to the public."

*Note:* See Appendix in Chapter 9 for discussion of variables. Negative coefficients for "ideology" and "income equality" indicate leftist political leanings. Negative coefficients for "economic freedom" and "liberalized government" indicate more laissez-faire and democratic positions, respectively.

*Sources:* 1990 World Values Survey (see Inglehart 1998). Data for Argentina, Brazil, and Chile.

history, is gradually developing with religious organizations leading the way.

This new social landscape has not only summoned clergy to action, but it has also challenged traditional scholarship in the field of religion and politics. Secularization theory – long the dominant paradigm in religious studies – holds little value in understanding a region that is witnessing an explosion in religious activity. Likewise, Daudelin and Hewitt (1995) point out that an exclusive focus on progressive Catholicism in the 1970s and 1980s led us to overlook the persistence of Catholic conservatism and to stereotype and underestimate the popularity of evangelical Protestantism among the poor. Cross-national and denominational research in the 1990s (e.g., Hallum 1996; Burdick 1993) helped to compensate for many of these weaknesses, but more work needs to done. Primary among the questions that need to be answered are how laws guaranteeing religious liberty are negotiated, implemented, and enforced. What have been the institutional roles of Catholic and Protestant leaders in the formulation of these laws? Does religious participation have a positive "spillover effect" for civil society? If so, what are the causal mechanisms by which this occurs?[23] How are religious organizations and symbols used to mobilize individuals for community participation, if this is indeed the case? Religious organizations historically have had long, successful track records in inspiring collective action. Knowing what makes religion such a potent mobilizing force will help us discern the dynamics of political and social life in the region. And finally, the findings generated from the study of Latin America have important implications for the study of religion and politics in other regions of the world, including parts of Europe, Asia, and Africa where similar trends toward increased religious pluralism and battles over religious freedom are playing out. Placing the study of religion and politics in a comparative global context as is being done in this edited volume is the proper step for understanding the spiritual dimensions of an ever-shrinking global community. The theoretical and empirical challenges are great, but the opportunities for learning abound.

## APPENDIX

Data for the discussion on religious and political attitudes were taken from the 1990 *World Values Survey* (WVS) (see Inglehart, et al. 1998)

---

[23] Studies of church and state tend to emphasize organizational and rule-based behavior, while "religion and politics" typically accentuates values, norms, beliefs, and ideologies/theologies. Obviously, no comprehensive understanding of Catholicism and Protestantism is possible without taking into account both dimensions, even though scholars concentrate on one or the other for analytical simplicity. See Levine (1987) for how these analytical dimensions have played themselves out in the study of Latin America.

using survey responses from the three South American countries included in the study – Argentina, Brazil, and Chile. Mexico was excluded from this study as the focus of this chapter is specifically on South America. Religious denomination was coded into a dichotomous variable – Catholic (0) and Protestant (1) – using variable 143 in the WVS. Protestants included "Mainline Protestants," "fundamentalist Protestants" and "other." The latter category may include Mormons and Jehovah's Witnesses as well as a number of spiritist sects in the region. Though "Mainline Protestants" may include "ethnic Protestants," a number of Mainline denominations (e.g., Presbyterians) do engage in proselytizing activities and thus were included in the analysis. The 1990 WVS provided no method for sorting out denominational affiliation in greater detail.

### REFERENCES

Barrett, David B., ed. 1982. *World Christian Encyclopedia*. Nairobi: Oxford University Press.

Berryman, Phillip. 1994. "The Coming of Age of Evangelical Protestantism." *NACLA Report on the Americas* XXVII (6): 6–10.

Brusco, Elizabeth E. 1995. *The Reformation of Machismo: Evangelical Conversion and Gender in Colombia*. Austin: University of Texas Press.

Burdick, John. 1993. *Looking for God in Brazil: The Progressive Catholic Church in Urban Brazil's Religious Arena*. Berkeley: University of California Press.

Cavendish, James C. 1995. "Christian Base Communities and the Building of Democracy: Brazil and Chile." In *Religion and Democracy in Latin America*. William H. Swatos, Jr. (ed.). New Brunswick: Transaction Publishers.

*Catholic Almanac*. Various Years. Garden City, NY: Doubleday & Co.

Coleman, Kenneth, Edwin Elcy Aguilax, and José Miguel Sandovel, et al. 1993. "Protestantism in El Salvador: Conventional Wisdom versus the Survey Evidence." In *Rethinking Protestantism in Latin America*. Virginia Garrard-Burnett and David Stoll (eds.). Philadelphia: Temple University Press.

Conferencia Episcopal Latinoamericano. 1984. *Las sectas en América Latina*. Buenos Aires: Editorial Claretiana.

Daudelin, Jean. and W. E. Hewitt. 1995. "Latin American Politics: Exit the Catholic Church?" In *Organized Religion in the Political Transformation of Latin America*. Satya R. Pattnayak (ed.). Lanham, MD: University Press of America.

Deiros, Pablo. 1992. "Protestant Fundamentalism in Latin America." In *Fundamentalisms Observed*. Martin E. Marty and R. Scott Appleby (eds.). Chicago: University of Chicago Press.

Della Cava, Ralph. 1993. "Financing the Faith: The Case of Roman Catholicism." *Journal of Church and State* 35 (1): 37–59.

Fleet, Michael and Brian H. Smith. 1997. *The Catholic Church and Democracy in Chile and Peru*. South Bend: University of Notre Dame Press.

Freston, Paul. 1993. "Brother Votes for Brother: The New Politics of Protestantism in Brazil." In *Rethinking Protestantism in Latin America*. Virginia Garrard-Burnett and David Stoll (eds.). Philadelphia: Temple University Press.

Froehle, Bryan T. 1995. "Religious Competition, Community Building, and Democracy in Latin America: Grassroots Religious Organizations in Venezuela." In *Religion and Democracy in Latin America*. William H. Swatos, Jr. (ed.). New Brunswick: Transaction Publishers.

Gill, Anthony. 1993. "To Fall from Grace: The Church-State Obsolescing Bargain in Latin America." Paper presented at the annual meeting of the American Political Science Association, Washington, D.C.

———. 1994. "Rendering Unto Caesar?: Religious Competition and Catholic Political Strategy in Latin America, 1962–79." *American Journal of Political Science* 38 (2): 403–425.

———. 1995. "The Institutional Limitations to Catholic Progressivism: An Economic Approach." *International Journal of Social Economics* 22 (9/10/11): 135–48.

———. 1996b. "The Struggle to Be Soul Provider: Catholic Responses to Protestant Growth in Latin America." In *Latin American Religion in Motion: Tracking Innovation, Complexity and Unexpected Change*. Christian Smith (ed.). Westport, CN: Praeger.

———. 1998a. *Rendering Unto Caesar: The Catholic Church and the State in Latin America*. Chicago: University of Chicago Press.

———. 1998c. "Government Regulation, Social Anomie and Protestant Growth in Latin America: A Cross-National Analysis." Working paper. University of Washington.

———. 1999. "The Economics of Evangelization." In *Evangelization and Religious Freedom in Latin America*, edited by Paul E. Sigmund (ed.). Maryknoll, NY: Orbis Books.

Gutiérrez, Gustavo. 1973. *A Theology of Liberation*. Translated by Caridad Inda and John Eagleson. Maryknoll, NY: Orbis Books.

Haggard, Stephan. and Robert R. Kaufman. 1995. *The Political Economy of Democratic Transitions*. Princeton: Princeton University Press.

Hallum, Anne Motley. 1996. *Beyond Missionaries: Toward an Understanding of the Protestant Movement in Central America*. Lanham, MD: Rowman & Littlefield.

Hennelley, Alfred T., ed. 1993. *Santo Domingo and Beyond: Documents and Commentaries from the Historic Meeting of the Latin American Bishops' Conference*. Maryknoll, NY: Orbis Books.

Hewitt, W. E. 1991. *Base Christian Communities and Social Change in Brazil*. Lincoln: University of Nebraska Press.

Huntington, Samuel. 1991. *The Third Wave: Democratization in the Late Twentieth Century*. Norman: Oklahoma University Press.

Hurtado, Alberto. 1992 [1941]. *¿Es Chile un país católico?* Santiago: Editorial Los Andes.

Iannaccone, Laurence R. 1990. "Religious Participation: A Human Capital Approach." *Journal for the Scientific Study of Religion* 29 (3): 297–314.

1994. "Why Strict Religions are Strong." *American Journal of Sociology* 99 (5): 1180–211.

Inglehart, Ronald, Miguel Basañez and Alejandro Moreno. 1998. *Human Values and Beliefs: A Cross-Cultural Sourcebook.* Ann Arbor: University of Michigan Press.

Johnstone, Patrick. 1986. *Operation World.* Bromley, U.K.: WEC Publications.

Kalyvas, Stathis. 1996. *The Rise of Christian Democracy in Europe.* Ithaca: Cornell University Press.

Keogh, Dermot (ed.). 1990. *Church and Politics in Latin America.* London: Macmillan.

Keshavarzian, Arang. and Anthony Gill. 1997. "State-Building and Religious Resources: An Institutional Theory of Church-State Relations in Latin America and the Middle East." Paper presented at the 1997 Annual Meeting of the American Political Science Association. Washington, D.C.

Lalive d'Epinay, Christian. 1969. *Haven of the Masses: A Study of the Pentecostal Movement in Chile.* London: Lutterworth Press.

Lehmann, David. 1996. *Struggle for the Spirit: Religious Transformation and Popular Culture in Brazil and Latin America.* Cambridge: Polity Press.

Levine, Daniel H. 1987. "From Church and State to Religion and Politics and Back Again." *World Affairs* 150 (2): 93–108.

*Religion and Politics in Latin America: The Catholic Church in Venezuela and Colombia.* Princeton: Princeton University Press.

1990. "How Not To Understand Liberation Theology, Nicaragua, or Both." *Journal of Interamerican Studies and World Affairs* 33 (3): 229–45.

1992. *Popular Voices in Latin American Catholicism.* Princeton: Princeton University Press.

1995. "Religious Change, Empowerment and Power: Reflections on Latin American Experience." In *Organized Religion in the Political Transformation of Latin America.* Satya R. Pattnayak (ed.). Lanham, MD: University Press of America.

Lipset, Seymour Martin. 1959. "Some Social Requisites of Democracy: Economic Development and Political Legitimacy." *American Political Science Review* 53: 69–105.

Mainwaring, Scott. 1986. *The Catholic Church and Politics in Brazil, 1916–1985.* Stanford: Stanford University Press.

Martin, David. 1990. *Tongues of Fire: The Explosion of Protestantism in Latin America.* Cambridge: Basil Blackwell.

Miguéz Bonino, José. 1999. "Argentina." In *Evangelization and Religious Freedom in Latin America.* Paul E. Sigmund (ed.). Maryknoll, NY: Orbis Books.

Moreno, Pedro (ed.). 1996. *Handbook on Religious Liberty around the World.* Charlottesville, VA: Rutherford Institute.

Poblete, Renato. 1965. *Crisis Sacerdotal.* Santiago: Editorial del Pacífico.

Serbin, Kenneth P. 1999. "Religious Tolerance, Church-State Relations, and the Challenge of Pluralism in Brazil." In *Evangelization and Religious Freedom in Latin America*, edited by Paul E. Sigmund (ed.). Maryknoll, NY: Orbis Books.

Sigmund, Paul E. 1990. *Liberation Theology at the Crossroads: Democracy or Revolution?* New York: Oxford University Press.

Stark, Rodney and Laurence R. Iannaccone. 1997. "Why the Jehovah's Witnesses Grow So Rapidly: A Theoretical Application." *Journal of Contemporary Religion* 12 (2): 133–57.

Stewart-Gambino, Hannah W. 1992a. *The Church and Politics in the Chilean Countryside.* Boulder: Westview Press.

1992b. "Introduction: New Game, New Rules." In *Conflict and Competition: The Latin American Church in a Changing Environment.* Boulder: Lynne Rienner.

Stoll, David. 1993. "Introduction." In *Rethinking Protestantism in Latin America.* Virginia Garrard-Burnett and David Stoll (eds.). Philadelphia: Temple University Press.

Vallier, Ivan. 1963. *Anglican Opportunities in South America.* New York: Bureau of Applied Social Research.

Verba, Sidney, Kay Lehmann Scholzman and Henry E. Brady. 1996. *Voice and Equality: Civic Voluntarism in American Politics.* Cambridge, MA: Harvard University Press.

Wiarda, Howard J. 1973. "Toward a Framework for the Study of Political Change in the Iberic-Latin Tradition: The Corporative Model." *World Politics* 25 (2): 206–235.

Willems, Emilio. 1967. *Followers of the New Faith: Cultural Change and the Rise of Protestantism in Brazil and Chile.* Nashville: Vanderbilt University Press.

A nne Hallum's account of the rise of evangelicalism and pentecostalism in Central America illustrates several consequences of the introduction of religious pluralism into a previously monopolistic religious
market. Hallum demonstrates that evangelical Protestantism has thrived
in Central America because the Catholic Church could legitimately be
characterized as a "lazy monopoly," leaving spiritual and other needs
unmet. The Central American case study also shows the variety of
responses available to a Catholic Church whose monopoly has been challenged, and the tension between the centralized structure of Catholicism
and the need for local adaptation and flexibility in pluralistic religious
contexts. In some Central American settings, a previously dominant
Catholic Church has managed to adapt to the transformation of local
and national religious markets, while, in others, the Church has
attempted to co-opt or suppress its new evangelical competitors. Finally,
Hallum directs our attention to some of the smaller scale, latent consequences of religious pluralism, and of experiential, personalized Protestantism. "Pentecostalism," in the variety of forms this tradition assumes
in Central America, is a potent source of "social capital," which can
empower previously marginalized people in the "private" spheres of
economic and family life. The Central American case nicely illustrates
that, in this region of the world, "the personal is political" in a very
profound sense.

# 10

# Looking for Hope in Central America
## *The Pentecostal Movement*

### *Anne Motley Hallum*

The five-hundred-year-old virtual monopoly of Roman Catholicism in Central America has given way to a religious marketplace in much of the region in less than thirty years. Today up to 25 percent of the population in this region are Protestants. In the trajectory of "One" dominant religion, to "Few," to "Many," Central America has moved from "One" to the category of "Many" in just one generation. Mainline Protestant churches have had a small presence in the region for a century, and the Maya indigenous religions have been quietly practiced for millennia in Guatemala, or blended with Catholicism. But an open, vibrant and competitive religious pluralism is very recent.

In this chapter, first we will define some important categories of Protestantism. Next, we will examine explanations from the research for why evangelicalism has taken hold in the region in the latter part of this century. Third, we will address the Catholic response to the explosive growth among evangelical Protestants, and finally we will tentatively explore some political implications and suggestions for research. Most Protestants in Central America are evangelicals, and most evangelicals are Pentecostals or neo-Pentecostals. For that reason, these terms will be used somewhat interchangeably in the chapter.

## EVANGELICALS IN CENTRAL AMERICA: DEFINING TERMS

It is difficult to obtain precise estimates of the size of the evangelical movement in Central America. Local Pentecostal Protestant churches are easily formed without registration or accounting; indeed, flexibility and ease of formation are major reasons for the spread of pentecostalism. In the absence of a door-to-door census, we must rely on educated estimates. Table 10.1 presents estimates that allow comparisons across countries. In my own research in Central America during the summers of 1990 through 1998, estimates of the scope of evangelical (i.e.,

Table 10.1. Estimated Percent Protestant, 1993

| Country | Percent Protestant | Number of Protestant denominations | Estimated population, 1995 |
|---|---|---|---|
| Chile | 27.9 | 60 | 14.3 |
| Guatemala | 24.1 | 215 | 10.6 |
| Brazil | 21.6 | 124 | 157.8 |
| El Salvador | 20.6 | 72 | 5.9 |
| Nicaragua | 17.3 | 79 | 4.4 |
| Panama | 16.7 | 50 | 2.6 |
| Honduras | 11.0 | 118 | 5.5 |
| Costa Rica | 10.7 | 179 | 3.3 |
| Bolivia | 9.3 | 120 | 7.4 |
| Argentina | 8.0 | 72 | 34.6 |
| Peru | 7.1 | 64 | n.a. |
| Paraguay | 6.0 | 24 | 5.0 |
| Venezuela | 5.3 | 51 | 21.8 |
| Mexico | 5.2 | 1,552 | 93.7 |
| Ecuador | 3.8 | 57 | 11.5 |
| Colombia | 3.8 | 63 | 37.7 |
| Uruguay | 3.6 | 25 | 3.2 |

*Source*: Johnston, Patrick. *Operation World*. 5th ed. Grand Rapids, MI.: Zondervan 1993. Holland, Clifton L., Director of Latin American Socio Religious Studies Program (PRO-LADES), 1998.

"Protestant") conversion by interviewees equaled or exceeded the figures in Table 10.1. In Guatemala, the true figure may be even ten percentage points higher than the data in this table, and at least one researcher states that "by 1990 Guatemala had the largest percentage of Protestants of any Latin American nation" (Garrard-Burnett 1998:1).

The Assembly of God church is the largest of these Protestant denominations throughout Central America, but it is joined by hundreds of others. In Guatemala, where Pentecostalism is particularly strong, informed figures are: approximately three million evangelicals (27 percent), two to three hundred evangelical denominations, and between 12,000 and 18,000 congregations (Smith 1998). The sheer number of denominations in Table 10.1 indicates the incredible diversity of the evangelical movement, so to clarify somewhat, the following categories are useful for analysis:

(1) Traditional or "historic" evangelical churches include Presbyterian, Mennonites, Episcopalians, Methodists, and Lutherans. Some of these groups have been in Latin America for approximately a century, but have few adherents relative to the population. For example,

Presbyterians have been in Guatemala since 1897, but for the first half of the twentieth century they remained at a fairly stable and unimpressive 1 to 2 percent of the population.

(2) Neo-Pentecostals are found primarily in urban areas and have grown in number among middle-class and upper-class professionals. Many of their leaders are trained in the United States, and many such churches maintain ties with North American denominations. Neo-Pentecostal doctrine stresses that God rewards good Christians with material wealth. Probably the top five denominations in this category are the urban congregations of: *Fraternidad Cristiana, La Familia de Dios, El Verbo, El Shaddai*, and *Elim*.

(3) Pentecostals are by far the largest and fastest-growing category of evangelicals, encompassing probably 80 percent of the members. These evangelicals are from the poorest sectors of society, both urban and rural, and they practice highly experiential, participatory worship with much singing, testifying, faith healing, and speaking in tongues (glossolalia). Material gain is not as central for the Pentecostals as for the Neo-Pentecostals.

The distinction between these three types of Protestants is important in sorting out contradictory claims about the impact of the evangelical movement in Central America.[1] Pentecostals are struggling with daily survival and are seldom interested in direct political participation, but there are signs of empowerment among these members at the level of community involvement. However, the urban and middle- to upper-class Neo-Pentecostals are often interested in participating in higher levels of government, especially regarding issues of reducing crime, and promoting a capitalistic economy and religious freedom.

## EXPLAINING THE GROWTH OF PROTESTANTS IN LATIN AMERICA

The relatively recent explosive growth of evangelicalism in Latin America has occurred for several reasons. First, several North American organizations targeted Central America in the 1970s for missionary activity, just as evangelical Protestantism was experiencing an resurgence in the United States. Nondenominational organizations such as the Latin American Mission, Calvary International, and Overseas Crusade International had more financial resources and energy for proselytizing in neighboring nations that they saw as vulnerable to godless communism

---

[1] For instance, Amy L. Sherman, in her book *The Soul of Development: Biblical Christianity and Economic Transformation in Guatemala* (New York: Oxford University Press, 1997), carefully defines the three categories of Protestants, but then uses them throughout her book as if they are interchangeable, which they are not.

in the 1970s and early 1980s. The missionaries in this period were "faith missionaries," who were usually not attached to a particular denomination and had a great deal of independence – and success – in the field.

Pentecostal churches spread at the local level as church members introduced family members and neighbors to the "new" religion, or sometimes became pastors themselves of a small church. The rapid spread of the churches was due to their ease of formation and pragmatic needs of the people that Catholicism apparently was not meeting. Almost ten years ago, renowned Catholic scholar Enrique Dussel made the following dramatic statement in an interview:

According to Rome, the threat posed by Protestantism is a serious one. A huge sector of the population that is poor and marginalized will be Protestant by the end of the century. In 10 to 15 years, more than 40 percent of Latin Americans will be Protestant. Rome blames liberation theologians, claiming they have concentrated on political instead of spiritual matters. According to the hierarchy, people have turned to sects [Protestants] out of their need for spiritual expression. For me, it's the opposite. The Vatican is in fact responsible for the people's turning to spiritual communities, even if they discourage participation in politics, are irresponsible and focus on individual salvation – like the fundamentalist sects – because the Vatican has no grassroots ministry. Sects offer the people a community. People know each other by name and the pastor is personally interested in them.

Thus, a second major factor explaining the growth of Protestantism is the lack of grassroots ministry because of chronic under-staffing of the Catholic Church in Latin America (see also Anthony Gill's Chapter 9 in this book). Only 15 to 20 percent of nominal Catholics participate actively in religious worship, primarily because of frequent vacancies in the pulpit and confessional. A single priest is usually responsible for a parish numbering 15,000 to 30,000, and he rotates to many different cathedrals each month. As Dussel notes above, community is missing in such a hierarchy, usually because the priest simply has too many parishioners for personal care or community-building activities.

Moreover, frequently priests are recruited from outside the country. In Honduras, for instance, in the late 1980s there were approximately 280 priests in the country and 220 of these were foreign (Inter-Hemispheric Education Resource Center 1988). This is a far cry from the neighborhood evangelical pastors who grew up in the village where they preach and are always available. Thus, Pentecostals oftentimes stepped into a religious community vacuum.

## PENTECOSTAL COMMUNITIES

A third reason that Pentecostal churches are growing is because among the rural and urban poor, Pentecostalism is associated with healing, resisting poverty, and resisting domestic violence. Historian R. Andrew Chestnut argues that faith healing of illnesses flowing from poverty is the critical element in the appeal of Pentecostalism in Brazil and through extrapolation, in much of Latin America. Chestnut reports that 46 percent of the women he interviewed had converted to pentecostalism seeking healing of physical illness. Furthermore, 80 percent of thirty years of testimonials compiled by the Assembly of God church in Brazil related to illness and faith healing (1997: 8). Chestnut describes the typical experience as follows: desperation from illness and unavailability of secular medicine in the slums; grateful acceptance of prayers for the power of healing; the healing experience itself; then conversion and lifestyle changes for the new Pentecostal. Chestnut makes two points regarding faith healing: First is the importance of a *"community* of spiritual medics," who provide emotional comfort and strength to the patient in their group; and second, that medical science now recognizes and is researching the therapeutic benefits of prayer and ritual acts (1997: 79–87).

The author presents a compelling and persuasive case for faith healing as the primary explanatory variable for the massive conversion to Pentecostal Protestantism. He dismisses hypotheses that pointed to urban anomie, millennial/apocalyptic expectations, or political manipulation as causes for the growth. Rather, he finds that people in the poorest neighborhoods of Latin America seek out the most available, effective, and affordable means of coping with health crises for themselves and their families. He points out that the strict obedience to scriptural laws by Pentecostals also means a healthier lifestyle because of the absence of excessive drinking and careless sex. In later chapters, Chestnut broadens his definition of health crises to include sickness of alcoholism, domestic violence and adultery, which somewhat dilutes his emphasis on healing.

Linda Green studied a village in Guatemala made up largely of widows and children because many of the men had been lost to the lengthy civil war. Green found that for these Maya women, Pentecostalism was a "religion of survival" (1993: 160). Church members worked together to build houses, plant and harvest corn, and also socialized nightly at services. In these churches, women pooled their meager resources, shared child-care needs, supported each other financially and emotionally during emergencies and in many cases, raised their standard of living.

Anthropologist Sheldon Annis conducted a detailed analysis of microlevel economic change in an indigenous Guatemalan town. Annis reported that evangelicals were wealthier than Catholics, were more likely to own a vehicle, and were more upwardly mobile – in part because they were more likely to work in occupations that led to owning their own business. Pentecostal children were more likely to go to school than were Catholic children. Pentecostals who remained in agriculture used more advanced farming than the subsistence Catholic farmers, planted high-yielding crops for sale, and fared better than Catholics in almost every measure of agricultural productivity (1987: 102–5). One rarely meets a Guatemalan who is not hard-working regardless of their religious beliefs; however, Pentecostals emphasize *accumulating* their earnings and practice an ascetic lifestyle that provides a bit more money to save.

Annis's research discovery in the Guatemalan town is, of course, highly reminiscent of Max Weber's analysis, *The Protestant Ethic and the Spirit of Capitalism.* Weber saw religion as a distinctive force for economic mobility decades ago. At least twenty independent case studies about evangelicals in Latin America by social scientists now report findings consistent with Sheldon Annis and Weber's original thesis.

Scholarly works on Pentecostalism in Latin America also note its value for helping women confront "machismo" – the complex of male behaviors such as excessive drinking, violence against women and children, chronic infidelity, abdication of household duties, and a general identification with the street culture rather than with the home. Elizabeth Brusco (1993) concludes from research in Colombia that what occurs with Pentecostal conversion is a transformation of male as well as female roles in a way that reduces inequality. Although admittedly controversial, Brusco insists that what occurs when men are transformed by Pentecostal conversion has deep significance:

The ideology of evangelicalism condemns aggression, violence, pride, and self-indulgence while providing positive reinforcement for peace-seeking, humility, and self-restraint. This applies to male as well as female members. . . . In evangelical households the husband may still occupy the position of head, but his relative aspirations have changed to coincide more closely with those of the wife. This last fact is key to the analysis of Colombian Pentecostalism and, I believe, constitutes a change of revolutionary proportions. (1993: 148)

Brusco suggests that after Pentecostal conversion, nominal patriarchy in the home and in the pulpit remains. But if men now share the domestic values of their wives and also measure success in terms of the stability of their homes and the achievements of their children, many of the deepest aspirations of Latin America's women would be attained.

In research in Central America, I repeatedly heard stories from Pentecostal families about how the women had converted first, brought other members of their families to the church, and gradually found their lives more stable. For instance, in a story that encompasses both faith healing and overcoming machismo, a young father, Jovani, described to me why he had become a Pentecostal:

My father had an illness in his intestine that was killing him with pain. We prayed over and over for him and he was cured. The doctor had said he would die, and they didn't understand why he didn't. It was a miracle from God. It was my girl-friend – now my wife – who first took me to her church to pray for my father. Now I'm a member. My parents are still Catholics. They didn't really mind when I became evangelical because they were so happy that I was out of the gang. They were afraid for me in the gang because it was dangerous. That was four years ago, and it was four years ago that I got this job [training teachers]. (1998)

### CATHOLIC RESPONSE

The Catholic hierarchy first ignored the evangelicals, assuming that like the historic Protestant churches they would have little consequence for the Catholic hold on Latin America. By the time of the Latin American Bishops' Conference (CELAM) in Santo Domingo in 1992, the evangelicals could be ignored no longer, and Pope John Paul II urged the bishops to defend their flocks against "the rapacious wolves" (*New York Times*, October 13, 1992). It seemed clear that the official stance of the Church in the light of this challenge would be confrontation. There have been reported incidents of physical confrontation in the streets among evangelicals and Catholics, and undoubtedly tensions have been high within countless divided families.

Yet the Church has also responded by attempting to reinvigorate their religious appeal. Some leaders experimented with a charismatic style of worship. The charismatic groups, in the manner of evangelicals, sing praise songs, hold prayer meetings and healing campaigns, and empha-size personal receiving of the Holy Spirit. The Vatican has shown some ambivalence about this trend, and instructed leaders of charismatic meet-ings and crusades not to allow Protestant speakers and to include the Catholic saints and Mary within the praise songs.

In 1999, the Latin American Bishops' Assembly in Quito, Ecuador called for a "New Evangelicalization" of urban as well as rural residents. In the official documents from the Assembly, the bishops did not denounce the evangelicals, but instead focused on being more creative and flexible in outreach efforts. Although the 1992 documents from Santo Domingo referred repeatedly to the evangelical invasion, virtually the only direct reference to the Protestant presence from the meeting in Quito was the following: "Meanwhile, the sects [evangelicals] and new religious movements are going in search of persons – at times in the manner of proselytizing. . . . Have we not lost in the Church the enthu-siasm and missionary impulse?" (CELAM). This change in tone from the hierarchy indicates a level of acceptance, of self-reflection, and of renewed dedication by Catholics to "try harder."

Progressive Catholics in Latin America who identify with teachings of liberation theology have undergone their own process of soul-searching in the past decade (Batstone, et al.). Anthony Gill's chapter in this book includes an excellent summary of liberation theology: the Catholic teaching prominent in the 1960s, 1970s, and early 1980s in Latin America that boldly challenged the Church to take the side of the poor rather than the elite and asserted that "evil is systemic," not just individual. But in the 1990s, the liberation theology adherents have not only been castigated by the Pope and conservative cardinals in the Church, but have seen their numbers dwindle just as the Pentecostal numbers climb.[2] Nevertheless, Progressive Catholics have often joined together with members of the historic Protestant churches (e.g., Methodists, Presbyterians, Mennonites, American Baptists) in development and assistance

---

[2] The Catholic Church in Guatemala has been consistently progressive and courageous during the thirty-six-year-old civil war in that country, which only ended in 1996. Hopes for a bright peaceful future in Guatemala were dimmed on April 27, 1998 with the brutal assassination of Auxiliary Bishop Juan Gerardi Conedera in the garage of his Guatemala City home. The murder was widely assumed to be politically motivated because it occurred two days after Bishop Gerardi released a 1,400-page report about wartime atrocities, with the tragically ironic title *Guatemala: Never Again!* This powerful document was prepared as a supplement to the United Nations Truth Commission Report that had been negotiated in the Guatemala Peace Accords. The Catholic Church hierarchy in the country was dissatisfied with the "no individual names" directive which weakened the impact of the U.N. Truth Commission work. In contrast, the report compiled by the Guatemala Catholic Church (officially titled Project for the Recovery of Historical Memory or REMHI) describes 422 massacres in detail. It specifies that 401 of these were committed by the army or paramilitary squads, sixteen by the guerrilla forces, and that the responsibility for five of these civilian attacks could not be determined. One result of Bishop Gerardi's martyrdom has been an emotional outpouring in the nation and an increased interest in the report. The Catholic Church published 20,000 copies instead of the 3,000 originally planned.

With Gerardi's assassination, the most dramatic recent nexus for religion and politics in Guatemala has been a bitter and tragic throwback to the past. It illustrates at least two points about liberation theology for scholars: First, the political influence of its leaders and adherents far outweighs the absolute numbers which are very low. Secondly, individual leaders have more autonomy and impact than observers commonly assume. The Vatican has discouraged liberationist teaching in various ways as Anthony Gill's chapter points out, yet Church stances in Guatemala and elsewhere demonstrate that Church leaders in particular settings can resist Vatican pressure. Gill argues that "growing religious pluralism will push the Catholic Church . . . to less vocal and more moderate political positions." This is a rational prediction regarding most issues, but Catholic leaders still demonstrate great power when they challenge the elite in an extreme and prophetic way. A rational cost–benefit analysis of religious behavior will discount martyrdom because it is itself "irrational" and rare, when in reality it has a significant effect.

projects on behalf of the poor. This is a category of Catholic response we should not overlook; that is, cooperation with those ecumenical Protestants who feel much more affinity with liberation theology Catholics than with Neo-Pentecostals Protestants (Hallum, 1996: 91–5). Along these lines, Brian H. Smith (1998) has conducted a thorough review of the literature of religion and politics in Latin America, and he argues persuasively that a likely scenario for the long-term future will be for Progressive Catholics and Pentecostals to work collaboratively on behalf of the poor in their own communities.

Thus the Roman Catholic response to conversions to Protestantism in Latin America has been confrontation and angry denunciation of the sects; then compromise and efforts to emulate some aspects of Pentecostal worship style among Charismatic Catholics; and also cooperation in selective efforts to work with ecumenical Protestants in projects for the poor. After a generation of growth, the vast majority of Pentecostal churches in Central America have no financial ties with transnational organizations – they are local (Cleary and Stewart-Gambino, 1997; Hallum, 1997; Martin, 1990; Miller, 1994). It has thus become clear that the evangelicals are now too numerous and localized to be considered a passing phenomenon, and what seems to be emerging in Central America is an uneasy sharing of religious space. Traditional Catholics, Charismatic Catholics, liberation theology (Progressive) Catholics; and Mainline Protestants, Neo-Pentecostals, Pentecostals, indigenous religions and secularism all appear to be part of the societal-religious fabric that is far richer and more complex than it was just a generation ago.

## IMPLICATIONS FOR POLITICS AND RESEARCH

A logical place to begin examining political implications of evangelicalism in Central America is at the level of national electoral office, which brings us to Guatemala. Both President Efrain Rios Montt (1982–3) of the *El Verbo* church and President Jorge Serrano (1991–3) of the *El Shaddhai* congregation in Guatemala were Neo-Pentecostals, the first non-Catholic leaders in all of Central America.

Efrain Rios Montt participated in a coup overthrowing the dictatorship of General Romeo Lucas Garcia in 1982, and then promptly appointed himself president and dismissed the other members of the junta. Rios Montt had earlier converted to Protestantism through the efforts of California missionaries from Outreach Mission. Thus, conservative evangelicals in the United States were elated at his ascent to the presidency and no doubt agreed with his own assessment on radio broadcasts that he was sent by God to save Guatemala from sin and godless communism. However, he did not save Guatemala from the most brutal and extensive massacres of the thirty-six-year civil war. His detractors say that Rios Montt ordered the massacres and burning of hundreds of villages suspected of aiding guerrillas. His defenders say he had nothing to do with the atrocities and that he simply could not control the military at the height of the war. An obvious sign of his lack of complete control was his ouster by the officer corps in 1983 after just seventeen months in office.

However, Rios Montt remained visible through his radio sermons on behalf of the Neo-Pentecostal *El Verbo* church, and has stayed in the government as a popular "law and order" congressional candidate in a country besieged by crime. His party made a strong, amazing comeback in 1994 when they took the majority of the congressional seats in Guatemala, and later Rios Montt himself was chosen as leader of the congress, where he now presides. The story does not end there, however, because currently Rios Montt has lost political credibility through his alleged tampering with a new law in order to lower the taxing of alcohol – a scandal one newspaper dubbed "Guate-gate." It is even possible that he will be impeached as president of congress, an ignominious end for the long political career of Central America's first evangelical national leader (Smith, 2000).

The first *elected* evangelical leader in Central America was the Neo-Pentecostal member of the *El Shaddai* church, Jorge Serrano in 1990. He was an extremely conservative president, who met opposition from the people for his neoliberal politics of privatization and reduction of already meager social services. At the height of this popular opposition, Serrano suddenly attempted an *auto-coup* by dissolving the congress and the courts and partially suspending the Constitution – probably at the instruction of hard-line military powers. However, in a courageous turn of events, street demonstrations in Guatemala City and international protest at Serrano's power grab resulted in a "countercoup" by more moderate military leaders and Serrano was forced to step down. Eventually, Serrano was found to have embezzled approximately fourteen million dollars of government funds, and he fled the country to a comfortable exile in Panama.

Needless to say, the brutality of Rios Montt, the disgrace of Serrano, and the potential impeachment of Rios Montt from congress, are disillusioning events for Neo-Pentecostals who perhaps envisioned changing the world through political means (Hallum 1996: 106–14). However, it is important to remember the categories introduced earlier when analyzing these developments. Neo-Pentecostals are much more likely to be engaged in electoral politics than are Pentecostals, because they are already from the middle and upper-classes and because they do not want Catholic dominance to crowd them out of economic development. Jorge

Serrano won his landslide victory in 1991 by defusing the religious issue and appealing to Catholics as well as Neo-Pentecostals, in an election in which 55 percent of eligible voters did not participate. Nonvoters are concentrated in the poor majority sector, which includes Pentecostals – neither candidate was able to mobilize the votes of average Pentecostals. If anything, the stories of Serrano and Rios Montt reinforce the Pentecostal disdain from engaging in the corruption of worldly politics.

This is not to say, however, that religious pluralism in Central America, and the high rates of conversion to Pentecostalism do not have political implications. Rather, the political repercussions are much more likely to be at the local level and will appear more gradually than through dramatic presidential coups and elections. These developments are also more difficult to research than national elections.

In an excellent, candid review essay about research on Protestantism in Latin America, David E. Dixon observes that an understanding of major shifts in religious identity, such as that occurring in parts of Central America:

> requires more time and patience than political scientists have. Because Protestantism tends to proliferate among the lower socioeconomic strata, researchers must take the time to break through cultural, class, and gender barriers in order to evoke dependable, accurate responses to questions. . . . Anthropologists are on the whole more willing than other social scientists to spend time in poor neighborhoods. While this dedication is commendable, anthropologists do not always produce findings that convince other social scientists. (1995: 490)

Dixon then proceeds to call for cross-national surveys – more familiar to political scientists – to be used in conjunction with the cultural case studies (1995: 490). The good news is that there are now sufficient in-depth case studies to reveal cross-national similarities and differences, and to inform such surveys. Some research has been misleading, however, because of the conceptual error of lumping together Pentecostalism with Neo-Pentecostal political activity,[3] so it is crucial to maintain clarity on these classifications.

---

[3] An article by H. B. Cavalcanti is a clear example of such confusion. Cavalcanti examines one institution in Brazil, the Presbyterian denomination, and concludes that the whole Protestant movement in Latin America will become subsumed within the traditional authoritarian powers of their host countries. Without citing any of the recent studies cited here (except Martin, 1990), he makes this argument sharply at odds with the observations of numerous field researchers: "Once on their own, these groups [the Protestants in Latin America] become literalist, mystical, or esoteric, having less and less to do with everyday life." H. B. Cavalcanti, "Unrealistic Expectations: Contesting the Usefulness of Weber's Protestant Ethic for the Study of Latin American Protestantism." *Journal of Church and State* (Spring 1995): 289–309.

Studies of women in Pentecostal churches have also been misleading when they focus primarily on the official leadership roles and pastors of Pentecostal churches. It is well known that the "sisters" in the churches effectively run the worship services, head the various church committees, and are often the spiritual guiding force for the congregation as well as the household. As just one illustration, Chestnut found among his Brazilian sample that 80 percent of the women were spiritually gifted, twice as many as the men, and they were highly respected for these abilities (1997: 99). Pentecostal women apparently do not equate gaining the official titles of leadership with being spiritual leaders or with "succeeding" in the movement.

Brenda Brasher and Elizabeth Ozorak make similar points in their separate studies investigating why women are more religious than men when religion appears to be overwhelmingly patriarchal in structure. They both conclude that women experience and define power differently than men, and when scholars criticize or devalue religion *because* women are not official leaders in religious institutions, the scholars are employing the traditionally male esteem for *structural* power. Elizabeth Brusco's field research in Colombia led her to assert that the movement was empowering, and indeed "revolutionary," for the women. Also note the telling fact that two-thirds of the members of these voluntary organizations throughout Latin America are women.

Finally, studies that account for Pentecostal success because of its theological basis also miss the real story. In my own interviews, I found that the simple message of a *transforming* relationship with Christ is both an explanatory variable and a result of Pentecostal conversion. That is, people are drawn to conversion not by a complex theology, but by the possibility of dramatic change in their lives. The following quotation from a pastor in El Salvador is the typical attitude toward theology that I encountered and coincides with the research of Chestnut and others:

I don't care if the Lord is coming or if he will scratch everything with one simple act of his will, or if it will be a process. I don't care. What I need to care about is being closer to him. And if I'm closer to Him everything will be for the good. So I'm not worried about that. Yes, we have a statement about the Rapture [at the end of the world], but we work with a lot of churches, so we don't really teach that. (Enrique Nuncio 1995)

The nondenominationalism of the Pentecostals makes doctrinal statements much less important or revealing to researchers than the effects of the *core beliefs and practices*. Pentecostal teachings give confidence to women resisting spouse abuse because women experience higher self-esteem because of their beliefs, and this is reinforced in a supportive community. Both Pentecostal men and women are improving their standard of living in their neighborhoods and villages through microbusinesses, healthier lifestyles and the discipline of saving meager resources, as at least twenty field studies now attest. To see and analyze this societal impact of Pentecostalism social scientists must examine these neighborhoods and villages, not just the official pronouncements of institutions or political parties.

It would be premature to make predictions about the future direction of the Pentecostal movement in Latin America – it appears to be leveling off in some countries, and continuing to grow in others. One side effect of the 1998 hurricane disaster in Nicaragua and Honduras may be an upsurge in Pentecostal conversions as people look everywhere possible for help, and as churches coordinate their efforts to respond. In any case, a rich body of Latin American case studies now exists that shatters many stereotypes and initial negative expectations of the Pentecostal growth. If nothing else, it has brought authentic religious pluralism to Latin America and forced the Catholic Church out of complacency and into a healthy self-examination and attentiveness to parishioners. But beyond that change, for millions of poor in Latin America, this religious development is about empowerment. Whether this new found power will translate into political aspirations of human rights or labor activism, or simply having more respect in a peaceful home is a choice for each member.

Over time, however, one could speculate that the enhanced self-esteem, the healthier lifestyles, the lack of tolerance for corruption, and the community support structures would influence the broader political system. Anthony Gill's report of findings in the "*World Values Survey, 1990*" indicates that those active in religious organizations are more likely to be active in civic organizations eventually as well. This optimistic development for democracy may require more patience than many political science researchers have. But demonstrating extreme patience, Romero DeLeon Carpio, the former Procurator of Human Rights in Guatemala and former president, said the following when asked about the impact of religious and political changes: "Never before have human rights been respected here – economically, socially, or politically, or in the home – because there has been no democracy, either for the individual or the collective. But millimeter by millimeter, we are gaining true democracy" (Interview with author, 1995).

### REFERENCES

Annis, Sheldon. 1987. *God and Production in a Guatemala Town*. Austin: University of Texas Press.

Batstone, David, Dwight Hopkins, and Eduardo Merdicta (eds.). 1997. *Liberation Theologies: Postmodernity and the Americas*. New York: Routledge.

Bowen, Kurt. 1996. *Evangelism and Aspostasy: The Evolution and Impact of Evangelicals in Modern Mexico*. Montreal and Kingston: McGill-Queen's University Press.

Brasher, Brenda. 1998. *Godly Women: Fundamentalism and Female Power*. New Brunswick, NJ: Rutgers University Press.

Brouwer, Steve, Paul Gifford, and Susan D. Rose. 1996. *Exporting the American Gospel: Global Christian Fundamentalism*. New York: Routledge.

Brusco, Elizabeth. 1993. "The Reformation of Machismo: Asceticism and Masculinity Among Colombian Evangelicals." In *Rethinking Protestantism in Latin America*. Virginia Garrard-Burnett and David Stoll (eds.). Philadelphia: Temple University Press.

⸻ 1993. *Looking for God in Brazil: The Progressive Catholic Church in Urban Brazil's Religious Arena*. Berkeley: University of California Press.

Burdick, John. 1998. *Blessed Anastacia: Women, Race, and Popular Christianity in Brazil*. New York: Routledge.

Chestnut, Andrew R. 1997. *Born Again in Brazil: The Pentecostal Boom and the Pathogens of Poverty*. New Brunswick, NJ: Rutgers University Press.

Clawson, David. 1984. "Religious Allegiance and Economic Development in Rural Latin America." *Journal of Interamerican Studies and World Affairs*. 26 (November): 499–524.

Cleary, Edward L., and Hannah W. Stewart-Gambino, eds. 1997. *Power, Politics, and Pentecostals in Latin America*. Boulder, CO: Westview Press.

Coleman, Kenneth M., Edwin Eloy Aguilar, and José Miguel Sandoval, et al. 1993. "Protestantism in El Salvador: Conventional Wisdom versus the Survey Evidence." In *Rethinking Protestantism in Latin America*. Virginia Garrard-Burnett and David Stoll (eds.). Philadelphia: Temple University Press.

Cox, Harvey. 1996. *Fire from Heaven: The Rise of Pentecostal Spirituality and the Reshaping of Religion in the 21st Century*. Reading, MA: Addison-Wesley Publishing.

Dixon, David. 1994. "The New Protestantism in Latin America: Remembering What We Already Know, Testing What We Have Learned." *Comparative Politics* (July): 479–92.

Drogus, Carol Ann. 1995. "The Rise and Decline of Liberation Theology: Churches, Faith, and Political Change in Latin America." *Comparative Politics* (July): 465–77.

⸻ 1997. "Private Power or Public Power: Pentecostalism, Base Communities, and Gender." In *Power, Politics, and Pentecostals in Latin America*. Edward L. Cleary and Hannah W. Stewart-Gambino (eds.). Boulder, CO: Westview Press.

Dussel, Enrique. 1992. "The Problem is the Church's Unjust Structure," *Latinamerica Press*, 5 November 1992, 7.

Garrard-Burnett, Virginia. 1998. "Transnational Protestantism." *Journal of Interamerican Studies and World Affairs*. (Fall): 117–25.

Green, Linda. 1993. "Shifting Affiliations: Mayan Widows and Evangelicos in Guatemala." In *Rethinking Protestantism in Latin America*. Virginia Garrard-Burnett and David Stoll (eds.). Philadelphia: Temple University Press.

Hallum, Anne Motley. 1996. *Beyond Missionaries: Toward an Understanding of the Protestant Movement in Central America*. Lanham, MD: Rowman-Littlefield.

1997. "The Transformation of the Christian Right in Central America." In *Sojourners in the Wilderness: The Christian Right in Comparative Perspective*. Corwin E. Smidt and James M. Penning (eds.). Lanham, MD: Rowman-Littlefield.

Ireland, Rowan. 1991. *Kingdoms Come: Religion and Politics in Brazil*. Pittsburgh: University of Pittsburgh Press.

Kanagy, Conrad L. 1990. "The Formation and Development of a Protestant Conversion Movement Among the Highland Quichua of Ecuador." *Sociological Analysis* (Summer): 105–17.

Levine, Daniel H. and David Stoll. 1997. "Bridging the Gap Between Empowerment and Power in Latin America." In *Transnational Religion and Fading States*. Susanne Hoeber Rudolph and James Piscatori (eds.). Boulder, CO: Westview Press.

Mariz, Cecilia Loreto. 1994. *Coping with Poverty: Pentecostals and Christian Base Communities in Brazil*. Philadelphia: Temple University Press.

Martin, David. 1990. *Tongues of Fire: The Explosion of Protestantism in Latin America*. London: Blackwell.

Miller, Daniel R., ed. 1994. *Coming of Age: Protestantism in Contemporary Latin America*. Lanham, MD: University Press of America.

Ozorak, Elizabeth. "The Power, But Not the Glory: How Women Empower Themselves Through Religion." *Journal for the Scientific Study of Religion.* 35 (1): 28–36.

Sexton, James D. 1978. "Protestantism and Modernization in Two Guatemalan Towns." *American Ethnologist* 5 (May): 280–302.

Sherman, Amy. 1997. *The Soul of Development: Biblical Christianity and Economic Transformation in Guatemala*. New York: Oxford University Press.

Smith, Brian H. 1998. *Religious Politics in Latin America, Pentecostal vs. Catholic*. South Bend, IN: University of Notre Dame Press.

Smith, Dennis A. 2000. CEDEPCA. Guatemala City, Guatemala. Personal communication with author.

Turner, Paul R. 1979. "Religious Conversion and Community Development." *Journal for the Scientific Study of Religion.* September 18: 242–60.

Weber, Max. 1958 [1930]. *The Protestant Ethic and the Spirit of Capitalism*. New York: Scribner's.

S unil Sahu's account of Hindu politics in India, in the face of intense competition from other religious traditions and from secularism, illustrates several limitations of the role of religion in democratic politics. Sahu provides a fascinating account of the attempt of the Bharatiya Janata party to effect a transformation of Hinduism from a prophetic to a priestly political role. Even religious traditions that are candidates for dominance within a political culture experience several important constraints on their ability to impose a particular orthodoxy. In the case of the Indian BJP, an authentically Hindu Indian politics is inhibited by religious pluralism between traditions, diversity within the dominant tradition itself (perhaps a particular problem within Hinduism), and the lingering effects of secularism provided by postindependence reactions to the policies of a former colonial power. Sahu's essay also provides a clear example of the importance of detailed case studies, since religious conflict on the Indian subcontinent is exacerbated by memories and interpretations of specific historical events. Moreover, the Indian case illustrates that there are numerous and often contradictory aspects to concepts such as "secularism," "church-state separation," or "religious neutrality," which can permit elite-level attempts to manage religious conflict to have the effect of increasing the political salience of religion. Despite the tremendous numerical, historical, and ideological advantages Hinduism might have in India, the role of explicitly Hindu political parties is constrained.

# 11

## Religion and Politics in India

*The Emergence of Hindu Nationalism and the Bharatiya Janata Party (BJP)*

*Sunil K. Sahu*

India was partitioned in 1947 along religious lines, creating a Hindu-majority nation of India and a Muslim-dominated Pakistan. Although religion has been the most powerful single factor in the development of Indian civilization, the official ideology of the early Indian state, and of the dominant Congress party, was secular nationalism. Hindu nationalist parties and organizations such as the Hindu Mahasabha, the Ram Rajya Parishad, the Bharatiya Jana Sangh, and the Rastriya Swayamsevak Sangh (RSS) were of marginal importance before and after India's independence. Jawaharlal Nehru, with other leaders of the Congress and the framers of the Indian constitution, committed India to secularism, and the secular Congress party dominated Indian politics for half a century. In the last two decades of the century, however, there has been a resurgence of Hindu nationalist ideology made manifest by the Bharatiya Janata party (BJP), and a concomitant decline in the consensus on secular nationalism.

The BJP, which had won only two seats in the 1984 parliamentary elections, won 161 seats in the Lok Sabha (the lower house of parliament) in 1996, and formed a government that lasted only thirteen days. In March 1998, the BJP formed a minority government after winning 178 seats in the Lok Sabha. In elections held in October 1999, the BJP increased its numbers to 182 seats, and with its allies it secured a comfortable majority (302) in the Lok Sabha. These three elections over a four-year period have changed the nature of party politics in India. The

An earlier version of this chapter was presented at the 94th Annual Meeting of the American Political Science Association in Boston, September 1998. The author would like to thank Ted Jelen, Mehran Tamadonfar, M. Mohapatra, Clyde Wilcox, Marthe Chandler, K. P. Singh, and the anonymous manuscript reviewers for their comments on earlier drafts. He also thanks the Faculty Development Committee of DePauw University for providing support for this study.

Congress party is in a state of disarray, suffering a humiliating defeat in the election of 1999, when it won only 114 seats in the Lok Sabha. In the golden jubilee year of India's independence, Atal Bihari Vajpayee became the first prime minister since independence who was not associated with the Congress party. It had taken the Hindu nationalist and revivalist forces more than 50 years after independence, but 1998 will go down in history as the year of "Hindu Restoration" in India.

In this "post-Congress polity" (Yadav 1996: 99) of the 1990s, the BJP-led government has given India, for the first time since 1998, a conservative/rightist alternative to the liberal/centrist national governments that dominated the country for most of the time since independence. This chapter is an attempt to explain the factors that led to the sudden rise of the BJP in the last decade and why there was such a lack of support prior to 1980 for what the Rudolphs (1987: 36–47) call "confessional politics" – parties and organizations that acknowledge commitment to religion. I will consider reasons why Hindu nationalism has increased since the 1980s as Nehruvian secularism declined, and why there has been a rise in communal violence especially against Muslims and Sikhs. In addition, I will focus on how the BJP succeeded in expanding its political base though it could not realize its dream of creating a Hindu nation. Finally, I will consider the future of the BJP-led National Democratic Alliance (NDA) government that came to power in October 1999. First, however, it is important to describe the religious and political context of Indian politics.

## INDIA'S RELIGIOUS TRADITIONS IN HISTORICAL CONTEXT

While India houses all the major faiths in the world, Hinduism is its dominant religion and Islam its main religious minority. Hindus constitute more than 82 percent of the population, and Muslims at nearly 12 percent are far more numerous than Christians and Sikhs (both 2%), Buddhists and Jains (less than 1%). The massiveness of the Hindu majority has intimidated many Indian minority communities, especially Muslims and Sikhs, who have feared being overwhelmed. The Muslim demand for the creation of a separate and independent Islamic state of Pakistan, articulated by the Muslim League in 1940, was the manifestation of that fear. The creation of Pakistan in 1947, however, did not end the Hindu-Muslim conflict in India, because a large number of Muslims remained in the country. India's Muslim population is the fourth largest in the world.

Relations between Hindus and Muslims have always been difficult, for the two religions differ radically in their conception of deity, human sexuality, and social organization. The two communities lived side by side for more than one thousand years, but in the first half of the twentieth century there were hundreds of communal riots before independence and intense violence between the two following the partition of India in 1947. Thereafter, the two communities lived in relative peace until the mid-1960s. Since the Muslims had lost most of their political leaders to Pakistan, Indian Muslims supported and voted for the secular Congress party on the understanding that the Congress government would maintain Muslim Personal Law and other aspects of Muslim culture. However, with the reemergence of political action along religious and ethnic lines in the late 1960s, the Hindu-Muslim conflict escalated and violence against Muslims increased, culminating in the destruction of Babur's mosque by a mob of Hindu fanatics on December 6, 1992.

To fully understand the nature of this conflict, it is necessary to understand the theology and religious practice of the major religious traditions in India.

### The Hindu Tradition

Hinduism originated around 2000 B.C., and remains one of the most complex religions in the world. Hinduism is an open religion, and is the source of three other contemporary religions: Jainism and Buddhism, two reform movements in the sixth century B.C., and Sikhism in the fifteenth century A.D. Hinduism does not have an identifiable founder or a single religious text. There are three main Hindu deities: Brahma (the creator of the universe), Vishnu (its preserver), and Shiva (its destroyer), but beyond this core is a bewildering diversity. There are regional variations, as each cultural-linguistic area has its own tradition and local gods. Hindus worship different gods and goddesses, which are limited portrayals of the unlimited – ultimate reality that is formless, nameless, and without personality. Not all Hindus believe in the same things: some worship one god, others many; some go to the temple to worship, others to small shrines in their homes; some revere holy men and saints (yogis and gurus), others particular trees, animals, and stones.

Underlying this diversity in religious practice and doctrine is a core of common beliefs among Hindus based on ancient scriptures and sacred writings such as the four Vedas, the *Upanishads*, and the two great epics, *Ramayana* and *Mahabharata*. Hindus believe in the doctrine of birth, rebirth, and reincarnation or transmigration of souls. The *Upanishads* talk about the unity of the individual soul (*atma*) with the ultimate reality (*Brahman*). The goal of Hindus is to escape from the bondage of individual existence, which is temporary and painful, and to be one with the Brahman. The law of *Karma* (action), the moral law of causation, determines the sequence of rebirth. Thus, the existence of one's life and position in society is determined by one's action in previous births, and one's action in this life will determine whether one will be reborn as a human being, an animal, or a plant. Because Hindus aim at liberation from rebirth, and since liberation does not depend on any intervention from the gods, Hindus follow the provisions of a rule called *dharma* (duty or conduct). The *dharma* of a person is related to caste, a social grouping determined by birth (Mathur 1992).

Hindu society is hierarchical and is divided into four castes conforming to the law of spiritual progression and structural social relations. They are, in descending order of importance, the *Brahmanas* (priests and scholars), the *Kshatriyas* (political rulers and soldiers), the *Vaishyas* (merchants and cultivators), and *Sudras* (artisans and laborers). These four castes are further divided into more than three thousand occupational groups, to which every Hindu belongs. Outside the fourfold caste system are the untouchables, or outcastes, who do not have a caste status. Though not mentioned in the ancient scripture, they rank below Sudras because of the defiling tasks that they have traditionally performed. These untouchables, also known as *Harijans* (children of God – the name given by Mahatma Gandhi), or "schedule castes" (the category used in the constitution) or Dalits (since the 1970s), number about 150 million and have historically been subjected to oppression by upper-caste Hindus.

### The Muslim Tradition

Islam is a more recent import to India, and although there is much diversity in Islam it is far more unified than Hinduism. It was brought to India by the Muslim invaders in the early eighth century and was well entrenched by the thirteenth century, when the Delhi Sultanate was founded (1206). In the sixteenth century, the Moguls, a dynasty of Turkish rulers, established an empire and ruled most of India from 1526 to 1707. The empire formally ended in the mid nineteenth century with the onset of the British rule in India.

Islam, in contrast to Hinduism, is a staunch monotheistic religion. But like Hinduism, Islam is an all-encompassing way of life. Its injunctions and commandments concern virtually all facets of one's personal, family and civic life from diet and clothing to business ethics, marriage, divorce, and inheritance. The creed of Islam is that "There is no God but Allah, and Mohammad is his messenger." The five pillars or obligations of Islam – those things which one must do in order to be a good Muslim – include repetition of the creed, five daily prayers, almsgiving, the fast during the month of Ramadan, and the pilgrimage to Mecca. The major themes of the *Quran*, the scripture of Islam which is said to contain the exact words of Allah to the Prophet and which had more influence on its people than scripture of any other religion, include the oneness of God and the purpose of human existence. The *Quran* and the *Sunnah* form the basis of the Shari'ah, or Islamic laws, as they provide a complete code governing the whole range of human activities. Islam includes a controversial requirement of a Jihad, which takes on many meanings including in some contexts the necessity of a holy war against infidels (Hopfe 1983: 451).

## The Hindu-Muslim Interaction

During the Mogul era, many Muslim rulers forced Hindus to convert to Islam, destroyed and desecrated Hindu temples and schools, and forbade public worship of Hindu idols and the building of new temples or repair of old ones. During the Muslim rule of India, there was mutual hostility between religious leaders of both communities, but there was mutual acceptance among ordinary citizens. Some Muslim rulers, notably Akbar, followed a policy of broad religious tolerance and equality of treatment for all his subjects (Smith 1963: 64). The close interaction between the Hindus and Muslims over centuries has resulted in the two cultures deeply influencing each other. For example, Indian Muslims developed, under the influence of Hinduism, their own form of occupation-based caste distinction, although Islam is egalitarian and inclusive. Muslim culture, on the other hand, has deeply influenced Indian art and architecture, literature and cuisine and, more recently, cinema and popular culture. By the early period of British rule, Hindus and Muslims had become tolerant of each other and were living peacefully side by side in different parts of India and sharing in the development of social and cultural traditions.

However, a series of factors led to the revival of the old enmity and hostility between the two communities in the decades preceding India's independence. Late in the nineteenth century, the Hindu reform and revival movement exacerbated tensions that were further heightened by the rise of Hindu extremism within the Indian National Congress at the turn of the twentieth century. During the independence movement, Hindu and Muslim organizations, and even the Congress party used religious symbols to mobilize people (Madan 1989: 137). The British policy of divide and rule increased religious hostility, by introducing a system of "communal" and "special" representation, and separate electorates had sown the seeds of communal politics, which seriously undermined the Congress's effort to speak for Hindus as well as Muslims and become the sole voice of Indian nationalism. The disproportionate benefits derived by Hindus but not by Muslims from the introduction of English education further contributed to the problem.

These tensions reached a nadir during the final years of the struggle for independence. Religious differences per se did not cause violence, confrontation, and enmity between the two communities. Rather, the Muslim League used religious differences to mobilize popular support for the creation of an independent Islamic state, and the Congress leaders contributed to the process by showing unwillingness to accommodate the demands of the Muslim leaders. The history of communal conflict during the era of nationalist movement has thus shaped the approach to secularism in independent India.

## THE SIKH TRADITION, THE DEMAND FOR PUNJABI SUBA, AND THE POLITICS OF KHALISTAN

Although Hindu-Muslim conflict has taken center stage in the history of religion and politics in India in the twentieth century, there have been conflicts and movements involving other non-Hindu religious minorities, notably the Sikhs who demanded the creation of a Punjabi-speaking province in the 1960s and a separatist movement for *Khalistan* (Land of the Pure) in the 1980s. Sikhism, founded by Guru Nanak, a Hindu, at the beginning of the sixteenth century, when Muslim rule was being consolidated, is a reformist and monotheistic religion. A blend of Hindu devotionalism and Muslim piety (Larson 1995: 23) Sikhism emphasizes the unity of Godhead, forbids worship of idols, and opposes the Hindu caste system. But the Sikh tradition is closer to Hindu traditions than to Muslim traditions. Most Hindus, therefore, regard Sikhism as a part or subset of the Hindu fold, which has given rise to the Sikh concern over how to maintain internal orthodoxy and the separateness of the Sikh religious identity and not be absorbed by Hinduism.

The persecution of the Sikhs and the execution of two gurus (religious teachers) by Mughal rulers had led to a martial tradition among Sikhs. Because many Sikh Gurus were also rulers of the Sikh kingdoms, there is no separation of religion and state in Sikhism. The British annexed the Sikh kingdom in the nineteenth century, and Sikhs remained loyal to the British and were rewarded with land and jobs, especially in the British army. However, the Sikhs moved away from the British and supported the Congress, especially after the Amritsar Massacre (1919) in which 379 Indians were killed and 1200 wounded by British troops.

With the introduction of democratic reforms and India's independence in 1947, the Sikhs lost the privileges previously extended by the British to religious minorities. A large number of Sikhs lost rich farmlands to Pakistan due to partition. Because they were not adequately compensated for the losses, this grievance gave birth to the agitation for a separate Punjabi-speaking province in India. This political pressure was spearheaded by the organization Akali Dal. The Sikh demand for a Punjabi Suba was based on linguistic and ethnic, not religious, differences with the Hindi-speaking population of the Punjab and was consistent with the Congress government effort, in the 1950s and early 1960s, to reorganize states along linguistic lines (Brass 1994: 193–4). However, the crisis and turmoil in Punjab in the 1980s, involving the Sikh secessionist movement, terrorism and Hindu retaliation, differed sharply from their earlier demand for a Punjabi Suba. In this instance radical Sikhs clashed violently with moderate Sikhs and with Hindus in their claim to protect and promote the interest of the faith and the community (Stern 1991, p. 124). The demand for a Sikh state in a constitutionally secular India was unacceptable to the central government.

The Sikh terrorism and violence which engulfed and paralyzed Punjab was India's most important political issue in the mid-1980s. The violence was the unintended consequence of the power struggle in Punjab between the Congress party and the Akali Dal. Although the Akali Dal did not have majority support in this majority Sikh province, Indira Gandhi sought to minimize their political clout by encouraging a split in the group. She encouraged the extreme Sikh faction within the Akali Dal to break away from their party, and later she supported Bhindranwale, leader of the Sikh Student Federation and a popular militant preacher, to further weaken the Akali Dal. The Akali Dal responded by mobilizing the forces of religious nationalism, through the chain of Sikh's temples available to the party, in order to unite its power base. Thus the Congress party's mobilization to split the Akali Dal and the latter's counter-mobilization led to the rise of Sikh militancy, violence and civil disorder that took on a political life of its own, increasingly out of control of both the Akalis and the national government (Kohli 1990, p. 360).

In an effort to curb Sikh terrorism, which took the lives of twenty to fifty people monthly between 1982 and 1987, Mrs. Gandhi ordered a military raid on the Golden Temple in Amritsar, the holiest shrine of the Sikhs, to flush out the terrorists who had taken refuge and hoarded a large cache of arms and weapons. According to the official count, 576 people were killed in the raid and some parts of the Golden Temple were destroyed, infuriating Sikhs all over the country (Hardgrave and Kochanek 1993: 155–6). The Sikhs held Mrs. Gandhi personally responsible for the raid on their temple, and their rage was manifested in a mutiny by a small number of Sikh soldiers and ultimately Mrs. Gandhi's assassination (October 31, 1984) by two of her own Sikh bodyguards. The assassination sparked violence against Sikhs by Hindus in Delhi and elsewhere, often with the complacency of the local Congress leaders; it was the worst violence against the Sikhs since the partition. Although

Rajiv Gandhi, who succeeded his mother as prime minister after her assassination, signed an accord with the Sikh leaders in 1985, it took many years to restore peace and order in Punjab. After a prolonged period of president's rule in Punjab, State Assembly and Lok Sabha elections were held in February 1992.

## INDIA AS A SECULAR STATE

India is constitutionally a secular state. The leaders of the nationalist movement in India recognized that the British had intentionally polarized Indians along religious and communal lines in the first four decades of this century: separate electorates for the Muslims were introduced in 1909 and in 1919, and in 1935 the same principle was extended to other minority religious communities. Therefore, the Congress denounced the colonial policy of divide-and-rule that had hardened vertical divisions along sectarian lines. Determined to change this situation after independence, the Congress leaders sought to create a political, legal, and constitutional system that would give security and a sense of fairness to India's religious minorities, especially the Muslims. The framers of the constitution had witnessed the horrors of violence between Hindus and Muslims following India's partition in 1947 that took nearly a million lives: India's approach to secularism was informed by the lessons of partition that "religious politics kills" (Rudolphs 1987: 38).

The 44th amendment to the Constitution (1976) guarantees the secularization of law so that all citizens would be granted equal rights by the state (Baird 1981: 393). The state, under the constitution, observes an attitude of *sarvadharma sadbhava* (goodwill, neutrality, and impartiality toward all religions). This meant that reserved seats and separate electorate for religious minorities were eliminated. Neutrality and impartiality does not mean complete separation of church and state, however. Unlike the United States, India explicitly provides for state support of religious institutions such as Hindu temples and Muslim mosques and for educational institutions that impart religious instructions such as Aligarh Muslim University and Banaras Hindu University (Smith 1963, pp. 130–2). Indeed, the constitution permits taxation for the benefit of all religions but not for "any particular religion" (Article 27), and it is permissible for the state to provide subsidy to the Muslims undertaking pilgrimage to Mecca.

Implementation of the secular state inevitably led to tensions and contradictions. Article 26 guarantees every religious group or denomination "the right to establish and maintain institutions for religious and charitable purposes; to manage its own affairs in matters of religion; to own and acquire and administer movable and immovable property." But freedom of religion was compromised by constitutional sanctions for extensive state interference in religious affairs such as requiring all public Hindu temples to be open for worship by ex-untouchables (Smith 1963: 133). In guaranteeing the fundamental principle of equality and nondiscrimination, the constitution provides that "The state shall not discriminate against any citizen on grounds only of religion, race, caste, sex, or place of birth or any of them" (Article 15 [1]). Yet this principle was compromised by the reservation of seats for the Schedule castes and Scheduled tribes in federal and state legislatures (Articles 330 and 332) and by the enactment of the Hindu Code Bill (1955–6) which codified laws for Hindus, but not for Muslims and Christians, in the areas of marriage, succession, guardianship, adoption, and maintenance.

The Nehruvian vision of a secular state was somewhat at odds with the views of Mahatma Gandhi, who emphasized the inseparability of religion and politics and the superiority of the former over the latter. For Gandhi, as Madan explains, "religion was the source of absolute value and hence constitutive of social life; politics was the arena of public interest. Without the former the latter would become debased" (Madan 1997: 344). Gandhi applied Hindu ethical values to the nationalist movement and used Hindu religious concepts such as "truth force," and "nonviolence" political tactics.

The militant Hindus and their radical organization, the Rashtriya Swayamsevak Sangh (RSS), opposed both the secular nationalist and the Gandhian views. They considered Gandhi's attitude toward Muslims to be "appeasement" and saw the Nehru government's effort to treat all religions equally as giving non-Hindu religions special protection (Frykenberg 1986). Hindu revivalists were marginalized in the freedom movement, and were further discredited in the immediate aftermath of independence because of the assassination of Mahatma Gandhi on January 30, 1948 by former RSS member Nathuram Godse, a fanatic Hindu nationalist.

Many Hindus opposed secularism, both on principle and because they saw inherent contradictions in its implementation. The Nehru government attempted to maintain "its simultaneous commitment to communities and to equal citizenship" (Rudolphs 1987: 38–9). Thus it refrained from endorsing a uniform civil code that might conflict with Muslim personal law, which occupied such a central place within Islamic religion. Hindu civil law codified the right for women to inherit some of their patrimony, for example, but this did not apply to Muslims. Muslim men were permitted four wives, and allowed easy access to divorce with no alimony or appeal. Nehru had hoped that the Muslim leadership would eventually reform their personal law, but the leadership remained orthodox in its doctrine.

Thus the Nehru government pursued secularism by "protect[ing] and maintain[ing] religious institutions of all faiths; allow[ing] colleges sponsored by Sikhs and Muslims, as well as by Hindus, to be incorporated into state universities; and permit[ting] aspects of traditional Islamic law pertaining to marriage, divorce, and inheritance to apply to members of the Muslim community." This approach to secularism was paradoxical, as Nehru sacrificed certain important principles of the secular state, such as a uniform civil code, in order to build up the confidence of religious minorities in the non-communal secular nature of the Indian state (Smith 1963: 290–1). Hindu nationalists interpreted this approach as merely pandering to religious minorities, especially Muslims, for electoral gain.

## HINDU NATIONALISM

The Rashtriya Swayamsevak Sangh (RSS) is at the core of Hindu nationalism. The RSS was founded in 1925 and drew its ideology from the writings of V. D. Savarkar, who argued that "virtually everyone who has ancestral roots in India is a Hindu and collectively they constitute a nation" (Savarkar 1969). In his *Essentials of Hinduism* (1922) and other writings, Savarkar advanced the concept of *Hindutva* (Indianness), which equated Hindu religion with ancestral Indian roots and nationhood (Savarkar 1969). His writings sought to create a Hindu identity and militancy, and to that end he objectified Muslims and the British as the Other (McGuire and Reeves 1994: 10.)

Golwalkar made explicit the role of non-Hindu in a Hindu nationalist state: The non-Hindu people in Hindustan must either adopt the Hindu culture and language, must learn to respect and hold in reverence Hindu religion, must entertain no ideas but those of glorification of the Hindu race and culture, i.e. they must not only give up their attitude of intolerance and ungratefulness towards this land and its age-old traditions but must also cultivate the positive attitude of love and devotion instead – in a word they must cease to be foreigners, or may stay in the country, wholly subordinated to the Hindu nation, claiming nothing, deserving no privilege, far less any preferential treatment – not even citizens' rights. (Quoted in Malik and Singh 1994: 159)

In the ideology of *Hindutva*, Hinduism is presented as a "unified cultural and religious system," and the diversity within Hinduism is either downplayed or completely ignored (Shekon 200: 36–7). The "family" of political parties and organizations involved in the resurgent Hindu nationalist movement such as the BJP, the RSS with 125,000 branches, a youth wing and 3,000 full-time instructor-propagandists, the mammoth Vishwa Hindu Parishad (VHP) and its youth wing, the Akhil Bharatiya Mazdoor Sangh (the largest trade union organization), all sub-

## Table 11.1. The Sangh Parivar (Family)

| Organization | Number (in millions) |
| --- | --- |
| Bharatiya Janata party | 17 |
| Rashtriya Swayamsevak Sangh | 2.5 |
| Akhil Bharatiya Kisan Sangh | 8 |
| Akhil Bharatiya Mazdoor Sangh | 4.5 |
| Adivasi Kalyan Kendra | 2.3 |
| Fishermen's Co-op Societies | 2.2 |
| Vivekananda Medical Mission | 1.7 |
| Adhyapak Parishad | 1.8 |
| Vivekananda Kendra | 1.8 |
| Bharatiya Vikas Parishad | 1.8 |
| Deen Dayal Shodh Sansthan | 1.7 |
| Rashtriya Sevika Samiti | 1.8 |
| Akhil Bharatiya Vidyarthi Parishad | 1.8 |
| Janata Yuva Morcha | 1.8 |
| Shikha Bharati | 2.1 |
| Vishwa Hindu Parishad | 2.8 |

*Sources: India Today International*, September 28, 1998, p. 16; *India Abroad*, May 1, 1998, p. 1.

scribe to the ideology of *Hindutva* as formulated by Savarkar and Golwalkar, although tactical differences between them remain. See Table 11.1.

### THE GENESIS AND HISTORY OF BJP

The roots of the BJP are found in its predecessor, a Hindu nationalist party called the Bharatiya Jana Sangh, founded in 1951. The Jana Sangh focused on cultural issues, calling for "one country, one nation, one culture, and the rule of law." The party emphasized that "the partition of India was the biggest tragedy that could fall on the country" and it believed that "the future welfare of India and Pakistan demand[ed] a reunited India" and that "it will work towards this end, keeping this as its goal and aim." The Jana Sangh concentrated its activities mainly in the Hindi heartland, especially in Uttar Pradesh, Madhya Pradesh, and Delhi, and had a special appeal to the northern states.

The party was largely isolated in the 1950s because the head of the party's central secretariat, the Hindi chauvinist Deen Dayal Upadhyaya, maintained ties with the militant RSS, which limited the ability of the party to appeal to moderate Hindu traditionalists. The party won only 3, 4, and 14 seats, respectively, in the first three parliamentary elections.

### Table 11.2. BJP/Jana Sangh Election Results:
1952–98

| Election | Number of seats | Votes (%) | Seats (%) |
|---|---|---|---|
| 1952 | 3 | 3.1 | 0.6 |
| 1957 | 4 | 5.9 | 0.8 |
| 1962 | 14 | 9.4 | 2.8 |
| 1967 | 35 | 9.41 | 6.73 |
| 1971[a] | 22 | 7.4 | 4.24 |
| 1977[a] | 93 | | |
| 1980 | 16 | | |
| 1984 | 2 | 7.4 | 0.89 |
| 1989 | 86 | 11.4 | 5.7 |
| 1991 | 120 | 19.9 | 22.0 |
| 1996 | 161 | 20.3 | 29.5 |
| 1998 | 178 | | 32.7 |
| 1999 | 182 | | 33.5 |

[a] The Jana Sangh contingent in the Janata party.

In the 1967 elections, the Jana Sangh joined in a broad anti-Indira Ghandi coalition, and won thirty-five seats in parliament and participated in united front governments in many states, notably Bihar, Punjab and Uttar Pradesh. The participation of the Jana Sangh in the anti-Congress camp, especially in the JP movement (1973–5) in which the Jana Sangh and the RSS provided much of the cadre for agitation in Delhi, Bihar, and Gujarat, finally gave the party the acceptance it needed.

When Mrs. Gandhi imposed the Emergency Rule in June 1975, the top Jana Sangh leaders, along with JP and other opposition leaders, were put in jail. In February 1977, Mrs. Gandhi ended the Emergency Rule and parliamentary elections were held. On the eve of this election the Jana Sangh temporarily merged with three other noncommunist opposition parties to form the new Janata party, a coalition united only in its opposition to Mrs. Gandhi's Emergency Rule. The Janata party won the election and formed a government, but the coalition unraveled and the party was badly beaten in the 1980 elections. In the aftermath of the 1980 elections, the Jana Sangh contingent left the Janata party to form the Bharatiya Janata party (BJP).

## THE BHARATIYA JANATA PARTY (BJP)

After leaving the Janata party, the Jana Sangh contingent recognized that the old image of a party that gave a narrow Brahminic interpretation of Hinduism had limited its appeal. The party's leaders wanted to expand their base and become a truly national party. By acquiring a new name the party sought to show voters that it had evolved from the narrow and strident "Hindi, Hindu, Hindustan" politics of the Jana Sangh to become a more mature and benign formation which would use its organizational and behavioral distinctiveness to occupy the anti-Congress space (Chatterjee 1996, p. 89). With that goal in mind the BJP adopted the ideology of Gandhian socialism, although the party has shifted its ideological emphasis and strategy several times since it was founded in 1980. The history of the party is of six distinct periods.

### Phase I: The Moderate BJP (1980–6)

In an effort to change the old Jana Sangh image, the BJP tried to maintain distance from the RSS and adopted the ideology of "Gandhian socialism." At the same time, the Congress party was slowly moving away from Nehru's secularism, with Mrs. Gandhi making an open appeal for Hindu votes. Mrs. Ghandi lost the Muslim vote for the first time in the 1977 elections, and although she regained Muslim support in 1980 she also appealed to the upwardly mobile Hindu middle castes.

Her son Rajiv Gandhi played on the fear of the Hindu voters in 1984 when, following the assassination of Prime Minister Indira Gandhi, he campaigned against Sikh extremism and on behalf of national unity. The Rajiv government did very little in response to the violence committed by Hindus against the Sikhs, especially in Delhi following the assassination of his mother by two of her Sikh bodyguards. The Congress party won an unprecedented victory in 1984, 401 seats, by appealing to anti-Sikh sentiments among Hindu voters, and in doing so limited the BJP to only two seats in parliament. This election suggested to BJP leaders that a Hindu voting bloc was indeed possible, but that they would have to win it from Congress (Chatterjee 1996: 91).

### Phase II: BJP's Two-Track Strategy (1986–9)

The BJP strategy in the aftermath of its 1984 electoral defeat was two-pronged. On the one hand, it remained a part of the mainstream anti-Congress opposition that crusaded against corruption in the Rajiv Gandhi government. On the other hand, the BJP carved out a base of its own through the mass mobilization of RSS and VHP.

The old Jana Sangh hard core once again played an important role within the party, working closely with the VHP and the RSS. In 1986, a Supreme Court ruling granted alimony to a seventy-five-year-old woman divorced by her Muslim husband in the Shah Bano case. The ruling enraged orthodox Muslims, who claimed that it violated their personal law, and the Congress party soon passed the Muslim Women (Protection of Rights on Divorce) Act in 1986, overturning the decision. In the Shah Bano case Rajiv Gandhi gave the Hindu nationalists and the BJP an issue they used to effectively mobilize Hindu support.

Many Hindus, especially those in the upper caste, were angry at the government's policies in the Shah Bano case. When the Ram Janmabhoomi temple was opened (February 1986) to Hindus for worship after thirty-seven years, it gave the Hindu nationalists an even greater issue with which to mobilize support and unite the Hindus.

## Phase III: The Militant BJP (1990–2)

The 1989 election resulted in the formation of a minority National Front government under the leadership of V. P. Singh, which was supported by the BJP and the left parties. However, within months the BJP abandoned the guise of moderation when it demanded that the Ram Janmabhoomi temple in Ayodhya be handed over to "the Hindus" (for details, see Elst 1990). Many Hindus believed that the Mogul emperor Babur built a mosque on the birth site of the popular god king Rama after demolishing an existing Rama temple, though there is no historical evidence to support the claim (see Gopal 1990: 11–20). The mosque was one of the oldest and most sacred places for Muslims, and Rama's birthplace one of the most important sites for Hindus. Hindu nationalists demanded that the mosque be dismantled and that the historic Ram Janmabhoomi temple be rebuilt.

In 1885, the Hindu application to build a temple on the site was denied by the court, and in 1949 the court locked the building in response to the demand of the Muslims to remove the idols of Rama, which had been installed by a group of Hindus who briefly took over the mosque following the partition of India. The mosque remained locked until February, 1986, when the Faizabad District Judge ordered opening of the building for Hindu worship. Thus by the time the BJP endorsed the VHP demand for the liberation of Ram Janmabhoomi, Ayodhya had already been transformed into a national issue. The efforts made by the VHP through its Religious Council and the Ram Birthplace Liberation Ritual had caught the imagination of Hindus all over India.

The most effective mobilization strategy of the VHP was the consecration of temple bricks, begun on September 30, 1989. As many as 110 million Hindus in India and many Hindus abroad participated in the worship of bricks at the local level, and these bricks were then sent to Ayodhya for the building of a temple (Chatterjee 1996: 100). Interest in the issue was heightened when national television broadcast its version of Hindu epics *Ramayana* and *Mahabharata*. *Ramayana* was an eighteen-month long series that attracted an estimated 100 million devoted viewers, and "this was followed by the even more successful *Mahabharata*, the greatest of Hindu epics, in 91 weekly episodes" (Hardgrave and Kochanek 1993: 182).

When the BJP supported the Ram Janmabhoomi liberation, the movement gained extra legitimacy. The BJP was supporting the United Front government and therefore considered it as part of the establishment. BJP support also helped BJP solidify its already growing support base. In the past few years the party had succeeded in expanding its support among the emerging middle class in small towns all over India. This new party base was jealous of the cosmopolitan English-speaking elites, and also fearful of competition from lower castes who were guaranteed 27 percent of government jobs by a new government policy (Chatterjee 1996: 105).

The mobilization of Hindus behind the BJP in this time was aided by regional and international developments in the 1980s – Zia ul-Haq's Islamization in Pakistan, the impact of the Khomeini revolution on the rise of Islamic fundamentalism in many Muslim countries, and the conversion of Scheduled caste Hindus to Islam in Meenakshipuram in Tamil. The Hindu nationalist organizations succeeded in uniting the Hindus not so much through common religious belief, but more through shared hostility toward Muslims.

Relying on the organizational strength of the RSS and the VHP and their ability to mobilize the Hindu population, BJP leader Advani announced in September 1990 a 10,000 kilometer journey in a chariot (Rath Yatra) in a style that Lord Rama may have used, from Somnath temple in Gujarat to Ayodhya. The Rath Yatra, however, was stopped by the government. Advani was arrested, and the BJP withdrew its support of the government, which collapsed. The new government of Chandra Shekhar lasted only four months.

In the 1991 election, the BJP campaigned on a platform that emphasized Hindu identity and nationalism, and it effectively exploited the Ayodhya issue and anti-Muslim hostilities. During the election campaign the identity of the party became virtually indistinguishable from that of the RSS, the VHP and Bajrang Dal. The BJP won 119 seats in parliament and power in four states, Himachal Pradesh, Madhya Pradesh, Rajasthan, and Uttar Pradesh (U.P.). But gaining power only at the state level, especially in U.P., and not at the center, presented a problem for the party. As the party in power in U.P. (where Ayodhya is located), the BJP could no longer continue putting pressure on the central government to hand over Babri mosque to the Hindus. Therefore, the BJP strategy changed following the 1991 election.

### Phase IV: A "Responsible" National Party in Search for Power
### (1992–8)

The 1991 election marked the beginning of a new phase for BJP in which it started projecting the image of a "responsible" national party interested in capturing state power in a manner similar to other parties. Yet the forces of Hindu nationalism that they had inflamed could not be controlled, and in December 1992 Hindu nationalists destroyed the Babri Masjid, leading to the worst communal violence in India since partition. Neither the VHP nor the BJP were able to fully control the movement.

The destruction of the Babri Mosque exhausted *Hindutva* as an electoral platform for the BJP, which immediately tried to distance from Hindu organizations, in particular the RSS and the VHP. In the 1993 state elections, BJP lost its majority in all four states it had controlled. Therefore, the BJP officially moved away from the Ram Janmabhoomi movement, although party documents routinely mentioned Ayodhya as an important issue. Moreover, the party scrupulously maintained distance from the demands of the Hindu nationalist organizations to gain control over shrines in two other cities in Uttar Pradesh.

The BJP quickly shifted its focus to issues of corruption, unstable coalitions, and good governance. The party even made overtures to the Muslims when Advani declared that "we can't afford to have such a large section of society outside our area of concern" (quoted in *India Today*, September 22, 1997: 17). In an effort to broaden the support base of the party, the BJP sought to co-opt the backward castes into the party, an effort that lead to increased support among these castes and Dalits (see Ahmad, Bhaumil, and Mishra 1997: 12–16).

This shift of emphasis was obvious in the strategy of the BJP in the 1996 and 1998 parliamentary elections. In 1996, while the party identified five issues in the Lok Sabha elections – the Ayodhya temple issue, Article 370 of the constitution dealing with the status of Kashmir, infiltration of foreigners, the Uniform Civil Code, and economic nationalism – the BJP campaign focused on the nonideological slogan, a "vote for change" (see Pai 1996: 1175). The party entered into pragmatic alliances with three regional parties, and the BJP won 161 seats and became the largest single party in parliament. On the eve of the 1998 parliamentary election, the BJP was hard at work projecting the image of a middle-of-the-road party that was playing conventional politics by skillfully entering into electoral alliances with regional parties. So successful was the new strategy that a leading news magazine commented: "Thanks to a series of incremental deals, beginning with Kalyan Singh's decimation of the Congress in Uttar Pradesh last October, the BJP and its allies have today become a factor in almost all major states, barring Kerala and

West Bengal" (*India Today*, December 29, 1997: 19). Thus the road that led the BJP to power was circuitous, from moderate part through radical Hindu nationalism to pragmatism.

### Phase V: The BJP in Power (March 1998–9 elections)

In power the BJP's most significant action was the testing of five nuclear weapons in May 1998, which prompted the Pakistani government to also test nuclear weapons, dramatically escalating border tensions, which then led to American economic sanctions. The BJP's strong defense policy has struck a favorable chord with the public. The May 1998 nuclear test, which was accepted across ideological and party lines as a desirable move by India, helped boost the image of the BJP as a party capable of decisive action and a strong security policy, and the diplomatic and military victory in the Kargil war with Pakistan made Prime Minister Vajpayee one of the most popular non-Congress leaders of independent India.

The BJP also showed pragmatism in dealing with religious issues. This was best seen in its decision to impose a ban on a controversial play that sought to dramatize the Hindu nationalist ideology and justification of the man who killed Mahatma Gandhi in 1948. The play quickly became a national political issue when the Gandhians, the Congress, and other opposition party leaders protested in parliament that the play denigrated Mahatma Gandhi and eulogized his assassin, Nathuran Godse. The BJP did ban the performance, much as the Congress party had in 1986 banned the publication of Salman Rushdie's *Satanic Verses*.

Similarly, in October 1998, the BJP withdrew, under pressure from its allies and the opposition, a controversial recommendation for making the teaching of Sanskrit, the classical Indian language, and Hindu religious texts mandatory in schools, and the proposal to bring about changes in the rights of minorities, guaranteed under the constitution, to run their own educational institutions (*India Abroad*, October 30, 1998: 4). In both cases, BJP leaders acted out of political expediency, demonstrating that they are capable of compromise to remain in power.

### Phase VI: BJP's Caretaker Government and Its Victory in the 1999 Elections

Following the dissolution of the parliament in April 1999, the Election Commission set elections dates between September and early October, giving the BJP the opportunity to lead a caretaker government for the longest period in India's history. During the next one hundred days, a series of events improved the image of the BJP. Inflation reached an all-time low, India won a military and diplomatic victory over Pakistan in the Kargil war, and the government announced India's draft nuclear

Table 11.3. Ministers in the First BJP Government: Partywise Breakup

| Party | Cabinet ministers | Ministers of state |
|---|---|---|
| BJP | 11 | 14 |
| Shiv Sena | 1 | – |
| Independents | 2 | 1 |
| TRC | 1 | – |
| Lok Shakti | 1 | – |
| Akali Dal | 1 | 1 |
| Samata | 1 | – |
| BJD | 1 | 1 |
| AIADMK | 2 | 2 |
| PMK | – | 1 |
| Arunachal Congress | – | 1 |
| TOTAL | 21 (plus prime minister) | 21 |

*Source*: *India Today*, March 10, 1998, p. 11.

doctrine. The BJP was also helped by a leadership crisis within the Congress party, and the creation of a breakaway faction.

The BJP-led NDA won a comfortable majority in the Lok Sabha, thereby forming a stable government for the first time since 1996. Its victory can be attributed to several factors. First, since the BJP was in power for over seventeen months prior to the election, it was perceived as a party capable of governing the country. Second, the BJP, unlike the Congress party, is a cadre-driven party; most of the 125,000 RSS *Shakhas* and one million active Sangh *Parivar* members work for the BJP candidates in their areas, and it is the only party that conducts training camps for its polling agent. Third, the party has evolved from a narrow, urban Hindi-based party in the 1980s to a national party with a broad support base in the late 1990s. The party has expanded its base from a limited geographic area and support from middle-class Hindu men in 1984 to an established presence in all areas, except Kerala and the Northeast, and support in both rural and urban areas.

Fourth, by forging National Democratic Alliance with twenty-three political parties, the BJP has expanded its support across caste spectrum: the upper castes through the BJP, the other backward castes (especially Kurmis and Koeris) through the Samata party, and the Dalits through Janata Dal (U) leader Ram Vilas Paswan. Because most of the key players of backward caste politics are now BJP's coalition partners, the future of backward caste politics is bleak (see Table 11.3).

Fifth, the BJP succeeded in portraying the Congress party as a party lacking in vision, discipline, and honest leadership. Finally, unlike the

Table 11.4. Ministers in the Second BJP Government:
Partywise Breakup

| Party | Cabinet ministers | Ministers of state |
|---|---|---|
| BJP | 16 | 31 |
| JD (U) | 4 | 2 |
| TC | 1 | 1 |
| DMK | 2 | 2 |
| SS | 1 | 1 |
| BJD | 1 | 1 |
| PMK | – | 2 |
| MSCP | – | 1 |
| MDMK | – | 1 |
| NC | – | 1 |
| IND | – | 1 |
| TOTAL | 25 (plus prime minister) | 44 |

Source: *http://www.indiadecides.com/cabinet.shtml.*

previous national elections in India and similar to the campaign style in
the United States, the 1999 election campaign did not seriously focus on
issues, policy, and ideological differences. Instead, candidates of all political parties, especially the BJP and the Congress party, resorted to personal attacks, dirty talks and dirty tricks (*India Abroad*, September 13,
1999: 12–19). In such an environment the BJP stood to gain more than
other parties. With 68 percent job approval rating of the Vajpayee regime
in September, the BJP fashioned the 1999 election, with a great degree
of success, into a presidential style leadership contest between Vajpayee
and Sonia Gandhi. Although most people were satisfied with the
Vajpayee government's performance, incumbency was an asset and not
a liability for the BJP.

## FUTURE OF SECULARISM IN INDIA

What does the rise of a religious party to power in India in 1998 and its
electoral victory again in the 1999 parliamentary elections tell us about
the future of secularism in India? Punjab is now peaceful and politically
stable, and Sikh nationalism is no longer a political force. The BJP used
Hindu nationalism to mobilize and expand its support base, but its
victory in 1999 was due not so much to its religious appeal but to the
party's superior organization and its appeal to middle classes, and upper-
caste groups whose interests were no longer represented by the Congress
party. Yet once in office BJP has steered away from the more combative
language of Hindu nationalism.

But the contradictions inherent in the constitutional provisions regarding secularism remain to be resolved. The paradoxical approach of the Congress governments of excluding Muslims and Christians from the Uniform Civil Code while simultaneously pursuing Hindu votes resulted in communalization of politics in 1980s and the rise of the BJP to power in the 1990s. Similarly, the BJP in office has not dealt with the issue of the Uniform Civil Code, one of the most salient issues of the Hindu nationalist movement.

The debate on the nature of Indian secularism and its future continues. Some scholars, notably Madan (1992), have argued that secularism is a Western concept not suited for India because India's policy of religious neutrality does not recognize the integral role of religion in people's lives in India. Others (Hasan 1996; Engineer 1995) continue to believe that a genuine commitment to secularism and the religious neutrality of the state is the only hope for peace and tolerance in a multi-religious and culturally diverse society like India's.

## CONCLUSION

When Vajpayee formed the BJP-led government in March 1998, there was exuberance on the part of Hindu nationalists and skepticism and fear on the part of secular liberals and Muslims. The record of the party in power since March 1998 has belied the expectations of the staunch Hindu nationalists and to some extent allayed the fears of its liberal critics. As the party heading a minority coalition government (1998–9), the BJP demonstrated flexibility and pragmatism over ideology and accommodated the demands of its coalition partners. From 1998 to 1999 the prime minister and other BJP leaders showed extreme sensitivity to the need of keeping the coalition together so that they stay in power.

The BJP took the pragmatic course, putting the goal of Hindu *Rashtra* and *Hindutva* aside and moving the party toward the center from its previous position on the right. The party moved to amend India's Patents Act (1970) to ensure that it conforms with the obligations under the trade-related intellectual property rights (TRIPS) of the Uruguay Round of multilateral trade negotiations of the General Agreement on Tariffs and Trade (GATT) treaty, signed by India in 1994 but not yet ratified by the parliament. This decision came as a big disappointment to the RSS, which has vehemently opposed the liberalization of the Indian economy in the 1990s and India's signing of the GATT. Prime Minister Vajpayee denounced the December 1998 attacks on the homes of the Christian minority and their churches in Gujarat, a state ruled by the Hindu nationalist party, which were alleged to have been committed or incited by the hard-line affiliates of the BJP (the RSS, the VHP, the Hindu Jagran

Manch, and the Bajrang Dal) (*The New York Times*, January 23, 1999: A1–5).

After winning the 1999 election and forming the second coalition government, the BJP has demonstrated continued pragmatism. For example, the party has resisted the pressure of the RSS to raise the temple issue once again. Although the pragmatic approach to politics and policy may keep the BJP-led NDA coalition together, the Vajpayee government is likely to come under pressure from the RSS and other members of the Sangh family to carry out the agenda of *Hindutva*. Because the BJP relies on the RSS for an electoral presence, it would find it difficult to take a policy position distant from that of the RSS.

The challenge of moderating BJP's Hindu nationalist ideology is thus serious, and the party will have to address a dilemma: If it wants to become a mainstream national party with a broad base of political support across the country, it must move to the center. But if the party is less willing to compromise its ideological purity and unable to find new issues around which it could energize and mobilize the core support base, the BJP would lose the momentum it has gained since 1996, and if Sonia Gandhi remains in control of the Congress party and makes no serious mistakes in the near future, the Congress party will regain some lost ground and can once again emerge as the leading party in national politics.

Nevertheless, the fragmentation of polity along caste and regional lines is almost complete, and the possibility of the BJP or the Congress party commanding a majority in the Lok Sabha in the foreseeable future is remote. The divisions of Indian society in terms of caste, class, religions, regions, languages, and ethnicity; the federal system; the decline of the hegemonic Congress party and the rise of regional and caste-based parties; and the long term effect of Nehruvian secularism on intellectuals, opinion makers and a large number of Indian elites point toward a future in which the party in power must be pragmatic, not ideological, and a more centrist approach to politics and policy is to be expected. However, the Nehruvian vision of modernization, which considered religion as a backward-looking ideology and therefore an impediment to progress, has been challenged and the debate on secularism continues.

### REFERENCES

Ahmad, Farzand, Saba Naqvi Bhaumil, and Subhash Mishra. 1997. "Double Speak Duo." *India Today*, (September 22): 12–16.
Baird, Robert D. 1981. "Secular State and the Indian Constitution." In *Religion in Modern India*. Robert Baird (ed.). Delhi: Manohar Publications.
Bazter, Craig. 1969. *The Jana Sangh: A Biography of an Indian Political Party*. Philadelphia: University of Pennsylvania Press.

Brass, Paul. 1994. *The Politics of India Since Independence.* 2nd ed. New York: Cambridge University Press.

Chakravarti, Sudeep and Shefali Rekhi. 1998. "Business Confidence Shaken and Stirred." *India Today* (July 13): 24–28.

Chatterjee, Manini. 1996. "The BJP: Political Mobilization for *Hindutva.*" In *Religion, Religiosity and Communalism.* Praful Bidwai, Harbans Mukhia, and Archin Vanaik (ed.). New Delhi: Manohar.

Chibber, Pradeep K. 1999. *Democracy Without Associations: Transformation of the Party System and Social Cleavages in India.* Ann Arbor: University of Michigan Press.

Dasgupta, Swapan and Smruti Koppikar. 1998. "Nathuram Godse on Trial Again." *India Today* (August 3).

Dixit, Prabha. 1986. "The Ideology of Hindu Nationalism." In *Political Thought in Modern India.* Thomas Pantham and Kenneth L. Deutsch (ed.). New Delhi: Sage.

Duara, Prasanjit. 1991. "The New Politics of Hinduism." *Wilson Quarterly* (Summer).

Elst, Koenraad. 1990. *Ram Janmabhoomi vs Babri Masjid: A Case Study in Hindu-Muslim Conflict.* New Delhi: Voice of India.

Engineer, Asghar Ali. 1992. "Secularism and Communalism." In *Secularism in India: Dilemmas and Challenges.* M. M. Sankhdher (ed.). New Delhi: Deep and Deep: 236–46.

Frykenberg, Robert Eric. 1986. "Revivalism and Fundamentalism: Some Critical Observations with Special Reference to Politics in South Asia." In *Fundamentalism, Revivalists and Violence in South Asia.* James W. Bjorkman (ed.). Riverdale, MD: Riverdale Company.

Gopal, Sarvepalli, ed. 1990. *Anatomy of a Confrontation: The Babri Masjid-Ramjanmabhoomi Issue.* New Delhi: Viking.

Gopalkrishnan, I. 1998. "World Banks's Gloomy Outlook on Economy." *India Abroad* (August 21): 24.

Hansen, Thomas Blom. 1999. *The Saffron Wave: Democracy and Hindu Nationalism in Modern India.* Princeton: Princeton University Press:

Hardgrave Jr., Robert L., and Stanley A. Kochanek. 1993. *India: Government and Politics in a Developing Nation,* 5th ed. New York: Harcourt Brace Jovanovich.

Hasan, Mushirul. 1996. "The Changing Position of Muslims and the Political Future of Secularism in India." In *Region, Religion, Caste, Gender and Culture in Contemporary India.* T. V. Sathyamurthy (ed.). Delhi: Oxford University Press, pp. 200–28.

Hopfe, Lewis M. 1983. *Religions of the World,* 3rd. Ed., New York: Macmillan Publishing Co.

Jain, Girilal. 1990. Quoted in *Ram Janmabhoomi vs. Babri Masjid: A Case Study in Hindu-Muslim Conflict,* by Koenraad Elst. New Delhi: Voice of India.

Kohli, Atul. 1990. *Democracy and Discontent: India's Growing Crisis of Governability.* Cambridge: Cambridge University Press.

Kothari, Rajni. 1970. *Politics in India.* New Delhi: Orient Longman.

Larson, Gerald James. 1995. *India's Agony over Religion*. State University of New York Press.

Madan, T. N. 1997. "Secularism in Its Place." In *Politics in India*. Sudipta Kaviraj (ed.). Delhi: Oxford University Press.

——— 1989. A Religion in India." *Daedalus*, Vol. 118, No. 4.

Malik, Yogendra K. and V. B. Singh. 1994. *Hindu Nationalists in India: The Rise of the Bharatiya Janata Party*. Boulder, CO: Westview Press.

Manifesto of All India Bharatiya Jana Sangh, New Delhi, 1951. Quoted in Craig Bazter. *The Jana Sangh: A Biography of an Indian Political Party*. Philadelphia: University of Pennsylvania Press, 1969.

Mathur, K. S. 1992. "Hindu Values of Life: Karma and Dharma," In *Religion in India*. T. N. Madan (ed.). New York: Oxford University Press, pp. 62–77.

McGuire, John and Peter Reeves, 1994. "Ayodhya, the BJP and *Hindutva*: An Interpretation." *South Asia*, XVII (Special Issue).

Mookerjee, Shyama Prasad. "The Bharatiya Jana Sangh." Quoted in B. D. Graham, 1990. *Hindu Nationalism and Indian Politics: The Origins and Development of The Bharatiya Jana Sangh*. New York: Cambridge University Press.

Nayar, K. S. 1998. "Political Will Needed for Economic Revival." *India Abroad* (August 21): 24.

Pai, Sudha. 1996. "Transformation of the Indian Party System: The 1996 Lok Sabha Elections." *Asian Survey*, XXXVI (12).

Rajgopal, P. R. 1987. *Communal Violence in India*. Delhi: Uppal.

Rudolph, Lloyd I. and Susanne H. 1987. *In Pursuit of Lakshmi: The Political Economy of the Indian State*. Chicago: University of Chicago Press.

Savarkar, V. D. 1969. *Hindutva: Who Is a Hindu?* Bombay: Veer Savarkar Prakashan. Quoted in Mark Juergensmeyer, *The New Cold War?: Religious Nationalism Confronts the Secular State*. Berkeley: University of California Press.

Sekhon, Joti. 2000. *Modern India*. Boston: McGraw Hill.

Smith, Donald Eugene. 1963. *India as a Secular State*. Princeton: Princeton University Press.

——— (ed.). 1966. *South Asian Politics and Religion*. Princeton: Princeton University Press.

Stern, Robert W. 1991. *Changing India: Bourgeois Revolution on the Subcontinent*. New York: Cambridge University Press.

Yadav, Yogendra. 1996. "Reconfiguration in Indian Politics: State Assembly Elections, 1993–5." *Economic and Political Weekly*, 31(2 and 3): 99.

The Japanese case exhibits some fascinating similarities and contrasts with accounts of religious politics in Western nations. In a manner similar to the Iberian nations, Shinto has historically been a component of national identity in Japan, and has been associated with a discredited former regime. Perhaps more importantly, the theological flexibility and "fluidity" of both Shinto and Japanese Buddhism may have provided a means by which religious pluralism does not lead to political conflict. Unlike the United States, the existence of multiple religious traditions does not occasion higher levels of religious participation, and, unlike the Indian case, the presence of multiple religions does not appear to increase religious prejudice or the political assertiveness of religious bodies. The Japanese case directs our attention to the content, rather than the form, of religious beliefs. The fact that neither Shinto nor Buddhism are religions based primarily on sacred texts makes doctrinal disputes unlikely. Further, neither Japanese religious tradition makes the strong exclusivist claims of monotheistic faiths such as Judaism, Christianity, and Islam. Toyoda and Tanaka argue that this "non-Western" understanding of political religion may provide the basis for a genuinely ecumenical political culture. Conversely, this sort of religious flexibility may reduce the role of religion as a "prophetic" public critic, or the potential of religion to provide social capital to Japanese citizens.

# 12

# Religion and Politics in Japan

*Maria A. Toyoda and Aiji Tanaka*

Although politics and religion were once tightly fused in Japan, today religion plays a weak role in politics and society. The mosaic of religions and sects that exist in Japanese society – including Buddhism, Christianity, Confucianism, Shinto, Taoism, and the many "new religions" that mix aspects of Buddhism and Shinto – does not create or reinforce political cleavages. Although once religion played an important role in politics in society, in the postwar period religion has become far less relevant to politics.

In the nineteenth century and prewar and wartime periods of the twentieth century, religious ideology was central to the political notions of the Japanese state and nation. Religious worship of the emperor, militarism, imperialism, and nationalism were tightly intertwined. After Japan's surrender in World War II, these doctrines were suppressed. Subsequently, religion in contemporary postwar Japanese society is viewed by most observers as politically irrelevant, or at most on the political periphery.

In this chapter, we explain this dramatic shift by focusing on the fluid nature of religious theology, and how political elites have historically sought to integrate new doctrines, and to reinterpret traditional religion in order to use religion as part of the solution to pressing political problems. We begin with an overview of Japan's two main religions, Shinto and Buddhism, their origins, and the ideological as well as geopolitical conditions that helped to foster syncretism between them. We next discuss how these two religions affected the process of nation and state building, and how new geopolitical threats beginning in the nineteenth century led to innovative formulations of religious ideology, centering on a state-led interpretation of Shinto principles. We then turn to the period following Japan's defeat in World War II and show how an entirely new geopolitical situation led to further dramatic changes in the religious landscape. In the final sections, we look more closely at the changed role of religion in the postwar period.

## RELIGION IN CONTEXT: GEOPOLITICAL OBSERVATIONS AND THE CHARACTER OF JAPAN'S MAJOR RELIGIONS

A snapshot of religious practice and public attitude towards religion in Japan today presents a few puzzles. For instance, in an *Asahi Shimbun* poll in 1995, most Japanese claimed to have a Buddhist altar in their home, even though in an NHK poll that same year nearly three-quarters of respondents claimed not be religious at all.[1] In the same *Asahi Shimbun* poll, a majority of Japanese also claimed to have a household Shinto altar, even though a 1994 *Yomiuri Shimbun* study revealed that only 5 percent of the respondents claimed that their family traditionally practiced Shinto, versus 80 percent whose family were traditionally Buddhists. Clearly Japanese religiosity is complex.

Many observers find answers in the basic character of Japan's major religions, Shinto and Buddhism. One of the more striking characteristics of these religions, as they are practiced in Japan, is that they depend almost entirely on professional clergy as spiritual practitioners, and not on lay participation. Rarely are there services or formal gatherings in either faith, except during seasonal festivals (*matsuri*) where the atmosphere most often resembles a marketplace, and the religious connection is hardly noticeable. Daily private or family rituals related to these religious beliefs, such as prayers and offerings to the deceased at the home altar, are more often than not perfunctory and routine.

This sometimes leads to comparisons between the "softer" variety of Buddhism practiced in Japan, and the more reverential, "harder" varieties of Buddhism popularly practiced in places such as Thailand, where most males spend a brief part of their youth in the priesthood, and career monks are relatively influential in politics. In contrast, the role of the priesthood in Japan is quite minor and often does not extend beyond their ritual services.

This is not to say that the Japanese are essentially nonreligious, but it underscores a certain spiritual division of labor in society. Professional clergy in many Asian cultures serve a function quite distinct from the ones they are often associated with in the West. They are, as one noted

---

[1] Some of the data utilized in this chapter were originally collected by *Asahi Shimbun*, NHK (Japan Broadcasting Company), Yomiuri Shimbun. The data was obtained from the Japan Public Opinion Location Library, JPOLL, Roper Center for Public Opinion Research, University of Connecticut. Neither the original collectors of the data, nor the Roper Center, bear any responsibility for the analyses or interpretations presented here.

scholar puts it, specially trained and prepared for the task of communicating to the deities, "The priest's liturgical training and rigorous observance of purifications and abstinences entitle him to a proximity to deity impossible for the layman" (Hardacre 1986). In other words, most formal manifestations of worship are best left to the professionals on behalf of laymen. Understanding this "nonprotestant" take on the practice of religion may help explain the seemingly complex attitudes toward religion in Japan. When religious elites are responsible for interceding with deities, average citizens are likely to be less involved with religion.

Yet historically religion has played a major role in Japanese politics. Perhaps because Buddhism and Shinto relied on elite leadership and practice to spread, they were both more malleable to political elites. The relationship between politics and religion in Japan has been driven, in part, by external, geopolitical forces and by the pursuit of nationalist goals. Post-World War II Japanese attitudes toward religion are a reflection of the country's new domestic priorities, shaped by United States-led Cold War-era geopolitics.

Historically, Japanese attitudes have been shaped by international threats and by domestic politics. Japan has, on the one hand, been relatively free of the domestic ideological and political divisiveness engendered by religion. On the other hand, throughout Japan's long history, international and geopolitical forces have had powerful influences on religious affinities, and national attitudes about religion. Japan has been mainly characterized by cultural and linguistic homogeneity, geographic isolation, and Japan's relationship to its continental neighbors during its earlier history, and its relationship to the United States in the post-World War II period.

In the next few sections, we develop this theme of reaction, looking at the role of religion during three distinct periods in Japanese political history. First, we look at the introduction of Buddhism into Japan, which came in reaction to developments on the Asian continent from about the sixth century. We explain how the syncretism of Buddhism and pre-existing, indigenous Shinto beliefs prevented any enduring or robust political cleavages. Next, we look at the growing and more formal ties between religious belief and the concepts of nationalism and emperor worship following the Meiji Restoration through to the end of World War II. We then turn to the postwar period, the relative decline of religious belief and patriotic fervor following surrender, and the era of economic reconstruction under the United States security umbrella. The chapter concludes with an analysis of religious groups and political parties, the nationalistic and religious resurgence in the 1980s and 1990s, distinct from that of the Meiji through Showa periods, and a look ahead to an even more complex relationship between politics and religion in a rapidly changing Japan.

## RELIGION AND ELITE POLITICS IN THE EARLY NATION: BUDDHIST AND SHINTO SYNCRETISM

Although Japan has two major religions – Buddhism and Shinto – the relationship between them is best characterized as cooperation rather than competition. The indigenous belief in Shinto, or the Way of the Gods, has coexisted with the imported Buddhist religion for more than fourteen centuries, since Buddhism's formal introduction into Japan in the sixth century.

Scholars believe that Shinto began in Japan around 500 B.C., as a form of ancestor worship. Japanese mythology claims an unbroken, mystic line running from the Sun Goddess, to the legendary Yamato tribe that is the alleged source of the Imperial family, down to the Japanese people. Early Shinto, like many of the pagan forms of worship that arise in agrarian cultures, postulates a close link between countless gods and humanity, with no concept of tension between the creator or creators and the created. This sense of unity and homogeneity would become, many centuries later, the basis for a reinterpreted version of Shinto that stressed racial purity and superiority.

In Shinto, ancestors are the grantors of good things, and worship is primarily in daily rituals and in festivals, like *Obon* that welcomes the spirits of the past. Primitive Shinto, therefore, was an intensely local and personal affair, deriving from the worship of the tutelary deity of each clan (the *uji-gami*). As political leadership began to coalesce around the personality of the emperor and the agrarian nobility, the *uji-gami* of the imperial family and of other powerful clans eventually were adopted as the tutelary deities of the Japanese nation. However, Shinto retained a wide variety of local practices, customs, traditions and rituals that often put conceptions of family and clan above those of nation.

The clannish character of early Shinto, therefore, meant that it was unsuited to the task of unifying political and national interests through its ideology, lacking formal and central organization, and a universal creed or doctrinal aspirations. Indeed, the intense localism and family ties of Shinto made the task of creating a unified nation more difficult. As historian, George Sansom (1958), wrote,

[U]nlike such great religions as Buddhism or Christianity [Shinto] was not something which added to or contributed to national life, but was rather an expression of the most intimate and vital sentiments of the Japanese people. In that sense it somewhat resembles the pagan cults of Greece and Rome, in their archaic strata. It is not a religion whose principles demonstrably arise from historical events. It is not the product of a revolution in ideas. Unlike Buddhism or Christianity or Islam, it has no founder, no inspired sacred book, no teachers, no martyrs, and no saints.

It was precisely this lack of national inspiration in Shinto that led Japanese rulers to turn to the relatively vibrant possibilities for national coherency that were inherent in Buddhism.

*Mahayana*, or the Greater Wheel variant of Buddhism, originated in India and probably came to Japan via Korea. There was initially strong opposition to the new religion from certain powerful clans in Japan, and this was partly tied to factional strife between various clans for leadership. But by the end of the sixth century, Buddhism was firmly established, and it was the dominant religion between the eighth and fifteenth centuries.

Buddhism was not a religion initially taken up by the populace; rather, it was the religion of the elite and the aesthetes, in part because Buddhism was so infused with the arts, music, and literature of China. But there was more than just the transmission of artistic and literary culture that attracted early adherents to Buddhism. Japan's leaders wanted to import Buddhism because it was better suited to nation building than was Shinto. Sansom notes: "It is a notable testimony to the interest in problems of government that Japanese leaders were feeling at this time – and which they have continued to display ever since – that Buddhism should have commended itself to the ruling class as a system of belief beneficial to the state."

Japan faced formidable military and diplomatic hurdles during this period. Relations with China were strained, and the Chinese Court viewed the Japanese Court as upstart barbarians. During the seventh century, Japan allied with the Kingdom of Paikche against the Chinese T'ang forces and was soundly defeated. Japan clearly lacked the central organization necessary for mounting effective resistance against the Chinese, whose pressure on the Korean peninsula continued for some time to come. The potential threat from the Mongol invaders was already evident. Recognizing these dangers, Japanese elites helped pave the way for the spread of Buddhism.

Buddhism was especially important in persuading the nobility of the usefulness of the idea of nationhood, and in drawing their loyalty to the nation instead of the traditional family or clan ties stressed by Shinto. Like other great world religions such as Islam and Catholicism, Buddhism provided the universal principles that helped to transcend parochialism and facilitate political centralization.

The elite took concrete steps to foster syncretism between the new religion and the existing system of Shinto worship, in order to facilitate the spread of Buddhism. Shinto gods were enshrined in Buddhist temples and some Shinto deities were named *bodhisattvas*, or Buddhist deities (Kiyota 1982). Conversely, Buddha was initially regarded as merely one of the more powerful *kami*, or Shinto gods. However, by the seventh century, the Buddha's message had become more distinct.

The elite role in developing the eventual Shinto-Buddhist syncretism was an important one, for their compatibility was not obvious at the start. Shinto is still most often associated with the trait of groupism – the *uji*, or clan – and locality, while Buddhism stresses greater universality. And while Shinto stresses ready acceptance of and harmony with the physical world, Buddhism views the world as the transient source of suffering, and the physical as something which believers strive to overcome. Yet there was the essential element of tolerance present in both religions that allowed the relationship between them to provide the ideological foundation for pursuing future nationalistic goals. Ultimately, though, it was careful elite shepherding and the tolerant and flexible application of Buddhist doctrine by Japan's leaders that helped transcend the contradictions between the local and the national, and the worldly and other-worldly.

The introduction of Buddhism helped mold a Japanese nation that was relatively unified for several hundred years. By the beginning of the sixteenth century, however, the country fell back into civil war and fighting between the *daimyo*, or feudal lords. Buddhist sects during the Middle Ages, especially the militant Nichiren, or Lotus, sect grew immensely in power, feeding off the *daimyo* conflicts. During this time, Portuguese traders and missionaries introduced Christianity, which had great appeal because many in the military and in the general populace saw the Buddhist sects as too powerful, and its clergy corrupt. By the end of the sixteenth century, however, a series of edicts were issued which ultimately expelled Christianity and most foreigners from Japan through the closing of all major trading ports except one in Nagasaki. The Tokugawa shogunate soon consolidated its power and ruled Japan for 250 years of relative peace.[2] While trade continued to take place with the Dutch and Portuguese through Nagasaki, Japan, for all intents and purposes, was a closed nation until the coming of Perry's Black Ships.

---

[2] Many scholars believe that one of the important motives behind the expulsion of Christianity was the popularity it had among the *daimyo* of the western provinces, and the advantages they had, relative to the *bakufu*, in trade with the Portuguese and the Dutch. Nagasaki port was controlled by the *bakufu* which, subsequent to the closing of all other ports, held a monopoly on foreign trade.

## THE RELIGION OF EMPIRE, NATION, AND STATE

Japan enjoyed considerable flows of trade and information with China and the West through the tightly controlled port of Nagasaki, but the coming of the American warships in 1854 came as an enormous surprise. After twenty-seven other attempts had failed, Japan was finally forced open by four American ships, commanded by Matthew Perry, who came demanding trade.

The Japanese domestic economy was soon thrown into disarray by the entry of the West, whose traffic in Japanese coin with China, and demand for silk and tea drove up prices in Japan (LaFeber 1997). Beginning in 1858, Japan was forced to sign a number of treaties that gave foreigners advantageous fixed tariff duties. Under such pressures, the Tokugawa shogunate, which proved unable to resist Western demands, fell to rebel forces. In 1868, in what is called the Meiji Restoration, a youthful emperor was proclaimed the nominal head of state. Little more than two decades later, a diet was established along with a party system, a constitution, and a "transcendental cabinet" (i.e., one that stood independent of political parties) of oligarchs to run the government.

The Meiji Restoration brought rapid and momentous change to both Japan's political and social realms. It came at a time of dramatic change in global economics and colonial geopolitics. Though a latecomer to the exclusive club of nations engaged in imperial conquest, Japan quickly met the membership requirements, defeating two continental powers in war – China in 1895 and Russia in 1905. Once again, politically driven developments in religion came to the service of the state to help it cope with the vast geopolitical changes that had occurred during the previous two and half centuries of relative isolation.

One of the most urgent tasks for the Meiji oligarchy was to instill in ordinary Japanese the principles of national pride, uniqueness, the sense of "public-spiritedness," and to unite and mobilize them behind the goals of a Greater Japan. This task was complicated by the rapid social shifts brought by industrialization and economic development, and by strongly centripetal forces of loyalty to local and family interests.

Japan's elite believed that a national consciousness was a prerequisite to building a modern nation. Religion proved invaluable in this task. This was finally achieved through the development of a state ideology centered on the figure of the emperor as a divine and benevolent ruler. Carol Gluck (1985) explains,

[T]he oligarchs, the bureaucrats, and their ideologues, realizing that some explanation was necessary to secure the cooperation of the people through the rigors of economic development and international expansion, created a state orthodoxy around the figure of the emperor and them imposed it upon the people. . . . By moralizing and mystifying the nature of the state, politics was depoliticized. All that was required of the citizen was loyal and willing submission, and this he is said to have given as a result of an indoctrination that began in his elementary school years and extended eventually into almost every quarter of his social life.

At the beginning of the nineteenth century, two main strains of Shinto gained prominence. The first, called *jinja* or shrine-based Shinto, maintained the traditional forms of worship and a clergy closely aligned with the state. In a departure from the long-held custom of coexistence and syncretism, this version of Shinto was elevated and separated from Buddhism as a symbol of the imperial state (Davis 1992). This "revised" Shinto was to become the basis for Japan's ultranationalist and militarist movements. The second type, known as *kyouha*, or sectarian Shinto, was the outgrowth of over a dozen sects founded by charismatic individuals, many of who claimed to have supernatural powers or special knowledge. These latter versions of Shinto had wider popular appeal, penetrating into Japanese society far more than the official, revised Shinto. In addition to these two main strains, local versions of Shinto continued to be practiced. But the shrine-based version of Shinto played the most important political role.

The Meiji government allowed Christian teaching in Japan in 1873, and in 1889 it guaranteed freedom of religion in the constitution, but it also made Shinto the official state religion. Shinto priests were assigned the task of developing a religious ideology that would glorify the emperor and the state. The traditional Shinto emphasis on unity was translated during the Meiji period into an emphasis on the homogeneity of the Japanese people; who were different from the outsiders on Japan's threshold.[3]

While the emperor had always been revered as a figure descended from the gods, state, or Shinto shrine, made this especially explicit, through its coordinated system of national education, press media (during a period of rapidly increasing literacy), and neighborhood shrines. The modern Japanese idea of nation physically manifest in the emperor was promulgated through religious symbolism, and nationalism and patriotism were expressed in religious ritual. Yet these attempts to manipulate Shinto led to decreased popular participation in the religion (Gluck 1985). Much of the populace soon regarded Shinto as imperial ritual, not as religion. So while the idea of nation was served by shrine Shinto,

---

[3] Buddhists, as Davis notes, were not silent on the subject of Japanese imperialism: Many mainstream sects supported the Russo-Japanese War as a necessary means for achieving order in East Asia.

popular spirituality was not. As a result, some people turned to other religions, including Christianity, while others became less active in religion.

The failure of shrine Shinto to gain a mass following led the Shinto priests to lobby to provide government funding for Shinto shrines, and to assure that national holidays were observed everywhere. The movement gained support among military circles and among bureaucrats in the Ministry of Education. The Ministry had an administrative and social reach that extended beyond the schools. Through directives, the Ministry penetrated through to many levels of society, seeking to standardize not only what students learned in the classroom, but also civic morality in general. In 1939, the Ministry of Education was given broadranging power to regulate religion under the Religious Bodies Law.

Through official edict, then, nationalism and religion were interwoven. Increasingly, militarism and imperialism were added to the mix, as conflict with the Western powers mounted. Following a short experience with party-led democracy during the Taisho period, government rule returned to the so-called "transcendental cabinets" staffed mostly by military leaders.

Throughout the 1930s, the military increased its power relative to civilian institutions. Tight controls were placed on the press, on associations, and on religious practice. One scholar estimated that 1,800 Christians were arrested during this period, and that members of some Shinto and Buddhist sects were persecuted for teachings that were critical of the state (Beasley 1981). When war broke out, the military used religious symbolism to mobilize the population for sacrifice, and to help prepare its fighting forces for death. The best-known examples of this symbolism is the *kamikaze*, or "divine wind," which called for suicide attacks from the air, and other forms of self-sacrifice, such as strapping a mine on one's back and diving under an enemy tank, or becoming human torpedoes underwater.

The interweaving between religion, militarism, and nationalism had a tremendous impact that endures today. So closely was Shinto tied to war that the invocation of religion in official ceremonies in Japan continues to raise great domestic and international controversy.

### POSTWAR RELIGION AND NATIONALISM ON THE POLITICAL PERIPHERY

The postwar period brought a significant break in the connection between Shinto and nationalism and militarism. In October 1945, following Japan's surrender, the Allied Powers issued a directive for religious freedom and the dismantling of state Shinto: "All financial support from public funds and all official affiliation with Shinto and Shinto shrines are prohibited and will cease immediately" (Kobayashi 1957).[4] On New Year's day, 1946, the emperor renounced his claim to divinity. Soon afterward, legal protections for religious organizations were established.

After the end of World War II, a new Japanese constitution was promulgated in 1947 under the guidance of the Allied Occupation Forces. It contains two articles concerning religion. Article 20 guarantees freedom of religion for all citizens, but also prohibits any religious groups from receiving special privileges from the state or from exercising political influence: "No religious organizations shall receive any privileges from the State, nor exercise any political authority." Article 89 reinforces Article 20 by prohibiting the use of public funds or public finances for any religious organization or group and its activities.

The Religious Corporation (Legal Person) Law was established in 1951 to provide religious organizations with legal status to engage in their activities. In accordance with this law, the government established the Religious Corporation Deliberative Council and an Office of Religion in the Department of Cultural Affairs. Despite these legal provisions, however, nationalistic impulses with religious overtones persisted within the ranks of Japan's political, intellectual and bureaucratic elite.

After Japan's defeat, the public immediately rejected militarism and nationalism, but the Japanese right-wing did not share this change of heart. In the early postwar years, the Allied Powers sought to purge Japan's militarists as part of the Occupation reforms in 1946 and 1947. Amnesty was granted to thousands who were imprisoned for opposing the government in the prewar and war periods. But, in 1951, the United States, perceiving a threat in the international communist movement, convinced Prime Minister Yoshida to reinstate prewar conservatives and militarists, because of the shortage of trained and qualified leaders. Many militarists assumed high positions in the diet, in major financial institutions and in companies. Although many remained quietly unrepentant of their militarism, they realized that military rearmament was impossible.

Japan faced the enormous task of rebuilding its infrastructure, its government and society, and its economy. Several provisions were made under the Occupation that made it impossible, and indeed unnecessary, to rebuild the military. Article IX of the Constitution renounced war as the sovereign right of the Japanese nation. Equally important were the provisions of the Mutual Security Agreement, signed in 1954 and revised

---

[4] Kobayashi notes, however, that financial dependence on the government was not very large to begin with.

in 1960, tying Japan both economically and militarily to the United States.

Although religious nationalists objected to the reduction of the emperor's status, they were pleased that the office was retained. They were reluctant to renounce the capacity for war, but the resources and energies that had gone into the war machine would now be focused and dedicated to the process of economic rebuilding. As one observer put it, Japan was allowed to flourish economically in the "American Greenhouse" (Hellman 1987). Within a generation, Japan was on track to becoming an economic superpower, marking its return as a developed nation by both hosting the Olympics and joining the OECD in 1964.

By then, religion-based nationalism was eclipsed by so-called "economic values." Japan had made a remarkably smooth and rapid transition both politically and socially to a system of Western-style democracy. The political basis for this rapid redevelopment was the system of one-party dominant rule, which began in 1955 when the two right-wing Liberal and the Democratic parties merged to form the Liberal Democratic party. The LDP enjoyed nearly forty years of uninterrupted rule, fortified by a combination of close ties with Japan's powerful and conservative bureaucracy, and with big business, and by pork barrel politics aimed at farmers and small- and medium-sized business people. Religious conservatism continued to play a shadow role in LDP politics, but the primary political emphasis was on economic bargaining with voters.

## INSTITUTIONALIZED DEMOCRACY: ECONOMIC VOTING AT THE FOREFRONT, RELIGIOUS CONSERVATISM IN THE SHADOWS

The LDP during its heyday was the classic "catch-all party" described by Kirscheimer (1966), basing its appeal in large part on the party's ability to represent "transcendental" interests by concentrating on economic rather than ideological issues that might have shattered its mosaic of support. One faction of the party was composed of nationalistic hard-liners, many of whom retained a commitment to State Shinto. The LDP appealed to war veterans and their families, and to Shinto shrines that exerted their influence through campaign contributions.

Yet the nationalist right-wing faction of the LDP did not push for nationalist and militarist policies, for two reasons. First, cold war-driven policy in the United States shaped Japanese conservatives' own policies. The United States provided a security umbrella, allowing Japan to devote much of its resources to economic development. Second, the majority of Japanese, especially urban, white-collar workers, strongly rejected nationalist appeals.[5] LDP leaders realized that economic, not ideological, voting was the main reason for their electoral success.

The only other party with a more explicit religious appeal was the Clean Government party, or Komeito, established in 1964, which is affiliated with the Soka Gakkai cult. At its height, Komeito was the third strongest party in the diet, but this did not provide the party with any real access to policy making. Japanese voters are generally quite negative toward the concept of religious parties. One cross-national study, conducted by the Leisure Development Center of Japan in 1979, shows that the Japanese, compared with five other nations, had the most negative reactions to religious parties (see International Value Study Council, 1980).

It is possible that the relationship between religion and politics may change again in the twenty-first century, however. Many Japanese leaders now support a more independent foreign policy from the U.S., for many reasons. Moreover, the United States now urges Japan to shoulder greater responsibility for its own defense; this was evident in public calls for Japan to contribute more resources to the Persian Gulf War. These events have occurred at a time of growing sense of Japanese confidence stemming from its economic power, thus providing the opportunity for nationalist voices to once again be heard.

### POSTWAR REVIVAL OF NATIONALISM?

The postwar preoccupation with economic success clearly moderated nationalist sentiments in Japan. The majority of Japanese citizens are pacifists who wish to undo the legacy of their prewar militarism. But unlike Germany, where repentance has become an integral part of national politics, Japan has to a much lesser extent confronted its past. The government has not dealt well with issues that have recently resurfaced from the war, such as the evidence of great atrocities committed by Japanese soldiers, and the reparations demanded by former female

---

[5] One high-profile incident shows how quickly the nationalist rhetoric was rejected by Japan's populace. In 1970, the novelist and devotee of martial arts and philosophy, Mishima Yukio committed ritual suicide after failing to rouse soldiers to action on behalf of the honor of the emperor. Mishima, and his personal militia, called the Shield Society (Tate no Kai), appealed to the officers at the Ichigaya Station to demonstrate that they had not lost their national spirit and martial devotion to the emperor. When ridiculed, he resorted to the samurai practice of *sepukku*, or suicide by self-disembowelment, in order to preserve honor. Many Japanese, however, characterized his suicide as an act of disgrace. This reaction may have signified more the fear of revived militarism on the part of the populace, and less any actual disgust with Mishima's solution. But it serves to illustrate the degree to which the citizenry and the military were both on guard against the resurgence of militarism.

sex slaves in Korea and the Philippines. Part of the intractability stems from LDP hard-liners, who have crafted an economic nationalism message that draws on religion.

Two broad types of nationalist sentiment have been voiced in recent years, one "benign," the other less so. The relatively benign type of nationalism might be characterized as "GNP Nationalism." Scholars who coined this phrase saw the new nationalist rhetoric as "a boastful pride in Japan's company unions, lifetime employment, and management styles, not to mention takeout sushi shops, pinball parlors, and the Bullet Train" (Kato 1988). This characterization did not link economic nationalism to religion.

The second, harder-line version of nationalism did explicitly refer to many of the same concepts of racial purity and divine origin that was advanced during the Meiji through Showa periods. Once again, the Ministry of Education was at the forefront of this movement, issuing directives in the 1980s calling for the singing of Japan's national anthem, the saluting of the flag, and the teaching of respect for the emperor in the schools. School textbooks that have been approved have underplayed Japanese aggression leading up to and during the war, and do not mention the wartime atrocities that have more recently been documented. In the cultural and academic quarters, the 1980s and 1990s were periods of revival for "nationalist" anthropology and archaeology, which gave credibility to and promoted popular ideas regarding the mystical nature of the origin of the Japanese race. The Kyoto School, headquartered at the prestigious Minpaku National Ethnological Museum, was the main proponent of thise views that helped to revive the unsettling, though this time more implicit, concept of Japanese racial superiority.

This hard-line nationalist view was common among right-wing members of the LDP, especially those aligned with Prime Minister Nakasone, whose friendly relationship with Ronald Reagan was interpreted as a symbol of Japan's ascendance to the status of an international power. In the 1970s, the right wing of the LDP party formed an action group, known as the Seirankai, which focused on shrine Shinto principles of race, often referring to the Japanese as the "Yamato race" descended from a single ancient tribe.

The Yasukuni Shrine controversy underscores the influence of the LDP right wing with respect to matters of religion and nation. With the backing of the Japan Association of Bereaved Families (JABF), the LDP attempted to nationalize the management of the Yasukani Shrine.[6] The LDP argued that the Yasukuni Shrine was exempt from constitutional articles forbidding government from helping to finance religious

[6] See Murakami 1986 and Kobayashi 1979.

organizations, because the shrine paid tribute to Japan's war dead. The LDP submitted this bill five times from 1969 to 1974, each time encountering strong objections from the opposition parties in the diet, and from non-Shinto religious groups, including many influential Buddhist sects and Christian organizations.[7] Finally hardliners backed official annual visits of the prime minister to the Shrine every August 15, on the anniversary of the end of World War II in the Pacific, despite the fact that the Legislation Bureaus of both houses of the diet and the Cabinet Legislation Bureau judged the official visits to be unconstitutional.[8]

The subsequent bursting of Japan's economic bubble in the 1990s curbed nationalist rhetoric, and the 1993 collapse of LDP rule silenced the most vociferous members of its right wing. But with additional tensions in the region at the end of the twentieth century, including instability on the Korean peninsula and uncertainty about the course of China's political and economic development, there is renewed talk of Japan's future defense capabilities and international role. In April 1999, the outspoken nationalist, Shintaro Ishihara, won the Tokyo governorship (a high-profile, though not especially powerful position), calling for a firmer stance against the United States and China, and United States return of Yokota Air Base in western Tokyo. Whether this signals resurgence of nationalist rhetoric grounded in religion remains to be seen.

## RELIGION TODAY

While the idea of a Japanese nation is still rooted in religious principles and myth, it is clear that the role of religion in politics does not constitute the classic " 'friend-foe' positions of tight-knit religious or ideological movements to the surrounding community," that was described by Lipset and Rokkan (1990) in their study of European political cleavages. Religion as ritual still permeates daily life: construction projects are opened by Shinto purification ceremonies, weddings are still largely Shinto, while funerals are Buddhist, shrines and temples are wealthy, and even sumo wrestling retains its ritual, religious character. But religious relevance to daily lives and political goals of Shinto and Buddhism has largely been lost.

In more recent years, the influence of the main religions has declined as a result of mobility and urbanization, which have undermined the traditional *ujigami*, or neighborhood organization, centered on shrines

---

[7] See Kobayashi 1979.

[8] In 1997, however, the Japanese Supreme Court ruled that the donation of public funds to the Yasukuni shrine violated the Constitution. The suit against the Yasukuni shrine, which is Shinto, was brought by Buddhists who have long protested the donations government officials made to Shinto shrines.

or temples. Another effect of greater mobility is that multigenerational family life, which traditionally has been the locus for transmitting religious belief and respect for ancestors, is also declining in modern Japan.

Surveys show that only 25 percent of Japanese consider themselves to be religious, and only 4 percent regularly visit a shrine, temple, or church. Nearly all of religious Japanese consider themselves to be Buddhists; only 3 percent identify with Shinto and only 2 percent are Christians. Only about 15 percent of the respondents between the ages of 20 and 29 years have religious beliefs, compared with about half of those who are 55 or older. Generational replacement is therefore creating a more secular Japan.[9]

However, where the mainstream religions have declined in influence, new religions have found an increasing number of followers; they "constitute the most vital sector of Japanese religion today." (Hardacre 1986) Some of these "new" religions can actually be traced back to the early nineteenth century, as well as the postwar period; others represent different sects of Buddhism that have formed around some charismatic leader. There are new religious groups, often called cults, which are increasingly active. Many have increasingly international appeal and a diverse range of political and business interests. Increasingly, these new religions have turned to information technology, such as the internet, in order to spread their message and gain new followers.

Soka Gakkai, which is based on the teachings of the ancient Nichiren Shoshu sect, is one major example. It is a nongovernmental organization (NGO) member of the United Nations, with its own school system, and a major university in Tokyo that has overseas campuses. The Soka Gakkai has also penetrated many other countries, including the United States, through its social and youth clubs. The Komeito party is the Soka Gakkai's political arm, and it derives much of its wealth from member contributions and various business interests, including real estate and education. Its platform can loosely be described as grassroots social welfare advocacy, internationalism, and adherence to non-nuclear principles. In 1993, Komieto was one of eight parties in the coalition that unseated the LDP government. Soon afterward, the Komeito disbanded and formed the New Frontier party (NFP) in coalition with several former LDP members and members of the Social Democratic party. NFP itself suddenly disbanded in 1997, and the New Komeito was formed in 1998. In the July 1998 Upper House elections, Komeito won nine seats,

---

[9] We should note that the data also indicate a strong pattern of increase in religious belief based on life-cycle changes, a phenomenon that is common to many societies. That is, people become more religious as they age.

carrying over thirteen seats, for a total of twenty-two out of 262 seats, a small but growing share.

Another example is the doomsday cult, Aum Shinrikyo, which came to the world's attention when it released sarin nerve gas into the Tokyo subway system in March 1995. The Aum has claimed between 40,000 to 60,000 members worldwide, with the majority of followers in Russia. The Aum religion is based on an eclectic mixture of Buddhism and belief in the Hindu god of destruction, Shiva; it is centered on the teachings of its guru, Shoko Asahara. Asahara claimed that through the practice of yoga and other meditation, he had attained the highest possible level of consciousness and lived in a constant state of nirvana (Senate Government Affairs Subcommittee on Investigations 1995).

Investigations following the subway gassing revealed that the Aum was extremely well-organized and that it had recruited young followers from the most elite Japanese universities, especially scientists. Using their legal status and tax privileges as a religious organization, they amassed a fortune in real estate and housing. Though Asahara and his deputies were arrested and put on trial, and the Aum has been stripped of its status as a religious organization, after the arrests the government no longer considered the cult a threat and chose not to use the antisubversion law to ban it. At the end of the 1990s, the cult claimed it was making a comeback, with their main income coming from computer sales (Associated Press 1999). Their website also listed other ventures, such as "salvation tours" to Bhutan, Zaire, and India.

These newer religions, in contrast to the Buddhist and Shinto, base their appeal on participatory worship styles. It appears that the new religions have succeeded by filling gaps left by the discrediting of the traditional religions. The newer religions are also free of the nationalist and militarist associations that continue to burden Shinto and Buddhism and, therefore, appeal especially to younger generations and to urban white-collar workers who have progressive social outlooks. While incidents like the subway gassing have brought disrepute to some cults, the membership of others continues to grow both domestically and internationally.

## CONCLUSION: TOWARD A NONWESTERN UNDERSTANDING OF RELIGION AND POLITICS

Clearly the history of religion and politics in Japan is different from the Western cases offered in this volume. Ideological flexibility has been the hallmark of the interplay between religion and politics. The relationship between politics and religion is characterized by both flexibility of doctrine and flexibility of application by political elites.

Neither Primitive Shinto nor Buddhism offers a fixed canon, and therefore provides no orthodoxy that opposes the proliferation of divergent interpretations. This has meant that elites have been able to mold Shinto and Buddhism to their political goals. In response to both foreign-inspired and domestic crises in Japan's predemocratic past, the leadership harnessed certain elements of these religions to raise national consciousness and bolster the power of the central government. The most important step in cultivating a cohesive national ideology came early when the elite encouraged the complementary coexistence of Buddhism and Shinto, combining the sense of unity and commonality found in Shinto with the universalist and orderly teachings of Buddhism, which encouraged the more general idea of a nation. Later elites manipulated Shinto to create a vehicle to mobilize public support and sacrifice for war. In the postwar period, elites have focused on economic productivity, and have not attempted to manipulate religion to help that cause.

This sense of ideological flexibility has carried over into other, non-religious issue areas in Japanese politics. This frequently creates a sense of ambiguity that some Western observers find frustrating. But understanding the historical and doctrinal foundations for religion in politics constitutes the first step toward understanding this case. Religion does matter in the politics of contemporary Japan, not in the way we are accustomed to seeing it matter in Western politics, but to the extent that it provides the historical basis for today's civic culture.

### REFERENCES

Beasley, W. G. 1981. *The Modern History of Japan*. 3rd. ed. London: Weidenfeld and Nicolson.

Davis, Winston. 1992. *Japanese Religion and Society*. Albany, NY: State University of New York Press.

Gluck, Carol. 1985. *Japan's Modern Myths*. Princeton: Princeton University Press.

Hardacre, Helen. 1984. *Lay Buddhism in Contemporary Japan: Reiyukai Kyodan*. Princeton: Princeton University Press.

⎯⎯⎯ 1986. *Kurozuikyo and the New Religions of Japan*. Princeton: Princeton University Press.

Hellman, Donald. 1987. "Japanese Politics and Foreign Policy: Elitist Democracy Within an American Greenhouse." In *The Political Economy of Japan: The International Context*. Vol. 2. Stanford, CA: Stanford University Press.

Institute for International Mathematics. 1953–1988. Cross-National Comparative Social Survey. Division of Humanities and Social Sciences. Tokyo, Japan.

International Value Study Council. 1980. 13-kakoku Kachikan Chousa Deeta Bukku (The 13 Nations Value Survey Data Book). Tokyo: Youka Kaihatsu Sentaa.

Kato, Shuichi. 1988. "GNP Nationalism." Japan Quarterly 35 (January–March): 2–7.

Kirchheimer, Otto. 1966. "The Transformation of the Western European Party System." In *Political Parties and Political Development*. Princeton: Princeton University Press.

Kiyota, Minoru. 1982. *Gedatsukai*. Los Angeles: Buddhist Books International.

Kobayashi, Sakae. 1957. *Changes in the Japanese Religions After World War II*. Microfilm. Master of Sacred Theology thesis. NY: Union Theological Seminary. Kobayashi Takasuke. 1979. "Yasukuni" Mondai, Tokyo: Kyoikusha.

LaFeber, Walter. 1997. *The Clash: A History of U.S.-Japan Relations*. New York: W. W. Norton.

Lipset, Seymour Martin. and Stein Rokkan. 1990. "Cleavage Structures, Party Systems, and Voter Alignments." In *The West European Party System*. New York: Oxford University Press.

Murakami, Shigeyoshi. 1986. *Yasukuni Jinja*. Tokyo: Iwanami.

*New York Times*. 1999. "Tokyo Will Not Track War Criminals." *New York Times Online*. February 24 (Accessible through http://www.nyt.com).

Office of the Prime Minister, Youth Problem Headquarters. 1984. Nippon no Seinen: Dai-3-kai Sekkai Seinen Isshiki Chousa Houkokusho (Japanese Youth: A Report of the Third World Youth Survey). Tokyo: The Ministry of Finance Printing Office.

Roper Center. 1999. JPOLL Results (Accessible through http://roper1.ropercenter.uconn.edu.).

Sansom, George. 1958. *A History of Japan to 1334*. Vol. 1. Stanford: Stanford University Press.

Sopko, John. and Alan Edelman. 1995. *A Case Study on the Aum Shinrikyo*. October 31 Staff Statement. Washington, D.C.: Senate Government Affairs Permanent Subcommittee on Investigations.

Stoetzel, Jean. 1983. Les Valeurs du Temps Present: Une Enquete Europeenne. Paris: PUF.

The treatment of religious politics in the United States provided by Clyde Wilcox and Ted Jelen serves to illustrate two important themes. First, the United States case demonstrates that national political institutions and legal standards can have a profound effect on the manner in which religious belief is manifested in political activity, and, indeed, on the religious composition of the population itself. The religious vitality and diversity that distinguishes the United States from other Western nations may be the result of the strong autonomy of U.S. churches, and the lack of governmental support these institutions receive. At various points in U.S. history, religion has served a vital prophetic role as social critic, and as an important source of political mobilization. The decentralized nature of U.S. politics creates multiple access points for religiously motivated citizens. Second, the combination of religious diversity and religious vitality that characterizes the United States creates a tension between the possibility of a strong public presence for religiously motivated values and the tendency for religious beliefs to be relegated to a private sphere of activity. The relatively high levels of religiosity which characterize American citizens frequently inspire a desire to translate religious values into public policy, while the diversity of U.S. religion renders the achievement of political success difficult for religious activists. Specifically, attempts by religious activists to assert a more "priestly" role in U.S. politics have usually been rebuffed.

# 13

# Religion and Politics in an Open Market

## Religious Mobilization in the United States

### Clyde Wilcox and Ted G. Jelen

The role of religion in American politics contradicts many conventional understandings. In an era when the citizens of Christian-majority nations are becoming increasingly secular, Americans remain remarkably devout. In a world in which many nations have established religious monopolies and others experience significant strife between religious groups, religious life in the United States is remarkably diverse, and the quiet competition between religious groups for adherents and voice in public life is generally intense but is also peaceful and even friendly. In a country best known for the "separation of church and state," religion insinuates itself into politics and government in myriad, complex ways.

The unique character of American political institutions and culture often leads students of comparative politics to ignore the United States, or to treat it as a exceptional case with little to contribute to larger efforts at theory building. This might seem especially true in the area of religion and politics, for in many ways the United States is unique. Yet the U.S. case may have important implications for the comparative study of religion and politics. The ever-growing religious diversity in the United States may have implications for other nations, where longstanding religious monopolies face new competition. Moreover, it may well be that the devotion and diversity of American religion are related, and if so this may suggest that the U.S. case can help us refine our theories of societal religiosity.

Although the United States is known for its constitutional provisions separating church and state, religious groups are very active in American politics. In 1988, two ordained ministers sought the presidency, and others have served in Congress, in state legislatures, and city councils representing both parties. Throughout the past decade, white evangelical churches have distributed voters' guides prepared by the

Thanks are due to Dorothy Brown and Ken Wald for helpful comments.

Christian Coalition implicitly endorsing Republican candidates, while African American churches have registered voters on church property, invited Democratic candidates to address the congregation, and even offered their basements to campaign activities. The Catholic Church has lobbied Congress about abortion and health care, liberal Protestant denominations lobbies work for increases in the minimum wage and for racial justice, and conservative Protestants have sought to ban abortions and to influence public school curricula. Religious groups have petitioned courts directly in cases involving religious freedom or the public displays of Christian symbols, and have filed briefs as "friends of the court" on behalf of plaintiffs on a range of issues. Religious groups have marched on Washington, blockaded abortion clinics, and harbored illegal refugees from Latin America.

This religious mobilization is unique in its intensity, and in its diversity. Religious mobilization in the United States is especially interesting because seldom do all major religious groups support the same side of a controversial political issue. Before we can examine religious mobilization into politics more closely, however, it is important to understand the religious context, the constitutional context, and the political context for this activity.

## THE RELIGIOUS CONTEXT

In the sixteenth and seventeenth centuries, the United States served as an outlet for religious unrest in Europe. Minority religious communities in Europe found in the New World an enticing opportunity to build a bit of heaven on earth. At first the shoreline was dotted with colonies dominated by differing religious traditions, each not terribly tolerant of the others. The Puritans of Massachusetts were not especially welcoming of the Quakers of Pennsylvania or the Catholics of Maryland, for example, but gradually pockets of limited tolerance developed. By the time of the Revolution, most colonies had established churches, but religious involvement was uneven. Despite religious establishment, the colonies at the time of the founding tolerated a wide diversity of religious faiths. By 1776, there were already more than ten denominations in the United States with significant followings (Finke and Starke 1992).

After the Revolution, westward expansion created the opportunity for religious competition, and some denominations, especially Methodists and Baptists, dramatically expanded their membership while the established churches served a smaller portion of the religious population. During this period, the portion of the public who attended church appears to have increased as well. The faiths that prospered during this period engaged in substantial evangelizing: The Methodists sent out preachers who rode their horses along circuits of churches, often holding revival services in each church they entered.

In the middle of the nineteenth century, the tension over the slavery issue resulted in splits in many Protestant denominations. The effects of these splits are still evident today in denominations such as the Southern Baptists. Other denominations such as the Presbyterians have reunited in recent years but retain considerable regional differences.

In the latter decades of the nineteenth century into the early twentieth century, several substantial Catholic migrations from Europe challenged the Protestant hegemony. Between 1850 and 1926, the percentage of U.S. Catholic citizens increased from 5 to 16 percent (Finke and Starke 1992). In much smaller numbers, Jews emigrated from Europe into urban areas, especially New York.

In the 1920s, American Protestantism experienced great doctrinal unrest. Eastern seminaries began to grapple with scientific advances, especially the theory of evolution, and developed modern theologies that stressed the importance of improving social conditions. Orthodox Protestants resisted this modernization, and many denominations and individual churches split as the fundamentalist movement was formed. At the same time, a movement of imminent spiritual worship styles spawned a number of Pentecostal churches. By the 1960s, modernist Protestant churches, frequently referred to as "Mainline" Protestants, were declining in numbers, while more orthodox Protestants – fundamentalists, Pentecostals, neo-evangelicals – were gaining members.

Over the last two decades, increasing numbers of immigrants with non-Judeo-Christian faiths have moved into America's largest cities, especially on the East and West coasts. Mosques, temples, and shrines now coexist in urban and surburan America with Protestant and Catholic churches. Although these new religious groups do not yet constitute a sizable portion of the populace, they do pose new challenges to U.S. society. Immigration has also begun to change the nature of Christian denominations; Hispanic immigrants are becoming an ever-increasing portion of American Catholics, while Korean immigrants are now a noticeable constituency in the Presbyterian church.

Any census of American religion will necessarily be controversial, and social scientists have developed a large and contentious literature on how to measure religious affiliation. One of the largest studies, a survey of more than 100,000 Americans, found that more than 86 percent of Americans are Christians. Slightly more than one in four are Catholic, slightly less than one in five are affiliated with one of the many Baptist denominations, and the rest are scattered among other major Protestant groups. More than 8 percent of Americans were not affiliated in any way with a religious institution (Kosmin and Lachman 1993).

The study reported that more than 3 percent were non-Christians, including nearly 2 percent who were Jews. Other religious traditions – Buddhists, Muslims, Hindu, and others – totaled less than 1 percent of the population. It is likely that these numbers have grown over the past decade, and they are certainly higher in major urban centers, where the unique religious garb of various non-Christian faiths are a common sight.

The diversity of religious life in major U.S. cities is seen in a ten-mile stretch along New Hampshire Avenue, in Montgomery County, a suburb of Washington, D.C. Included in this small area are a synagogue, a mosque, a Cambodian Buddhist temple, a Hindu temple, a Unitarian church, and 29 Christian churches, including 3 Catholic (one of which is Ukrainian), 1 Ukrainian Orthodox, 2 Seventh Day Adventist, 2 Jehovah's Witnesses Kingdom Hall, and 21 Protestant churches. The Protestants range from Presbyterian, United Methodist, and Lutheran to a large and growing nondenominational Bible church. Some of the Protestant and Catholic churches serve particular immigrant communities, including the Choong-Moo Evangelical Church of Washington, the Sung Hwa Presbyterian Church, the Our Lady of Vietnam Roman Catholic Church. Although the many religious citizens and residents worship different gods in different languages, they have joined together to lobby government about zoning, and to remove graffiti from a mosque (Levine 1997).

At times, this diversity is significantly undercounted by a census of churches. One small Presbyterian church in Wheaton, Maryland (another Washington suburb) is home to four different congregations, speaking three different languages. After a worship service by a relatively sedate, older congregation of Presbyterians, an affluent congregation of Taiwanese Presbyterians meet and worship in Chinese. Still later the New Baptist Creation Church, an African-American congregation headed by a forceful woman pastor, meets for a lively service. In the late afternoon, the Iglesio Pentecostal Christo Rey (Christ the King Pentecostal Church) holds a Spanish-language service that attracts immigrants from El Salvador, Nicaragua, and Guatemala and which often lasts more than four hours (Ruane 1999)

The cacophony of religious voices in suburban Washington is not echoed in Fairmont, West Virginia, a small city some 230 miles west of Washington. Yet Fairmont has more than fifty Christian churches representing a remarkable range of doctrine and practice, including several churches independent of any denomination. These churches all meet in established buildings, but other Fairmont citizens congregate in storefronts that are rented by the month, in rented space in the nearly empty shopping mall outside town, or even in living rooms, so there are even more congregations than churches.

After a concerted effort by political science scholars to improve measurement of religious denominations, the National Election Study – a large, national survey conducted around American elections – has a master list of more than one hundred Christian denominations, and includes Jewish and non-Judeo-Christian categories as well. In 1996, the survey of 1700 included respondents from more than fifty different Christian denominations, four distinct Jewish traditions, and Muslims, Buddhists, Hindu, and Native American religions. Yet the diversity of denominations does not tell the entire story, for within many of these denominations, individual congregations form cohesive communities that may preach diverse social, moral, and political messages (Wald, Owen, and Hill 1988; Jelen 1991).

The United States also has a remarkably high level of religious belief and observance, a fact that makes the country an outlier in the well-established relationship between socioeconomic development and religious observance. Citizens of the United States are more likely to believe in a personal God, in an afterlife, in heaven, and especially in Satan and hell than are citizens of Europe. They are more likely to attend church weekly or more often, and to pray regularly. Data from the 1996 National Election Study show that more than half of Americans pray daily; more than 30 percent pray several times a day. Moreover, well over a third report that religion provides a great deal of guidance in their daily lives.

Taken together, these data might seem to imply that the U.S. case has little in common with other developed nations. Yet in recent years, scholars have increasingly argued that these two distinctive features of American religion are related, and that the diversity of American religion helps explain the high levels of religiosity of its citizenry. Finke and Stark (1992) argue that U.S. citizens became more involved with religion as new, more vigorous denominations rose to challenge established churches. Using a theoretical approach that focuses on "market share" and the emergence of new theological products, the authors argue that in countries with religious monopolies, religious indifference is widespread. This is true for two reasons. First, a dominant church cannot target its appeals to meet the diverse spiritual needs of citizens, because it must appeal to all. Second, monopolies tend to be "lazy," and make little effort to hold onto market share because they lack competition. In contrast, in the United States older denominations, with lower "costs" of membership (fewer demands for piety, infrequent meetings, smaller financial contributions) are continually challenged by new, more sectlike religious groups that set higher "costs" but offer a more vigorous religious experience. This "new paradigm" of the sociology of religion suggests that the United States is more religious precisely because it has so much diversity (Warner 1993). Thus the American experience might well have some implications for countries in which established religious monopolies face new competition.

## THE ONE, THE TWO, THE MANY? DIVERGENT VIEWS OF AMERICAN RELIGIOUS DIVERSITY

Although there is widespread agreement that the United States has remarkable religious diversity, there is less consensus on precisely what that means for American society, and the role of religion in politics. Some observers have argued that although there are important differences in worship styles and religious doctrine, there is a prevailing Judeo-Christian ethos that underlies a consensus on fundamental values. One of the earliest articulations of this view was by Alexis de Tocqueville, who wrote that:

In the United States, religion exercises but little influence upon the laws and upon the details of public opinion, but it directs the customs of the community, and by regulating domestic life, it regulates the state. Christianity . . . reigns without obstacle, by universal consent; the consequence is . . . that every principle of the moral world is fixed and determinant, although the political world is abandoned to the debates and experiments of men. Thus, the human mind is never left to wander over a boundless field. (1945: 314–15.)

This view is held by many scholars today. Reichley (1985) argued that the Judeo-Christian consensus in America is a vital, indispensable support for democracy. He argued that secular value systems cannot provide the moral basis to maintain the cohesion and vitality of a free society, and that the theist-humanist values of Judaism and Christianity are the source of most of America's stability and its dynamism. Wald (1992) argues that "certain patterns of religious thought, habitual ways of reasoning about God and humankind, made it easier for certain ideas to take root in American society" (p. 67). Among these ideas are contractual, limited government. (For a critique of this "consensual" view of American religion, see Segers and Jelen 1998).

One of the manifestations of this common religious culture is the existence of a "civil religion," a concept sometimes also referred to as a public theology or the religion of democracy. Many Americans interpret the nation's history in religious terms, and viewing the United States as "one nation, under God" (Bellah 1975). Some believe that the United States is a favored nation in God's sight, perhaps even a new chosen people, a idea taken from the Puritan view that the passage to the New World to establish the new religious community resembled the journey of Jews toward the promised land, and involved a special covenant with God (Wald 1992).

Although not all scholars see civil religion as a useful concept, others point to the priestly role of presidents, who generally close their speeches by asking for God's blessing upon the nation and citizenry. Many important historical figures, such as President Abraham Lincoln, evoked God's will to justify the Civil War and to sanctify the sacrifice of fallen soldiers. Other presidents have asserted America's divine purpose, and used that language to exhort the people to follow their proffered policies. Civil religion does more than rally Americans behind wars and policies, it increases support for the political system more generally: children who view the nation in transcendent terms are more likely to have positive attitudes toward political authority (Smidt 1982). Yet civil religion does more than reify the state, it also has a prophetic element. Indeed, those who see America as God's chosen people are often especially critical of government policies that might seem to be inconsistent with their interpretations of God's will.

Although some scholars see the Judeo-Christian tradition as a foundation of the American consensus on values and on limited government, others see the religious diversity of America distilling into two divergent forces engaged in a "culture war" to influence American values and policy. According to this thesis, cultural modernists, including secular citizens and mainline Protestant churches, seek to promote a tolerance for diversity and an individualist moral ethic, while cultural conservatives, led by orthodox evangelical Protestant churches, seek to support moral conformity, enforced through the power of law (Hunter 1991; for a more nuanced view see Green, Guth, Smidt, and Kellstedt 1996).

The progressive elements of this coalition would include secular Americans, and social movement such as the feminist and gay and lesbian movement that sought to promote gender equality and to decrease discrimination against gays and lesbians. It would also include most Jews, and the leadership and many members of mainline Protestant denominations, which in recent years have often uneasily endorsed abortion rights and have in some cases "married" gay or lesbian couples, or ordained openly gay or lesbian clergy. In most cases, the liberalism of the clergy and activist elites within these liberal Protestant denominations exceeds that of many members in the pews, and there have been often bitter disputes within the denominations over these issues, especially gay rights. This was evident in the 1990s when the Presbyterians first adopted language that proposed that sexual relationships be evaluated according to whether the relationship is supportive and nonexploitative, rather than whether it exists in the bounds of marriage or whether it is heterosexual. Later in the decade, the denomination's General Assembly adopted an amendment that mandated that individuals engaged in non-marital sexual relationships of all types not be ordained as lay activists. The denomination, like most liberal Protestant churches, remains divided on gay rights.

Although there is considerable diversity among the members of this modernist coalition, many of the Mainline Protestant churches have cooperated closely in the past several decades, and some have even merged into new bodies such as the United Methodists and the Evangelical Lutheran Church of America. In the 1960s, this liberal coalition was quite active in politics, providing much of the moral force behind the movement to end racism and the Vietnam War. Today the Mainline churches focus much of their communitarian activity on bettering social conditions on earth, trying to alleviate the problems of poverty, racism, and discrimination, which they believe are the sources of much suffering and sin. The Wheaton Presbyterian Church, discussed above, has a congregation that quilts and rolls bandages for the needy. Others have developed volunteer networks to provide hospice to AIDS patients, to shelter refugees from Central America, to teach English to immigrants, to feed or shelter the homeless, and provide refuge and counseling to battered women.

On the other side are a coalition of evangelical, fundamentalist, and Pentecostal Protestant churches, along with some conservative Catholics and Orthodox Jews, whose leaders and members promote traditional morality, including traditional gender roles, a ban on most or all abortions, and strictures against homosexual conduct. These moralist churches are less likely to merge denominations, because the doctrinal differences among them remain highly salient. Yet the members of these churches may well work together in political organizations that fight abortion, or on behalf of political candidates who promote traditional family values.

Although these orthodox churches were once on the sidelines of American politics, in recent years a social movement aimed at mobilizing conservative Christians into Republican politics has had some success. The Christian right has encouraged activists to register to vote, to work within the parties to influence nominations and party rules, and to run as candidates (Green 1997; Rozell and Wilcox 1996). Today these orthodox Christians provide the activist base of the Republican party and dominate party politics in many states (Rozell and Wilcox 1996).

Many scholars see American religion increasingly dividing into these two camps, and becoming increasingly associated with the two major political parties (Wuthnow 1988; Guth, Green, Smidt, et al. 1997). Yet other scholars suggest that the American religious scene is much more multifaceted. They note that Catholics do not fit neatly into this two-party system, for Catholic religious elites stake very conservative positions on some social issues while supporting liberal, communitarian policies to deal with poverty and social problems. There is evidence that Catholic laity also do not fit neatly into the culture wars (Jelen 1997). African Americans do not fit well either – their religion is generally evangelical and many hold conservative views on social and moral issues, but support progressive economic and racial policies (Hertzke 1993; Wilcox 1990). Moreover, within the dominant religious coalitions, there are clear divisions. Fundamentalist religious leaders are quite critical of Pentecostal religious practices – fundamentalist Jerry Falwell once stated that those who spoke in tongues had "eaten too much pizza the night before" (Slansky 1989).

The question is more than a purely academic one, for Hunter (1991) predicted an escalating culture war that might lead to the same kind of violence that has characterized religious struggles in other parts of the world. Indeed, the firebombing of abortion clinics and the murder of abortion providers raises the specter of a cultural conflict escalating beyond control. If there are many voices, rather than two, then such an escalation seems less likely.

## THE CONSTITUTIONAL CONTEXT

Although the founders did not anticipate the incredible diversity of contemporary American religion, they did worry about the dangers of religious conflict. The First Amendment to the Constitution contains the following: "Congress shall make no law respecting an establishment of religion, or prohibiting the free exercise thereof." These two short clauses – commonly referred to as the "establishment clause" and the "free exercise clause" – have been the subject of much litigation, and of an enormous amount of scholarly analysis. Legal scholars have focused entire articles on specific words, such as what it means to ban laws about "an" establishment of religion.

The establishment clause clearly bans an official religion for the nation, but beyond this there is little agreement as to what it means. Some legal thinkers, often called "accommodationists," suggest that the establishment clause permits the government to establish policies that support all religion, or perhaps Christianity in general. Under this view, a spoken prayer in public schools that uses language endorsed by one specific denomination would be banned, but a more generic prayer would be permitted. "Separationists," in contrast, hold that the establishment clause forbids the government from upholding religion in general, and that the government must be neutral not only between religions, but also between religion and no religion. Separationists frequently cite Thomas Jefferson's call for a "high wall of separation" between church and state, a phrase that the public supports but does not appear to fully understand (Jelen and Wilcox 1995).

Differences in the "correct" interpretation of the establishment clause are, to a large extent, based on the different conceptions of the public role of religion. Accommodationists generally believe that there is a consensus in the United States on moral and many religious issues, and that this then makes a generally neutral, yet supportive relationship between church and state desirable. Because the practical effects of religion are generally held to be positive, government can (and should) encourage an active role for religion in public life. Conversely, separationists tend to view religion as a source of conflict and tension, both between religions and between religious and less religious citizens in the "culture wars," and thus tend to support a much less visible public presence for religion (see Jelen 2000).

In practice, the meaning of these clauses is contingent on Supreme Court doctrine and decisions. In general, the Court has taken a separationist position on the establishment clauses, striking down laws that have a religious purpose, have the effect of advancing or inhibiting religion, or involve "excessive entanglement" between church and state. Thus the establishment clause has been interpreted to prohibit the display of religious symbols such as crosses or nativity scenes on public property, although they may be included in a larger secular display. In other words, the nativity scene cannot stand alone on city property, but it can be displayed along with other Christmas symbols, such as a Christmas tree and a Santa Claus. This ruling has led a number of cities to display menorah candle sets in December as well, a practice that many Jews complain distorts the meaning of this holiday to fit with Christian desires to display Christmas symbols. The establishment clause has also been interpreted to ban prayer and moments of silence in public schools, including at school graduation, and to ban public support for secular schools. In recent years, the Court has moved toward a slightly more accommodationist stance, for example allowing student religious groups to meet on public school property if other student organizations are given that right.

The "high wall" of separation has many holes. United States money contains the phrase "In God We Trust," the pledge to the flag was amended in the 1950s to include the phrase "one nation, under God," prayers begin each day's work in Congress, Moses is visible in a frieze in the Supreme Court, and presidents typically close their national speeches by asking God's blessing on the nation. Most Americans support these public acknowledgments of the dominant Judeo-Christian culture.

There is also some disagreement as to the meaning of the free exercise clause. Not all religious behavior is protected – human sacrifice can be banned, for example – but the extensive religious diversity in the United States provides for many more nuanced and difficult cases. Some scholars and legal experts offer a communitarian understanding of the clause, suggesting that prevailing community standards can limit some kinds of unconventional religious behaviors that might offend the moral sensibilities of the majority (Reichley 1985). Others propose a more libertarian view, that all religious behavior should be protected unless there is a compelling state interest in limiting it. Thus a communitarian understanding of the free exercise clause might allow a ban on Satan worship, which would offend the majority in the community, while a libertarian view would allow such worship.

Again, the communitarian-libertarian controversy is largely based on different analyses of the nature of religious pluralism in the United States. Communitarians tend to argue that, because religion is a source of social cohesion and government legitimacy, religious free exercise can be limited in a neutral manner. Government (and, by extension, popular majorities) may proscribe practices permitted or required by particular religions, provided that such regulations apply neutrally to religious and secular behavior alike. By contrast, libertarians tend to regard religious values as sources of *individual* empowerment, and as a means by which the power of government and public opinion may be limited (Jelen 2000).

Throughout U.S. history the Supreme Court has generally taken a more libertarian stance, holding that government can regulate religious practice only when there is a compelling state interest, where the religious practice is not central to the religion under consideration, or when the regulation does not pose a substantial infringement on the practice of that religion (Robbins 1993). The Court upheld the religious rights of Americans to refuse to salute the flag and to refuse to fight in wars. The Amish were permitted to withdraw their children from public schools at a relatively young age in order to socialize them into their faith.

In recent years, however, the Court has handed down a series of rulings that appear to limit the free exercise of religious minorities, including the longstanding Native American practice of using peyote (a hallucinogenic drug made from cactus plants) in religious ceremonies, and the rights of Orthodox Jews to wear religious headgear under army helmets. In response, a broad coalition of religious groups successfully lobbied Congress to pass the Religious Freedom Restoration Act, but the Court later overruled significant portions of that act.

The growing diversity of American religion raises new issues of free expression on a daily basis. School boards struggle over issues of special attire for Sikh boys and Muslim girls, employers and schools struggle to deal with dietary laws, holy days, and other religious requirements of their increasingly diverse constituents, and communities which have incorporated Christian symbols into larger secular displays face requests from Buddhists that their statues be displayed on special days. Although Americans generally support religious freedom for minority religious groups, their tolerance wears thin quickly. One survey showed that nearly all residents of Washington, D.C. would allow religious freedom to all groups, but nearly one in five would ban religious headgear in public schools, and fewer than one in four would allow animal sacrifice, a practice explicitly protected by the Supreme Court in a case involving a Santeria church in Florida (Jelen and Wilcox 1995).

Of course, many issues involve both establishment and free exercise issues. Should a student prayer group be allowed to meet on public school property after classes, as other students groups do? Can students present book reports on the Bible or other religious books? In recent years, accomodationists have increasingly recast their arguments into the language of free exercise, hoping to get a more friendly reception in the Court and in the larger society.

Finally, it should be noted that the separation of church and state has never been interpreted to mean that churches cannot serve a prophetic function to criticize the state, and to support political issues and causes. Indeed, many proponents of a "high wall" of separation argue that separation permits religious bodies to be more critical of government, and more active in moral pronouncements.

## THE POLITICAL CONTEXT

The American political system has several unique characteristics that makes it easier for interest groups and social movements to mobilize, and to influence politics. First and probably most important is the porous, undisciplined nature of American parties. Nominees for office by the Democratic and Republican parties are selected not by party leaders, but by voters in primary elections, caucuses or conventions. Candidates for party nomination run against one another in part by staking different positions on issues, many of which are of great interest to religious bodies. There is no binding party platform for American parties; Democrats and Republicans can be for or against legal abortion, for or against civil rights protections for gays and lesbians, for or against a voucher system that would provide government money to parents who send their children to religious schools. The lack of final control over nominations also denies American political parties the source of discipline that exists in most countries, for elected officials who deviate from party policy cannot be denied the ballot in the next election.

American parties are not membership organizations, and this means that any citizen that registers as supporting the party can vote in a primary election or caucus. Indeed, in some states there is no party registration, and any citizen can vote in the primary election of either party, so long as they vote in only one. This makes American political parties exceptionally open to penetration by social movements. Groups and movements can use parties to nominate their candidates and to endorse their policy proposals in party platforms, they can even take over party organizations at the local, state, or even national level. In the 1960s, the civil rights and peace movements exerted significant influence within the Democratic party, and both movements had substantial bases in various religious communities. In the 1980s and 1990s, the Christian Right won control of many local and state party organizations, dominated national nominating conventions, and exerted substantial influence on party platforms (Rozell and Wilcox 1996, 1997).

Because the United States has only two, large political parties that serve as coalitions of interests, parties depend on groups to reach potential voters, to use their infrastructure to support political campaigns, and to lend their resources to political action. For many years Democratic candidates have depended on black churches to help them reach African-American voters, and GOP candidates have counted on the Christian Right to help them reach orthodox white Protestants. Thus parties and religious groups have a symbiotic relationship, and parties try to mobilize religious constituencies through political and religious groups. Indeed, in the 1990s the Democratic party lent its resources to the creation of the InterFaith Alliance, a liberal religious coalition that opposes the Christian Right.

The lack of party discipline means that any member of the national, state, or local legislature is free to vote however she wants on any issues, thus presenting an opportunity for religious and other groups to seek to win her support. This opportunity comes at a cost, for to assemble a majority in a legislative chamber groups cannot count on discipline from a party leader. As a consequence, religious groups often form coalitions among themselves, and with other secular organizations.

The separation of powers at the national, state, and local level presents many opportunities for religious mobilization. Groups can try to help elect a president, and approach the executive for political support. Ronald Reagan lent rhetorical support to conservative Christians for school prayer and abortion, but failed to push their agenda in Congress or the courts. Bill Clinton has made public pronouncements about free exercise for students in public schools, and asked the Justice Department to clarify the law for school principals. Presidents can also appoint members of religious and quasireligious organizations to executive positions: Reagan appointed a high-ranking official of the Moral Majority (a Christian right organization of the 1980s) to the Department of Education, and had as his domestic policy advisor a man who later was head of a Christian Right group. Congress can pass laws in which minor phrases affect policies of great concern to religious groups, and the courts can strike down laws or practices that affect churches.

American federalism means that national, state, and local governments make policies, and thus are targets of influence. Local governments display Christian symbols, determine the curriculum and textbooks of local schools, zone property in ways that affect churches, and regulate businesses. State governments pass laws on abortion, homosexuality, and medical care for the poor.

The American political system thus provides multiple opportunities for religious involvement in politics. Political parties and other interest groups urge religious groups on to greater involvement, because they seek the political support that religious groups can provide. These political characteristics are especially important because of the religious diversity in the United States. Unlike countries with established religious monopolies, the values and moral policies of the United States are frequently contested, and religious groups often take intensely different positions on them. Catholic bishops condemn capitalism, while Baptists exhort its potential to create better lives for all. Assemblies of God pastors condemn abortion, while the Religious Coalition for Reproductive Freedom seeks to promote pro-choice policies. Fundamentalists condemn homosexuality as a sin, while some liberal Protestant churches perform marriages of homosexual couples. In a country that takes its religion seriously, where many faiths compete to define the national moral character and to embody their interpretations of God's laws into those of the nation, it is natural that religious citizens are mobilized into political action regularly.

## RELIGIOUS MOBILIZATION IN A PLURALISTIC COUNTRY: A BRIEF HISTORY

Religious constituencies have been mobilized into politics throughout American history, and have led to some of the most important policy changes in the nation's history. Yet the pluralistic nature of American religion has generally meant that religious voices have been divided on most controversial policy issues, and rarely have the main religious bodies mobilized together behind a cause. The outcome of many of these disputes has hinged on the size of the religious constituencies and the degree of their mobilization, the degree of religious opposition, the strength and unity of other political actors in the system, and prevailing public sentiments.

Even on slavery, an issue on which all religious bodies in America are united in hindsight, there was considerable religious division. In the north, religious groups formed the nucleus of the emancipation movement. Religious women constituted a sizable portion of the activist core of the antislavery movement, religious rhetoric was frequently used to motivate the faithful, and Quaker and other churches provided important infrastructure.

Yet many religious bodies were deeply divided by the slavery issue, mainly along regional lines. The Methodist Church denounced slavery, then quickly suspended this language. In the north, individual Methodist churches continued the struggle to end slavery, while in the south and border states the church sought instead to save the souls of slaves. Other churches, especially the Baptists and Presbyterians, experienced heated internal conflicts over the slavery issue. Eventually these denominations all split, in some cases creating denominations that persist today. Southern religious organizations supported the confederacy and the continuation of slavery, while northern organizations became more active in the emancipation movement (Smith 1972; Eighmy 1987).

Many of the religious women who played an active role in the abolition of slavery saw a clear connection between the emancipation of slaves and greater liberty for women, especially the right to vote. Many of the women who congregated in a small church in Seneca Falls in 1848 were devoutly religious, and argued that women should have an increased voice in politics precisely because their religious values would improve society. Although religious women, often organized into local and state groups, played a critical role in advancing the cause of women's equality, many churches opposed suffrage and women's equality. Northern evangelical churches joined in this crusade, but many southern Protestant churches remained in opposition.

Some religious women sought to link women's suffrage with the prohibition of liquor. The Women's Christian Temperance Union, formed in 1874 by women representing some sixteen states, promoted both suffrage and bans on the sale of alcohol. The WCTU appealed directly to women in orthodox Protestant churches, and played a key role in building a broader coalition on behalf of women's rights. Because of the WCTU, many conservative religious women who might otherwise have opposed women's equality were drawn to the movement. In the context of a united fight against the evils of liquor, arguments that women had an important role to play in bringing better values to politics and society met with more receptive ears.

The larger temperance movement represented a coalition of evangelical and liberal Protestants, in both the North and South, and of many Catholics as well. Their efforts to enact local and state-wide bans on alcohol eventually culminated in a Constitutional amendment that extended these bans to the entire country. Although many denominations were not actively involved in promoting Prohibition, few religious voices were raised in opposition.

These early waves of religious mobilization were largely successful – slavery was abolished, women won the right to vote, and the sale of alcohol was banned for a time. None of these successes would have been possible without the active involvement of religious bodies and activists, although in each case there was critical support from more secular institutions. In only one case – Prohibition – was there anything approaching a single religious voice, and even in that case significant elements of the religious community sat on the sidelines.

Early in the twentieth century, American Protestantism became deeply divided over whether they should accommodate modern teachings, especially evolution. This was a time of great religious upheaval, in which orthodox fundamentalists split from their modernist brethren to establish fundamentalist denominations and congregations. The fundamentalists mobilized to oppose the teaching of evolution in public schools. Fundamentalist religious organizations such as the World Christian Fundamentals Association (WCFA), as well as denomination-centered groups such as the Bible Crusaders of America (Baptists), lobbied state legislatures, held public rallies, and engaged in public debates (Wilcox 1991). Yet liberal Protestant churches had made their peace with Darwin, and had even incorporated the theory of evolution into a doctrine that focused on improving social conditions on earth so as to usher in the Second Coming of Christ. Although liberal churches did not actively mobilize in opposition to the fundamentalist efforts, they did quietly provide different council to elected officials from their denominations, and sometimes engaged the fundamentalists in public debates. The fundamentalist antievolution crusades were the first wave of Christian right activism in the twentieth century.

In the late 1950s and early 1960s, there was a substantial and highly contested mobilization to end racial segregation and discrimination. Most important was the role of African-American churches, especially in the South, which provided the infrastructure and leadership for the movement. Blacks met in churches throughout the South to plan their campaign, and ministers and lay leaders led a campaign of civil disobedience that included protest marches and sit-ins. In the North, Mainline Protestant churches and some Catholic parishes provided support, including endorsements, cash contributions, and volunteers. In the South, a few white religious leaders endorsed the movement, but many others opposed it publicly. As northern white religious leaders joined black preachers to lead protest marches that sometimes led to confrontations with civil authorities, many southern religious leaders decried the active involvement of religion in politics. Some prominent evangelists such as Billy Graham worked quietly to integrate his religious rallies, but the Rev. Jerry Falwell had black protestors removed from his church and arrested. The role of southern evangelicals in resisting desegregation and full civil rights for African Americans is a great source of embarrassment today for many activists in the tradition, who have apologized individually and collectively.

The Religious left also mobilized in the early 1970s to oppose the Vietnam War. In some cases entire denominations spoke mainly with one voice: the Quakers through the American Friends Services Committee counseled young men to resist the draft, and carried food and medicine to North Vietnam. A number of Baptist denominations endorsed the war, which they saw as a battle against atheistic communism. The Catholic Church was divided, partially along ethnic lines. Some priests led campaigns of protest and civil disobedience, while others, represented ethnic constituencies from countries dominated by communists supported the war. In Mainline Protestant churches opposition to the war grew, and many specific congregations were active in the antiwar movement.

Late in the 1970s, religious conservatives mobilized on a variety of issues: secularization of public schools, abortion and policies that made it easier for women to work outside the home, and the perceived decline of American military readiness. Aided by secular conservatives, the Christian Right of the 1970s included groups like the Moral Majority, Christian Voice, and the Religious Roundtable. Best known was the Moral Majority, which was centered in the Baptist Bible Fellowship (BBF) denomination of founder Jerry Falwell. The BBF was and is a very decentralized denomination where individual religious entrepreneurs build their own churches, and Falwell was one of the group's greatest success stories.

The Moral Majority built state and some county organizations by recruiting mainly BBF pastors to head the organizations (Guth 1983; Liebman 1983). This proved an especially effective way to establish an organization on paper, but it also ultimately limited the organization's growth for several reasons. The BBF clergy were busy building churches and church schools, and thus had little time for real political activity. More importantly, they were quite intolerant of other religious groups, and did not welcome Pentecostals, Catholics, and other potential allies. As a consequence, studies revealed that an overwhelming majority of the members of local Moral Majority chapters were Baptists, particularly BBF members (Wilcox 1992). The Moral Majority was disbanded a decade after its founding, primarily because it had difficulty raising money.

Many Mainline Protestant churches opposed the efforts of the Moral Majority and other Christian Right groups. While the Moral Majority pushed for larger defense budgets, liberal religious groups called to reduce those budgets and to redirect the money to programs to combat hunger and poverty. While the Moral Majority sought to return women to their "traditional" role as homemakers, liberal churches increasingly ordained women as ministers. It was not until the 1990s, however, that liberal religious leaders began to organize to oppose directly the Christian right.

In the mid and latter 1980s, presidential campaigns by two Baptist preachers mobilized significant religious resources into electoral politics. In 1984 and again in 1988, Rev. Jesse Jackson, an African-American civil rights leader, used the infrastructure of the black religious community to raise money, recruit volunteers, and make important speeches, as he sought the Democratic presidential nomination. During his campaigns, Jackson preached on Sundays in large black churches, and encouraged the congregants to register, to vote, and to encourage others to do the same. His campaign often passed the collection plate to raise the money needed to fly him to his next event (Hertzke 1989).

In 1988, Pat Robertson, a leading figure on conservative religious television, sought the GOP nomination. Although Robertson was a Baptist, he had strong ties to the Pentecostal community, which provided him with most of his support (Green and Guth 1988; Wilcox 1992). Robertson won few delegates, but he raised record amounts of money from those who regularly donated to his *700 Club* television program. More importantly, after he conceded defeat, his supporters continued to work within the party, and gained control of a number of state and local GOP party organizations (Hertzke 1988; Rozell and Wilcox 1996, 1997).

## RELIGIOUS MOBILIZATION IN THE NEW CENTURY

At the outset of the twenty-first century, religious groups remain active in mobilizing their members into politics. Although most of the Christian right groups of the 1970s are defunct or moribund, a new set of groups has emerged, and are much more effective. The Christian Coalition, formed out of the mobilization of the Robertson presidential campaign, distributes voter guides in churches on the Sunday before elections. Although these guides do not officially endorse a candidate, they make it clear that the Coalition supports the Republican party. They also lobby government, and have a sophisticated Washington office. In general, the organization is pragmatic, counseling conservative Christians to compromise on important issues and to work incrementally for change (Wilcox 1996).

Like any social movement, the Christian Right is full of competing groups and competing leaders, each of which have a different view of how the movement should engage in politics. The Family Research Council takes a more puristic stand on social issues, and opposes compromise in many instances. It specializes in generating research that it uses in lobbying Congress and state legislatures, and also does voter mobilization. The Concerned Women for America, a group actually formed in the 1970s, enlists women in a moral crusade to retake America. It does grassroots lobbying, voter mobilization, and litigation. Many other groups focus on specific issue areas.

The contemporary Christian Right is not so deeply rooted in a few specific denominations as had been the Moral Majority. One estimate in the early 1990s suggested that perhaps half of the members of the Christian Coalition were Baptists, a quarter belonged to Mainline Protestant churches, 15 percent were Pentecostals, and the rest were scattered among a variety of other denominations, including some Catholic support (Rozell and Wilcox 1996). The Christian Coalition even reached out to Catholics and African Americans by founding special organizations such as the Catholic Alliance. There is evidence that other Christian right organizations of the 1990s also have an ecumenical base (Wilcox, Rozell, and Gunn 1996).

The Christian Right focuses on a variety of issues, including education, abortion, support for traditional families, opposition to gay and lesbian civil rights, and support for increased public acknowledgement of religion. Organizations and activists take a range of positions on each of these issues, with some favoring relatively moderate goals and others supporting radical action. For example, moderate Christian right activists seek to permit students to pray voluntarily in schools, and to read their Bibles in study hall, while more radical activists withdraw their children from public schools entirely and build Christian schools or teach their children at home.

Yet the Christian Right does not speak for all "people of faith," nor even for all Christians. A liberal Christian coalition has formed under the name of the Interfaith Alliance, with resources provided in part by the Democratic party. The Alliance has on its board of directors religious leaders from a variety of Christian denominations, as well as Jews and Muslims (http://www.tialliance.org/tia/page13.html; on March 3, 1999). It seeks to counter the activity of the Christian right in electoral politics, and to articulate a moderate to liberal voice on political issues. Even on abortion, American religion speaks with diverse voices in the twenty-first century. The Religious Coalition for Reproductive Choice includes a number of activists in Mainline Protestant denominations, as well as Jews and some Catholics. The liberal coalition does more than merely oppose the agenda of the Christian Right, however, it also pushes for more spending on social programs to aid the poor, on policies to ameliorate the effects of racism, and on other social reforms, and for separation of church and state.

The Christian right is firmly ensconced in the Republican party, while the Democrats helped found the Interfaith Alliance. The increasingly visible role of religious groups in electoral politics, and their clear alliance with the two major political parties, suggests the possibility of an emerging two-party system in American religion. As a simplifying metaphor, the two-party system is a useful way to conceive of the growing alliance between religious coalitions and the political parties. This alliance has consequences of the temper of the religious competition and debate, for political campaigns in the United States often rely on inflammatory rhetoric to sufficiently arouse party supporters to induce them to vote. In the 1990s, the religious rhetoric has become more heated: One Christian Right voters' guide in 1992 warned that "A Vote for Bill Clinton is a Vote Against God" (Wilcox 1997).[1]

Yet the Catholic Church does not fit neatly into these two parties, for it works to limit abortion but also to expand some programs to help the poor, to reduce military spending, and to oppose the death penalty. The awkward place of the Catholic Church in any two-party religious system was evident in its position on President Clinton's health care plan in 1993: The church supported national health insurance, but only so long as it did not pay for abortions. Many activists in the Catholic Church support a "seamless garment" of pro-life policies that include support for prenatal health care, nutrition programs, spending on education, and opposition to abortion, the death penalty, and nuclear weapons. This package does not neatly fit into either party, although it is closer to Democratic positions. Yet the salience of the abortion issue creates tension between Catholics and the Democratic party (Bendyna 1999).

Thus religious groups are very active in American politics, but they compete to define the moral and political character of the nation. Perhaps because of this competition, the sheer diversity of tactics that religious groups use to influence politics is dazzling. Many denominations, coalitions of denominations, political groups that organize around religion, and even some congregations lobby government to influence policy (Hertzke 1988). They work quietly in Congress to influence legislation, within the bureaucracy to influence implementation rules, and in the

---

[1] Although religious rhetoric has become more heated, it is still much more subdued than in earlier times. It was not uncommon early in the twentieth century to learn in fundamentalist churches that Catholic missionaries ate young children. In the midst of the heat of denominational birth early in the century, denominational barriers among Protestants were seen as a significant barrier to marriage.

White House to influence presidential initiatives, rhetoric, and executive orders. They litigate cases to influence policy on church-state separation, the free exercise of religion, and other issues, and file countless "friends of the court" briefs on key cases. Religious groups are not just active at the national level; indeed individual congregations are often quite active in local politics.

Religious groups are also active in electoral politics. They recruit candidates, sometimes from within their own ranks, and mobilize money and volunteers behind those candidates in intra-party disputes. The Christian Right is especially active in internal party politics, working to influence GOP platforms, nominations, and policies (Rozell and Wilcox 1996, 1997). African-American churches are also quite active in internal Democratic politics, and are major power bases for some candidates, many of whom have historically been religious leaders. Religious groups also provide financial support for candidates, generally through networks of individual donors. Indeed, even numerically small religious groups such as Jews and Buddhists can provide significant financial resources to candidates when they give in unison.

In pursuing these tactics, American religious groups frequently behave as ordinary interest groups. They join large and ad-hoc coalitions that might include secular groups that hold policy goals incompatible with the religious group. Indeed, the Christian Coalition lobbied together with their nemesis the American Civil Liberties Union in the 1990s to defeat some elements of lobby regulations. They sit down with other groups and party leaders to help plan campaign strategies that may involve framing issues in a somewhat deceptive manner. They bargain with party leaders to form the legislative agenda, pledging to deliver the support of their followers to policies that are not obviously in their self-interest.

Although American religious communities are generally in competition, they have on some rare occasions joined together in a single voice. In 1993, an unprecedented coalition of religious activists of all types pressured Congress to pass the Religious Freedom Restoration Act, a bill aimed at overturning some recent Supreme Court decisions that seemed to limit religious liberty for some groups. The effort was successful, although the U.S. Supreme Court eventually overturned the bill. This broad-based effort was an important exception to the general rule of religious competition.

## CONCLUSION

The United States is characterized by a remarkable level of religious diversity and devotion. As religious groups compete for adherents, they also compete to define the nation's moral and political character.

Throughout U.S. history, religious mobilizations have occurred within and across denominational lines, and have influenced the outcome of important social struggles. Yet almost always, religious groups organize on both sides of important American policy issues.

In doing "normal politics," American religious groups are frequently criticized for compromising their basic principles in pursuit of power. There is an uneasy tension, especially among conservative Protestants, between the desire to bring religious values to bear on politics, and the desire to stand back from politics and exercise prophetic criticism. It is difficult for religious leaders who have negotiated hard with politicians to later criticize those same politicians. In the 1970s, this was evident when evangelist Billy Graham slowly and somewhat reluctantly criticized President Nixon for Watergate (and especially for the profanity on taped conversations released to the public).

In doing normal politics, American religious groups often find themselves torn between the necessary compromises of the U.S. political system, and the need to retain their moral and religious vision. Because the United States has weak, coalitional parties, policy making frequently involves bargaining with other elements of the party coalition for access to the political agenda. To win concessions on moral issues, religious groups often find themselves forced to agree to fully support other policies that are at least outside their area of interest. Thus the Christian Coalition pledged to support the Republican party *Contract with America*, even though the document only peripherally addressed issues of concern to the Coalition's members. African-American religious groups found themselves forced to defend Bill Clinton during the impeachment hearings, despite his admission of immoral conduct.

There is therefore a consistent tension in American religion, between doing the hard work necessary to inject religious values into the political debate but compromising on key issues, or withdrawing and offering a prophetic criticism of the state but not working directly in politics. There appears to be a cyclical nature to the mobilization of religious communities in the United States: In the 1960s the religious liberals were mobilized while the conservatives were withdrawn; in the twenty-first century the opposite pattern holds. At the end of the twentieth century, however, there is some scattered evidence that the conservative Protestants may begin to withdraw from politics again. Important intellectual leaders have in recent years questioned the benefits of political action, and in 1999 Paul Weyrich, an instrumental social conservative, concluded that political action was not effective and that conservative Christians should withdraw and build their own communities.

Whether the Christian Right withdraws in the early years of the twenty-first century remains to be seen. What is clear, however, is that

American religion has a long history of mobilization and withdrawal, and that the Christian Right will "come again" into politics if it withdraws. Indeed, it seems inevitable that U.S. religious bodies will continue to compete for members and for a voice in defining government policy.

To date, that competition has been kept civil and even friendly, in part because it is conducted within a framework of dominant Judeo-Christian values. Although denominational differences in the United States sometimes are intense, the protagonists agree on much more than when the conflict is between two very different groups, such as Muslims and Hindus. Thus the "one" religious framework that dominates American politics provides a common core of values and assumptions to allow for limited conflict.

The competition is intense and becoming much more so, in part because as the two dominant coalitions form alliances with the major political parties, the parties exhort them to commit more resources and to take more polemical stands. Both sides work hard to mobilize their faithful to the polls, in order to have more influence within America's porous political parties, and therefore upon government. In recent years, the rhetoric of competition has become somewhat inflammatory, yet even if the two-party system solidifies it is likely to be conducted within the bounds of normal political discourse. And the divisions within the religious coalitions, which shift slightly depending on the issues and struggle to include a number of Protestant groups as well as the large Catholic bloc, assure that the discussion will remain civil.

It will be interesting to trace the impact of the growing numbers of the non-Judeo-Christian religious in America. To date the "many" have been primarily different Christian denominations and Jewish theological groupings. Already in major urban areas, there are other faiths that have sufficient numbers of adherents to pose public policy issues for government. Whether that competition will remain as civil and orderly if the nature of the competition expands dramatically is a question for the twenty-first century.

## REFERENCES

Bellah, Robert N. 1975. *The Broken Covenant: American Civil Religion in a Time of Trial*. New York: Seabury.

Eighmy, John Lee. 1987 (rev. ed.). *Churches in Cultural Captivity: A History of the Social Attitudes of Southern Baptists*. Knoxville: University of Tennessee Press.

Finke, Roger, and Rodney Stark. 1992. *The Churching of America, 1776–1990*. New Brunswick: Rutgers University Press.

Flexner, Eleanor. 1975. (rev. ed.). *Century of Struggle: The Women's Rights Movement in the United States*. Cambridge, MA: Belnap Press of Harvard Press.

Green, John C. 1997. "The Christian Right in the 1996 Elections: An Overview." In M. Rozell and C. Wilcox (eds.). *God at the Grassroots, 1996*. Lanham, MD: Rowman & Littlefield.

Green, John C., and James L. Guth. 1988. "The Christian Right in the Republican Party: The Case of Pat Robertson's Supporters." *Journal of Politics* 50: 150–165.

Green, John C., James L. Guth, Corwin E. Smidt, et al. *Religion and the Culture Wars: Dispatches from the Front*. Lanham, MD: Rowman & Littlefield.

Guth, James L. 1983. "The Politics of the New Christian Right." In A. Cigler and B. Loomis (eds.). *Interest Group Politics*. Washington, D.C.: CQ Press.

Guth, James L., John C. Green, Corwin E. Smidt, et al. 1997. *The Bully Pulpit: The Politics of the Protestant Clergy*. Lawrence, KS: University of Kansas Press.

Hertzke, Allen. 1988. *Representing God in Washington*. Knoxville: University of Tennessee Press.

1993. *Echoes of Discontent*. Washington, D.C.: CQ Press.

Hunter, James Davidson. 1991. *Culture Wars*. New York: Basic Books.

Jelen, Ted G. 1991. *The Political Mobilization of Religious Beliefs*. New York: Praeger.

1997. "Religion and Public Opinion in the 1990s: An Emperical Overview." In B. Norrander and C. Wilcox (eds.). *Understanding Public Opinion*. Washington, D.C.: CQ Press.

2000. *To Serve God and Mammon: Church-State Relations in the United States*. Boulder, CO: Westview.

Jelen, Ted G., and Clyde Wilcox. 1995. *Public Attitudes Toward Church and State*. Armonk, NY: M. E. Sharpe.

Kosmin, Barry A., and Seymour P. Lachman. 1993. *One Nation Under God: Religion in Contemporary American Society*. New York: Harmony Books.

Levine, Susan. 1997. "A Place for Those who Pray: Along Montgomery's 'Highway to Heaven,' Diverse Acts of Faith." *The Washington Post*, August 3, 1997: B1.

Liebman, Robert. 1983. "Mobilizing the Moral Majority." In R. Liebman and R. Wuthnow (eds.). *The New Christian Right*. New York: Aldine.

Reed, Ralph. 1994. *Politically Incorrect: The Emerging Faith Factor in American Politics*. Dallas: Word Publishing.

Moen, Matthew. 1990. "Ronald Reagan and the Social Issues." *Social Science Journal* 27: 199–207.

Reichley, A. James. 1985. *Religion in American Public Life*. Washington, D.C.: Brookings.

Robbins, Thomas. 1993. "The Intensification of Church-State Conflict in the United States." *Social Compass* 40: 505–527.

Rozell, Mark J., and Clyde Wilcox. 1996. *Second Coming: The New Christian right in Virginia Politics*. Baltimore: Johns Hopkins University Press.

1997. *God at the Grassroots, 1995*. Lanham, MD: Rowman & Littlefield.

1998. *Interest Groups in American Campaigns: The New Face of Electioneering*. Washington, D.C.: CQ Press.

Ruane, Michael. 1999. "A Church with Four Faces." *The Washington Post*, February 21, 1999: A1.

Segers, Mary, and Ted G. Jelen, 1998. *A Wall of Separation: Debating the Public Role of Religion*. Lanham, MD: Rowman & Littlefield.

Smidt, Corwin. 1982. "Civil Religious Orientations and Children's Perception of Political Authority." *Political Behavior* 4: 147–162.

Smith, H. Shelton. 1972. *In His Image But . . . : Racism in Southern Religion, 1780–1910*. Durham, NC: Duke University Press.

Stanton, Elizabeth Cady. 1971. *Eighty Years & More: Reminiscences 1815–1897*. Gail Parker (ed.). New York: Schoken Books.

Tocqueville, Alexis de. 1945. *Democracy in America*. Phillips Bradley (ed.). New York: Vintage.

Wald, Kenneth D. 1992. *Religion and Politics in the United States*, 2nd ed. Washington, D.C.: CQ Press.

Wald, Kenneth D., Dennis E. Owen, and Samuel S. Hill. 1988. "Churches as Political Communities." *American Political Science Review* 82: 531–548.

Warner, R. Stepehen. 1993. "Work in Progress Toward a New Paradigm for the Sociological Study of Religion." *American Journal of Sociology* 98: 1044–1093.

Wilcox, Clyde. 1990. "Blacks and the New Christian Right: Support for the Moral Majority and Pat Robertson Among Washington, D.C. Blacks." *Review of Religious Research* 32: 43–56.

1992. *God's Warriors: The Christian Right in 20th Century America*. Baltimore: Johns Hopkins.

1996. *Onward Christian Soldiers: The Religious Right in American Politics*. Boulder, CO: Westview.

Wilcox, Clyde, Mark J. Rozell, and Roland Gunn. 1996. "Religious Coalitions in the New Christian Right." *Social Science Quarterly* 77: 543–559.

Wuthnow, Robert. 1988. *The Restructuring of American Religion: Society and Faith Since World War II*. Princeton: Princeton University Press.

# 14

# The Political Roles of Religion

*Ted G. Jelen and Clyde Wilcox*

The chapters in this book have shown that religion can play a variety of roles in national and international politics. Clearly these roles are shaped by history, by culture, and by external forces in each country, by political institutions and the shape of civil society. Yet we also believe that these cases allow us to begin to formulate some cross-national generalizations about the political importance of religion. We are still far from any single unified theory of religion and politics, but some useful, mid-level, cross-national generalizations have emerged from the work of the contributors to this collection. Although some of the expectations raised in the introduction have been supported by the case studies, more often our attempts at more general understandings of the political roles of religion have been modified by encounters with empirical data.

The essays in this collection are intended to describe and explain the "style" of religious politics in a variety of national and regional settings. To some extent, the nature and extent of religious conflict and/or consensus constitutes the broadly defined "dependent variable" in this inquiry. At the outset of this volume, we suggested that the nature of religious politics in a given setting is likely to be a function of two general independent variables: the structure of the religious "market" in a particular nation, and the content of the religious creed or creeds in question. Based on the case studies in this collection, we offer some tentative generalizations about these relationships.

## THE ONE, THE FEW, AND THE MANY: THE IMPORTANCE OF RELIGIOUS MARKET STRUCTURE

The several cases with dominant religious traditions included in this volume provide little evidence that dominant religious traditions provide a sacred canopy that provides a seamless explanation of the personal and the political. Clearly religious and secular elites sometimes try to build a mutually reinforcing relationship between regimes and religion. In some instances (predemocratic Iberia, certain Latin American nations such as Chile and Israel) there have been visible and conscious efforts by political elites to identify particular regimes with religious traditions. In others (India, various Islamic countries, and in some ways the United States) religious leaders have attempted to co-opt the machinery of the state for religious purposes. The greatest success has been in Iran, where the Islamic revolution led to the creation of a government that is officially Islamic and where religious officials have significant direct input on policymaking. Yet even in Iran there is a lively debate among Muslims who have different visions of the state. Thus, the model of the "sacred canopy" has few, if any, contemporary instances in the politics of the nations of the world. In terms of the vocabulary we laid out in the introductory essay to this volume, the "priestly" function of religion is extremely problematic in modern national politics.

There seem to be at least three reasons why this is so. First, several of the works in this book have shown that there is no necessary connection between a nation's religious composition and the relationship of church and state. Although the examples in the preceding paragraph suggest that a dominant church or a state may find it advantageous to identify with the other entity, it is also clear that faith traditions which are numerically dominant will not necessarily support or seek support from political elites. In some instances, such as contemporary Spain and Portugal, religion has effectively been politically neutralized because of past close identification between Catholicism and discredited authoritarian regimes. In others, such as Poland and Brazil, a numerically dominant Catholic Church has served as an important source of opposition to a particular regime. Indeed, the case of Poland is instructive, in that, under the communist regime, the Polish church can be described as having represented the Polish *nation* in opposition to the Polish *state*.[1] Yet after the fall of that state, the role of the church in the polity is far more ambiguous. Thus, it is difficult to generate reliable generalizations concerning the ability and willingness of political regimes and locally dominant religious traditions to cooperate. There is no simple relationship between the presence or absence of a dominant faith tradition and the propensity of leaders of that tradition to play either a priestly or prophetic political role.

Second, several of the chapters presented here suggest that the very concept of a religious "tradition" is malleable indeed, and that the identity of a religious tradition with which citizens may identify may vary according to the social and political context. Dominant religious groups

---

[1] We are indebted to Nathalie Frensley for this insight.

may fragment into competing theological elements, which may sap their power to dominate the political realm. Perhaps the clearest example of this phenomenon is the recent history of the Christian Right in the United States, which sought to unite and mobilize various traditions within the evangelical community. In the early 1980s, Christian right leaders such as Jerry Falwell and Pat Robertson suggested that the United States is a "Christian nation," whose culture and politics was animated by adherence to a "Judeo-Christian tradition." Indeed, the concept of a "Moral Majority" (which came to be the name of Falwell's political organization) implied a general consensus on the essential elements of a religious-moral order. Yet these organizations continually battled religious particularism, where fundamentalists and charismatics and neoevangelicals disagreed about religious doctrine and resisted unification into a single tradition (Green 1995; Jelen 1991; Wilcox 1992).

Kenneth Wald's chapter on Israel suggests that a similar phenomenon of religious disaggregation is an important feature of religious politics in Israel. The presence of formidable external threats to Israeli national security (which are at least partially mobilized by religious concerns) has not prevented the occurrence of something resembling a "culture war" between the Haredim and more secular Israeli Jews. One might also anticipate a similar fragmenting effect among Hindus in India. It has been suggested (Gold 1991) that the mobilization of a faith tradition as decentralized and doctrinally flexible as Hinduism has been quite difficult historically, and may only occur in response to external threats to the political environment, such as the independence movement from Britain during and after World War II or the presence of a large, politically assertive Islamic minority. Indeed, Sunil Sahu's account of the Indian BJP in this book suggests that it is difficult to sustain support for a unified Hindu political party, and that the history of the BJP is characterized by drastic surges and declines in popular support. The general point here is that some faith traditions have theological or contextual characteristics that render sustained political unity quite difficult.

Third, locally dominant religious traditions may be limited internally. Clearly, not all faith traditions are equally vulnerable to the effects of fragmentation and religious particularism: Catholicism and Islam are less vulnerable though not completely immune (but see Finke and Wittberg 2000). However, such dominant religions do appear subject to the "lazy monopoly" phenomenon described in the introduction. To summarize briefly, it is often argued that those religions that enjoy monopoly or quasi-monopoly status lack competitive incentives to respond to the needs and desires of potential members. As such, religious observance in such settings is usually lower than that observed in more competitive religious markets. The existence of nominal adherents to a dominant religious tradition may thus create a market for other religious competitors, as has been observed in Latin America. The chapters by Anthony Gill and Anne Hallum strongly suggest that the failure of Roman Catholicism to actively engage its adherents, and to provide sufficient personnel to meet religious needs, created an opening for the evangelizing efforts of conservative (and especially Pentecostal) Protestants. Conversely, the existence of a large, religiously uncommitted population may create a market for secular ideologies, as well as for alternative religions. The chapter by Timothy Byrnes on Poland suggests that, in the politics of post-revolutionary change, Catholicism is forced to contend with a variety of secular competitors.[2]

Thus, in the contemporary world, the "sacred canopy" model of religious politics no longer seems viable. One possible exception to this generalization is the Republic of Ireland. Despite a religious monopoly, and a quasi-established status, Roman Catholicism appears to dominate Irish politics in a manner quite similar to that advanced by Berger (1969). Michele Dillon's chapter on religious politics in Ireland shows that Catholicism shapes Irish politics in direct and indirect ways. Not only have Irish public policies on such matters as abortion and divorce been historically consistent with Catholic doctrine (although divorce has recently become legal in Ireland), Roman Catholicism appears to dominate the shape and vocabulary of Irish political discourse.

This "Irish exceptionalism" may already be eroding, however. Church attendance rates have dropped in Ireland rather dramatically in recent years, although rates are still high compared with other Christian nations. Among those under thirty-five, regular mass attendance rates hover at less than 40 percent, and nationwide attendance has dropped more than 17 percent in the last four years. At the same time, agreement with church policy on contraception, celibacy for priests, and women in the clergy has reached record lows.[3] The clergy in Ireland are aging and rapidly declining in numbers. It may well be that as Ireland becomes more industrialized, and is further integrated into the European Union, Catholic dominance over Irish politics will be reduced. Ireland will of course remain a Catholic country for the foreseeable future, but the areas of social and political life over which the Church is regarded as authoritative are likely to contract over time (Burns 1992; Casanova 1994).

We suggested in the introduction that religiously motivated political activity in pluralistic markets might be dampened, and that the political

---

[2] As Paul Manuel has shown in the chapter on religious politics on the Iberian peninsula, this generalization seems to apply to Spain and Portugal as well.

[3] "Mass and the Masses," *The Irish Times on the Web*, February 5, 1998.

demands made by religious groups would tend toward demands for autonomy, rather than for the enactment of religious values into public policy. Religious competition might focus more on winning converts than on winning control of government to enact policies. In the United States and Latin America, manifestly political activity has tended to be less visible than in other countries. In the United States, the most obvious exception to this generalization – the Christian Right – has been less active in recent years. Some Christian right leaders have called for a scaling back of partisan politics and a return to the business of saving souls. Although the religious aspect of the movement may have been minimized, many activists have become ensconced in the Republican party (Green, Rozell, and Wilcox 2000), thereby shifting the locus of the debate. Similarly, Anne Hallum's account of the effects of Pentecostal versions of Protestantism in Central America have not resulted in an increase in religiously motivated political activity, but have instead been focused on individual spiritual and economic "empowerment." Decentralized, often very small, congregations have assumed the role of improving the religious and material circumstances of their members, without attempting to alter the political structure in which such circumstances may exist.

Of course, religious competition that is "extramural" has not been shown to reduce political activity. Religious politics on the Indian subcontinent remain as vigorous and contentious as ever, and the existence of multiple religious traditions in European nations such as Germany do not prevent political mobilization in response to the sudden presence of *new* religious movements (such as Scientology) or large groups of Muslim immigrants. Indeed, the very rationale for religiously motivated political activity in such settings is often the presence of religious "outsiders" who are perceived to pose a threat to prevailing religious or political practices. We hypothesize that the market metaphor which underlies "supply-side" theories of religious adherence and participation is simply irrelevant when the possibility of religious switching seems remote. As the chapter on India in this book makes evident, Hindus do not seriously consider conversion to Islam and vice versa (for a more detailed argument, see Kurtz 1995).

A second expectation of religious pluralism is that pluralism will change the nature of political demands made by religious actors. Rather than seeking dominance or quasi-establishment, members of minority religions will tend to seek autonomy for religious beliefs and practices. Again, a very clear example can be derived from the Christian Right in the United States. Confronted with the limiting effects of religious particularism (see especially Reed 1994), Paul Weyrich has recently urged conservative Christians to create alternative social institutions, and to seek protection by government to create a community in which they can practice their beliefs. Similarly, regimes in Western Europe (Monsma and Soper 1997) and Israel have provided publicly defined spaces in which religious belief may be practiced, and the Indian regime provides a similar space for Muslims and other non-Hindus. In the language of U.S. constitutional law, the emphasis in religiously pluralistic regimes tends to shift from one of religious "establishment" to one of the "free exercise" of religion.

However, as the chapters in this book make clear, the granting of religious "autonomy" is no simple matter in an era in which modern governments routinely provide a variety of services to citizens. Is religious freedom enhanced if services such as tax exemptions, educational subsidies, or exemptions from otherwise valid laws are granted to members of particular denominations? For example the issue of educational tax vouchers featured prominently in the presidential election in the United States, and the U.S. Supreme Court seems poised to take on the issue as well. Is the granting of such tax exemptions (which are used to offset the costs of tuition at private institutions) necessary to permit members of certain religious groups the right to educate their children in their faith tradition (which would seem to be included in the right to religious "free exercise"), or does such preferential treatment under the tax code constitute an unlawful "establishment" of religion?

Similarly, one might argue that the Israeli regime elevates the Haredim to a specially favored status with the concessions made to Orthodox Judaism. As Kenneth Wald has noted in this book, one of these concessions is exemption from military service for many, which is certainly an important prerogative in a nation in which national security considerations are extremely salient. Conversely, we have already noted the potentially discriminatory consequences of exempting Muslims from certain aspects of India's civil code in "private" areas such as divorce. It is likely the case that Muslim women in India are denied certain essential features of state protection by the regime's attempts to accommodate Islamic values in the civil law.

This point can be generalized. In modern nations, religious autonomy cannot be granted by an absence of government action or regulation. Very few modern organizations (religious or secular) are able to forego completely the services offered by government (see Jelen 2000). Therefore, modern governments must constantly determine which services enhance religious autonomy and which result in religious discrimination, and in which cases religious autonomy would undermine important state functions. To use American legal language, the same government policy can often be described as enhancing or enabling religious free exercise, or as constituting religious "establishment" or discrimination. Such legal

and political ambiguity surrounding religious politics in religiously pluralistic societies seems likely to provide the basis for continuing conflict
over the proper relationship between God and Caesar.

## THE POLITICS OF THEOLOGY RECONSIDERED

It also seems likely that the nature of religious politics in a given setting
is, in some sense, contingent on the content of the faith traditions under
consideration. In this book, we have seen the relationship between different religious traditions, or between church and state, range from a
cooperative stance of syncretism and accommodation to one of violent
conflict over religious values.

The Japanese case is particularly instructive in this regard. The chapter
by Toyoda and Tanaka shows that the traditions of Buddhism and Shinto
coexist easily in Japan, with many Japanese citizens embracing aspects
of both. This case study suggests that there is no necessary conflict
between non-monotheistic faith traditions. The fact that we do not
encounter religious syncretism in any of the other chapters in this volume
(all of which involve at least one monotheistic tradition) lends credence
to the hypothesis that the spread of monotheistic Semitic religions
(Judaism, Christianity, and Islam) is an important source of religious conflict in the contemporary world.

Indeed, it might be argued that monotheism is a critical feature of
many of the patterns presented in this collection. The market metaphor
on which various "supply-side" theories of religion are based (and which
underlie several of the studies in this book) assume that religious goods
are both scarce and costly. While time, energy, and money are obvious
sources of religious costs, it seems likely that the demands for exclusivity made by various traditions also inhibit religious syncretism, and
thereby enhance the potential for religious conflict. A priori, it would
seem likely that cultural proximity, intermarriage between members of
faith traditions, and the increased secularism of at least some aspects of
social and political life would render the melding of religious traditions
a plausible effect of religious pluralism. The fact that genuinely ecumenical sycretism is such an unusual phenomenon is a powerful testa-
ment to the power of monotheism. The First Commandment appears to
have profound political consequences (Kurtz 1985).

Finally, several of the chapters in this collection have highlighted the
unique aspects of political Islam. As the studies presented here suggest,
Islamic leaders have not reached a stable relationship or accommodation
with political authorities in any setting in which Muslims constitute a
majority (Iran, Egypt, Algeria). Moreover, Muslims appear to be
regarded as unwelcome strangers in jurisdictions in which adherents of
Islam are a minority (India, Western Europe). A revitalized Islam poses

special questions and problems for the relationship between the sacred and the secular.

This may be true for several reasons. The politics of Islam is complicated by geopolitical forces, and by nationalistic and anti-colonial sentiments among many political activists. Thus it may be that the difficulty in reaching a stable relationship between religion and politics is primarily related to regional politics, and not to Islam itself. If Islam was the dominant religion in Europe while Catholicism dominated in the Middle East, we might instead be pondering the special case of Catholicism instead of Islam.

It may also be, however, that there are doctrinal roots to the tension. The theology of Islam may make its leaders less willing or able to reach the flexible accommodations with the state that characterize the Catholic Church. Perhaps paradoxically, the centralized nature of Catholicism has enabled the Church to adapt to changing historical and cultural conditions, and to create different arrangements with different regimes at the same time in history. The First and Second Vatican councils can be seen as generally successful attempts to retain religious and political plausibility in a modernizing, increasingly pluralistic world. Indeed, Vatican II, with its emphasis on the Church as the "People of God," provides an explicit justification for national churches to adapt to local political environments and religious markets.

In a much different manner, Protestant Christianity also contains theological resources that may enhance the adaptability of Protestant churches. It is important to recall that the root of the term "Protestantism" is "protest," and that the Protestant movement was born by an explicit separation from a then hegemonic Catholic Church. Individual autonomy and the voluntary nature of church membership are important tents of Protestantism, and the process by which Martin Luther founded the Lutheran Church served to legitimate further fragmentation within Christian Protestantism. What this implies for politics is that one very common adaptive strategy for Protestant clergy and laity is the possibility of schism. If membership in a particular denomination seems incompatible with other political, economic, or social realities, the possibility of founding new religious organizations is specifically legitimized by the very nature of Protestantism itself (see especially Finke and Stark 1992). Thus, Protestant Christianity contains the doctrinal means by which particular denominations or congregations may adapt to, or resist accommodating, the prevailing secular culture.[4]

---

[4] In the course of doing some fieldwork in local Protestant congregations in the Middle West, one of us frequently heard the joke about the two Baptist ministers stranded on a desert island. Within a week, each had founded his own church, and the extent of their cooperation was to help each other with the construction.

By contrast, it is possible that contemporary Shi'ite or Sunni Islamic doctrine makes such accommodation or resistance to the secular culture harder. Lacking a globally centralized source of authority, it possible that Islamic leaders in various countries do not have the religious authority to modify their religious doctrine or emphases. Yet in previous times Islam did reach relatively stable accommodations with states, even states that made few concessions to special social arrangements implied by Islamic doctrine.

This is emphatically not to say that Islam, any more than Christianity or Judaism, is a dogmatically inflexible faith tradition. There is great richness and variety in Islam, and Mehran Tamadonfar's comparison of Islamic politics in Egypt, Algeria, and Lebanon clearly shows that Islamic leaders can and do create a variety of responses to different national and cultural settings. Rather, we are suggesting the possibility that contemporary Islam emphasizes universalistic doctrine more than in the past, and that this makes local accommodations more difficult to negotiate. If this is true, then perhaps one reason may lie in the current revitalization of Islam, which, like all such movements, stresses purity of doctrine over pragmatic politics.

We would predict, however, that, over time, Islamic forces in different nations will reach some sort of stable relationship with the non-religious aspects of the local culture. We can see no clear reason why Islam might be exempt from the generalization that the "sacred canopy" model of religious politics is no longer viable in the contemporary world. Therefore, Islam, like Christianity, will be forced to find and to define its place in various political cultures. The fact that such a phenomenon has not yet occurred is undoubtedly attributable to the abrupt shift in international economic relations over the past three decades. The changes in global power relationships occasioned by the shifts in the supply and demand of petroleum have likely provided the setting in which Islam has become a potent political force. While we do not expect the political role of Islam to diminish as the politics of energy are inevitably transformed, we would anticipate that the various political roles of Islam eventually will stabilize.

## CONCLUSION

Thus, the chapters in this book indicate that religion is a promising and important element in the study of comparative politics. The recent work of Samuel Huntington (1996) suggests that religion, to a substantial extent, defines the cultural contexts of particular societies. Moreover, many religions, such as Catholicism and Islam, are sufficiently transnational in scope to provide a means by which different cultures can be compared and contrasted in a relatively straightforward manner.

Further, the works presented here suggest that the nature of religious "markets" in particular nations can provide a useful source of comparison between societies in which the content of prevailing religious beliefs differs enormously. We would suggest that this book demonstrates that the prospect of "intercivilizational" comparison of religious politics is both a promising avenue for future research into comparative politics and a daunting challenge to the "scientific" aspirations of political science as an academic discipline. Religion appears to be politically mobilized, mobilizable, or demobilized dependent on whether religion is regarded locally as a source of unity, controversy, or diversity. The studies in this collection have taken us a considerable distance in understanding the various political roles religion may assume within different cultural or institutional contexts.

### REFERENCES

Berger, Peter. 1969. *The Sacred Canopy: Elements of a Sociological Theory of Religion*. Garden City, NY: Anchor.

Burns, Gene. 1992. *The Frontiers of Catholicism: The Politics of Ideology in a Liberal World*. Berkeley: University of California Press.

Carter, Stephen L. 1993. *The Culture of Disbelief: How American Law and Politics Trivialize Religious Devotion*. New York: Basic Books.

Casanova, Jose. 1994. *Public Religions in the Modern World*. Chicago: University of Chicago Press.

Finke, Roger, and Rodney Stark. 1992. *The Churching of America: 1776–1990*. New Brunswick, NJ: Rutgers University Press.

Finke, Roger, and Patricia Wittberg. 2000. "Organizational Revival from Within: Explaining Revivalism and Reform in the Roman Catholic Church." *Journal for the Scientific Study of Religion* 39: 154–70.

Gold, Daniel. 1991. "Organized Hinduism: From Vedic Truth to Hindu Nation." In Martin E. Marty and R. Scott Appleby (eds.). *Fundamentalisms Observed*. Chicago: University of Chicago Press: 531–93.

Green, John C. 1995. "Pat Robertson and the Latest Crusade: Religious Resources and the 1988 Presidential Campaign." *Social Science Quarterly* 74: 157–68.

Huntington, Samuel S. 1996. *The Clash of Civilizations and the Remaking of World Order*. New York: Simon and Schuster.

Jelen, Ted G. 1991. *The Political Mobilization of Religious Beliefs*. New York: Praeger.

2000. *To Serve God and Mammon: Church-State Relations in the United States*. Boulder, CO: Westview.

Jelen, Ted G., and Clyde Wilcox. 1998. "Context and Conscience: The Catholic Church as an Agent of Political Socialization in Western Europe." *Journal for the Scientific Study of Religion* 37: 28–40.

Kurtz, Lester. 1997. *Gods in the Global Village: The World's Religious in Sociological Perspective.* Thousand Oaks, CA: Pine Forge Press.

MacIntyre, Alasdair. 1973. "Is a Science of Comparative Politics Possible?" In Alan Ryan (ed.). *The Philosophy of Social Explanation.* New York: Oxford University Press: 171–88.

Moen, Matthew C. 1992. *The Transformation of the Christian Right.* Tuscaloosa, AL: University of Alabama Press.

Monsma, Stephen V., and J. Christopher Soper. 1997. *The Challenge of Pluralism: Church and State in Five Democracies.* Lanham, MD: Rowman & Littlefield.

Reed, Ralph. 1994. *Politically Incorrect.* Dallas: Word.

Wilcox, Clyde. 1992. *God's Warriors: The Christian Right in 20th Century America.* Baltimore: Johns Hopkins University Press.

# Index